AI-POWERED AUTOMATION FOR BUSINESS

Real-World Workflows and Tools

Eleanor Stratton

Reactive Publishing

CONTENTS

PREFACE

Over the past decade, AI and automation have evolved from buzzwords into essential drivers of business efficiency and innovation. Whether you're a seasoned executive seeking to optimize your operations, a manager eager to streamline processes, or an entrepreneur exploring new avenues for growth, the content ahead has been meticulously crafted to meet your needs. We delve into foundational concepts, like the true nature of AI-powered automation and its historical evolution; explore its transformative impact on sectors as diverse as healthcare, retail, finance, and manufacturing; and unveil the tangible benefits that come from embracing a culture of intelligent automation.

The journey through this book is structured to engage both your intellect and your imagination. In the early chapters, you'll encounter clear definitions and breakthrough insights into pivotal technologies such as machine learning, natural language processing, and robotics process automation. These discussions are not just technical—they are the building blocks for real-world applications that are reshaping industries across the globe. As you move further, you'll discover how to identify automation opportunities within your own organization, perform rigorous cost-benefit analyses, and design robust strategies that tie technology to clear business objectives.

Every chapter has been designed with you in mind, addressing practical questions and offering robust frameworks to overcome common challenges. From understanding the nuances of integrating AI into customer relationship management and supply chain logistics to refining your marketing, finance, and human resources operations, this book is a comprehensive roadmap for any leader eager to drive change. With detailed case studies and actionable strategies, we highlight both success stories and lessons learned from failures, painting a realistic portrait of a dynamic, evolving industry.

What truly sets this book apart is its focus on the human element in the face of technological transformation. It's not only about the power of automation but also about cultivating an innovative, agile culture where every member of your team feels empowered to contribute to the digital revolution. You'll discover how to foster transparency, encourage continuous learning, and create an environment where risk-taking and experimentation are heralded as stepping stones to success.

Our aim is to provide you with the tools to think creatively and implement solutions that resonate emotionally and practically with your business goals. As you explore strategies for implementing AI systems, mitigating risks, and ensuring compliance and ethical integrity, you'll gain the confidence to navigate the complexities of today's digital landscape while remaining true to the core values that define your organization.

This is more than a book—it's a call to action. Embrace the promise of AI-powered automation and envision a business landscape where technological agility and human ingenuity coexist harmoniously. Let this guide inspire you to reimagine your workflows, challenge conventional wisdom, and ultimately, drive sustainable growth in an era of rapid change.

Welcome to your journey into the future of business automation. Let's transform challenges into opportunities and ideas into innovations, together.

Happy reading,

Elenor Stratton

CHAPTER 1: DEFINITION OF AI AUTOMATION

Artificial intelligence automation involves using AI technologies to perform tasks that typically require human intelligence, but with little to no human intervention. Unlike traditional automation, which depends on fixed rules and scripts, AI automation learns from data patterns, makes decisions, and improves over time. This adaptability allows systems to manage complex processes such as natural language understanding, image recognition, and predictive analytics—tasks once thought beyond the reach of automation.

Take customer support as an example. Instead of relying on simple rule-based chatbots that respond only to predefined queries, AI-powered assistants can interpret a wide range of questions, understand context, and even anticipate customer needs before they are explicitly stated. This not only streamlines the support process but also personalizes interactions in real time. Such flexibility highlights AI automation's value—it moves beyond merely automating repetitive tasks to enhancing business processes with intelligent decision-making.

At its foundation, AI automation combines several branches of artificial intelligence: machine learning models that detect patterns and improve predictions; natural language processing (NLP) algorithms that parse and generate human language; computer vision systems that analyze images and videos; and robotic process automation (RPA) tools enhanced by AI capabilities. Together, these elements enable workflows to respond dynamically rather than follow rigid sequences.

In finance departments, for example, invoice processing traditionally required manual data entry prone to errors. Today, AI-powered systems use optical character recognition (OCR) to scan invoices, classify expenses automatically by vendor or category with trained models, flag inconsistencies for review, and update accounting ledgers—all without direct human input. This integration of perception (OCR), classification (machine learning), and action (ledger updating) demonstrates how AI automation weaves multiple technologies into a seamless process.

Understanding the difference between conventional rule-based automation and AI-driven systems is crucial for businesses considering technology investments. Traditional automation performs well in structured environments where inputs are predictable—such as generating reports from standardized spreadsheets or moving files based on fixed criteria. But as variability increases—different document formats, evolving customer inquiries, or fluctuating supply chain conditions—AI's learning capabilities become essential. It can detect subtle changes in data trends or user behavior that static programs cannot handle efficiently.

Consider a retail company automating inventory management. A rule-based system triggers reorder alerts when stock falls below set thresholds but cannot predict demand spikes caused by seasonal trends or marketing campaigns unless manually updated. In contrast, an AI system analyzes historical sales data along with external factors like weather patterns or social media sentiment to forecast demand more accurately and adjust reorder points dynamically.

Another important aspect is how AI automation systems improve through embedded feedback loops. These systems continuously collect operational data after deployment —whether tracking success rates in resolving customer queries or accuracy in fraud detection—and refine their models accordingly. This ongoing evolution stands in stark contrast to fixed-script automations that remain static until manually reprogrammed.

It is also important to clarify what AI automation does not represent: it is not a magical replacement for all human roles nor a plug-and-play solution requiring zero oversight. While some routine functions can be fully automated—such as sorting incoming emails into categories—many processes still need hybrid approaches where humans manage exceptions or make nuanced judgments beyond current algorithmic abilities.

The practical impact of AI automation spans industries —from healthcare automating patient record triage with NLP tools to manufacturing deploying robotic arms guided by computer vision for quality control inspections. Each application reflects the core idea: machines performing intelligent actions autonomously or semi-autonomously based on learned insights rather than hard-coded instructions alone.

At its core, AI-powered automation blends adaptive intelligence within automated workflows, transforming traditional task execution into responsive, continuously improving systems capable of handling complexity at scale. This foundational understanding paves the way to explore its profound effects on efficiency, cost savings, and innovation across modern business environments.

Historical context and evolution

Tracing the roots of AI-powered automation reveals a journey shaped by technological breakthroughs and evolving business priorities. Early automation efforts, dating back to the Industrial Revolution, centered on mechanizing manual labor—steam engines replaced human muscle, and assembly lines standardized production. These foundational changes set the stage, yet automation remained largely mechanical and deterministic for more than a century.

By the mid-20th century, programmable logic controllers (PLCs) and basic computer automation enabled businesses to replace repetitive clerical tasks with scripted processes. However, these systems operated strictly on predefined rules. For example, early manufacturing robots followed fixed motion patterns without adapting to environmental changes or unexpected anomalies. While effective, they lacked the ability to learn or adjust.

The landscape began to shift with the rise of artificial intelligence research in the 1950s and 1960s. Although AI's ambitions initially exceeded its practical reach, gradual improvements in machine learning algorithms during the 1980s and 1990s expanded automation beyond simple rule-based logic. Businesses experimented with expert systems—programs encoding specialized knowledge to support decision-making—but these too proved brittle when faced with novel data or unstructured inputs.

A pivotal turning point arrived with the explosion of big data and advances in computational power in the early 21st century. As vast datasets became accessible and cloud infrastructure scaled rapidly, machine learning models grew more sophisticated, enabling pattern recognition across complex information. Automation evolved from rigid scripting toward making predictions, dynamically classifying inputs, and even generating content autonomously.

This progression is evident in customer service tools: simple Interactive Voice Response (IVR) systems that once directed callers through fixed menus gave way to chatbots powered by natural language processing (NLP), which understand intent rather than just keywords. Starting around 2015, conversational AI agents began delivering context-aware responses by analyzing prior interactions and integrating sentiment analysis—marking a shift not just toward smarter automation but toward interfaces that blend machine intelligence with human nuance.

Automation's evolution also mirrors changing organizational priorities. Initially focused on cost reduction and efficiency—minimizing errors or accelerating throughput—the emphasis has expanded to enhancing decision quality and customer experience. The adoption of agile methodologies and continuous improvement philosophies encouraged iterative deployment of intelligent systems capable of self-tuning based on real-time feedback rather than infrequent upgrades.

In supply chains, for example, automated inventory tracking progressed from barcode scanners counting stock at fixed intervals to IoT-connected sensors streaming live data analyzed through predictive analytics platforms. This integration of AI interpreting sensor data alongside cloud computing orchestration has fostered resilient ecosystems that proactively adjust to disruptions.

Alongside technical advances came cultural shifts within organizations embracing AI-driven workflows. Early skepticism gave way as pilot programs demonstrated measurable ROI; yet successful adoption required reimagining roles where humans complemented machines rather than competed with them. The narrative shifted from "automation replacing jobs" to "automation augmenting workers," highlighting a vital lesson: true success depends on harmonizing technological capability with organizational change management.

Looking at the broader economic impact, studies show AI-powered automation has significantly boosted productivity in sectors like finance, healthcare diagnostics, and retail logistics over the past decade. JPMorgan Chase's COIN platform, for instance, automates contract reviews that once took lawyers thousands of hours annually—a striking example of cognitive tasks once considered immune to mechanization now within reach.

Challenges remain along this path: legacy infrastructure complicates integration; ethical concerns about algorithmic bias have surfaced; regulatory frameworks often lag behind rapid innovation cycles. These obstacles underscore why understanding this history is essential—not as mere nostalgia but as guidance for navigating future advancements responsibly.

AI-powered automation did not emerge overnight nor spring fully formed from laboratories; it is the product of decades-long convergence among hardware capabilities, algorithmic breakthroughs, data accessibility, and evolving business needs. Recognizing this layered history equips organizations with perspective—acknowledging both the potential benefits and inherent complexities embedded in these technologies.

In sum, appreciating this historical arc clarifies why modern AI automation represents more than improved efficiency: it embodies a fundamentally new paradigm of adaptive systems that learn continuously while reshaping how work itself is conceptualized across industries worldwide.

Importance for modern businesses

AI-powered automation is no longer just a tool for incremental improvements; it has become essential for gaining a competitive edge in today's dynamic business environment. Organizations leveraging AI can respond swiftly to evolving markets and increasingly complex customer demands. Where traditional manual processes once caused inevitable delays and inefficiencies, AI-enhanced workflows now continuously adapt and optimize, making older methods appear costly and outdated.

Take customer service, for example. Companies that adopt AI-driven chatbots drastically reduce wait times from minutes to seconds, all while providing round-the-clock availability. Beyond speed, these systems analyze past behaviors, preferences, and sentiment cues to personalize each interaction, delivering tailored experiences at scale. This not only boosts customer satisfaction but also drives loyalty and revenue growth—benefits that extend well beyond mere cost savings.

In manufacturing, AI transforms maintenance strategies by shifting from reactive repairs to proactive interventions. Sensors embedded in equipment feed data into machine learning models that detect subtle performance shifts signaling potential failures. So, downtime decreases significantly, inventory of spare parts shrinks, and technicians focus on targeted tasks rather than routine checks. This operational agility leads to higher throughput and improved margins, crucial for maintaining profitability amid intense global competition.

Financial institutions similarly benefit from AI automation. Fraud detection systems employ sophisticated anomaly detection algorithms to uncover suspicious transactions faster and more accurately than human analysts alone. Meanwhile, accounting departments use AI tools to reconcile large volumes of invoices, flag inconsistencies instantly, and generate compliance-ready reports with minimal manual effort. Automating these tasks frees skilled professionals to concentrate on strategic planning rather than routine bookkeeping.

Beyond improving efficiency, AI-powered automation enhances strategic agility. In today's markets, operational excellence is no longer enough; continuous innovation and adaptability are vital. Firms using AI can quickly experiment with new products or service models by leveraging automated data analysis and simulation tools that offer near real-time insights into customer behavior or supply chain performance. Take this example, retailers employing AI-based demand forecasting can dynamically optimize inventory across multiple locations, avoiding costly stockouts or excess stock.

AI also enables scalability that was once prohibitively expensive or complex. Startups can compete with established players by automating core functions such as marketing outreach or customer onboarding without proportionally increasing headcount. Larger enterprises integrate fragmented legacy systems into unified workflows using AI solutions, streamlining collaboration across departments and accelerating initiative launches.

However, realizing these advantages requires more than acquiring technology—it demands a shift in organizational mindset. Leaders must align automation efforts with clear business outcomes like revenue growth, risk reduction, and improved customer lifetime value rather than pursuing automation for its own sake. Without this focus, projects risk becoming isolated technical exercises with limited impact.

A practical example highlights this point: a mid-sized logistics company initially deployed an AI-driven route optimization system without incorporating driver feedback. Although the algorithm suggested routes that were efficient on paper, it failed to account for local realities such as seasonal traffic patterns or delivery window restrictions imposed by regulations. After integrating human insights and continuously retraining models with operational data, the company reduced fuel costs by 15% and noticeably improved delivery times.

From a financial perspective, McKinsey reports that companies embedding AI into core processes see productivity gains of up to 40%, decision-making speeds increase by half, and operating costs drop by as much as 30%. These improvements translate directly into greater shareholder value and increased capacity for reinvestment in innovation.

It is important to recognize that AI automation reshapes workforce roles rather than simply replacing jobs—a nuance often overlooked in public discussion. Machines handle routine cognitive tasks while employees focus on exception management, strategic initiatives, and relationship building —areas where human judgment remains essential. The most successful organizations embrace this shift as an opportunity to augment human potential rather than supplant it.

Still, challenges persist: legacy infrastructure can slow deployments; data silos limit model accuracy; cultural resistance impedes adoption; and regulatory uncertainty restricts experimentation in sensitive sectors like healthcare and finance. Overcoming these barriers requires deliberate governance frameworks centered on transparency, ethics, and ongoing stakeholder engagement.

In summary, AI-powered automation's true significance lies not just in enhancing operational metrics but in fundamentally transforming how companies compete and deliver value at scale. When advanced technologies are paired with strategic clarity and organizational readiness, formerly cumbersome processes become agile engines driving sustained growth in volatile markets.

Key technologies involved

Understanding the technologies behind AI-powered automation is crucial for unlocking its full potential in business. These technologies form an interconnected ecosystem, each contributing distinct capabilities that together transform complex workflows. Machine learning, natural language processing, computer vision, robotic process automation, and cloud computing combine to create adaptable systems that drive efficiency and innovation.

Essentially of most AI applications lies machine learning (ML), which enables systems to identify patterns in data without needing explicit programming for every scenario. Take, for example, a customer support chatbot trained on thousands of past interactions: instead of relying on fixed scripts, it continuously improves responses by learning from ongoing conversations. Businesses can develop supervised learning models using Python libraries like scikit-learn or TensorFlow to classify inquiries or forecast inventory needs. Take this example, a retailer might use a random forest classifier to spot high-value customers by analyzing purchase histories and engagement metrics, refining the model as new data arrives.

Natural language processing (NLP) extends AI's reach into human communication—both text and speech. Techniques such as sentiment analysis, named entity recognition, and language translation have advanced rapidly. Consider automated email triaging: an NLP model can categorize incoming messages into support requests, billing questions, or feedback without manual effort. Frameworks like spaCy and Hugging Face's Transformers simplify building these models. Real-world applications include virtual assistants that not only interpret commands but understand context —differentiating between "shipment delays" and "order cancellations" to route queries appropriately.

Adding another layer of perception, computer vision enables machines to interpret images and video streams. Manufacturing often leverages computer vision for quality control—detecting defects by analyzing product images in milliseconds using convolutional neural networks (CNNs). Tools like OpenCV combined with deep learning frameworks make such solutions accessible without massive hardware investments. A typical setup might involve capturing images on production lines, preprocessing them through normalization and augmentation, then training a CNN to distinguish acceptable products from flawed ones using labeled datasets.

Robotic Process Automation (RPA) complements these AI capabilities by automating repetitive, rule-based tasks traditionally done by humans within software interfaces. Unlike ML or NLP—which extract intelligence from data patterns—RPA operates at the user interface level, mimicking actions such as data entry across platforms lacking APIs. Imagine an accounts payable clerk manually inputting invoice details into legacy ERP systems daily; an RPA bot can replicate those mouse clicks and keystrokes faster and error-free around the clock. Platforms like UiPath and Automation Anywhere offer visual design tools for creating bots without coding skills initially while supporting advanced scripting for customization.

The surge in big data has propelled AI automation further by providing vast and diverse information that enhances model accuracy over time. Integrating AI algorithms with big data platforms—such as Hadoop clusters or cloud warehouses like Amazon Redshift—enables real-time analytics essential for responsive automation workflows. For example, a logistics company might combine GPS tracking data with weather forecasts to dynamically optimize delivery routes using predictive analytics built in Apache Spark environments.

Meanwhile, Internet of Things (IoT) devices serve as continuous data sources feeding AI systems. Sensors embedded in machinery monitor temperature fluctuations or vibration patterns, generating signals analyzed by anomaly detection algorithms that alert maintenance teams before failures occur—a classic case of predictive maintenance. Securing IoT connections requires robust middleware supporting protocols like MQTT alongside edge computing capabilities to minimize latency.

Cloud computing significantly lowers barriers to deploying AI-powered automation at scale by providing flexible infrastructure on demand alongside pre-built AI services such as Google Cloud's AutoML or Microsoft Azure Cognitive Services. This eliminates the need for large upfront investments in servers or specialized staff just to begin experimenting with intelligent automation projects. Instead, companies access scalable compute resources coupled with advanced toolkits through managed platforms.

To see how these technologies work together, consider an insurance company automating claims processing end-to-end. Incoming claim documents arrive via email, where NLP parses their content; attached photos undergo computer vision analysis for damage assessment; RPA bots extract information from unstructured text fields and populate internal databases; meanwhile, machine learning models assess fraud risk to prioritize claims—all running seamlessly on cloud infrastructure that also leverages real-time IoT sensor feeds from involved vehicles.

Security is woven throughout this technological fabric: encryption protects data transmitted between IoT sensors and cloud services; role-based access controls secure RPA environments; bias mitigation techniques improve fairness during ML training; and audit trails ensure compliance—especially vital in regulated industries like healthcare or finance.

Mastering these technologies requires more than technical knowledge—it calls for strategic alignment with business objectives and existing IT ecosystems. Through experimentation and iterative development, organizations can discover the right mix that accelerates efficiency while preserving agility.

 the landscape of AI technologies powering automation is rich and multifaceted: machine learning provides adaptability; NLP unlocks human communication; computer vision adds perceptual insight; RPA delivers operational consistency; big data fuels deeper understanding; IoT offers continuous context; and cloud platforms enable scalable deployment. Navigating this constellation equips businesses not only to automate but to innovate boldly amid rapid change.

Benefits over traditional methods

The advantages of AI-powered automation become strikingly clear when compared with traditional business methods. Conventional workflows often depend heavily on manual input, repetitive tasks, and rigid rule-based systems. While these approaches have supported organizations for decades, their drawbacks—slow response times, error-prone processes, and inflexibility—are increasingly apparent in today's fast-paced environment.

Speed and scalability illustrate this contrast well. Traditional automation can efficiently handle predefined tasks but struggles when faced with variability or unexpected scenarios. In contrast, AI systems adapt dynamically to new data patterns or customer behaviors without requiring constant human intervention. For example, a legacy order processing system may reject any request outside a strict template, causing delays or requiring manual fixes. Meanwhile, an AI-driven workflow equipped with machine learning models can interpret diverse inputs, intelligently flag anomalies, and escalate only truly exceptional cases for review—significantly reducing bottlenecks.

Accuracy improvements also stand out against older methods. Humans inevitably make errors—such as data entry mistakes or oversight during audits—and conventional software often lacks the sophistication to detect subtle inconsistencies beyond hard-coded rules. Consider invoice processing: traditional OCR (Optical Character Recognition) tools may misread characters, necessitating laborious manual verification. By comparison, AI-enhanced OCR combined with natural language understanding can parse varied invoice formats, spot irregularities like duplicate payments or mismatched amounts, and learn from corrections to improve over time.

Cost efficiency emerges not just from automation itself but from the resource optimization enabled by AI insights. Tasks that once required entire teams can be offloaded to intelligent bots working 24/7 without fatigue or downtime. Meanwhile, predictive analytics help guide inventory management to avoid overstocking or stockouts—common drains on working capital in retail and manufacturing sectors alike. Take this example, a consumer electronics company integrated AI forecasting into its supply chain system and cut excess inventory by 30% within six months while improving order fulfillment rates.

Traditional methods tend to operate in silos; departments often maintain separate datasets and systems that don't communicate well with each other. AI-powered solutions thrive on data integration and cross-functional collaboration. Cloud-based platforms consolidate information streams—from sales and marketing to logistics and customer service—enabling real-time insights that support proactive decision-making rather than reactive firefighting.

Risk management and compliance monitoring also benefit significantly from AI's capabilities. Manual checks are time-consuming and sometimes subjective; they can miss subtle signs of fraud or regulatory breaches hidden within large volumes of data. Machine learning models trained on historical incidents detect anomalies faster and flag potential issues earlier. For example, banks continuously use AI to analyze transaction patterns, identifying suspicious activities far more effectively than rule-based filters alone.

Employee empowerment is another important outcome. Rather than replacing workers—a common misconception —AI tools relieve employees from mundane chores so they can focus on higher-value tasks that require creativity or strategic thinking. A marketing team using automated content generation software spends less time drafting standard emails and more time crafting brand strategy that machines cannot replicate.

In practical terms, implementing AI-driven automation leads to shorter cycle times across multiple business functions—from onboarding new clients in days instead of weeks to closing monthly financial reports hours earlier without sacrificing accuracy. The cumulative effect is agility: businesses respond faster to market shifts, evolve customer services more smoothly, and accelerate innovation cycles.

A concrete example comes from an insurance provider that replaced its batch-processing claims system with an integrated AI platform combining NLP document analysis and RPA-driven data entry bots. So, claim resolution times dropped by 40%, operational costs fell substantially due to reduced overtime expenses, and customer satisfaction scores rose thanks to quicker payouts.

Transitioning away from rigid workflows toward adaptive intelligence isn't always simple but delivers undeniable gains in competitiveness and resilience compared with legacy methods reliant on manual oversight or static programming logic.

Taken together, these benefits explain why businesses across sectors prioritize AI-powered automation—not as a luxury but as a necessary shift for survival and growth amid relentless market pressures.

In summary: improved speed with flexible exception handling; superior accuracy through continual learning; cost savings via optimized resource use; enhanced risk detection beyond rigid checks; integrated data enabling proactive strategies; and empowered personnel focusing on impactful work—all surpass what traditional systems alone can deliver.

These advantages lay the foundation for companies to build smarter operations—not only automating tasks but fundamentally transforming how work gets done.

Common misconceptions

Misconceptions about AI-powered automation often cloud strategic decision-making and hinder progress in many organizations. One common myth is that AI will completely replace human jobs, making entire teams obsolete. While AI does automate repetitive and routine tasks, it more often enhances human capabilities rather than eliminating roles altogether. For example, in financial auditing, AI tools process vast amounts of data to flag anomalies, but expert auditors remain essential for interpreting results and making final decisions. This narrative overlooks how businesses shift human talent toward higher-value activities such as strategy, innovation, and customer engagement.

Another misunderstanding is the belief that AI implementations are "set and forget." Many expect instant, flawless automation once AI tools are deployed. In reality, successful integration requires ongoing monitoring, tuning, and training as new data patterns emerge or business needs change. Take this example, a retailer using AI-driven inventory forecasting must regularly recalibrate models to account for seasonal shifts or promotional campaigns. Overconfidence in initial deployments can lead to overlooked errors or declining performance—risks that proactive governance frameworks help mitigate.

Some assume that AI automation is only feasible for large enterprises with extensive data resources and deep pockets. This view ignores the growing democratization of AI through cloud platforms and open-source projects. Small and medium-sized businesses can now adopt affordable, scalable solutions without investing in costly infrastructure. A local logistics firm, for example, combined robotic process automation (RPA) with natural language processing (NLP) chatbots to efficiently manage customer inquiries, achieving measurable cost savings within months despite a modest budget.

There is also a misconception that AI systems require vast amounts of perfectly clean data before they can deliver value. While high-quality data improves accuracy, modern machine learning algorithms are designed to tolerate noise, missing entries, or incomplete datasets by using techniques such as imputation or transfer learning. Early-stage pilots often succeed using whatever data is available and then improve outcomes over time as more feedback is incorporated. For example, a marketing agency began with limited customer segmentation data but gradually enhanced its predictive models by integrating campaign results.

Confusion also arises around the differences between AI

and traditional automation methods like rule-based systems or macros. These approaches are sometimes treated as interchangeable, yet their capabilities differ significantly. Rule-based automation performs well in fixed scenarios but struggles with variability or ambiguity. AI excels in these complex contexts by learning from examples and adapting dynamically. Take this example, a customer service center relying on a rules engine could only handle scripted FAQs, whereas an AI-powered virtual assistant understands diverse queries and responds contextually.

Many assume that adopting AI automatically leads to improved business outcomes without recognizing the need to align technology with clear objectives and processes. Deploying an advanced chatbot won't enhance customer experience if underlying workflows remain inefficient or if staff aren't trained to collaborate effectively with the tool. A global insurer discovered that automating claims processing yielded little benefit until case assignment protocols were optimized and agents were equipped with real-time analytics dashboards.

Security concerns also fuel misunderstandings. Although AI introduces new risks such as adversarial attacks or data privacy issues, these challenges are neither unique nor insurmountable compared to traditional IT threats. Organizations often perceive AI as inherently less secure due to its complexity; however, employing rigorous encryption, access controls, and audit trails can effectively mitigate vulnerabilities when integrated thoughtfully during design.

Finally, some executives expect AI automation to be plug-and-play technology requiring minimal organizational change management. In reality, cultural resistance often poses a greater barrier than technical hurdles. Employees may fear job loss or mistrust opaque algorithms that impact their work. Transparent communication paired with inclusive training transforms skepticism into collaboration

—as demonstrated by a manufacturing plant where frontline workers co-designed an RPA rollout plan, resulting in higher acceptance rates.

By understanding these misconceptions, leaders can approach AI automation pragmatically rather than idealistically or fearfully. Appreciating the nuanced interplay between humans and machines helps set realistic expectations while fostering environments conducive to experimentation and continuous improvement.

These insights enable organizations to harness AI's potential judiciously—balancing enthusiasm with critical assessment —and ultimately drive meaningful business transformation without falling prey to oversimplifications or hype-driven pitfalls.

CHAPTER 2: THE IMPACT OF AI ON BUSINESS EFFICIENCY

Speed and accuracy enhancements

S peed and accuracy are among the most evident benefits AI brings to business automation. Take a customer support center that once managed thousands of calls daily: introducing AI-powered chatbots not only reduces wait times but also enhances the quality of responses. Unlike rigid FAQ systems, these chatbots use natural language processing to understand and address diverse customer needs in real time, cutting resolution times from minutes down to seconds. The airline industry offers a clear example, where AI virtual assistants instantly handle rebooking or refund requests, freeing human agents to focus on more complex issues.

Beneath these visible improvements lies a complex system of data ingestion and predictive analytics. In manufacturing,

AI sensors continuously monitor equipment, detecting anomalies that would escape human notice. This early warning accelerates maintenance workflows, prevents costly downtime, and improves production line accuracy. Unlike traditional scheduled checks based on fixed intervals, AI-driven predictive maintenance adapts dynamically to actual machine conditions. Take this example, General Electric reportedly saves millions annually by using AI diagnostics to anticipate turbine failures before they happen.

Speed enhancements extend beyond operations into data processing as well. Financial institutions, once burdened by manual reconciliation, now rely on machine learning algorithms that analyze transactions quickly and with near-perfect precision. These models, trained on historical data, flag inconsistencies or potential fraud almost instantly. JPMorgan Chase's COiN platform exemplifies this approach —it scans thousands of legal documents in seconds, replacing hundreds of hours of manual labor. The outcome is faster turnaround times and reduced errors without compromising compliance.

Accuracy improvements also strengthen decision-making by reducing human biases and errors in interpreting data. Sales forecasting, traditionally reliant on subjective judgment and spreadsheets, benefits from AI models trained on extensive historical data that uncover subtle patterns. Retailers like Walmart use such systems to optimize inventory across regions, minimizing both overstock and stockouts—achievements difficult to reach with manual methods alone.

Maintaining a balance between speed and accuracy is critical. For example, in healthcare claims processing, AI-based Optical Character Recognition (OCR) automates rapid digitization of paper forms, but additional anomaly detection algorithms verify data integrity before approvals proceed. This layered validation cut processing times by 40%

while ensuring compliance remained intact.

To capture these gains effectively, businesses should begin with process audits to identify bottlenecks where delays or errors have the greatest impact. Prioritizing these areas for AI adoption—such as automating invoice processing or customer data entry—lays the groundwork before tackling more complex tasks like demand forecasting. A typical integration process includes:

1. Data collection: Consolidate high-quality datasets relevant to the task.

2. Model selection: Choose algorithms suited to the problem—for example, classification models for sorting documents or regression for trend prediction.

3. Pilot testing: Deploy AI solutions in controlled settings to measure performance.

4. Feedback integration: Refine models based on real-world results.

5. Full deployment: Scale successful pilots across departments.

Consider a mid-sized logistics company that implemented AI-based route optimization software. By dynamically adjusting delivery schedules using traffic and weather data, pilot runs cut average delivery times by 15%, resulting in fuel savings and improved customer satisfaction.

Such improvements require ongoing refinement as data evolves and business needs shift. Establishing dashboards that track metrics like response times and error rates helps maintain accuracy while uncovering new opportunities for speed gains.

leveraging AI to enhance both speed and precision provides a competitive advantage. Shorter cycle times coupled with improved quality control elevate customer experiences and drive better financial performance across workflows.

Cost reductions

Cost reduction is a key motivator for adopting AI in business automation, with many organizations realizing significant savings across various functions. In accounts payable, for example, AI-powered optical character recognition (OCR) and workflow automation transform the traditionally labor-intensive process of invoice handling. These technologies extract data from invoices, verify it against purchase orders, and automatically route exceptions, cutting processing costs by up to 70%. One multinational retailer reported nearly halving its invoice handling staff after implementing such automation, allowing employees to focus on higher-value tasks instead.

Beyond reducing headcount, AI also drives smarter resource allocation that minimizes operational waste. Manufacturing plants, for instance, use AI to optimize energy consumption in real time by analyzing sensor data streams. This helps machines to run during non-peak production windows rather than following rigid schedules, a dynamic approach that has helped companies like Siemens save millions annually on energy without compromising output. Similarly, AI enhances supply chain management through demand forecasting that prevents costly overstock and frees up capital otherwise tied in idle inventory.

Reducing errors is another important avenue for cost avoidance. Manual data entry often introduces mistakes that cause delays and rework downstream. AI-powered automated data validation dramatically lowers error rates; one financial institution using machine learning for transaction monitoring cut exception handling costs by 40%. Early anomaly detection reduced expensive audits and investigations. In insurance claims processing, AI accelerates fraud detection by rapidly cross-referencing large datasets, saving millions that might have been lost to false claims.

Optimizing labor costs doesn't always mean reducing jobs; more often, it enhances workforce productivity through intelligent automation tools. Chatbots, for example, handle routine customer inquiries around the clock, freeing service agents to tackle complex issues more effectively. This shift improves employee satisfaction while lowering support center expenses. A telecom provider experienced a 30% reduction in call center costs after deploying conversational AI assistants that resolved common problems instantly.

Successfully implementing cost-effective AI requires careful vendor evaluation and a realistic view of hidden expenses. Licensing fees can escalate if usage grows beyond initial estimates, and cloud computing costs for large-scale model training sometimes take organizations by surprise. Budgeting should cover not only upfront investments but also ongoing maintenance, staff training, and integration efforts. Creating detailed total cost of ownership (TCO) models that compare different automation scenarios— accounting for both direct and indirect costs—is a best practice.

To illustrate the financial impact concretely: imagine a mid-sized company processing 10,000 invoices monthly at an average labor cost of (5 per invoice, amounting to)50,000 in direct labor expenses each month. Implementing an AI system that reduces manual effort by 60% yields monthly savings of (30,000 or)360,000 annually. After factoring in system maintenance costs (around (5,000 per month) and an initial implementation investment ()100,000 amortized over three years), net annual savings remain substantial at roughly (240,000.

These figures don't capture intangible benefits such as improved compliance and enhanced customer satisfaction, which often add even greater value. For example, automating regulatory reporting through AI helps minimize fines due to errors or missed deadlines—risks that are difficult to quantify but can have severe financial consequences.

In practice, some organizations underestimate the importance of scaling cost-saving initiatives carefully. Deploying automation too broadly before refining workflows can lead to wasted investments and stakeholder frustration. A phased rollout with pilot projects allows teams to address process-specific challenges affecting ROI before expanding deployment.

leveraging AI for cost reduction involves more than just technology—it requires aligning initiatives strategically with organizational priorities and continuously monitoring performance. When done thoughtfully, AI not only cuts expenses but also transforms operational models toward greater efficiency and resilience.

As Peter Sondergaard from Gartner aptly put it, "Information is the oil of the 21st century, and analytics is the combustion engine." The greatest cost savings come when companies harness their data through intelligent automation—fueling smarter spending that keeps them competitive today and adaptable tomorrow.

Improvements in customer service

Customer service has undergone a profound transformation with the introduction of AI-powered automation, fundamentally changing how businesses engage with their customers while boosting satisfaction and loyalty. A key example is the widespread adoption of AI-driven chatbots and virtual assistants in frontline support. These systems efficiently manage a broad range of routine inquiries —such as order status updates, product information, and troubleshooting—around the clock without human involvement, delivering immediate responses. Take this example, a leading e-commerce platform reported that after implementing AI chatbots, their average customer wait time fell from several minutes to under 10 seconds, leading to a 40% increase in first-contact resolution rates. This level of responsiveness helps reduce frustration and enhances convenience, directly supporting customer retention.

Beyond speeding up response times, AI personalizes interactions by leveraging data-driven insights. Machine learning algorithms analyze past purchases, browsing habits, and customer feedback to tailor recommendations and support conversations. One telecom company, for example, uses AI models to predict which customers may encounter service issues by examining network usage alongside previous complaint data. Customer service agents receive alerts with suggested solutions before problems escalate, enabling proactive outreach instead of reactive troubleshooting. This strategy contributed to a 15% reduction in churn within a year—a clear boost to customer lifetime value.

Another significant benefit is the consistency AI brings to service quality. Unlike human agents—whose performance can fluctuate based on experience or workload—AI systems maintain uniform standards for accuracy and tone. Natural Language Processing (NLP) empowers chatbots to grasp nuanced questions and respond with appropriate empathy or urgency, simulating human-like interaction while eliminating variability that often frustrates customers. Achieving this level of sophistication requires ongoing training with diverse conversation logs and regular audits to fine-tune responses and avoid robotic or inappropriate replies.

AI also streamlines the collection and analysis of customer feedback, accelerating service improvement cycles. Sentiment analysis tools scan social media posts, emails, and surveys to quickly identify trends or emerging issues. For example, a travel agency applied AI analytics to millions of reviews and uncovered widespread dissatisfaction linked to delays from a specific booking partner. With this insight, they renegotiated terms and improved accountability —actions that would have been impossible without automation at scale. Additionally, predictive models help forecast peak demand periods, allowing businesses to optimize call center staffing or enhance self-service options accordingly.

Despite these advantages, technology cannot fully replace the human touch. The most effective deployments use AI as an augmentation tool rather than a substitute. Complex cases are smoothly escalated from automated systems to specialized agents armed with contextual information gathered earlier in the interaction. This hybrid approach alleviates agent burnout by offloading repetitive tasks while preserving empathetic resolution where it matters most.

To illustrate, consider a CRM platform like Salesforce Einstein: its 'Einstein Bots' feature enables chatbots to handle FAQs by uploading typical queries and responses into a knowledge base. Simultaneously, Einstein Analytics monitors metrics such as average handling time and customer satisfaction via real-time dashboards. Workflow rules can be configured so unresolved issues automatically escalate to human agents along with complete chatbot conversation history, ensuring seamless handoffs.

Nonetheless, businesses must stay mindful of potential drawbacks like over-automation that may alienate customers who prefer human contact or privacy concerns around storing sensitive data. Transparent communication about AI's role fosters trust; customers who know when they're interacting with bots tend to be more forgiving of occasional mistakes.

enhancing customer service through AI-powered automation depends on balancing speed, personalization, and empathy at scale. When done well, it delivers measurable benefits—including higher satisfaction scores, increased repeat business, and operational efficiencies—that drive profitability forward without compromising brand integrity.

Streamlining operations

Efficiency in business operations depends on minimizing friction and accelerating workflows. AI-powered automation plays a crucial role by managing complex, multi-step processes that previously required extensive manual oversight. Rather than automating isolated tasks, streamlining operations means integrating disparate systems, synchronizing data flows, and eliminating bottlenecks to create a seamless operational ecosystem.

Consider order fulfillment as an example—a process involving numerous interconnected steps, from inventory checks to shipping logistics. Traditional methods often face delays caused by manual handoffs or siloed information. AI-driven workflow automation can close these gaps effectively. Take this example, robotic process automation (RPA) bots can extract order details from emails or web portals, cross-reference inventory databases instantly, trigger restocking alerts if necessary, and initiate shipping requests—all without human intervention. This end-to-end automation significantly reduces cycle times.

To illustrate, imagine an e-commerce company leveraging Microsoft Power Automate to streamline order processing:

1. Trigger: A new order email arrives containing structured data.

2. Data Extraction: An AI model parses the email to identify product SKUs, quantities, and customer information.

3. Inventory Validation: The system queries the ERP database to verify stock availability.

4. Decision Branch: If stock is sufficient, the workflow proceeds; otherwise, it generates a purchase requisition.

5. Shipping Request: The process sends a shipment initiation request to the logistics platform's API.

6. Customer Notification: An automatic confirmation email with tracking details is sent to the customer.

This streamlined sequence reduces manual involvement from dozens of steps to primarily monitoring exceptions—such as out-of-stock items or incorrect addresses—that are flagged automatically for human review.

Beyond speeding up fulfillment, this approach enhances accuracy by eliminating common transcription errors and ensures real-time synchronization across departments that might otherwise operate independently.

A similar transformation occurs in finance operations. Invoice processing traditionally involves verifying vendor details, matching purchase orders with received goods, and routing approvals through multiple managers—a slow and error-prone procedure when documents are misplaced or approvals delayed. AI-powered intelligent document processing (IDP) uses optical character recognition (OCR) to scan invoices, extract key fields like invoice number and amount, match them against digital purchase orders, and route them for approval automatically based on predefined rules.

For example, using Python open-source libraries:

```python
import pytesseract

from PIL import Image
```

```
import re

\#\# Load invoice image
invoice_img = Image.open('invoice_sample.png')

\#\# Extract text using OCR
text = pytesseract.image_to_string(invoice_img)

\#\# Extract invoice number assuming format: Invoice \#: 12345
match = re.search(r'Invoice \#:*(+)', text)
invoice_number = match.group(1) if match else None

print(f'Extracted Invoice Number: invoice_number')
```
` ` `

From this point, custom scripts can connect with ERP APIs to verify amounts and automate approval workflows based on thresholds—cutting days off payment cycles while improving cash flow visibility.

Operational streamlining also extends into human resources processes such as onboarding new hires or handling employee requests. Bots integrated with HR platforms like Workday or BambooHR can automatically assign training modules aligned with role profiles, schedule orientation sessions by syncing calendars across departments, and track completion status—all without requiring HR staff to manage each step manually.

One notable challenge involves ensuring interoperability among legacy systems that may lack support for modern

APIs or standardized data formats. Middleware platforms or custom connectors often bridge these gaps but must be carefully designed to maintain data integrity during transfers.

The benefits of smoother operations go beyond internal efficiency—they translate directly into improved customer experiences. Fewer errors in order fulfillment mean reduced returns; faster invoice payments strengthen vendor relationships; timely onboarding accelerates employee productivity—all delivering measurable value back to the bottom line.

In summary, streamlining operations through AI-powered automation requires a comprehensive understanding of business processes combined with strategic integration of technology tailored to address specific pain points. Success comes not from simply deploying tools but from aligning them thoughtfully across the entire organizational workflow landscape for maximum impact.

Case studies: Success stories

Success in AI-powered automation is best understood through real-world examples—companies confronting challenges, capitalizing on opportunities, and fundamentally transforming their operations. These case studies demonstrate how technology adoption delivers measurable benefits while highlighting the complex interplay among people, processes, and tools.

Consider UiPath, a leading RPA vendor whose client stories span multiple industries yet share common themes: rapid deployment, clear ROI, and scalability. One mid-sized insurance firm dramatically shortened claims processing from days to hours by implementing an RPA workflow. This system automatically extracted data from claim forms using intelligent document processing, verified policy details against databases, and routed exceptions for human review only. The outcome was a 70% reduction in manual labor hours alongside a 50% boost in customer satisfaction scores.

In retail logistics, DHL leveraged AI-driven predictive analytics to revolutionize inventory management across its global warehouses. By combining machine learning models trained on historical shipment data with real-time sensor inputs from IoT devices, they optimized stock levels—cutting overstock by 25% while avoiding stockouts that previously delayed deliveries. The system continuously refines forecasts through feedback loops, illustrating automation that not only executes tasks but also learns and improves over time.

JPMorgan Chase's COIN platform (Contract Intelligence) offers another compelling example. Before automation, contract reviews consumed thousands of lawyer-hours annually—a tedious but critical task prone to errors. COIN uses natural language processing to swiftly analyze legal documents and flag anomalies or risky clauses for further review. This AI-driven tool reduced review time by approximately 360,000 hours per year while minimizing costly mistakes that might have slipped through manual checks.

Shifting to marketing automation, Sephora embraced AI-powered personalization engines that analyze customer browsing behavior and purchase history. By integrating AI with their CRM system, Sephora dynamically tailored email campaigns to individual preferences. This approach increased campaign click-through rates by nearly 15%, driving significant online sales growth without additional advertising spend.

Smaller-scale implementations also offer valuable lessons due to their simplicity. Take this example, a regional accounting firm automated invoice approvals using Microsoft Power Automate combined with AI-based OCR tools like Azure Form Recognizer. The workflow extracted invoice data automatically, cross-checked vendor details against internal systems, and routed approvals based on configurable rules:

- Invoice amount ≤)1,000 → Auto-approve

- Invoice amount > (1,000 → Route for manager approval

- Duplicate invoices flagged for manual intervention

This straightforward solution halved approval cycles and freed staff to focus on client advisory work instead of administrative tasks.

These success stories reveal several recurring factors critical to effective automation:

1. Clear problem definition: Targeting well-understood bottlenecks or high-volume tasks where errors or delays carry significant costs.

2. Incremental rollout: Piloting projects within limited scopes before scaling mitigates risk and builds stakeholder confidence.

3. Human-in-the-loop design: Automation workflows often include exception handling points that require expert judgment rather than fully replacing people.

4. Data quality emphasis: Clean input data is essential for reliable AI outputs; many failures trace back to poor or inconsistent datasets rather than flawed algorithms.

5. Cross-functional collaboration: Engaging IT teams alongside business units early avoids siloed efforts that can stall progress.

The airline industry provides a notable example with

Delta Airlines' AI-powered chatbot used during irregular operations such as weather disruptions or mechanical issues. Capable of handling rebooking requests across web chat and mobile app channels simultaneously during peak disruptions like snowstorms, the bot dramatically cut wait times while maintaining near-human accuracy and personalized interactions.

These examples also highlight common pitfalls: underestimating change management challenges can breed resistance; neglecting cybersecurity during integration risks exposing sensitive data; failing to align automation initiatives with broader business strategy can limit impact beyond quick wins.

The lesson is clear: success demands blending technological expertise with operational insight and human-centered design principles. Automation isn't magic—it requires careful planning paired with adaptability as systems evolve after deployment.

For practitioners embarking on their own automation journeys, consider this distilled checklist:

- Identify high-volume repetitive tasks ripe for automation using process mining tools.

- Prioritize initiatives that deliver clear ROI within manageable scopes.

- Select tools compatible with existing infrastructure but flexible enough to evolve.

- Engage end users early through workshops or pilots to gather feedback.

- Establish upfront metrics—such as cycle time reduction and error rate improvements—and monitor continuously.

- Develop training programs addressing new

workflows and cultural shifts.

- Implement governance policies covering security standards and ethical considerations.

To illustrate practical implementation further: imagine a medium-sized manufacturing firm automating its quality assurance documentation process using Python scripts combined with OCR libraries like Tesseract and integration into SharePoint for records management:

```python
import pytesseract

from PIL import Image

import os


def extract_text_from_image(image_path):

img = Image.open(image_path)

text = pytesseract.image_to_string(img)

return text


def process_quality_docs(folder_path):

documents = [f for f in os.listdir(folder_path) if f.endswith('.png') or f.endswith('.jpg')]

qa_reports =

for doc in documents:

path = os.path.join(folder_path, doc)

text = extract_text_from_image(path)

\#\# Extract relevant info - e.g., batch number
```

```
batch_line = [line for line in text.split('') if "Batch Number:" in
line]

batch_number    =    batch_line[0].split(":")[1].strip()    if
batch_line else "Unknown

qa_reports[doc] = batch_number

return qa_reports


folder = './quality_docs'

reports = process_quality_docs(folder)

print("QA Reports Batch Numbers:", reports)
` ` `
```

This script automates extraction of key metadata from scanned QA forms—a task previously done manually—and feeds the results into downstream workflows such as automated compliance reporting or alerts when batches fail inspection criteria.

Across these examples, the tangible impact ranges from millions of dollars saved annually down to hours reclaimed weekly—explaining why organizations across sectors invest heavily in AI-powered automation today.

it's not just about efficiency gains but unlocking agility: responding faster to market changes; reallocating talent toward strategic initiatives; consistently delivering superior customer experiences—all indispensable advantages in increasingly digital and competitive landscapes.

Employee roles transformation

Automation is reshaping employee roles in ways that extend beyond simply replacing tasks. Rather than displacing workers outright, AI tools often enhance human capabilities by shifting responsibilities toward higher-value activities.

Take customer service representatives as an example: routine inquiries that once consumed much of their time are now handled by AI-powered chatbots. This shift allows staff to focus on complex issues requiring empathy and nuanced judgment—qualities machines have yet to master.

In finance departments, automation changes accountants' work from manual data entry to strategic analysis. Robotic process automation (RPA), for instance, can automatically reconcile bank statements or flag suspicious transactions. So, financial professionals transition from number crunchers to advisors who interpret AI-generated insights to guide budgeting and investment decisions. This evolution demands new competencies in understanding AI outputs and communicating findings effectively.

This changing landscape also calls for continuous learning. Employees must adapt not only by developing technical skills but also by embracing mindsets that prioritize collaboration with AI systems. A marketing analyst today partners with predictive analytics platforms that analyze vast datasets to forecast trends. The human role involves validating algorithmic suggestions and crafting creative campaigns based on those insights. Such collaboration improves effectiveness but requires comfort with data-driven decision-making.

Despite these opportunities, resistance to changing roles remains a significant challenge. Workers may feel threatened by automation or uncertain about their future contributions. Organizations that succeed in managing this transition do so through transparent communication and targeted training programs, clearly demonstrating how AI augments rather than replaces jobs. For example, a logistics company retrained warehouse staff to operate and maintain autonomous vehicles instead of performing manual picking tasks exclusively. This approach reduced turnover, maintained morale, and improved operational efficiency.

Automation can also flatten hierarchies by decentralizing decision-making. With AI systems providing near-real-time analytics, frontline employees gain authority to act swiftly without waiting for managerial approval on routine matters. In retail settings, store managers equipped with AI dashboards adjust inventory or pricing dynamically based on local demand signals. Empowering employees in this way increases engagement and responsiveness but requires trust and accountability frameworks.

However, not all impacts are positive. Job roles that rely heavily on repetitive or rule-based tasks risk obsolescence unless workers are reskilled promptly. Industries such as manufacturing and data entry are experiencing significant workforce shifts where automation displaces certain positions while creating new ones focused on system oversight, maintenance, or continuous improvement initiatives.

A practical example of automation enhancing rather than replacing human roles can be seen in HR processes. An AI-driven candidate screening tool integrated into recruiters' workflows filters resumes based on criteria like skills, experience, and certifications, drastically reducing initial review time. Recruiters then concentrate on interviews and assessing cultural fit—the aspects machines cannot accurately evaluate. This hybrid model streamlines hiring while preserving the essential human element.

A typical workflow might proceed as follows:

- Job requisition entered into the HR system
- AI analyzes incoming resumes for keyword matches and ranks candidates
- Recruiters receive a shortlist for manual review
- Selected candidates proceed to automated scheduling tools for interviews

- Interviewers provide feedback through integrated platforms that feed back into AI models for continuous learning

In this scenario, the recruiter's role evolves from gatekeeper to strategist and relationship builder—skills technology complements but does not replace.

transforming employee roles successfully depends on designing automation with human-in-the-loop principles rather than pursuing full autonomy indiscriminately. Balancing machine efficiency with human creativity builds resilient organizations prepared for long-term success.

Potential risks and challenges

Automation offers tremendous potential but comes with inherent risks and challenges that, if ignored, can undermine its benefits. A critical concern is data quality. AI systems rely heavily on accurate, comprehensive, and well-structured data to perform effectively. The adage "garbage in, garbage out" remains true—poor or biased data can produce flawed outcomes, misinformed decisions, or even discriminatory practices. Take this example, a predictive hiring tool trained on historical recruitment data reflecting past biases may unintentionally reinforce those biases, marginalizing qualified candidates from underrepresented groups. Maintaining clean and representative datasets requires continuous auditing and validation.

Integration complexity presents another significant hurdle. Many organizations operate with legacy systems developed over decades—fragmented software architectures, outdated databases, and siloed processes are common. Introducing AI-powered automation often means connecting these disparate elements, a task that can be technically challenging and costly. For example, a retail chain automating inventory management might face difficulties linking new AI forecasting tools with existing point-of-sale and supply chain platforms without disrupting daily operations. Without careful planning, downtime or data mismatches can erode trust in automation solutions.

Resistance to change also ranks among the major obstacles. Employees frequently fear job displacement or loss of control when automation is introduced. Cultural inertia can stall adoption, especially if leadership does not clearly communicate the purpose behind AI initiatives or provide sufficient retraining opportunities. At one mid-sized manufacturing firm, initial backlash arose as workers viewed robots as threats rather than collaborators. Management addressed this by involving employees early in pilot projects and offering skill development workshops focused on robot maintenance and programming— gradually turning skeptics into advocates.

Security vulnerabilities tend to increase with AI integration as well. Automated systems connected to multiple data sources expand the attack surface vulnerable to cyber threats. For example, ransomware targeting AI-driven supply chains could disrupt logistics networks by corrupting critical scheduling algorithms or demand forecasts. To protect sensitive business functions, strong cybersecurity measures—such as encryption, access controls, and regular penetration testing—must accompany automation deployments.

Legal and regulatory uncertainties further complicate implementation. As governments worldwide work to establish fair and transparent AI governance, organizations may encounter compliance risks amid ambiguous or evolving standards. Regulations like GDPR impose strict rules on collecting and processing personal data through AI tools—particularly in customer-facing applications such as chatbots or recommendation engines. Failure to comply can lead to substantial fines and reputational harm.

An often-overlooked risk involves overreliance on automation outputs without sufficient human oversight. Blind trust in AI predictions or decisions can result in serious errors when algorithms encounter situations beyond their training or reveal unexpected biases. Consider a financial institution using an AI model for credit scoring: neglecting periodic validation of model assumptions or human review might lead to unfair loan denials or exposure to high-risk borrowers. Incorporating human-in-the-loop mechanisms ensures accountability and enables corrective feedback.

Cost overruns and underestimated timelines commonly derail AI projects as well. Organizations frequently misjudge the resources required for data preparation, model training, system integration, and employee upskilling. Take this example, a large enterprise automating customer support discovered initial cost projections doubled after realizing extensive customization was necessary to align off-the-shelf tools with unique workflows. Realistic budgeting should include contingencies for unforeseen technical challenges.

Finally, ethical dilemmas emerge around transparency and explainability of AI decisions—especially in regulated sectors like healthcare or finance where stakeholders demand clear reasoning behind automated outcomes. Black-box models obscure how inputs translate into outputs, making it difficult to build trust among users and customers alike. Employing interpretability frameworks or rule-based systems helps clarify decision pathways but may sometimes reduce predictive accuracy.

Addressing these diverse challenges calls for a holistic approach that combines technological rigor with organizational readiness and ethical mindfulness. Effective risk mitigation includes comprehensive data governance programs, phased implementation with pilot testing, ongoing employee engagement initiatives, cybersecurity tailored for AI environments, proactive compliance monitoring, and fostering a culture where humans retain final authority over critical processes.

By recognizing these risks upfront, businesses can avoid pitfalls while unlocking the full potential of AI automation —transforming challenges into stepping stones rather than obstacles on the path forward.

Sector-specific impacts

Certain industries have embraced AI-driven automation in distinctly different ways, shaped by their unique operational demands, regulatory frameworks, and customer expectations. Understanding these sector-specific dynamics is essential for businesses aiming to implement AI solutions effectively, as a uniform approach rarely achieves success.

In manufacturing, for example, robotics and AI-powered predictive maintenance have transformed production lines. Instead of waiting for equipment failures, companies now use sensor data combined with machine learning models to predict breakdowns before they occur. Embedding vibration sensors on machinery allows real-time data to feed anomaly detection algorithms—such as recurrent neural networks trained on historical failure patterns. When potential issues are identified, maintenance teams receive advance alerts, enabling them to schedule repairs without disrupting production. This not only minimizes downtime but also streamlines inventory management for spare parts and optimizes labor allocation.

The retail sector leverages AI to automate inventory control and personalize customer interactions in real time. Amazon's demand forecasting models illustrate this well: they integrate sales history, seasonal trends, and external factors like weather or local events to optimize stock distribution across warehouses globally. On the customer-facing side, natural language processing (NLP) powers chatbots that guide shoppers through product selections smoothly, reducing friction and increasing conversion rates. Some retailers go further by using computer vision to analyze shopper behavior in physical stores—tracking foot traffic or shelf engagement—to refine store layouts and promotional tactics dynamically.

In financial services, AI has deeply impacted risk assessment and fraud detection. Traditional credit scoring has evolved into sophisticated ensemble models that incorporate vast alternative data sources—transaction histories, social signals, even device fingerprinting—to evaluate loan eligibility with improved accuracy and fairness. Take this example, banks may deploy AI systems combining gradient boosting trees with explainable AI methods like SHAP (SHapley Additive exPlanations). This not only flags high-risk borrowers earlier but also provides compliance teams with transparent insights into decision factors, a crucial advantage amid regulations such as GDPR and the Fair Credit Reporting Act. Similarly, fraud detection systems use unsupervised learning algorithms to sift through millions of transactions daily, identifying anomalies that could evade human scrutiny.

Healthcare presents a complex landscape where AI's promise is balanced by strict regulations and privacy concerns. Automated image analysis using convolutional neural networks assists radiologists by highlighting suspicious regions in X-rays or MRIs, effectively serving as a second opinion. However, rigorous validation and regulatory approvals—such as FDA clearance requiring extensive clinical trials—are mandatory before these tools can be deployed widely. Beyond diagnostics, robotic process automation (RPA) helps manage administrative tasks like patient scheduling and claims processing, freeing medical staff to focus more on direct patient care.

Logistics and supply chain management have been reshaped

by real-time tracking systems integrated with AI analytics. For example, DHL uses AI-driven route optimization algorithms that consider traffic conditions, delivery windows, vehicle capacities, and driver performance metrics to reduce fuel consumption and ensure timely deliveries. Predictive analytics also help anticipate demand shifts influenced by economic indicators or geopolitical events, allowing procurement teams to adjust orders proactively.

Energy companies apply AI to optimize grid operations and predict maintenance needs for infrastructure such as wind turbines and pipelines. IoT sensors connected through cloud platforms continuously monitor equipment health, feeding data on temperature fluctuations, vibrations, or pressure changes into machine learning models that forecast failures or inefficiencies across vast terrains.

Even legal services benefit from automation tailored to their workflows. Contract review software powered by NLP scans thousands of documents rapidly to identify clauses linked to compliance risks or financial exposure—a process once requiring extensive manual labor. This automation shifts lawyers' focus from document review to strategic advising.

These examples highlight the importance of customizing AI automation to fit industry-specific requirements—not just in technology but also in aligning with regulatory demands and operational nuances. While supply chain firms might prioritize integrating IoT data streams into predictive inventory models, healthcare providers must ensure compliance with HIPAA while maintaining AI functionality.

A concrete illustration can be found in automotive manufacturing: General Motors combines robotics with AI-driven visual inspection systems on assembly lines. Cameras capture every production stage, and computer vision algorithms detect defects like paint flaws or missing components more quickly than human inspectors. Quality metrics are logged in centralized databases accessible across the company for ongoing improvement initiatives.

On the other hand, small businesses in hospitality employ simpler automation tools suited to their scale—chatbots managing reservations or sentiment analysis bots interpreting customer reviews using algorithms trained on hospitality-specific language nuances.

Businesses pursuing sector-specific automation must carefully balance integration complexity against anticipated benefits. Some industries require stringent cybersecurity due to sensitive data handling; others need scalable architectures to accommodate seasonal demand fluctuations.

recognizing these sector-specific differences enables organizations to invest wisely in automation technologies that enhance core processes without causing disruption. As Andrew Ng aptly noted, "AI is the new electricity," but just as electricity's impact depended on tailoring applications —from lighting homes to powering factories—the same principle applies to AI.

By understanding where their industry lies on this spectrum, companies can set realistic expectations around implementation timelines, ROI projections, and required skill sets—essential factors when crafting sustainable automation strategies aligned with both immediate needs and long-term goals.

The future outlook

Emerging trends in AI-powered automation are transforming business landscapes at an unprecedented pace. As industries deepen their adoption of intelligent systems, innovation increasingly blends autonomy with enhanced collaboration between humans and machines. Rather than simply replacing tasks, future AI frameworks aim to augment decision-making, creativity, and operational agility across sectors.

This evolution is driven in part by the fusion of advanced machine learning with real-time data streams from Internet of Things (IoT) networks. On manufacturing floors, for example, sensor arrays continuously monitor equipment health. The next step involves AI systems that not only detect anomalies but also autonomously adjust machine parameters to optimize performance. This shift from reactive to proactive maintenance requires new architectures capable of edge computing—processing data locally with minimal latency. Companies like Siemens are already developing industrial AI platforms that embed intelligence directly into hardware controllers, enabling instantaneous responses without relying on cloud connectivity.

Alongside these technological advances, hybrid human-AI teams are becoming the norm. The augmented workforce concept emphasizes AI tools that assist employees with complex problem-solving rather than fully automating roles. Financial analysts, for instance, no longer need to sift manually through vast amounts of market data; instead, they rely on explainable AI dashboards that highlight anomalies or trends flagged by predictive models. This collaboration enhances both accuracy and trust, which are essential for broader organizational acceptance. BlackRock's Aladdin platform exemplifies this approach by integrating human expertise with AI insights in portfolio management.

As AI capabilities embed more deeply into ecosystems, new business models emerge. Subscription-based access to AI services democratizes high-level tools for small and medium enterprises (SMEs), allowing companies to scale automation flexibly in response to demand fluctuations instead of making costly upfront investments. Platforms like UiPath Marketplace offer prebuilt automation components accessible on demand, enabling rapid deployment without extensive coding expertise—a particularly valuable feature for industries with seasonal or cyclical cycles.

The convergence of 5G networks with AI further accelerates transformation by enhancing connectivity and data throughput across devices and locations. Logistics providers leverage 5G-enabled sensors to achieve near-instantaneous supply chain visibility, feeding predictive analytics engines that dynamically adjust shipment routes based on traffic or weather conditions. In agriculture, drones equipped with 5G transmit multispectral imaging data for AI-powered crop monitoring in real time, facilitating precise interventions that increase yield while minimizing resource use.

Decentralized AI architectures are also gaining traction through blockchain integration and edge computing clusters. These models distribute data processing and decision-making across networks rather than relying solely on centralized cloud services, improving security, privacy, and resilience. In healthcare, for example, patient data can remain within hospital firewalls while AI algorithms operate locally—preserving compliance with stringent regulations while delivering personalized diagnostics or treatment recommendations. Companies like Ocean Protocol are pioneering marketplaces for decentralized data sharing that could fuel future collaborative AI ecosystems.

As innovation races forward, ethical standards and governance frameworks strive to keep pace by emphasizing transparency and accountability in AI deployments. Organizations face increasingly complex regulatory environments across jurisdictions and must balance innovation with safeguards against bias or misuse. Tools offering model explainability, audit trails, and bias detection become indispensable; IBM's AI Fairness 360 toolkit helps developers identify discriminatory patterns during model training—a crucial step toward responsible automation adoption.

Simultaneously, advances in natural language understanding are revolutionizing human-machine interaction. Conversational agents evolve beyond scripted responses into context-aware collaborators capable of handling nuanced requests across languages and domains. Sales teams may soon rely on virtual assistants that automatically draft customized proposals based on client histories, while customer service centers employ multilingual chatbots that detect sentiment shifts mid-conversation to prioritize escalation when needed.

Looking further ahead, tight integration between AI and augmented reality (AR) or virtual reality (VR) promises immersive environments for training and remote collaboration. Field technicians wearing AR glasses overlaid with real-time diagnostic information from embedded AI models can reduce errors and accelerate repairs—even in unfamiliar settings.

Global collaboration is also accelerating innovation cycles as companies engage in cross-border research partnerships leveraging shared datasets and open-source algorithms. While competition remains intense, knowledge sharing drives collective progress in fields like drug discovery and climate modeling where scale matters most.

Navigating this evolving landscape requires leaders who balance optimism about possibilities with pragmatic risk management grounded in data-driven insights. Embracing a forward-looking mindset means committing to continuous learning—not only about technology but also about shifting market dynamics shaped by policy changes and consumer expectations.

the future of AI-powered automation is neither utopian nor dystopian but a complex interplay of technical breakthroughs and human judgment shaping how businesses thrive amid uncertainty. Organizations willing to invest thoughtfully today stand poised to reap compound benefits tomorrow—embracing an era where agility ensures survival and innovation becomes an ongoing journey rather than a finite destination.

Balancing automation with human touch

Automation, even when driven by advanced AI, cannot fully separate from the human element. The key to successful AI adoption in business lies in balancing machine efficiency with human judgment. Over-automation risks alienating both customers and employees, while underusing AI means missing out on valuable productivity gains. Achieving this balance requires a clear understanding of where AI excels and where human insight remains essential.

Take customer service as a clear example. AI chatbots can handle thousands of routine inquiries simultaneously, quickly responding to common questions about orders or policies. Yet when more complex issues arise—such as billing disputes involving multiple accounts or emotional customer complaints—chatbots' scripted responses fall short. In these cases, smooth escalation to human agents preserves empathy and flexibility, preventing frustration that could harm brand loyalty. Many companies now use hybrid CRM workflows where AI triages queries using natural language processing (NLP) and sentiment analysis, but hands off cases to human specialists when confidence scores dip below certain thresholds.

Similarly, sales pipelines benefit from automation tools that score leads based on behavior patterns and historical data, prioritizing outreach effectively. Still, closing deals often depends on interpersonal dynamics—trust-building conversations and nuanced negotiations—that remain beyond AI's reach. The best approach leverages AI for lead qualification and routine follow-ups while reserving human salespeople for personalized engagement during critical decision points.

This balance can be architected using workflow automation platforms like Microsoft Power Automate or UiPath integrated with communication tools such as Slack or Zendesk:

1. Incoming customer requests enter a centralized ticketing system.

2. AI-powered algorithms classify tickets by urgency and complexity.

3. Simple issues trigger automated responses or self-service knowledge base links.

4. Complex tickets flagged with low confidence scores automatically alert human agents via Slack.

5. Agents review enriched context from AI analytics dashboards before engaging customers.

6. After resolution, customer feedback is collected to continually train AI models.

Such a design ensures machines handle volume efficiently without sacrificing the personal touch crucial for customer satisfaction and retention.

On the manufacturing floor, balancing autonomy with human oversight is equally important. Predictive maintenance systems analyze sensor data to forecast equipment failures, scheduling interventions that reduce downtime and costs. Despite high accuracy—some models cut unplanned outages by over 30%—final decisions about maintenance timing often incorporate operator input, accounting for production schedules or supply chain factors invisible to algorithms.

In financial services, fraud detection vividly illustrates this partnership. Machine learning models scan millions of transactions daily to flag suspicious activity—far beyond what humans could handle at scale. Yet compliance officers manually review flagged cases to confirm intent and legal relevance before escalation; mishandling false positives can be costly both financially and reputationally.

Consider invoice processing automation integrating Python scripting into an ERP system:

- Step 1: Optical Character Recognition (OCR) extracts invoice data automatically.

- Step 2: A machine learning classifier verifies vendor authenticity using historical records.

- Step 3: Anomalies—like mismatched amounts or unexpected vendors—trigger manual review flags.

- Step 4: Accounts payable staff receive detailed exception reports highlighting discrepancies alongside AI-generated suggestions.

- Step 5: Staff resolve exceptions; their corrections feed back into model retraining pipelines for improved accuracy.

This iterative loop showcases how AI's speed combines with human contextual judgment to enhance reliability without overwhelming manual workloads.

Achieving this balance also demands cultural shifts within organizations. Employees must be trained not only on new tools but on collaborative mindsets that trust yet critically verify AI outputs instead of blindly accepting or dismissing them out of fear or skepticism. Leaders play a pivotal role in communicating that automation complements rather than replaces human roles, reducing resistance and fostering productivity improvements.

Embedding "human-in-the-loop" checkpoints at strategic stages mitigates risks tied to over-reliance on automation—such as ethical blind spots or unintended biases embedded in training data—a concern extensively discussed by experts like Kate Crawford in algorithmic accountability.

And, blending automation with human interaction opens new opportunities for innovation through augmented intelligence approaches, where machine suggestions accelerate creativity rather than constrain it—for example:

- Marketing teams refining AI-generated content drafts to better reflect brand voice.

- Product developers using simulation outputs while iterating designs based on experiential insights.

combining machine efficiency with uniquely human capabilities creates workflows resilient enough to adapt dynamically as market conditions evolve—a necessity in today's volatile business environment.

Ignoring this delicate interplay risks pitfalls ranging from diminished customer experience and employee disengagement to compliance failures under complex regulations demanding transparency and fairness in automated decisions.

For sustainable success, businesses must recognize that technology alone isn't enough; thoughtful integration strategies preserving essential human judgment ensure automation acts as an enabler—not a dictator—of business processes.

Practically speaking, start small by automating discrete tasks while preserving manual override options; monitor outcomes closely; solicit continuous feedback from frontline workers; then iterate toward workflows that naturally blend the best of both worlds rather than imposing changes top-down.

This nuanced balance distinguishes fleeting hype around "AI replacing humans" from enduring transformation, where machines empower people to work faster and smarter—a reality already unfolding across industries worldwide.

CHAPTER 3:
UNDERSTANDING
AI TECHNOLOGIES

Machine learning basics

T ake a common business problem like sorting incoming emails into categories such as spam, inquiries, or orders. Initially, engineers might create keyword-based filters—marking emails containing words like "discount" or "free" as spam. However, this method is fragile and often fails when spammers change tactics or when legitimate emails use those keywords in different contexts. Machine learning models overcome this by analyzing thousands of labeled emails, picking up on subtle patterns beyond obvious keywords—such as word combinations, sender behavior, or timing—to classify new messages more accurately.

To illustrate, consider a basic email classification example using Python's popular scikit-learn library. Suppose you start with a dataset of emails labeled by category:

```python
```

from sklearn.feature_extraction.text import TfidfVectorizer

```python
from sklearn.model_selection import train_test_split
from sklearn.naive_bayes import MultinomialNB
from sklearn.metrics import classification_report

\#\# Sample data: list of emails and their labels
emails = [
Huge discount on electronics!",
Your order has been shipped",
Meeting scheduled for tomorrow",
Win a free vacation now!",
Invoice attached for your recent purchase
]
labels = ["spam", "order", "inquiry", "spam", "order"]

\#\# Convert text data into numerical vectors
vectorizer = TfidfVectorizer()
X = vectorizer.fit_transform(emails)

\#\# Split into training and test sets
X_train, X_test, y_train, y_test = train_test_split(X, labels, test_size=0.4)

\#\# Train a Naive Bayes classifier
model = MultinomialNB()
```

```
model.fit(X_train, y_train)

\#\# Predict categories of test emails
predictions = model.predict(X_test)

print(classification_report(y_test, predictions))
` ` `
```

Breaking down the steps:

- Text vectorization: The raw email text is converted into numerical feature vectors using TF-IDF (term frequency-inverse document frequency), which highlights the importance of words.

- Train-test split: The data is divided to fairly evaluate how well the model performs on unseen examples.

- Model training: The Multinomial Naive Bayes algorithm learns to differentiate categories based on training data.

- Evaluation: The classification report provides precision and recall metrics to assess accuracy.

While this example is simple, it highlights how machine learning can automate time-consuming tasks like sorting emails—freeing customer support or marketing teams from manual work.

Machine learning's applications extend beyond classification into regression analysis, widely used for forecasting sales or demand. Imagine managing inventory for an online retailer: predicting future product demand helps optimize stock levels and minimize holding costs. Linear regression models relate past sales data to factors such as seasonality or promotional activities.

A practical way to explore this is through Excel:

1. Organize historical weekly sales data with columns for Week Number (A), Sales Volume (B), and Advertising Spend (C).

2. Use Excel's Data Analysis Toolpak to run regression:

3. Navigate to Data > Data Analysis > Regression.

4. Set Sales Volume as the dependent variable (Y Range).

5. Set Advertising Spend as the independent variable (X Range).

6. Review the output, noting coefficients that indicate how much sales change per advertising dollar.

7. Apply the regression equation to forecast sales for upcoming weeks based on planned ad budgets.

This hands-on method enables managers without coding experience to quickly access predictive insights—a key advantage of AI-enhanced decision-making.

Unsupervised learning offers another dimension where algorithms identify hidden patterns without labeled data. Clustering techniques, for example, segment customers by behavior without predefined groups. A retail chain might use this approach to discover distinct buyer personas from purchase histories and tailor promotions accordingly.

Here's a brief illustration using k-means clustering in Python:

```python
```

from sklearn.cluster import KMeans

import numpy as np

```
\#\# Simulated customer purchase frequencies across two product categories
data = np.array([
[5, 1], \# Customer A buys 5 electronics and 1 clothing item
[2, 4],
[6, 0],
[1, 5],
[7, 2]
])

kmeans = KMeans(n_clusters=2)
kmeans.fit(data)
print("Cluster assignments:", kmeans.labels_)
` ` `
```

The algorithm automatically groups customers with similar purchase profiles, allowing marketing teams to design targeted campaigns for each segment—improving engagement and return on investment compared to broad, untargeted efforts.

Despite its power, machine learning's success hinges on high-quality data—a truth echoed by AI pioneers like Andrew Ng who emphasize that "data beats algorithms." Poor or biased training data can lead even advanced models to produce unreliable results that misinform decisions or perpetuate mistakes.

Addressing this requires dedicating effort early on to clean datasets thoroughly by:

- Removing duplicates and erroneous records.
- Handling missing values through imputation.
- Balancing class distributions to prevent skewed predictions.

And, continuous retraining helps models adapt as business conditions evolve—whether due to shifting seasonal trends or changing customer preferences.

Deploying machine learning within automated workflows also demands attention to computational resources and system architecture. Cloud platforms such as AWS SageMaker or Azure ML offer scalable environments that enable efficient model deployment at enterprise scale without heavy infrastructure investments.

Looking beyond algorithms themselves reveals a broader impact: machine learning enables smarter automation by allowing systems to improve autonomously over time— surpassing the limitations of rigid rule-based tools like macros or simple robotic process automation bots.

At its core, machine learning transforms raw data streams into actionable intelligence that drives dynamic workflow automation—from sorting communications and forecasting demand to personalizing user experiences. This foundation empowers businesses to achieve efficiency gains unattainable through manual effort alone.

Yet true mastery involves not only applying machine learning but understanding its limits and operational demands well enough to design sustainable solutions aligned with organizational goals. Complex models are not always the best fit; sometimes simpler heuristics offer more reliable results with lower risk and overhead.

Striking this balance is key to successful AI-powered automation initiatives across industries today.

Natural language processing (NLP)

Natural language processing (NLP) expands AI automation beyond raw data analysis into the intricate domain of human communication. While machine learning often focuses on structured data, NLP empowers systems to interpret, understand, and generate human language, enabling meaningful business interactions. From automating customer inquiries to extracting insights from unstructured documents and supporting intelligent assistants, NLP connects complex language patterns with practical workflows.

Take a customer support center receiving thousands of emails and chat messages daily. Traditional keyword-based filters may misclassify requests or overlook the true intent behind them. In contrast, NLP models assess context, sentiment, and intent together—distinguishing, for example, between a complaint about product quality and a simple delivery status inquiry. This nuanced understanding is essential for accurately routing tickets or generating responses that feel personalized rather than robotic.

A concrete example involves building an NLP pipeline using Python's spaCy library, known for its speed and linguistic precision. Imagine automating the extraction of key details like dates, product names, and issue descriptions from support emails:

```python
import spacy

\#\# Load pre-trained English model
nlp = spacy.load("en_core_web_sm")
```

```
\#\# Sample email text

email_text = ""

Hello team,

I ordered the X200 headphones last week but received a
defective pair.

Can you please arrange a replacement by next Monday?
Thanks!
"


doc = nlp(email_text)


\#\# Extract named entities (e.g., products, dates)

for ent in doc.ents:

print(ent.text, ent.label_)
` ` `
```

In this snippet, the nlp object tokenizes and annotates the email. Named entity recognition (NER) highlights 'X200 headphones' as a product and 'next Monday' as a date. These extracted details can then drive automated workflows —triggering inventory checks or scheduling replacements without manual intervention.

Beyond extraction, sentiment analysis adds another layer of understanding. Identifying whether customer messages express frustration or satisfaction helps prioritize urgent cases. Open-source libraries like TextBlob and commercial APIs such as Google Cloud Natural Language provide tools for sentiment scoring. Take this example:

```python
from textblob import TextBlob


feedback = "The delivery was late and the package was damaged.


analysis = TextBlob(feedback)

print("Sentiment polarity:", analysis.sentiment.polarity) \# Negative value indicates dissatisfaction
```

A polarity score near -1 reflects negative sentiment, while positive values indicate satisfaction. Integrating these insights into CRM systems enables businesses to flag unhappy customers proactively before issues escalate.

Supporting multiple languages is increasingly important for global operations. Transformer-based models like BERT and GPT have transformed multilingual understanding by capturing deep contextual nuances across languages. Though deploying these models requires significant computational resources, cloud services often offer managed endpoints that allow businesses to scale efficiently without heavy infrastructure investments.

Text summarization further enhances productivity by automatically condensing lengthy documents—such as legal contracts or technical manuals—into concise bullet points tailored for decision-makers. Approaches range from straightforward frequency-based methods to advanced abstractive models capable of generating natural summaries specific to various domains.

In real-world applications, combining rule-based systems with machine learning often yields robust NLP pipelines.

For example, insurance companies deploy hybrid solutions where predefined patterns identify policy numbers while ML models classify claim types from free-text descriptions. This approach accelerates claims processing while reducing errors.

Despite these advances, NLP faces ongoing challenges. Language ambiguity demands continuous model refinement and domain-specific tuning. Detecting sarcasm remains particularly difficult; misinterpretations can lead to flawed automation decisions that waste resources or frustrate customers further.

Data privacy also plays a critical role. Handling sensitive communications requires strict controls on data access and anonymization to comply with regulations like GDPR or CCPA—especially when using third-party APIs that involve transmitting data externally.

Mastering NLP tools gives businesses powerful automation capabilities across customer service, marketing personalization, compliance monitoring, and more. However, the greatest benefit comes from seamlessly integrating these capabilities into existing systems. Embedding an NLP module within a CRM platform can automatically classify tickets as they arrive; coupling this with workflow engines triggers downstream actions without manual intervention.

A typical integration flow might look like this:

1. Data ingestion: Incoming customer emails enter a message queue.

2. NLP processing: Each message undergoes entity extraction and sentiment analysis.

3. Classification: Messages are tagged based on features (e.g., 'urgent complaint,' 'refund request').

4. Automation triggers: Tickets route automatically

to specialized teams; pre-written replies dispatch where appropriate.

5. Feedback loop: Results track over time to retrain models and improve accuracy.

Implementing such end-to-end pipelines transforms labor-intensive communication tasks into streamlined operations running around the clock with minimal human oversight—freeing staff to focus on more complex problem-solving.

NLP's development has reshaped how businesses engage customers at scale while maintaining quality interactions—a balance once thought achievable only with large teams. Its diverse toolkit—from entity recognition and sentiment analysis to summarization—enables organizations not just to automate but genuinely understand the textual data that drives their success.

This deep understanding forms the foundation of intelligent automation strategies that honor both operational efficiency and human experience—the essential duality defining modern AI-powered business workflows today.

Computer vision applications

Computer vision extends AI automation into interpreting and understanding visual information—a vital capability for businesses working with images, videos, or real-time sensor data. Unlike natural language processing, which focuses on text and speech, computer vision algorithms analyze pixels to identify objects, detect anomalies, or extract meaningful patterns. This visual intelligence enables automation across a wide range of industries, from quality control in manufacturing to customer behavior analysis in retail.

Take a production line where defects must be detected quickly to prevent faulty products from reaching customers. Manual inspection is often slow and susceptible to human error. In contrast, computer vision systems powered by convolutional neural networks (CNNs) excel by learning the features that distinguish acceptable parts from flawed ones. Take this example, an automated camera setup might capture images of circuit boards moving along a conveyor belt, while a trained model classifies each board based on the presence of defects.

Implementing such a system typically involves several key steps:

1. Data collection: Assemble thousands of labeled images showing both defective and non-defective components.

2. Preprocessing: Normalize image sizes and apply augmentations like rotations or flips to improve model robustness.

3. Model training: Use CNN architectures such as ResNet or MobileNet tailored for image classification tasks.

4. Deployment: Integrate the trained model with real-time cameras and alert systems on the production floor.

Below is an example using Python's TensorFlow library to build a simple image classifier for defect detection:

```python
import tensorflow as tf

from tensorflow.keras import layers, models

from tensorflow.keras.preprocessing.image import ImageDataGenerator


\#\# Set up data generators for training and validation

train_datagen = ImageDataGenerator(rescale=1./255,
```

```
rotation_range=20,
horizontal_flip=True,
validation_split=0.2)

train_generator = train_datagen.flow_from_directory(
'dataset/train',
target_size=(150, 150),
batch_size=32,
class_mode='binary',
subset='training'
)

validation_generator = train_datagen.flow_from_directory(
'dataset/train',
target_size=(150, 150),
batch_size=32,
class_mode='binary',
subset='validation'
)

\#\# Build a simple CNN model
model = models.Sequential([
layers.Conv2D(32,          (3,3),          activation='relu',
input_shape=(150,150,3)),
```

```
layers.MaxPooling2D(2,2),

layers.Conv2D(64,(3,3), activation='relu'),
layers.MaxPooling2D(2,2),

layers.Conv2D(128,(3,3), activation='relu'),
layers.MaxPooling2D(2,2),

layers.Flatten(),
layers.Dense(512, activation='relu'),
layers.Dense(1, activation='sigmoid')
])

model.compile(loss='binary_crossentropy',
optimizer='adam',
metrics=['accuracy'])

\#\# Train the model
history = model.fit(train_generator,
epochs=10,
validation_data=validation_generator)
` ` `
```

This code creates data pipelines that automatically handle normalization and augmentation—crucial steps to improve accuracy amid real-world variations in lighting and orientation. The binary classifier distinguishes defective parts (label 1) from good ones (label 0). While simplified here for clarity, practical implementations often involve fine-tuning hyperparameters or leveraging transfer learning from pretrained models like VGG16 to boost performance on smaller datasets.

Beyond manufacturing inspections, computer vision drives many other applications. Automated inventory tracking uses barcode and QR code scanning embedded in mobile apps or warehouse robots. Retailers employ facial recognition technologies (though these require careful ethical consideration) to analyze foot traffic and measure shopper engagement with displays—enabling dynamic optimization of store layouts based on real-time insights.

In logistics, computer vision integrates with autonomous vehicles or drones to improve parcel identification and sorting accuracy. For example, Amazon Robotics deploys sophisticated visual systems that guide robots through warehouses while avoiding obstacles—a combination of object detection algorithms and spatial mapping techniques known as SLAM (Simultaneous Localization and Mapping).

Common building blocks in computer vision workflows include:

- Object Detection: Identifying instances of predefined classes (e.g., products on shelves) using models like YOLO or Faster R-CNN.

- Image Segmentation: Precisely delineating pixel regions belonging to objects for detailed analysis in medical imaging or quality inspection.

- Optical Character Recognition (OCR): Extracting text from images—key for automating invoice processing or reading shipping labels.

- Video Analytics: Tracking motion patterns over

time for applications like security monitoring or crowd management.

For businesses exploring computer vision today, cloud platforms offer managed services such as Google Cloud Vision API or Microsoft Azure's Computer Vision. These services lower the barrier to entry by abstracting complex model training and infrastructure management. They provide features like landmark recognition or text extraction accessible through simple REST calls:

```python
from google.cloud import vision

client = vision.ImageAnnotatorClient()

with open('product_image.jpg', 'rb') as image_file:
content = image_file.read()

image = vision.Image(content=content)
response = client.object_localization(image=image)

for object_ in response.localized_object_annotations:
print(f'object_.name                                    at
object_.bounding_poly.normalized_vertices')
```

This snippet retrieves localized objects within an image along with bounding boxes normalized relative to image dimensions—making it easy to overlay detections on user interfaces.

Despite its promise, adopting computer vision comes with

challenges: variability in image quality can affect accuracy; dataset bias may cause rare defect types to be missed; real-time processing demands low-latency hardware; privacy concerns arise when identifying individuals without consent.

Nonetheless, integrating computer vision into business workflows often yields measurable efficiency gains—cutting inspection times from minutes per item down to seconds while improving consistency beyond human capabilities. It also enables scaling operations without proportionally increasing workforce size—a critical competitive advantage.

computer vision transforms visual data into actionable insights seamlessly embedded within automation pipelines. By turning manual tasks into precise machine-driven processes, it accelerates productivity across sectors ranging from manufacturing floors to customer-facing retail environments.

Robotics process automation (RPA)

Robotic Process Automation (RPA) transforms routine workflows by assigning repetitive, rule-based tasks to software "robots." Unlike traditional automation—which often demands deep integration or custom coding—RPA works at the user interface level, mimicking human interactions with existing applications. This approach allows businesses to boost efficiency without the need to overhaul legacy systems.

Consider an accounts payable department overwhelmed by manual invoice entries. Rather than hiring additional staff or waiting for IT to build complex integrations, an RPA bot can log into the invoicing platform, extract data from emails or PDFs, input that information into accounting software, and flag exceptions for human review. This leads to faster processing and fewer errors—all without disrupting established systems.

An RPA solution generally consists of three key components:

- Bot Development Environment: Tools such as UiPath Studio or Automation Anywhere Designer enable users to visually create workflows through drag-and-drop interfaces.

- Bot Runner: The runtime environment where bots carry out their assigned tasks based on schedules or triggers.

- Control Center: A centralized dashboard for managing bots, monitoring their performance, and handling exceptions.

To illustrate, here's a simple example using Python and the open-source RPA Framework (built on Robot Framework). Imagine you want a bot to download daily sales reports from a web portal and save them locally.

```python
from RPA.Browser.Selenium import Selenium

from RPA.FileSystem import FileSystem


browser = Selenium()

fs = FileSystem()


try:

browser.open_available_browser('https://salesportal.example.com/login')

browser.input_text('id=username', 'your_username')

browser.input_text('id=password', 'your_password')

browser.click_button('id=login-button')
```

```
browser.wait_until_element_is_visible('xpath=//
a[contains(text(),"Daily Sales Report")]')

browser.click_link('xpath=//a[contains(text(),"Daily        Sales
Report")]')


download_path    =    fs.join_path(fs.get_current_directory(),
'downloads', 'daily_sales_report.csv')

fs.create_directory(fs.join_path(fs.get_current_directory(),
'downloads'))


browser.download_file(download_path)


finally:

browser.close_all_browsers()
` ` `
```

This script automates logging into the portal, navigating to the report, downloading the CSV file to a designated folder, and closing the browser—replacing what would otherwise be a repetitive daily task.

RPA excels at automating processes involving structured data: invoice processing, order entry, employee onboarding forms, customer data updates, and more. It's particularly valuable in organizations reliant on multiple legacy applications that lack APIs but still depend heavily on user interfaces.

However, effective RPA deployment starts with careful process analysis. Not every task suits automation. Ideal candidates are rule-based with minimal exceptions and stable interfaces; otherwise, bots may fail frequently and require human intervention—undermining efficiency gains.

Returning to invoice processing: if invoices come in highly variable formats with inconsistent fields or handwritten notes, pure RPA may struggle. Integrating AI-powered document understanding tools—like optical character recognition (OCR) or natural language processing (NLP)—can help extract unstructured data before passing it along to bots for structured input.

This leads to hybrid workflows where AI handles variability and decision-making while RPA manages repetitive transactional steps. For example:

1. AI extracts supplier name, invoice number, and total amount from scanned documents.

2. RPA inputs this extracted data into ERP systems.

3. Bots route any anomalies flagged during extraction or entry to human reviewers via email notifications.

Scaling an RPA program also requires robust governance: establishing development standards; defining change management policies; and deploying monitoring dashboards to track bot health and measure ROI.

Many organizations underestimate maintenance overheads —bots need regular updates as applications evolve (e.g., UI changes can break scripts). Monitoring tools like UiPath Insights or Automation Anywhere Analytics help identify bottlenecks and trigger timely fixes.

From a cost perspective, RPA delivers quick wins with relatively low upfront investment compared to full system replacements. Still, it's important to avoid "bot sprawl"— uncontrolled proliferation of bots can create inefficiencies and security vulnerabilities without proper oversight.

To put ROI into perspective for invoicing:

- Manual processing time per invoice: 5 minutes
- Average invoices per month: 10,000
- Labor cost per hour:)20

Manual monthly labor cost = (5/60) * 10,000 * (20 =)16,666

If an RPA bot reduces processing time by 80%, monthly savings approach (13,333—potentially covering licensing costs within months depending on vendor pricing.

In customer service centers, RPA bots ease frontline workloads by automating routine ticket categorization or status updates across platforms lacking API connectivity. This frees human agents to focus on complex inquiries requiring empathy and judgment.

Despite its accessibility and power, caution is needed against over-reliance on surface-level automation without addressing underlying process inefficiencies. Sometimes processes must be redesigned before automation can deliver lasting value—a point emphasized by Gartner analyst Craig Le Clair: "Automation should amplify good processes—not patch broken ones."

Robotic Process Automation unlocks significant potential by bridging manual labor gaps within existing IT ecosystems with minimal disruption. When thoughtfully combined with AI-driven components that handle complexity and variability, it becomes a foundational element of modern business automation strategies—streamlining operations while enabling resources to focus on higher-value activities.

AI and big data integration

Integrating AI with big data transforms vast volumes of raw information into actionable intelligence, empowering smarter business decisions. While big data delivers the scale —volume, velocity, and variety—AI brings the analytical power needed to uncover meaningful patterns and generate predictive insights from these extensive datasets. Together, they enable businesses to move beyond traditional reporting and embrace dynamic, real-time analysis that evolves as new data arrives.

Take, for example, a global retailer handling millions of customer interactions daily—transactions, social media comments, website clicks, and supply chain updates. These massive datasets are difficult to manage using conventional analytics, which often yield only surface-level summaries. However, AI algorithms like machine learning models trained on historical purchasing behavior can reveal subtle trends such as emerging product preferences or detect anomalies indicating potential supply chain disruptions. This level of insight supports proactive inventory management and targeted marketing campaigns, reducing waste and boosting sales efficiency.

Essentially of integrating AI with big data lies a multi-layered process. It begins with data ingestion— the automated collection and consolidation of structured and unstructured information from diverse sources like databases, IoT sensors, cloud platforms, and streaming services. Technologies such as Apache Kafka or Amazon Kinesis facilitate this continuous data flow with minimal latency. Next comes data preprocessing: cleansing inconsistent entries, standardizing formats, and enriching records to ensure high-quality inputs for AI models.

The following Python example illustrates these foundational steps by cleaning a raw sales dataset before training a machine learning model:

```python
import pandas as pd

from sklearn.model_selection import train_test_split

from sklearn.ensemble import RandomForestClassifier
```

```python
\#\# Load raw sales data
data = pd.read_csv('sales_data.csv')

\#\# Remove rows with missing values
data_clean = data.dropna()

\#\# Convert categorical variables to numeric codes
data_clean['region_code']                                        =
data_clean['region'].astype('category').cat.codes

\#\# Define features and target variable
X = data_clean[['units_sold', 'price', 'region_code']]
y = data_clean['promo_success']

\#\# Split the dataset into training and testing subsets
X_train, X_test, y_train, y_test = train_test_split(X, y,
test_size=0.2)

\#\# Train a Random Forest Classifier to predict promotion
success
model = RandomForestClassifier()
model.fit(X_train, y_train)

\#\# Evaluate model accuracy
accuracy = model.score(X_test, y_test)
```

```
print(f'Prediction accuracy: accuracy:.2f')
```
` ` `

This snippet highlights essential practices: cleaning incoming data to ensure reliability, encoding categorical features for compatibility with machine learning algorithms, and training a model to forecast outcomes such as promotional success—key for optimizing marketing investments.

Organizations often deploy AI and big data solutions on scalable cloud infrastructures like Google Cloud or Azure. These platforms offer integrated tools that combine storage (e.g., BigQuery), analytics pipelines (Dataflow), and AI services (AutoML), streamlining the journey from massive datasets to complex algorithm deployment.

Yet integrating AI within big data environments is not without challenges. Data silos persist as departments collect overlapping but uncoordinated information, resulting in inconsistencies. Compliance with privacy regulations such as GDPR further complicates matters when handling sensitive personal data. Robust governance frameworks become crucial—not only to manage access rights but also to maintain thorough data lineage so decision-making can be audited transparently.

A practical example comes from logistics giant DHL, which processes millions of shipment tracking points daily. By combining historical shipment data with real-time sensor feeds on temperature and location through machine learning models, they can predict delays and reroute shipments proactively. This approach significantly reduces missed delivery windows while optimizing fuel consumption through smarter route planning.

For businesses aiming to harness this integration effectively:

1. Conduct a comprehensive inventory of existing

data assets across departments.

2. Identify high-impact use cases where large datasets intersect with key decision-making challenges.

3. Build modular architectures that allow incremental adoption—starting with automated ingestion and preprocessing pipelines.

4. Select AI techniques aligned with specific needs —clustering for customer segmentation; anomaly detection for fraud prevention; natural language processing for sentiment analysis.

5. Implement monitoring dashboards that track model performance alongside data freshness indicators.

6. Regularly retrain models as new data accumulates to sustain accuracy and relevance.

The fusion of AI and big data also enables continuous learning systems—adaptive frameworks that refine predictions based on live feedback loops. This allows organizations to respond swiftly when market conditions change unexpectedly.

integrating AI with big data reshapes how businesses perceive information—not merely automating analysis but transforming static repositories into intelligent engines that drive strategic agility. Companies mastering this synergy unlock competitive advantages across every operational layer—from personalized customer experiences to optimized supply chains—making AI-powered automation an essential capability rather than just a technological add-on.

The role of IoT

The Internet of Things (IoT) plays a vital role in the AI automation ecosystem by bridging the physical and digital worlds through an extensive network of sensors, devices, and machines. This network generates a continuous stream of real-time data that feeds AI algorithms, transforming raw sensory inputs into actionable business intelligence. Unlike static datasets, IoT data is highly granular and constantly updated, enabling precise monitoring and control over operational environments.

Take, for example, a manufacturing plant outfitted with hundreds of IoT sensors embedded in its machinery to monitor temperature, vibration, and energy consumption. These sensors produce terabytes of telemetry data daily —an overwhelming volume for traditional analytics tools to process effectively. AI addresses this challenge by interpreting patterns within the data flood. Machine learning models can detect subtle anomalies that humans might miss, predicting equipment failures before they occur. This proactive maintenance approach not only reduces downtime but also extends the lifespan of costly assets.

Supporting this IoT-driven AI automation is a layered architecture: edge devices collect data locally; edge computing nodes perform initial filtering or analysis near the source to minimize latency; and cloud platforms handle comprehensive modeling and long-term storage. Take this example, an autonomous warehouse robot gathers positional and obstacle detection data on-site while transmitting summarized status reports to a cloud system that optimizes fleet coordination.

To illustrate how IoT integrates with AI for business automation, consider a simplified Python example analyzing sensor data streams. Suppose temperature readings from multiple factory machines are collected in CSV format:

```python
import pandas as pd
```

```
from sklearn.ensemble import IsolationForest

\#\# Load sensor temperature data
data = pd.read_csv('machine_temps.csv')

\#\# Assume columns: 'machine_id', 'timestamp', 'temperature'
data['timestamp'] = pd.to_datetime(data['timestamp'])

\#\# Focus on one machine's recent temperature readings
machine_data = data[data['machine_id'] == 'M01'].sort_values('timestamp')

\#\# Use Isolation Forest for anomaly detection
model = IsolationForest(contamination=0.01)
machine_data['anomaly_score'] = model.fit_predict(machine_data[['temperature']])

\#\# Filter anomalies (score == -1)
anomalies = machine_data[machine_data['anomaly_score'] == -1]

print(f"Anomalies detected:anomalies[['timestamp', 'temperature']]")
` ` `
```

This example employs an unsupervised learning method —Isolation Forest—to identify unusual temperature fluctuations that may signal potential faults without requiring prior labeled failure data. Early detection of such outliers enables operations teams to act proactively rather than reacting to breakdowns after they occur.

Beyond manufacturing, IoT's impact spans various industries. In logistics, GPS trackers provide live vehicle locations, allowing AI-driven predictive analytics to adjust routes dynamically. Retail environments use smart shelves equipped with weight sensors to monitor inventory levels automatically; combined with AI forecasting demand trends, these systems trigger replenishment orders without human intervention.

However, leveraging IoT for effective AI automation presents challenges. Ensuring reliable connectivity across widely distributed devices is critical, as is managing security risks inherent in exposed endpoints. Additionally, inconsistent or noisy sensor data can complicate analysis, while integrating heterogeneous communication protocols within legacy IT infrastructure requires careful planning. Selecting appropriate standards—such as MQTT or CoAP —and enforcing rigorous device management policies are essential steps for successful implementation.

Scalability is another key consideration. Platforms must accommodate exponential growth in connected devices and data volume while maintaining real-time responsiveness. Cloud providers increasingly offer specialized IoT services integrated with machine learning capabilities—Amazon AWS IoT Analytics and Microsoft Azure IoT Hub are notable examples—that streamline building end-to-end pipelines from sensor ingestion through predictive insights delivery.

For businesses beginning their journey into IoT-enhanced AI automation, a strategic approach helps ensure success:

1. Identify critical processes where real-time monitoring can reduce risks or costs.

2. Map existing physical assets suitable for sensor instrumentation or retrofitting.

3. Select pilot projects targeting high-impact areas like equipment maintenance or supply chain visibility.

4. Define clear metrics to measure improvement, such as mean time between failures (MTBF) or inventory turnover rates.

5. Build cross-functional teams combining domain experts with data scientists experienced in IoT datasets.

6. Plan integration strategies that ensure smooth interoperability between device networks and core enterprise systems.

By embedding IoT into AI-powered workflows, organizations gain unprecedented visibility into their operations—transforming passive infrastructure into intelligent systems capable of anticipating needs and continuously optimizing performance. This shift moves businesses from reactive problem-solving toward predictive autonomy, unlocking efficiency gains unattainable through isolated technologies alone.

At its core, the Internet of Things elevates artificial intelligence from abstract models to practical decision-making engines grounded in physical reality—a foundational capability for any enterprise pursuing modern automation at scale.

Cloud computing and AI

Cloud computing is revolutionizing how AI-powered automation is deployed and scaled within businesses. Unlike traditional on-premises infrastructure, cloud platforms provide virtually unlimited computational resources on demand, allowing organizations to run complex AI models without heavy upfront investments. This flexibility enables companies to start small—testing algorithms with limited data—and then scale seamlessly as workloads increase or new use cases arise.

Take the example of training deep learning models, which traditionally demanded specialized hardware clusters. Today, cloud services such as Amazon Web Services (AWS), Google Cloud Platform (GCP), and Microsoft Azure efficiently handle these tasks. These providers offer managed AI tools ranging from prebuilt machine learning frameworks to custom model training pipelines, eliminating the operational overhead of maintaining infrastructure. Take this example, a retail company exploring customer segmentation can use AWS SageMaker to prepare data, train models, and deploy predictions—all within a unified environment accessible via web interfaces or APIs.

The synergy between cloud and AI extends beyond raw compute power. Cloud storage solutions enable centralized data lakes that consolidate vast amounts of structured and unstructured information for analysis. Imagine a financial firm processing millions of daily transactions: storing this data in cloud object storage supports both real-time querying and batch processing, which feed AI-driven fraud detection systems. Combining streaming data ingestion tools like Apache Kafka with scalable storage architectures ensures continuous model retraining and ongoing performance improvements.

Security and compliance remain top priorities when handling sensitive business data in the cloud. Leading providers address these concerns through advanced encryption protocols, identity and access management controls, and certifications that comply with regulations such as GDPR and HIPAA. Businesses can configure virtual private clouds (VPCs) and implement role-based access controls to limit data exposure while benefiting from global availability zones that reduce latency for distributed teams or IoT devices.

Platform-as-a-service (PaaS) offerings further accelerate AI development cycles by removing the need for manual server configuration. Data scientists gain access to managed Jupyter notebooks or AutoML pipelines directly through browser interfaces. For example, a marketing analytics team aiming to predict campaign ROI might upload historical performance metrics into Google BigQuery—a fully managed serverless database—and then use built-in AutoML Tables to generate predictive models without writing extensive code.

For smaller businesses concerned about complexity, cloud vendors provide no-code or low-code AI tools integrated into broader automation suites. Microsoft Power Platform combines AI Builder components with workflow automation in Power Automate, allowing users to create intelligent processes—such as invoice processing or customer follow-ups—with minimal technical expertise. This democratization empowers non-technical staff to build AI-powered workflows that enhance operational efficiency.

However, reliance on cloud infrastructure also brings challenges like vendor lock-in and cost management. Consumption-based pricing models can lead to unexpectedly high bills if usage scales unpredictably—particularly when leveraging GPU instances for deep learning tasks. Implementing resource governance policies, including budget alerts and automated shutdowns for idle instances, is crucial for sustainable operations.

A practical example illustrates this balance: an e-commerce company wanting to automate product categorization using image recognition might start by uploading labeled images into Azure Blob Storage. They would then create an Azure

Machine Learning workspace to configure a convolutional neural network (CNN) using the Python SDK:

```python
from azureml.core import Workspace, Dataset

from azureml.train.dnn import TensorFlow


\#\# Connect workspace

ws = Workspace.from_config()


\#\# Register dataset

dataset    =    Dataset.File.from_files(path='azureblob://
product_images/')

dataset.register(workspace=ws, name='ProductImages')


\#\# Define TensorFlow estimator for CNN training

estimator = TensorFlow(source_directory='./src',

entry_script='train_cnn.py',

compute_target='gpu-cluster',

framework_version='2.4',

use_gpu=True)


\#\# Submit experiment

experiment    =    Experiment(workspace=ws,
name='ProductCategorization')

run = experiment.submit(estimator)
```

After training, the model deploys as a web service endpoint in Azure Container Instances for real-time predictions integrated into their inventory management system—streamlining workflows that previously required manual tagging.

Beyond deployment flexibility, cloud-native AI fosters collaboration across dispersed teams through shared workspaces and version-controlled model repositories. It supports continuous integration/continuous deployment (CI/CD) pipelines tailored for machine learning (MLOps), enabling rapid iterations based on user feedback or market changes without disrupting live services.

Successful adoption depends on aligning organizational processes with cloud capabilities rather than simply migrating existing workloads wholesale. Effective strategies include managing data lifecycles by archiving stale datasets cost-effectively while prioritizing fresh inputs for time-sensitive predictions. Additionally, serverless functions can automate preprocessing triggered by new data arrivals without requiring persistent server maintenance.

cloud computing transforms artificial intelligence from a niche technology confined to specialized labs into an accessible engine driving scalable automation across industries. By reducing technical barriers and enhancing agility, businesses that embrace this synergy gain powerful advantages: faster innovation cycles combined with operational resilience built on flexible infrastructure tailored to evolving demands.

Trends in AI technology

AI technology is advancing rapidly, transforming the possibilities of automation within businesses. One of the most notable developments is the emergence of foundation models—large-scale, pre-trained AI systems designed to adapt to a wide range of tasks with minimal retraining.

Examples like OpenAI's GPT series and Google's PaLM illustrate a shift away from creating specialized AI from scratch toward harnessing versatile, general-purpose engines. This helps companies to deploy a single language model across diverse applications, from customer support chatbots to automated report generation, significantly reducing development time.

Alongside this, multimodal AI systems are gaining traction by integrating various data types such as video, audio, sensor inputs, and tactile feedback. This fusion allows for richer context and more precise decision-making than models focused on a single modality. Take this example, retailers using in-store analytics might combine video feeds with customer behavior data to dynamically optimize product placement—offering insights beyond what traditional single-mode AI can provide.

Edge AI is another growing trend driven by the need for lower latency and enhanced data privacy. By processing information closer to its source rather than relying solely on centralized cloud servers, organizations —especially in manufacturing and healthcare—can make real-time decisions critical to their operations. Predictive maintenance algorithms running directly on factory-floor devices exemplify this approach, detecting anomalies immediately and triggering preventative actions without cloud dependency.

Transparency in AI is becoming increasingly important as well. Explainable AI (XAI) frameworks help demystify complex black-box models by revealing how decisions are made. With rising regulatory scrutiny and stakeholder demands for accountability, businesses are adopting tools like SHAP values and LIME to interpret feature importance in predictive models. For example, financial institutions use XAI techniques to validate credit risk assessments, fostering trust with clients while meeting compliance requirements.

At the same time, the democratization of AI tooling is expanding access beyond traditional technical experts. Low-code and no-code platforms such as Microsoft's Power Platform and Google's AutoML empower business users to build intelligent automation workflows without extensive programming knowledge. This trend accelerates innovation cycles but also highlights the need for governance frameworks to ensure responsible use.

Emerging hybrid AI architectures further enrich the landscape by combining symbolic reasoning with neural networks. These systems integrate rule-based logic to encode explicit domain knowledge alongside machine-learned patterns, enhancing both interpretability and adaptability. In complex fields like legal contract analysis or medical diagnostics, hybrid models improve accuracy and reliability by blending human-understandable rules with data-driven insights.

On the hardware front, specialized AI accelerators—including NVIDIA GPUs and Google TPUs—are becoming more accessible to mid-sized enterprises through cloud rentals or on-premises options. This broader availability enables faster training of sophisticated models while keeping costs manageable.

A growing emphasis on data-centric AI underscores a shift from fine-tuning model architectures toward improving dataset quality, annotation accuracy, and diversity. Organizations recognize that even the most advanced algorithms struggle with biased or incomplete data. Tools supporting active learning loops facilitate ongoing dataset refinement during deployment, enhancing overall performance.

While still largely experimental, quantum computing presents an intriguing future direction for AI. Researchers are exploring quantum algorithms that could accelerate optimization problems fundamental to machine learning training processes.

Finally, regulatory and ethical considerations are increasingly influencing AI development worldwide. Governments and industry groups advocate for standards addressing fairness, privacy, environmental sustainability, and accountability. So, organizations are embedding ethics into their AI strategies from the outset rather than treating them as afterthoughts.

To bring these trends into focus: imagine a logistics company deploying edge AI devices on delivery trucks that analyze sensor data in real time while syncing key summaries with cloud platforms powered by foundation models assessing global supply chain disruptions. Explainable AI modules ensure that rerouting decisions remain transparent and auditable by human operators, while no-code interfaces allow logistics managers to adjust automation rules on the fly without IT involvement.

Navigating these technological advances requires more than technical expertise; it demands strategic foresight. Investing in scalable infrastructure and cultivating multidisciplinary teams capable of integrating new paradigms into existing workflows will be essential for sustained success in automation-driven businesses.

CHAPTER 4:
IDENTIFYING
AUTOMATION
OPPORTUNITIES

Process mapping

P rocess mapping is fundamental to pinpointing where automation can have the greatest impact within a business. Rather than merely listing tasks, it involves visualizing workflows in detail—capturing every step, decision point, and handoff between people or systems. This detailed view helps organizations identify inefficiencies and bottlenecks that might otherwise remain hidden.

Begin by selecting a specific business process that is either critical to operations or characterized by repetitive manual work. For example, an accounts payable workflow in a mid-sized company offers a clear starting point. Document each action from invoice receipt through to final payment approval: receiving the invoice, verifying vendor information, matching purchase orders, entering data into accounting software, routing for approvals, and releasing payment. Tools like Microsoft Visio or free alternatives such as Draw.io can simplify this visualization.

Pay close attention to detail—small but time-consuming tasks like manual data entry or email follow-ups often present prime automation opportunities because they consume employee time without adding strategic value. Identify where delays frequently occur or errors tend to arise; for instance, invoices may stall awaiting manager sign-off or mismatched data could trigger rework cycles.

Once the process is fully mapped, try to quantify the time spent at each stage. This can be achieved through direct observation or by interviewing team members involved in those tasks. If manual data entry takes 30 minutes per invoice and the company processes 200 invoices monthly, automating this step could save around 100 hours each month—a clear efficiency gain.

To apply process mapping effectively, consider this step-by-step approach:

1. Select a process: Choose one with clearly defined inputs and outputs.

2. Gather information: Interview stakeholders and review relevant documentation.

3. Map steps: Use standard flowchart symbols—ovals for start/end points, rectangles for tasks, diamonds for decisions.

4. Identify pain points: Highlight areas prone to delays, errors, or redundancy.

5. Quantify effort: Estimate the time required for each task.

6. Validate map: Review the map with team members to ensure accuracy.

This method can be applied across various workflows—

such as customer onboarding or inventory restocking—to uncover further automation opportunities.

Take this example, a retail company mapped its order fulfillment process before integrating AI-driven automation and uncovered duplicate data entry between its e-commerce platform and warehouse management system. By automating data synchronization through APIs and deploying robotic process automation (RPA) bots to handle exceptions flagged by AI validation rules, they reduced order processing time by 40%. The detailed mapping was crucial in revealing hidden redundancies that might otherwise have been overlooked.

Process mapping also plays a vital role in planning for scalability. As businesses grow rapidly, manual processes often fail under increased volume. Visualizing workflows early helps distinguish which steps scale linearly and which become bottlenecks needing immediate automation.

However, some common pitfalls should be avoided: oversimplifying complex processes or neglecting input from frontline employees who understand daily realities can result in incomplete maps and misguided automation initiatives.

The true value of process maps lies in treating them as living documents—regularly updated as workflows evolve post-automation—to monitor improvements and catch emerging inefficiencies before they escalate. Incorporating tools that integrate with existing platforms can streamline this ongoing update process; many workflow management systems now offer built-in mapping features connected to performance dashboards.

process mapping is not just a theoretical exercise but a foundation for setting clear objectives aligned with broader business goals like reducing costs or enhancing customer satisfaction. Without it, there's a risk of automating inefficient processes rather than improving them.

Effective process mapping not only identifies repetitive tasks suitable for AI but also fosters cross-departmental understanding—a critical factor when managing change during automation adoption. When deciding which processes to automate first, the insights gained through comprehensive mapping provide an essential starting point by spotlighting where AI can fill gaps and supporting robust cost-benefit analyses down the line.

Defining business objectives

Defining clear business objectives is fundamental to the success of any AI automation initiative. Without a thorough understanding of what the organization aims to achieve, automation efforts risk becoming fragmented experiments rather than strategic investments. Well-articulated objectives act as a guiding compass, aligning technical possibilities with tangible business value and ensuring every automated workflow drives measurable results.

Begin by grounding your objectives in concrete business goals—whether that means reducing operational costs, accelerating time-to-market, enhancing customer satisfaction, or managing compliance risks. Take this example, a logistics company might set a goal to cut delivery times by 20% within a year, while a financial services firm could focus on detecting fraudulent transactions within minutes instead of hours. Defining precise targets like these helps prevent scope creep and concentrates efforts on what truly matters.

Using the SMART criteria—Specific, Measurable, Achievable, Relevant, and Time-bound—can bring clarity and focus. Instead of vaguely aiming to "improve efficiency," specify a target such as "reduce invoice processing time from 48 hours to 24 hours within six months." This specificity sharpens accountability and makes progress easier to track. In practice, many organizations find it valuable to develop objectives collaboratively across departments—incorporating insights from finance, operations, sales, and IT—to ensure alignment and shared ownership.

Balancing short-term wins with long-term transformation goals is another crucial consideration. Early automation projects should ideally deliver quick returns to build momentum and justify further investment. For example, automating data entry in sales reporting might take only weeks but immediately reduce manual errors. Meanwhile, broader ambitions—like reimagining the entire customer onboarding journey—require incremental steps supported by these smaller successes.

Consider the case of a mid-sized manufacturing company that set a primary objective of "achieving zero defects in product quality through predictive maintenance within one year." This clear goal led to targeted automation efforts: integrating IoT sensors for real-time equipment monitoring and deploying AI models for anomaly detection. Because the objective was concrete and directly linked to customer satisfaction and cost savings from reduced downtime, every step in the automation process had clear justification.

Prioritization plays an equally important role when selecting which processes to automate. Faced with numerous possibilities, organizations can use their objectives to rank opportunities based on expected impact and strategic relevance. A retail chain aiming to increase online sales might prioritize automating personalized marketing campaigns over back-office payroll tasks—even if both improve efficiency—because marketing automation directly drives revenue growth.

Aligning objectives with broader organizational KPIs fosters transparency and helps unite stakeholders around automation initiatives. For example:

- If the CEO is focused on improving customer retention rates this quarter, automating customer feedback analysis or support ticket triaging becomes a top priority.

- If compliance concerns dominate legal teams due to new regulations, automating audit trails or document verification will take precedence.

This clarity also streamlines vendor selection by enabling businesses to filter tools based on features that closely match prioritized objectives.

Documenting objectives thoroughly goes beyond simple statements. Creating a matrix that links each objective to relevant processes, expected benefits (quantified when possible), responsible teams, and timelines establishes an actionable roadmap guiding design and implementation. This approach ensures that automation remains an integrated business transformation effort rather than an isolated technology project.

For example, a healthcare provider aiming to improve patient scheduling efficiency by 30% within nine months while maintaining HIPAA compliance detailed specific KPIs (average scheduling time per patient), constraints (data privacy requirements), key stakeholders (scheduling staff and compliance officers), and phased timelines (pilot rollout in three months). With these documented needs, they were able to systematically evaluate AI tools for automated appointment reminders and rescheduling bots against clear criteria.

Finally, clearly defined objectives help identify risks inherent in automation plans—such as potential disruption to existing workflows or employee resistance—allowing organizations to proactively implement mitigation strategies like targeted training or phased deployments.

Without well-articulated business objectives underpinning AI initiatives, organizations risk drifting toward technology-driven solutions disconnected from real pain points or growth strategies. In contrast, when clear goals guide every decision—from process selection through tool evaluation—the journey toward impactful automation becomes more focused, manageable, and successful.

Prioritizing tasks for automation

Prioritizing tasks for automation demands a strategic approach that balances immediate impact with long-term sustainability. After clearly defining business objectives, the next step is to identify which processes offer the greatest return on investment when automated. Not every task lends itself equally well to automation—some deliver quick wins, while others require substantial resources with uncertain benefits. The key is to weigh these factors carefully to maximize value without overwhelming operational capacity.

Begin by pinpointing processes that are repetitive, rule-based, and high in volume. These characteristics often indicate prime candidates for automation. For example, data entry tasks like transferring customer information from emails into CRM systems consume countless hours but follow predictable patterns. Automating such workflows reduces errors and frees staff to focus on more complex problem-solving. In contrast, highly variable or creative activities—such as strategic planning or nuanced customer negotiations—tend to resist straightforward automation and should generally be deprioritized initially.

A common way to prioritize is by developing a scoring matrix that evaluates candidate processes across multiple criteria: frequency, complexity, potential cost savings, risk reduction, and alignment with strategic goals. Assign numerical values or weightings based on what matters most to the organization. For example, if cutting operational costs is a top priority, cost-saving potential might weigh more heavily than task frequency. This quantitative framework adds objectivity to what might otherwise be a subjective decision.

Consider a mid-sized insurance firm aiming to streamline claims processing. Applying such a matrix helped them identify three key subprocesses: initial claim data validation, fraud detection flagging, and manual report generation. While report generation was frequent, its complexity was higher due to varied formats; fraud detection required advanced AI models but promised significant risk mitigation; initial data validation was repetitive and rule-based with moderate savings potential. The firm chose to automate data validation first—achieving rapid efficiency gains—and then gradually moved on to fraud detection.

Scalability is another important consideration. A process with low current volume might become critical as the business grows or diversifies. Prioritizing scalable tasks ensures automation investments remain valuable beyond immediate gains. For example, an e-commerce company automating inventory updates during seasonal peaks must design systems capable of handling spikes in order volume without performance issues.

Equally important is assessing the degree of process standardization. Highly standardized workflows typically integrate smoothly with AI tools and robotic process automation (RPA). Conversely, processes riddled with exceptions or reliant on human judgment may require substantial upfront redesign or selective partial automation. Overlooking this can lead to costly projects that stall or underperform.

Mapping end-to-end workflows can reveal bottlenecks and redundant steps ripe for automation. Visual tools like swimlane diagrams enable stakeholders to see handoffs between departments and uncover inefficiencies hidden within organizational silos. One retail chain used such mapping to discover that customer returns processing involved multiple approval steps causing delays; automating approval routing cut processing time by 40%, significantly improving customer satisfaction.

Regulatory constraints and compliance risks must also factor into prioritization—especially in heavily regulated industries like finance and healthcare. Tasks involving sensitive data or legal judgments demand rigorous validation before automation to avoid costly violations.

Engaging frontline employees who perform these tasks daily provides invaluable insights into pain points and hidden complexities beyond what documentation reveals. Their involvement not only improves solution design but also fosters buy-in during implementation.

For example, a financial institution automating loan application reviews held workshops with credit analysts who identified inconsistent data sources causing downstream delays. Addressing those inconsistencies before automation ensured smoother deployment and more accurate decision-making models.

Once priorities are set, establishing phased implementation timelines aligned with resource availability helps maintain momentum without overwhelming teams or infrastructure. Early wins build stakeholder confidence while revealing unforeseen challenges that inform later phases.

To summarize an effective prioritization approach:

- Focus first on high-volume, repetitive tasks governed by clear rules.

- Use scoring matrices weighted according to strategic priorities.

- Evaluate scalability and process standardization.
- Employ workflow mapping for comprehensive insight.
- Involve frontline staff for qualitative feedback.
- Account for regulatory and compliance considerations.
- Plan phased rollouts balancing impact with feasibility.

By balancing these factors, organizations avoid the common pitfall of chasing every automation opportunity indiscriminately—an approach that often leads to fragmented efforts draining budgets without measurable returns.

In practice, thoughtful prioritization turns broad objectives into actionable projects with clear success metrics—such as reducing invoice processing time by 50% within three months or cutting customer onboarding errors by 30%. This focus enables teams to allocate resources effectively while delivering tangible business value early in their AI-powered automation journey.

Identifying repetitive processes

Repetitive processes often present the most accessible opportunities for AI-powered automation, but accurately identifying them requires more than intuition. These tasks are usually predictable, rule-based, and performed consistently across business operations. Examples include invoice data entry, customer email triaging, and inventory restocking notifications—activities that consume valuable time without requiring creative problem-solving. To pinpoint these processes effectively, a systematic approach grounded in process mapping and detailed workflow analysis is essential.

Start by gathering detailed data on daily operations: How frequently does each task occur? Who is responsible for it? Which systems are involved? Combining time-tracking exercises with employee interviews can reveal hidden bottlenecks and routine chores that might otherwise go unnoticed. Take this example, a mid-sized logistics firm discovered that frontline workers spent over 30% of their day manually updating shipment statuses across multiple platforms—a clear candidate for automation. Quantifying such repetitive activities helps prioritize those with the greatest potential for efficiency gains when automated.

One useful technique during this identification phase is Pareto analysis, which focuses on the 20% of tasks accounting for 80% of operational effort. Creating a task frequency matrix can also clarify priorities: listing business activities along one axis and measuring their frequency and complexity along the other. Tasks that occur often but are low in complexity emerge as prime automation targets. For example, a customer service department handling hundreds of similar inquiries daily might deploy natural language processing (NLP) chatbots to manage initial responses, significantly reducing human workload while maintaining quality.

Assessing error rates in repetitive tasks adds another important dimension. Manual data entry errors or misfiled documents tend to increase in highly repetitive workflows due to fatigue or oversight. An accounting team, for example, might spend days reconciling mismatched entries caused by inconsistent manual input—a situation well-suited for robotic process automation (RPA). Automating these error-prone tasks not only speeds up processing but also enhances accuracy, positively impacting financial reporting integrity.

Some repetitive processes cross departmental boundaries or require coordination between multiple systems—so-called cross-functional workflows. Order fulfillment illustrates this well, spanning purchase order reception, warehouse picking, and shipping updates. Mapping these end-to-end workflows exposes handoff points where delays or redundancies frequently occur. AI-driven orchestration tools can address these inefficiencies by enabling intelligent task routing and providing real-time status updates.

It's important to recognize that not all repetitive work fits neatly into automation frameworks. Some processes involve complexity or variability that challenge straightforward implementation. Legal review tasks, for example, often require nuanced judgment beyond AI's current capabilities, though AI can assist with document classification or flagging potential issues. Identifying such limitations early prevents costly missteps arising from attempts to automate processes that demand human expertise.

To illustrate this approach in practice, consider a simple Excel checklist tailored for small businesses:

1. List all core business activities in column A.

2. Record average frequency per week in column B.

3. Note average time spent per occurrence in column C.

4. Capture error rates or rework percentages in column D.

5. Indicate whether the task is rule-based (Yes/No) in column E.

6. Calculate total weekly time invested by multiplying frequency and time in column F.

Sorting this checklist by total time invested and filtering for rule-based tasks highlights strong candidates for AI automation solutions such as RPA bots or AI chatbots.

Beyond internal evaluation, benchmarking against industry

standards reveals common automation trends within your sector. Retailers often automate inventory counts; financial firms employ AI for compliance checks; manufacturers adopt predictive maintenance alerts powered by sensors and analytics.

Identifying repetitive processes is not simply a matter of ticking boxes—it requires ongoing collaboration between frontline employees and leadership to ensure automation initiatives align with actual operational pain points. When done well, this groundwork lays the foundation for scalable AI deployments that reduce manual drudgery and free capacity for higher-value work—an essential step toward maintaining competitive agility in today's marketplace.

Analyzing workflow efficiency

Workflow efficiency analysis builds on the identification of repetitive tasks by focusing on how processes actually perform under current conditions. Rather than simply listing activities, this approach examines the flow of work to uncover bottlenecks, redundancies, and handoffs that slow operations or drain resources. Efficiency encompasses more than speed—it also involves quality, reliability, and adaptability to evolving business demands.

Begin by mapping each process end-to-end with as much detail as possible. Visual tools like swimlane diagrams or value stream maps clearly show who is responsible for each step, when tasks occur, and where delays happen. Take this example, a customer onboarding process might reveal multiple approval stages spread across departments that cause significant lag. Identifying these chokepoints enables managers to consider how AI-powered automation could streamline decision-making or speed up information sharing.

Quantitative metrics play a crucial role in this analysis. Measures such as cycle time (total time to complete a process), lead time (elapsed time from initiation to completion), and throughput (units processed per unit time) provide concrete insights. Imagine a claims processing workflow that averages five days with frequent back-and-forth due to incomplete documentation; automating document verification can reduce cycle time, boosting throughput and customer satisfaction.

Evaluating error frequency alongside timing metrics adds further clarity. High error rates often point to complex manual steps or unclear instructions that trigger rework loops. Pinpointing stages prone to errors—like manual data entry fields or inconsistent handoffs—can guide the adoption of AI tools such as intelligent document processing (IDP) systems or robotic process automation (RPA) bots that standardize inputs and detect anomalies early.

Consider a practical example: an insurance company notices its policy renewal process is sluggish despite seeming straightforward. Workflow analysis reveals redundant data checks performed independently by different teams instead of sharing centralized databases. Implementing AI-driven knowledge management systems that consolidate and automatically update client information reduces duplicated effort and accelerates renewals.

Before rolling out automation, workflow simulation software can model potential impacts. By inputting current process parameters alongside proposed changes—such as adding an NLP-driven chatbot for initial customer queries —the simulation forecasts shifts in throughput, wait times, or error rates. This minimizes costly trial-and-error in live environments and builds stakeholder confidence through data-backed projections.

Cross-functional workflows deserve special attention since inefficiencies often emerge at departmental or system interfaces. For example, a manufacturing firm's order fulfillment may stall if inventory updates aren't promptly communicated to shipping teams due to incompatible software platforms. AI orchestration layers can serve as integrators here—monitoring triggers across systems and dynamically routing tasks based on availability or priority —transforming fragmented workflows into seamless pipelines.

Human factors also influence efficiency: employee fatigue, training gaps, or resistance to change can undermine theoretical gains projected on paper. Combining quantitative data with qualitative feedback from interviews or surveys provides a richer picture and helps ensure automation addresses root causes rather than symptoms alone.

For analysts managing workflow assessments in Excel, a practical approach includes:

- Listing each process step in column A.
- Recording average cycle times per step in column B.
- Entering observed error frequencies in column C.
- Noting dependencies on other departments or systems in column D.
- Assigning complexity ratings (e.g., Low/Medium/ High) in column E.
- Highlighting bottlenecks based on long cycle times combined with high error rates.
- Applying conditional formatting to flag priority intervention areas.

Pivot tables summarizing total delays by department or step type help pinpoint where targeted automation will yield the highest return on investment.

Efficiency improvements closely tie into scalability goals; a process that performs well under low volumes but falters under pressure signals a need for redesign before implementing AI solutions. Ongoing monitoring after deployment ensures improvements endure without new inefficiencies creeping in unnoticed.

analyzing workflow efficiency sharpens the perspective beyond identifying repetitive tasks alone—it reveals how smoothly those repetitions execute and uncovers opportunities for meaningful impact beyond simple task substitution. This focus lays the groundwork for strategic decisions that optimize resource allocation while sustaining service quality amid the growth challenges modern businesses face.

Ensuring scalability

Scalability becomes a crucial consideration once workflow efficiency is well understood. It's not enough for an automated process to perform adequately at current volumes; it must sustain—or ideally improve—performance as demand increases. Without scalability designed in from the outset, organizations risk bottlenecks, service degradation, or escalating costs during periods of heightened activity.

A common challenge lies in creating automation suited to today's workload but unable to handle higher transaction volumes or user interactions. For example, an AI-driven customer support chatbot may smoothly manage 100 queries daily but falter when traffic doubles, resulting in slow responses and errors. This often occurs because the infrastructure or logic wasn't built with growth in mind. Effective scalability planning requires anticipating these future demands.

Begin by modeling capacity. Assess how current systems behave as process volumes rise. Monitor resource usage —such as CPU load, memory consumption, and API call limits—to pinpoint thresholds where performance begins to degrade. Take this example, a financial reporting bot might run flawlessly overnight on small datasets but stall or crash when processing quarterly reports involving millions of transactions. Identifying these limits early informs whether system upgrades or architectural changes are necessary.

Architectural decisions significantly impact scalable automation. Cloud-native solutions often provide flexible resource allocation through on-demand computing power and storage. They support horizontal scaling—adding more service instances—or vertical scaling—increasing the capacity of individual servers—to accommodate workload fluctuations. Consider an e-commerce company using robotic process automation (RPA) for inventory updates: moving from a single-server RPA bot to distributed bots running in the cloud can ensure smooth handling of peak holiday seasons.

Designing modular automation components that operate independently yet coordinate effectively helps avoid single points of failure and enables targeted scaling. For example, an onboarding workflow with stages for document verification, identity checks, and data entry can be divided into separate bots or AI services. If document verification experiences heavy load spikes, that component alone can be scaled without overprovisioning the entire process.

Load testing plays a vital role in validating scalability assumptions. Simulating high-volume scenarios allows teams to monitor responsiveness, error rates, and recovery times under stress. Tools like Apache JMeter or Locust facilitate API and user interaction stress tests in controlled environments. Post-test analysis of logs can reveal unexpected latency or resource bottlenecks that might otherwise undermine automation performance during peak demand.

Automation scripts and models also require optimization for

scale. Batch processing algorithms may struggle with real-time requirements, whereas event-driven architectures offer faster reactions but introduce greater complexity. Balancing these trade-offs involves iterative refinement informed by monitoring data collected after deployment.

Scalability extends beyond technology to include human and organizational preparedness. As process volume and complexity increase, teams managing AI systems need clear protocols for monitoring performance and swiftly handling exceptions. Implementing real-time dashboards displaying KPIs such as throughput rates and error counts supports proactive management. For example, supply chain managers benefit from alerts triggered by predictive analytics tools flagging potential delays.

Collaboration across teams further supports scalability efforts. IT departments responsible for infrastructure must maintain close communication with business units defining workload patterns and priorities. Adopting DevOps principles—with continuous integration and deployment pipelines—enables frequent updates without disrupting live automation, which is critical when accommodating rapid growth or fluctuating demand.

Budgeting for scalability typically requires upfront investment balanced against long-term benefits. Since many cloud providers bill based on resource consumption, unplanned surges can cause unexpected cost spikes without proper governance. Implementing usage caps or autoscaling policies helps control expenses while preserving service quality.

A real-world example illustrates these points: A mid-sized logistics firm initially automated delivery scheduling successfully for a few hundred daily orders. However, seasonal peaks reaching thousands of orders caused system slowdowns due to a monolithic design relying on single-threaded processing. Redeveloping this solution into cloud-hosted microservices allowed elastic scaling across multiple instances, reducing processing times by over 70%. Continuous monitoring dashboards tracked queue lengths and latency, enabling proactive adjustments before customers were affected.

Conversely, some organizations fall into the trap of over-engineering scalability too early—investing heavily in infrastructure for growth that never occurs—leading to wasted resources without commensurate benefits. A lean strategy stages scalability efforts based on realistic growth forecasts supported by data rather than speculation.

In summary, practical steps include:

1. Analyzing current system loads to identify critical thresholds

2. Choosing cloud-based or scalable architectures favoring modular design

3. Conducting thorough load and stress testing before full deployment

4. Optimizing automation logic for high-throughput scenarios

5. Implementing real-time monitoring dashboards with alert mechanisms

6. Fostering cross-functional collaboration between IT and business teams

7. Managing scaling costs through policy controls and staged investments

Neglecting scalability risks undermining the benefits of automation under pressure; prioritizing it ensures workflows remain resilient and efficient amid business growth or market volatility. The ability to adapt operational intensity smoothly often distinguishes leaders from laggards in AI-driven transformation—and ultimately safeguards customer satisfaction alongside financial performance over time.

Change management considerations

Change management is often one of the most overlooked yet vital aspects of implementing AI-powered automation. No matter how advanced the technology, its success hinges on the people who use and are affected by it. Unlike routine software updates or hardware installations, AI initiatives frequently alter workflows, job roles, and decision-making processes, which can create uncertainty and anxiety among employees. Without deliberate and thoughtful change management, even the most sophisticated automation efforts risk stalling or backfiring.

Acknowledging the human element from the outset is essential. Resistance to change isn't simply stubbornness; it reflects a natural response to disruption. Employees may worry about job security, shifting responsibilities, or skill gaps. Leaders must cultivate transparency around why automation is being introduced, what it means for daily work, and how it benefits both the organization and individuals. For example, when a large insurance company automated claims processing with AI, frontline staff initially pushed back out of fear of layoffs. Leaders addressed this by holding interactive workshops to explain that AI would handle routine checks while freeing employees to focus on complex claims requiring judgment and empathy—an approach that helped reshape attitudes positively.

Open and multidirectional communication channels play a crucial role in this process. Top-down announcements alone rarely suffice. Instead, organizations should establish forums—whether virtual or in-person—where employees can voice concerns and offer feedback. Forming cross-functional ambassador groups that include representatives from impacted teams can be especially effective. These ambassadors serve as liaisons between management and frontline workers, sharing updates and surfacing issues before they escalate.

Training is another cornerstone of effective change management in AI adoption. It goes beyond teaching new software interfaces to include building complementary skills such as data literacy and critical thinking alongside machines. A financial services firm that rolled out an AI-driven fraud detection system paired it with tailored upskilling programs: employees learned not only how to operate the tool but also how to interpret AI-generated alerts and make nuanced decisions accordingly. This dual emphasis significantly boosted adoption rates and reduced errors compared to standard user training alone.

Embedding change into organizational culture requires ongoing reinforcement rather than one-time sessions. Regular pulse surveys or quick interviews help leaders track shifts in sentiment and uncover emerging challenges. Quantitative metrics—like system usage rates, error reports linked to user input, or support ticket volumes—also provide valuable insights into adoption hurdles that may need attention.

Resistance often arises when end-users aren't involved early enough in planning. Engaging employees during process mapping or pilot testing fosters ownership and trust. Take this example, a retail chain implementing AI for inventory forecasting invited store managers to test prototypes; their feedback on local demand patterns revealed gaps in the algorithm's initial design. Their participation accelerated improvements and created internal champions advocating for the system.

Navigating organizational politics is another important factor. Departments may compete for resources or attribute unrelated performance issues to automation, which can hinder progress. Clear governance structures that define decision-making authority, issue resolution protocols, and accountability help prevent confusion from derailing implementation.

Managing expectations realistically is equally critical to avoid disillusionment—a common pitfall in AI projects. Automation seldom works perfectly from day one; initial hiccups are inevitable as algorithms learn and processes evolve. Framing implementation as an iterative journey rather than instant perfection helps maintain patience and constructive mindsets.

Key practical steps for embedding change management include:

1. Conducting stakeholder analysis to identify key influencers and potential resistors

2. Designing tailored communication plans emphasizing transparency and benefits

3. Establishing feedback loops through ambassador programs or surveys

4. Developing comprehensive training covering both technical skills and mindset shifts

5. Encouraging early user involvement in pilots and design iterations

6. Defining governance roles to streamline conflict resolution

7. Setting realistic timelines with phased rollouts to manage expectations

Neglecting these human-centered strategies often results in costly delays or failed deployments despite technological excellence. Treating change management as an ongoing process rather than a checklist ensures that AI-powered automation delivers tangible business value—not just on paper but in everyday operations where people bring it to life.

while technology drives efficiency, people sustain transformation—their willingness to adapt remains the true linchpin of success in any automation journey.

CHAPTER 5: COST-BENEFIT ANALYSIS FOR AI AUTOMATION

Initial investment considerations

nitial investment considerations are fundamental to the success of any AI automation project. Unlike traditional software purchases, AI solutions typically demand a layered financial commitment that extends beyond the obvious costs of platform subscriptions. Organizations often underestimate these upfront expenses by overlooking the less visible but essential requirements such as customization, integration, hardware upgrades, and ongoing maintenance.

For example, a mid-sized logistics company implementing an AI-powered route optimization tool encountered more than just software licensing fees. They needed to upgrade their GPS hardware to handle real-time data feeds, hire a data engineer to prepare historical route data, and allocate internal IT resources to integrate the AI system with their existing fleet management software. These additional steps increased their initial budget by approximately 30%, highlighting how easily costs can escalate when all factors aren't accounted for.

Breaking down these investments clarifies the true financial scope:

- Software Licensing: Costs vary widely, often including per-user fees or tiered pricing based on data volume or API calls. Subscription models differ as well—some vendors offer monthly rates, while others require annual commitments with penalties for early termination.

- Hardware and Infrastructure: Although many AI solutions utilize cloud computing to reduce on-premise expenses, certain applications—especially those demanding low latency or high security—require dedicated servers or edge devices. Take this example, manufacturing plants using AI-driven quality inspection might invest in specialized cameras and GPU-enabled local servers.

- Data Preparation: High-quality input data is critical. Businesses frequently spend substantial resources on cleaning, annotating, or purchasing supplemental datasets. Sometimes, data preparation costs exceed those of the AI implementation itself.

- Personnel and Training: Deploying AI often necessitates hiring specialists like machine learning engineers or data scientists. Alternatively, existing staff may require upskilling through training programs, which carry their own costs and can temporarily affect productivity.

- Integration Expenses: AI systems rarely operate in isolation. Seamless connection with existing ERP or CRM platforms often involves custom API development or middleware procurement.

A realistic estimate of these categories requires careful assessment of current IT capabilities and business objectives. Utilizing spreadsheet models helps organize each cost area with projected amounts alongside contingency buffers —typically 10–20%—to cover unforeseen expenses. For example:

| Cost Category | Estimated Cost ()) | Notes |

| Software Licenses | 50,000 | Annual subscription |

| Hardware Upgrade | 20,000 | Edge devices + server upgrade |

| Data Preparation | 15,000 | Annotation & cleaning |

| Personnel Hiring | 60,000 | One full-time ML engineer |

| Integration | 25,000 | API development |

| Training Programs | 10,000 | Workshops + e-learning modules |

| Contingency (15%) | 27,000 | Buffer for unexpected costs |

| Total | 207,000 | |

Timing also plays a crucial role in managing investments. Many organizations adopt a phased approach: proof-of-concept pilots incur smaller upfront costs but can reveal additional requirements before scaling up. This strategy minimizes risk by validating assumptions early without committing large sums prematurely.

Take this example, a retail chain might deploy AI-driven inventory forecasting initially in select stores before rolling it out nationwide. The initial phase covers licenses and integration for those locations only; subsequent phases budget for scaling server capacity and expanded training based on pilot results.

Vendor contracts deserve close attention during budgeting as well. Key negotiation points include license flexibility (ability to scale users), maintenance fees, support levels (24/7 versus business hours), and exit clauses. Hidden charges related to "premium features" or "data overage" fees can significantly impact total cost if overlooked.

A healthcare provider automating patient appointment scheduling with AI chatbots encountered such challenges firsthand. Initial quotes seemed reasonable but failed to include regulatory compliance costs—such as HIPAA encryption standards—that required additional investments in secure cloud storage and legal consultations. Early collaboration with compliance teams helped identify these needs before finalizing contracts.

It's also important not to assume that cloud-based AI tools always minimize upfront capital expenses. While they often reduce hardware costs compared to on-premise solutions, subscription fees can accumulate substantial operational expenses over time if not carefully monitored and optimized.

evaluating initial investments means looking beyond the sticker price of the core product. Comprehensive budgeting must factor in infrastructure upgrades, personnel development, integration complexities, and legal compliance requirements. A pragmatic approach combined with thorough due diligence lays a strong foundation for realizing measurable returns without encountering unexpected obstacles early in the project lifecycle.

Estimating ROI

Estimating return on investment (ROI) for AI automation projects involves more than simply comparing costs and profits. It requires a thorough understanding of both direct and indirect effects, short-term improvements alongside long-term value, and the subtle benefits that traditional accounting methods often overlook. Unlike conventional software investments, where ROI calculations tend to be straightforward, AI projects add complexity because their outcomes frequently evolve as the system learns and scales.

A logical starting point is to quantify the most apparent savings, such as labor reductions from automating repetitive tasks. Take this example, automating invoice processing with AI can cut manual review hours by 70%, freeing staff for higher-value work. If an accounts payable team spends 1,000 hours monthly on manual tasks at a fully loaded labor cost of (30 per hour, automation could save 700 hours each month—equating to)21,000 in monthly savings or (252,000 annually. This alone establishes a solid baseline for ROI.

However, focusing only on labor efficiency misses other tangible benefits. AI's ability to improve accuracy leads to fewer costly errors and penalties. In finance departments, mistakes like duplicate payments or missed early payment discounts can amount to thousands in losses each month. Reducing error rates from 5% to under 1% through automation directly enhances profit margins without increasing revenue.

Speed improvements also add value. Faster processing cycles enable quicker turnaround times, which improve cash flow management—a critical concern for many businesses. For example, reducing invoice approval times from five days to two allows companies earlier visibility into cash commitments and better liquidity forecasting. Translating these operational gains into financial terms might involve calculating reduced interest expenses or strengthened supplier relationships.

Beyond immediate financial impacts lie intangible benefits that are often overlooked but essential in justifying investment. Enhanced customer satisfaction from faster response times or improved product quality via predictive maintenance can create competitive advantages that indirectly boost revenue. While these benefits are harder to quantify precisely, surveys and historical trends can provide reasonable estimates.

A structured approach to estimating ROI might include these steps:

1. Identify all impacted processes by mapping workflows affected by automation, including both direct tasks and supporting functions.

2. Calculate current costs, covering labor hours, error-related expenses, delay penalties, and other operational costs.

3. Project savings by estimating reductions in time spent, error rates, and delays based on pilot programs or vendor data.

4. Assign monetary values by converting time saved into payroll dollars and quantifying cost avoidance from fewer mistakes.

5. Incorporate indirect benefits using proxy metrics such as improvements in customer retention or employee satisfaction.

6. Adjust for implementation costs by deducting upfront investments and ongoing maintenance fees.

7. Model timelines to account for ramp-up periods when savings might be limited as teams adapt.

Consider a mid-sized e-commerce company implementing AI-driven chatbots for customer support. After automation, live agent calls dropped by 40%. Live agents cost)25 per hour, while chatbot operation averaged (5 per hour including software fees and maintenance. Before automation:

- Monthly live agent cost = 10,000 calls × 10 minutes per call ×)25/hour ≈ (41,667

After automation:

- Live agent calls = 6,000
- Chatbot calls = 4,000

Monthly costs break down as:

$(6,000 \times 10/60) \times)25 + (4,000 \times 10/60) \times (5 =)25,000 + (3,333 =)28,333$

This leads to monthly savings of (13,334 or about)160,000 annually. Subtracting annual AI platform fees of (50,000 yields a net gain near)110,000—a compelling ROI that also includes improved response speed and higher customer satisfaction.

ROI calculations further benefit from scenario planning —modeling best-case and worst-case outcomes helps set realistic expectations and identify risk thresholds. Sensitivity analysis can reveal which factors most influence returns; for example, whether accuracy improvements contribute the largest share of value or if integration delays extend timelines more than expected.

Many companies overlook ongoing operational costs after deployment—such as cloud computing expenses that rise with data volume or costs for retraining staff as algorithms evolve—which can erode ROI if not accounted for early.

Balancing quantitative models with qualitative factors provides a more comprehensive picture. Take this example, automating compliance reporting not only saves labor but also reduces risks of regulatory fines or reputational damage that could cost millions over time.

Despite challenges in precise forecasting, establishing a rigorous ROI framework enables informed decision-making grounded in measurable outcomes aligned with business strategy rather than relying on gut feelings or vendor promises alone.

In practice, combining financial models with pilot programs supplies empirical data that continuously refines assumptions—transforming theoretical ROI estimates into actionable performance indicators for teams and leadership alike.

This disciplined approach ensures investments in AI-powered automation are calculated steps toward sustainable efficiency gains and strategic advantages over competitors still dependent on manual processes or legacy systems whose hidden inefficiencies quietly drain resources every day.

Long-term financial planning

Long-term financial planning for AI automation goes beyond immediate cost savings and initial ROI estimates. It requires a strategic perspective that accounts for sustained investment, evolving technology, and organizational adaptability. While early excitement often focuses on quick wins—such as reducing manual labor or accelerating processes—the true financial benefit unfolds when companies consider how AI initiatives fit within broader fiscal frameworks over several years rather than just months.

One important distinction lies between capital expenditures and operational expenditures. Initial setup costs—including hardware upgrades, software licenses, and consulting fees—often appear as a lump sum investment. However, ongoing expenses like cloud service fees that scale with data usage, continuous model retraining, subscription renewals, and personnel training create recurring operational costs that must be carefully budgeted. For example, a retailer implementing AI-driven inventory forecasting might invest (200,000 upfront but then face annual cloud processing costs that increase by 15% each year as data volumes grow. Without accounting for these incremental increases, the long-term financial outlook can become misleading.

A comprehensive approach incorporates multi-year cash flow projections that include depreciation of AI assets and amortization of intangible investments such as proprietary algorithms or data acquisition. Companies should also evaluate the expected lifespan of their AI systems in relation to rapid innovation cycles; what is cutting-edge today may require significant upgrades within two to three years to remain competitive or compliant. Planning for phased reinvestments helps ensure budgets align with technology refreshes rather than reacting to urgent needs.

Scenario analysis further strengthens forecasting by considering variable adoption rates across departments and shifting market conditions. Take this example, a mid-sized logistics firm deploying AI-powered route optimization may experience slower adoption due to employee resistance or integration challenges. In this case, anticipated savings in fuel and labor might materialize partially or later than planned. Incorporating conservative adoption curves into financial models helps avoid overestimating returns while signaling when interventions are needed to sustain momentum.

Risk management is another crucial element within financial planning. Unexpected regulatory changes related to data privacy can lead to costly compliance adjustments, while cybersecurity breaches may result in remediation expenses and reputational damage that affect revenues. Including contingency reserves for such possibilities builds resilience against the uncertainties inherent in emerging technologies.

Aligning AI investments with broader organizational goals adds further value. For example, automating energy consumption monitoring not only reduces operational costs but also supports sustainability targets—a priority increasingly tied to investor relations and brand reputation. Capturing these indirect financial benefits calls for integrating non-traditional metrics into planning frameworks.

Consider a healthcare provider that introduced an AI-based patient scheduling system aimed at reducing no-show rates and optimizing staff utilization. The initial ROI focused on cutting administrative hours by 40%, translating to)300,000 in annual savings. Long-term financial planning also accounted for anticipated patient volume growth—estimated at 10% per year due to improved service capacity —and budgeted (50,000 every 18 months for algorithm updates. This forward-looking approach ensured steady budget alignment with evolving operational demands rather than unexpected expenditures.

Embedding AI financial planning within enterprise resource planning (ERP) systems enhances visibility and accountability across departments. Dashboards tracking actual versus forecasted AI-related expenditures allow finance teams to adjust assumptions promptly while providing business units with transparent cost-benefit data to support informed decisions.

Effective long-term financial management also depends on fostering cross-functional collaboration among finance professionals, IT teams, and operational managers. When these groups jointly establish key performance indicators tied to both financial outcomes and qualitative impacts—such as customer satisfaction or employee productivity—the resulting plans reflect a balanced understanding rather than siloed views prone to overly optimistic projections.

As automation becomes more embedded within an organization's ecosystem, continuous evaluation cycles are essential. Regular financial reviews aligned with technological milestones promote proactive adjustments instead of reactive responses, maximizing value extraction while controlling risk over time.

By integrating these considerations, long-term financial planning evolves from a static budgeting task into a dynamic strategic capability that anchors AI automation investments within sustainable business growth trajectories.

Evaluating intangible benefits

Evaluating intangible benefits can be challenging because these gains don't easily fit into spreadsheets or traditional financial models. Yet, they often play a crucial role in the overall success and sustainability of AI automation initiatives. Take improved employee morale, for example: while it may not show up directly on a balance sheet, reducing repetitive tasks can lower turnover rates and training costs over time. Likewise, building customer trust and enhancing brand reputation through more consistent AI-driven service delivery creates competitive advantages that indirectly boost revenue.

Consider how AI chatbots handling routine customer support free human agents to focus on complex issues. This shift improves job satisfaction and reduces burnout, leading to fewer sick days and less attrition—tangible cost savings that might otherwise go unnoticed. Similarly, faster decision-making enabled by AI analytics equips leadership teams with near real-time insights, helping them avoid costly mistakes that traditional ROI calculations often overlook.

Intangible benefits also extend to accelerating innovation. AI-powered tools streamline data gathering and pattern recognition, enabling teams to discover new market opportunities or optimize products more quickly. While difficult to quantify precisely, speed-to-market improvements are vital in competitive industries where delays can mean lost revenue or market share.

Capturing these values calls for blending qualitative

assessments with quantitative metrics. Organizations might use employee engagement surveys before and after automation projects, track Net Promoter Scores (NPS) to gauge shifts in customer sentiment, or analyze social media trends as proxies for brand impact. These indicators offer actionable insights beyond straightforward cost savings.

Risk mitigation is another key intangible benefit. AI systems that detect fraud patterns or ensure regulatory compliance help reduce exposure to penalties and legal costs. Take this example, a financial services firm using machine learning to spot anomalous transactions can prevent significant losses that might otherwise surface only during audits or investigations.

Integrating these factors into business cases requires cross-department collaboration. Finance teams need to interpret non-financial metrics, while operational units must communicate qualitative improvements in ways that resonate with executives focused on numbers. A balanced scorecard approach works well here by combining financial KPIs with customer, internal process, and learning-and-growth perspectives for a comprehensive view.

One often-overlooked aspect is the cultural shift driven by AI adoption. Automation that fosters transparency or empowers employees with augmented intelligence reshapes workplace dynamics positively, even if those changes aren't immediately visible. Recognizing this early helps organizations build ongoing support rather than encountering resistance later on.

For practical measurement, assigning proxy dollar values to certain intangibles based on comparable historical data can be effective. For example, calculating turnover cost reductions by multiplying average hiring expenses by decreases in attrition after automation bridges the gap between abstract benefits and financial planning without claiming exact precision.

embracing intangible benefits enriches the evaluation process by revealing AI's broader value within businesses. It encourages decisions informed not just by immediate returns but also by longer-term strategic advantages that sustain competitive positioning in rapidly evolving markets.

Comparing automation vendors

Selecting the right automation vendor can significantly impact the success of an AI initiative. With a crowded marketplace full of options—each promising transformative results—it's essential to adopt a structured evaluation framework rather than rely solely on marketing claims or feature checklists.

Start by aligning vendor capabilities with your specific business needs. For example, if automating invoice processing within finance is your priority, a vendor specializing in natural language processing (NLP) designed for document extraction and validation will likely outperform a general robotic process automation (RPA) provider. Clearly defining use cases early on helps narrow down vendors whose strengths directly support your workflows.

Integration compatibility is equally important. Many organizations operate legacy systems or multiple disparate platforms, so the vendor's solution must integrate smoothly without requiring extensive customization or causing disruptive downtime. During demos, request detailed architecture diagrams or API documentation to verify how their tools connect with your existing ERP, CRM, or data warehouses. Be cautious of vendors offering "one-size-fits-all" solutions that overlook these complexities—customizable APIs and middleware support are key indicators of adaptability.

Evaluating performance metrics provides insight into

a vendor's technological maturity. Don't accept stated accuracy rates for automated data extraction or predictive analytics at face value; instead, ask for case studies or pilot results demonstrating real-world effectiveness. Take this example, a vendor might claim 95% accuracy in customer sentiment analysis, but understanding how they handle ambiguous inputs or multilingual data is crucial before making a commitment.

Pricing models also warrant careful examination. Vendors often package services differently—some charge upfront licensing fees plus per-user costs, while others use subscription pricing based on transaction volumes or compute usage. Consider the total cost of ownership (TCO), including initial expenses, ongoing maintenance, support tiers, and potential scaling fees as automation adoption grows. It's helpful to request pricing scenarios reflecting projected usage over the first two to three years.

Security and compliance are non-negotiable factors, especially when handling sensitive customer data or operating in regulated industries like healthcare and finance. Inquire about certifications such as ISO 27001, SOC 2 Type II audits, and GDPR compliance measures the vendor has implemented. A strong security posture minimizes risks of breaches that could damage trust and lead to costly penalties.

Support services often distinguish similar offerings. Does the vendor provide dedicated onboarding teams? Are there comprehensive training modules for your staff? What is their average response time for technical queries? Negotiating a detailed service level agreement (SLA) upfront —with uptime guarantees and clear escalation procedures— helps avoid surprises during implementation.

To put this approach into perspective, imagine a mid-sized retailer evaluating AI-powered inventory management solutions. Vendor A offers advanced machine learning algorithms for demand forecasting but lacks flexible integration with the company's legacy warehouse management system (WMS). Vendor B provides slightly less sophisticated analytics but includes pre-built connectors tailored to popular WMS platforms along with comprehensive post-sale support. Although Vendor A's features look more impressive on paper, Vendor B aligns better operationally, resulting in smoother deployment and faster ROI.

Running proof-of-concept pilots with shortlisted vendors on limited-scope workflows is another practical step before full-scale rollout. This hands-on phase reveals hidden challenges like system latency or unexpected data inconsistencies that might not surface during presentations alone.

Don't overlook references from existing clients in similar industries or of comparable company size—peer feedback often uncovers critical insights about vendor reliability and responsiveness under pressure.

Summarizing evaluations into a weighted scoring matrix can help decision-makers objectively compare vendors across multiple criteria. Assigning scores based on fit to needs, technical robustness, cost-effectiveness, security standards, and support quality clarifies trade-offs rather than allowing any single factor to dominate the decision.

choosing an automation partner goes beyond technology; it involves building a collaborative relationship that supports continuous improvement as business demands evolve. The due diligence invested during selection lays the groundwork not only for choosing the right tool but also for ensuring sustainable success through partnership agility and shared vision.

By understanding these dimensions, what might initially seem like an overwhelming selection process becomes an informed strategy that balances innovation ambitions with practical realities—a decisive step toward unlocking AI's full potential within your organization.

Understanding hidden costs

Hidden costs often catch organizations by surprise during AI automation initiatives, eroding projected savings and extending timelines. While upfront expenses like software licenses and hardware are easy to identify, less obvious costs deserve equal attention. Neglecting these can strain budgets and dampen enthusiasm for future projects.

Data preparation is a prime example of such hidden expenses. AI systems rely on clean, well-labeled data, but most businesses contend with messy, inconsistent records that require extensive cleansing and normalization before use. Take this example, a retail company automating customer segmentation might find duplicate entries, outdated contact information, or mismatched formats within their databases. Addressing these issues typically involves dedicating skilled personnel or hiring external data specialists—costs often overlooked during initial budgeting.

Customizing AI tools to fit specific workflows adds another layer of complexity and expense. Off-the-shelf platforms rarely align perfectly with every business process. Take a manufacturing firm implementing predictive maintenance: integrating sensor data from legacy machines might require bespoke connectors or middleware development. This technical tailoring demands developer time and iterative testing, delaying deployment and pushing project costs beyond vendor quotes.

Employee training also represents a frequently underestimated factor. Successful adoption depends on user proficiency, making comprehensive training programs essential. A financial services provider automating fraud detection, for example, may need multiple sessions to help analysts interpret AI-generated alerts effectively. The hidden costs include not only training hours but also a temporary dip in productivity as staff adjust to new tools and workflows.

Ongoing maintenance and support are continuous financial commitments often overlooked at the outset. AI models degrade over time without regular updates or re-tuning —a phenomenon known as model drift. An e-commerce platform using AI for dynamic pricing must continually refine algorithms based on market trends and competitor actions to prevent revenue loss. Budgeting for monitoring infrastructure, expert oversight, and periodic retraining is crucial to sustaining automation benefits.

Licensing fees tied to usage volume can cause expenses to escalate unexpectedly. Many vendors employ tiered pricing structures where costs rise sharply after crossing certain transaction or user thresholds—a detail easy to miss without careful contract review. For example, a logistics company using route optimization software might see monthly fees double during peak shipment seasons, undermining fixed cost assumptions.

Regulatory compliance often introduces indirect costs when automating processes involving sensitive data or regulated activities. Meeting standards such as GDPR or HIPAA may require additional security measures, audit trails, or specialized reporting features within automation platforms —capabilities that sometimes carry premium price tags or necessitate third-party consulting.

Integration with legacy systems brings its own concealed challenges. Beyond initial compatibility assessments, risks include downtime during cutovers and subtle errors caused by partial synchronization between old and new applications. These disruptions can translate into lost revenue opportunities and require contingency budgets for rapid IT troubleshooting.

To manage these complexities effectively, organizations should conduct thorough "hidden cost audits" alongside traditional ROI analyses before committing to vendors or technology stacks. This approach involves assembling cross-functional teams—including finance, IT, compliance, and operations—to realistically map resource demands throughout the project lifecycle.

Consider a healthcare provider adopting AI-driven patient scheduling: early projections might focus solely on software purchase costs while overlooking expenses related to integrating with electronic health record systems (EHR), retraining staff amid evolving privacy regulations, and managing data governance overhead imposed by hospital policies.

Developing detailed cost models that incorporate contingencies for such factors enables decision-makers to understand the true financial impact rather than relying on optimistic vendor estimates.

Finally, negotiators should insist on contractual transparency regarding all potential fees—such as license renewals, API access charges, and premium support tiers —and demand clear service level agreements with defined penalties for underperformance.

Ignoring hidden costs not only threatens project viability but can also foster skepticism about automation's promised benefits within leadership ranks, undermining the momentum needed to scale successful AI initiatives enterprise-wide.

A realistic understanding of these unseen expenses empowers businesses to plan accordingly—allocating appropriate resources upfront while maintaining flexibility for adjustments—ultimately strengthening both financial control and operational resilience throughout their automation journeys.

Negotiating vendor contracts

Negotiating vendor contracts for AI automation solutions requires much more than a quick glance at price tags and delivery schedules. The complexity of AI tools, combined with often unclear pricing models and shifting service demands, calls for a strategic and detail-oriented approach that carefully balances cost control with operational flexibility.

Begin by examining the contract's pricing structure beyond the surface numbers. Vendors frequently use tiered or usage-based pricing schemes that can lead to unexpectedly high fees once certain thresholds are exceeded. Take this example, an organization implementing AI-driven customer service chatbots might initially find license costs attractive but then face steep increases as monthly active users or conversation volumes grow. It's crucial to request clear definitions of these usage metrics upfront and insist on caps or alerts to prevent budget surprises. A well-crafted contract will also include penalty clauses or renegotiation triggers if actual usage significantly surpasses projections.

Service level agreements (SLAs) are another essential element that often receives insufficient attention during negotiations. AI automation systems demand high availability and quick response times to avoid disruptions, yet vendors may offer generic SLAs that don't meet specific business needs. Insist on explicit performance guarantees covering uptime percentages, latency limits, data processing speeds, and support response times tailored to your industry context. For example, a financial institution automating fraud detection cannot tolerate prolonged downtime without risking regulatory penalties or financial loss. Include remedies such as service credits or termination rights if SLA breaches persist.

Intellectual property (IP) ownership and data rights also require careful scrutiny. Contracts must clearly specify who owns the outputs generated by AI models, who controls access to underlying datasets, and what happens to proprietary algorithms upon termination. Some vendors retain ownership of their trained models or restrict data portability, potentially locking clients into costly renewals or complicating future migrations. To protect your interests, negotiate clauses allowing data export in standardized formats and specify rights to customize or extend AI components internally.

Confidentiality and security provisions deserve close attention as well—particularly since AI automation often involves sensitive information. Ensure the contract mandates compliance with relevant regulations such as GDPR, HIPAA, or industry-specific standards like PCI DSS. It should detail encryption requirements for data at rest and in transit along with regular audit obligations to verify compliance. Given rising cyber threats targeting integrated systems, request commitments on vulnerability patching timelines and incident notification protocols.

Customization and integration support form another critical negotiation area. Most organizations need some level of tailoring—whether adapting workflows or connecting AI tools to legacy systems—and vendor willingness can vary widely. Contracts should clearly outline which customization services are included versus those billed separately; clarify expectations for developer collaboration; define change request procedures; and establish timelines for iterative testing cycles. For example, an e-commerce company integrating AI-powered recommendation engines will want assurances about API compatibility updates aligned with platform releases.

Training and knowledge transfer are frequently overlooked

but vital for successful adoption. Negotiate provisions for initial onboarding sessions tailored to different user roles as well as ongoing refresher courses or access to updated documentation as features evolve. Vendors may offer these only as optional add-ons—but declining them risks limiting workforce readiness and diminishing return on investment.

Additionally, be explicit about software updates, model retraining schedules, and maintenance responsibilities. Automation projects rely on continuous improvement due to model drift or changing business contexts; contracts must clarify who covers costs for scheduled upgrades versus emergency fixes. For example, an industrial firm deploying predictive maintenance will want assurances that updates minimize production downtime.

Termination rights merit particular scrutiny since disengagement costs can be significant otherwise. Ensure contracts allow exit without onerous penalties if performance goals aren't met within agreed timeframes —or if regulatory changes require discontinuation. Define transition assistance terms so vendors support smooth migration away from their systems while protecting intellectual property developed during the partnership.

Finally, transparency around hidden fees is non-negotiable: demand full disclosure of potential charges such as API call overages, premium support tiers, expanded data storage beyond initial limits, or additional licensing triggered by new feature deployments. Insist these fees be capped or negotiable before signing to avoid unexpected costs that could undermine project viability.

Effective negotiation strikes a balance between assertive questioning and collaborative dialogue—viewing the relationship as a partnership rather than a mere transaction often leads to better long-term results. As Satya Nadella said, "Every company is now a software company." Applying the same rigor to your AI vendor relationships as you do internally helps ensure alignment on objectives and accountability.

In summary, approaching vendor contracts with thorough due diligence—probing pricing details, securing robust SLAs, clarifying IP rights and security requirements—lays a solid foundation for sustainable AI automation success instead of costly pitfalls down the road. Being proactive saves time, money, and headaches while strengthening organizational confidence throughout today's complex digital transformations.

CHAPTER 6:
DESIGNING AN
AUTOMATION
STRATEGY

Setting strategic goals

Defining clear, strategic goals is the foundation of every successful AI automation initiative. Without well-articulated objectives, projects risk becoming technical experiments disconnected from real business value. Begin by asking: What specific outcomes should automation achieve? Are you aiming to reduce operational costs, improve customer satisfaction, accelerate time-to-market, or enhance compliance? Clarifying these targets guides every decision that follows.

Consider a practical example: a mid-sized logistics firm wanted to reduce delivery delays caused by manual scheduling errors. Their goal was straightforward—to cut average delivery times by 15% within six months through AI-powered route optimization. This focus helped them avoid chasing broad automation trends and instead concentrate on integrating predictive analytics with existing dispatch systems. The result was not only faster deliveries but also measurable cost savings from improved fuel efficiency.

To set such goals effectively, start with a workshop involving key stakeholders from business units, IT, and operations. Apply the SMART criteria—Specific, Measurable, Achievable, Relevant, and Time-bound—to create objectives that are both ambitious and realistic. Examples might include:

- Increasing invoice processing speed by 40% within 90 days

- Achieving 95% accuracy in customer query responses through AI chatbots by Q3

- Reducing employee onboarding time by 30% via automated workflows over the next quarter

Precise goals like these help prevent scope creep and make it easier to track progress.

It's also important to align these objectives with the broader corporate strategy to ensure AI initiatives support the company's long-term vision rather than operating in isolation. Take this example, if sustainability is a priority, explore how automation can drive greener operations—through AI-driven energy monitoring or waste reduction algorithms. Connecting tactical goals to strategic ambitions facilitates executive buy-in and smoother budget approvals.

Quantifying expected benefits strengthens this alignment further. Conduct baseline assessments before deployment to capture current metrics such as process cycle times, error rates, or customer satisfaction scores. These benchmarks provide a solid reference for measuring AI's impact later on. Skipping this step often leads to anecdotal claims of improvement that are difficult to verify during reviews.

Once goals are established, categorize them into short-term wins and long-term transformations. Quick wins—like automating repetitive data entry—deliver immediate value and build momentum, while longer-term objectives may involve complex machine learning models requiring sustained investment over years.

Understanding dependencies among goals is equally crucial. For example, reducing call center wait times might rely on deploying an AI routing system alongside chatbot support; sequencing these rollouts thoughtfully prevents bottlenecks. A visual roadmap with clear milestones keeps teams coordinated and aware of how each piece fits together.

At the tactical level, translate strategic goals into functional requirements that guide technology selection and workflow redesigns. If improving customer experience is a priority, prioritize tools with natural language processing capable of contextual understanding rather than simple keyword matching. Likewise, security-focused objectives demand AI platforms with built-in data governance from the outset.

Risk factors tied to each goal must be considered as well. Some initiatives depend heavily on data availability or regulatory compliance that require careful attention—for example, automating financial reporting involves strict audit trail requirements where overlooking details could result in costly violations.

Finally, never underestimate the human element in goal setting. Engage frontline employees who intimately understand daily challenges—they often uncover hidden opportunities for automation. Encourage iterative feedback loops so objectives can evolve responsively as projects progress.

Strategic goal setting in AI automation is far more than an administrative task—it determines whether technology investments deliver measurable business value or get lost in complexity. By clearly defining success and aligning it closely with overall strategy, organizations position themselves for focused execution that maximizes efficiency gains and competitive advantage.

Building a diverse team

Building a diverse team is often overlooked in the rush to adopt AI automation, yet it remains one of the most crucial elements for success. Diversity goes beyond demographic differences; it includes a wide range of skills, perspectives, and experiences that drive innovation and effective problem-solving. When forming your automation team, it's important to bring together not only data scientists and AI engineers but also business analysts, frontline workers, compliance experts, and end users. This combination ensures that solutions are practical, compliant, and closely aligned with day-to-day operations.

Consider a financial services company that initially staffed its AI project exclusively with technologists. While the system was technically sound, it missed key customer pain points because client-facing teams were excluded from the process. After expanding the team to include those voices alongside technical experts, they redesigned workflows that boosted customer onboarding by 25%. This example highlights how technical expertise alone falls short without incorporating domain knowledge.

Recruitment efforts should prioritize candidates who offer fresh perspectives or come from unconventional backgrounds. Take this example, professionals with experience in psychology or behavioral economics can provide valuable insights into customer behavior that might elude purely technical staff. Similarly, including team members with diverse educational backgrounds helps prevent tunnel vision; developers trained in the humanities may question assumptions around data bias or algorithmic fairness that others might overlook.

Organizational diversity adds another dimension: teams spread across departments or geographic locations are more likely to identify challenges invisible within siloed groups. Tools like dedicated Slack channels and regular cross-functional workshops create environments where ideas flow freely and potential problems surface early.

A practical starting point is mapping out the skill sets required to meet your project goals. If your focus is automating supply chain logistics, for example, you'll need logistics experts alongside data engineers skilled in predictive analytics and cybersecurity professionals familiar with vendor risk management. Evaluating your existing talent against these needs helps identify gaps.

Once those gaps are clear, targeted hiring or upskilling initiatives become possible. Internal training programs can develop current employees into capable contributors over time—often a cost-effective alternative to external recruitment amid tight labor markets. Partnering with universities that offer AI curricula or sponsoring employee certifications can further enhance relevant skills.

It's natural for communication styles within diverse teams to clash initially due to varying jargon or priorities. Structured frameworks such as Agile sprints combined with clear documentation standards help synchronize efforts without stifling inclusivity. Regular retrospectives provide opportunities to reflect on collaboration dynamics and improve processes.

Leadership plays a pivotal role in this environment. Leaders who model open-mindedness foster psychological safety, making team members feel comfortable sharing novel ideas or raising ethical concerns related to automation choices. Such an atmosphere encourages creativity rather than conformity.

For example, a healthcare provider formed a

multidisciplinary AI steering committee with clinical staff, IT security experts, legal counsel, and patient advocates. The resulting patient triage algorithm incorporated privacy safeguards along with performance metrics tailored for efficiency and fairness across demographic groups—a balanced outcome unlikely from a homogenous team.

Engaging stakeholders at various levels also promotes ownership throughout implementation. Frontline employees invited early on tend to support change more readily since their insights shape tools they will eventually use daily, reducing resistance often encountered when systems feel imposed rather than co-created.

In summary, key action steps include:

- Identifying essential skills aligned with automation objectives
- Assessing internal resources against hiring needs
- Encouraging interdisciplinary collaboration through workshops and digital platforms
- Investing in upskilling programs for existing staff
- Promoting leadership behaviors that emphasize inclusivity and psychological safety
- Establishing mechanisms for continuous feedback and adaptation

AI-powered automation demands more than technical expertise; it requires diverse human capital capable of recognizing nuances often missed by singular perspectives. A well-rounded team not only accelerates development quality and adoption but also helps mitigate risks related to bias and compliance—ultimately protecting investments in transformative technology.

Developing a roadmap

Developing a roadmap for AI-powered automation requires both precision and foresight. It goes beyond simply setting dates or checking off milestones; it involves crafting a strategic sequence of initiatives that balance immediate priorities with long-term goals. With clear strategic objectives defined and a diverse team in place, the next essential step is to outline how the automation journey will unfold in practical terms.

A thoughtfully designed roadmap breaks down the complex automation process into manageable phases. Starting with pilot projects focused on high-impact but contained areas of the business helps reduce risk while providing valuable insights. Take this example, a retail company might begin by automating inventory tracking before expanding efforts to customer service chatbots. This phased approach supports iterative learning and more effective allocation of resources based on early results.

One effective way to structure the roadmap is to divide it into four stages: Discovery, Development, Deployment, and Optimization. During Discovery, teams audit existing workflows, data sources, and technology infrastructure, cataloging pain points and bottlenecks uncovered during earlier process mapping exercises. This phase often reveals hidden complexities that can influence timelines or require adjustments in scope.

The Development stage moves from assessment to building or customizing AI solutions. Teams select the appropriate tools—whether off-the-shelf platforms or bespoke models—and begin integrating them into test environments. Rapid prototyping plays a key role here, enabling developers to iterate quickly based on feedback from end users or automated performance metrics. For example, if an AI-powered invoice processing tool struggles with certain vendor formats, the team can refine parsing algorithms without disrupting overall progress.

Deployment marks the shift from controlled testing to live operation within the business environment. Coordinating this phase involves IT, security, compliance, and user training teams working together to minimize disruption. Staggered rollouts can mitigate operational risks: a logistics company deploying route optimization AI initially within one regional hub before scaling nationwide experienced fewer system failures and faster adoption rates.

The final stage, Optimization, centers on continuous monitoring. Roadmaps should include explicit checkpoints to evaluate key performance indicators such as process cycle times, error rates, and employee satisfaction related to automation tools. Utilizing dashboards that combine AI-generated data with human feedback channels provides a comprehensive view of performance.

An effective roadmap also incorporates contingency plans for unexpected challenges—whether technical glitches or shifts in business priorities. For example, during deployment of an AI-driven customer support platform at a telecommunications firm, sudden regulatory changes required swift adjustments to data handling protocols without stalling project momentum.

To illustrate this approach concretely:

1. Discovery: Hold workshops with department heads to identify redundant tasks suitable for automation; document current manual effort metrics.

2. Development: Select an RPA (Robotic Process Automation) platform compatible with existing ERP systems; develop scripts to automate expense report approvals.

3. Deployment: Pilot the expense approval bot within

one finance division; conduct training sessions for users and IT support.

4. Optimization: Collect monthly reports on processing time reductions; gather user feedback through surveys; refine bot rules accordingly.

This stepwise process ensures each phase remains measurable and adaptable rather than rigid—a vital consideration given how quickly AI technologies evolve and business environments change.

Equally important is fostering cross-functional collaboration throughout the roadmap's lifecycle—not just at kickoff but as an ongoing dialogue among data scientists, operations managers, legal advisors, and frontline employees who interact daily with automated processes. This continuous engagement uncovers real-world usability issues early and promotes shared ownership of success metrics.

In practice, layering timeline visualization tools like Gantt charts with heat maps that indicate resource allocation or risk levels helps teams maintain situational awareness during execution. Visual cues can prompt timely interventions—for example, flagging integration bottlenecks that delay deployments so leadership can redirect efforts promptly.

designing an effective automation roadmap means aligning strategic intent closely with operational realities. This dynamic blueprint guides organizations through uncharted territory without losing sight of core objectives or stakeholder needs. Without careful planning and thoughtful sequencing over time, even promising AI initiatives risk faltering amid complexity or misaligned expectations.

Getting this right transforms abstract strategy into tangible progress and lays the foundation for sustainable competitive advantage—powered by intelligent automation solutions tailored precisely to a business's unique rhythm and scale.

Technology selection criteria

Selecting the right technology for AI-powered automation requires a careful balance between understanding your business needs and navigating the technical landscape. Rather than opting for the flashiest or most popular platform, success depends on aligning the tool's capabilities with your strategic objectives, existing infrastructure, and team expertise.

Begin by identifying the core functionalities essential to your operations. Take this example, a customer service team might prioritize natural language processing and chatbot integration, whereas finance departments may focus on robotic process automation (RPA) for tasks like invoice processing or fraud detection. Equally important is assessing interoperability—how smoothly the technology integrates with systems such as ERPs, CRMs, or data warehouses can greatly influence implementation speed. Choosing AI tools that function in isolation risks creating silos instead of seamless workflows.

Consider Microsoft Power Automate and UiPath as examples. Both provide strong RPA features but differ in customization and ease of use. Power Automate's tight integration with Microsoft 365 makes it an excellent choice for organizations deeply embedded in that ecosystem. In contrast, UiPath offers greater flexibility for complex automation across diverse platforms but may demand more technical expertise. Reflect on your team's skill set: if experience with Python scripting or cloud services is limited, vendor support and training become critical factors.

Security considerations also play a pivotal role. Industries such as finance and healthcare must comply with regulations like GDPR or HIPAA, so any AI solution should include built-in encryption, audit trails, and role-based access controls. Cloud-based services from providers like AWS or Google Cloud come with compliance certifications but differ in regional data residency options—a crucial factor for companies operating internationally.

Budgetary constraints often clash with feature expectations. Creating a weighted scoring matrix can help objectively compare options by assigning importance to criteria such as cost, scalability, ease of integration, vendor reputation, and post-deployment support. This structured approach reduces reliance on demos or marketing promises alone.

The maturity of the vendor ecosystem deserves attention as well. Established providers typically offer comprehensive documentation, active user communities, and frequent updates—elements that reduce implementation risks. Meanwhile, emerging startups may present innovative niche solutions tailored to specific industries, such as manufacturing defect detection through computer vision or real-time sentiment analysis in retail.

Conducting a hands-on proof-of-concept (PoC) can highlight subtle differences before full commitment. For example, a logistics company evaluating two predictive analytics platforms might find that one excels at integrating external weather data into delivery forecasts, while the other offers superior explainability of machine learning models but lacks easy connectors for third-party data. Pilot testing with live data helps determine which system better suits operational needs.

Licensing models also influence long-term costs and flexibility. Subscription-based SaaS often supports faster upgrades but involves ongoing payments without asset ownership; perpetual licenses may require higher upfront investment but avoid recurring fees. Evaluating these trade-offs through multi-year cost projections is advisable.

From an architectural standpoint, cloud-native versus on-premises deployments bring distinct considerations. Cloud solutions offer scalability and rapid provisioning but depend on reliable internet connectivity and raise concerns about sensitive data residing outside corporate firewalls. On-premises setups provide tighter control but entail higher initial hardware costs and ongoing maintenance efforts.

A practical checklist can guide your evaluation:

- Functional fit: Does it cover all key use cases?

- Integration capability: Can it seamlessly connect with existing systems?

- Scalability: Will it accommodate growing data volumes or transaction loads?

- Security & compliance: Does it meet relevant regulatory standards?

- Vendor support: What training and troubleshooting resources are available?

- User experience: Is the interface intuitive for end users?

- Cost structure: What are total ownership costs over 3–5 years?

- Deployment model: Does cloud or on-premises align better with your IT policies?

To illustrate this approach, imagine a mid-sized e-commerce business aiming to automate marketing campaigns using AI-driven personalization tools. They narrow their choices to two platforms: Platform A offers deep CRM integration but comes at a premium subscription price; Platform B is more affordable yet requires daily manual data exports between systems. Testing shows Platform A reduces campaign setup time by 40%, directly boosting sales velocity despite higher costs—providing clear evidence to inform their decision.

selecting technology is not a one-time task but an ongoing process aligned with evolving business goals and feedback loops established during earlier roadmap phases. Making informed choices lays the foundation for sustainable automation success; misalignment risks costly delays and underused investments.

Technology should enable innovation rather than constrain it within your organization's unique context. Balancing ambition with pragmatism ensures AI initiatives remain resilient amid shifting market dynamics and technological advances alike.

Security and compliance concerns

Security and compliance considerations often mark the dividing line between successful AI automation initiatives and costly failures. Overlooking these critical aspects when selecting or designing AI-powered solutions can lead to data breaches, hefty fines, and lasting damage to brand reputation. This is especially true in highly regulated industries such as finance, healthcare, and government, where security protocols must be integrated into every layer of the automation stack rather than added as an afterthought.

A fundamental starting point is data governance. Automation systems typically handle large volumes of sensitive information—from personal customer details to confidential business records—making it essential to encrypt data both at rest and in transit. Take this example, employing AES-256 encryption for stored data combined with TLS 1.3 for network communications helps prevent unauthorized access or tampering. Beyond encryption, implementing access controls like role-based access control (RBAC) or attribute-based access control (ABAC) restricts permissions strictly to authorized personnel or system components. Adding multi-factor authentication (MFA) further strengthens security by securing entry points against unauthorized users.

The choice of deployment architecture—cloud versus on-premises—also significantly affects compliance strategies. Cloud providers such as AWS, Azure, and Google Cloud offer extensive compliance certifications (including SOC 2 Type II and ISO 27001) that simplify adherence to industry standards. However, regional data residency laws like the EU's GDPR may require organizations to carefully select cloud regions or adopt hybrid deployments to ensure data remains within designated jurisdictions. On-premises solutions provide greater direct control but also place increased responsibility on organizations for patch management, intrusion detection systems (IDS), and physical hardware security.

Auditability is another essential pillar of compliance. Automated workflows must generate detailed logs capturing who accessed what data and when, as well as documenting automated decision-making processes where applicable. For example, an AI-driven loan approval system should maintain immutable records of evaluation criteria to support regulatory reviews or dispute resolution. These logs not only facilitate internal audits and external compliance assessments but also enable forensic investigations if incidents occur.

Industry-specific regulations add further layers of complexity while offering clear guidance. The Health Insurance Portability and Accountability Act (HIPAA), for example, mandates strict controls over Protected Health Information (PHI) in medical AI applications—requiring encrypted storage, rigorous user authentication, and timely breach notifications. Similarly, financial services must comply with frameworks such as Sarbanes-Oxley (SOX) and the Payment Card Industry Data Security Standard (PCI DSS).

Awareness of these requirements should influence not only tool selection but also workflow design, ensuring that only processes fully manageable within compliance boundaries are automated.

Integrating privacy-by-design principles throughout development and deployment provides a practical approach to meeting these challenges. This involves minimizing collected data to what is strictly necessary ("data minimization"), applying anonymization techniques like masking or tokenization where feasible, and designing clear opt-in consent flows that inform users about how their information will be used by automated systems.

Consider a retail chain deploying AI-based customer segmentation tools: collecting purchase histories alongside demographic details without documented explicit consent risks violating regulations across multiple jurisdictions. Incorporating automated consent management modules linked to CRM systems helps enforce compliance dynamically while preserving customer trust.

Incident response planning must not be overlooked either. Despite best efforts, breaches or system failures remain possible—especially given the complexity of AI decision logic that can obscure vulnerabilities. Establishing clear protocols for detection, containment, notification, and remediation ensures preparedness when incidents arise. Examples include:

- Monitoring anomaly detection alerts from network activity and AI model behavior

- Assigning responsibilities across IT security teams for swift investigation

- Preparing communication templates aligned with legal requirements for breach notifications

On the technical side, adopting secure coding practices

reduces attack surfaces in custom automation scripts or APIs that integrate disparate systems—a common source of vulnerabilities if neglected during integration.

Vendor due diligence also plays a crucial role since many organizations rely on third-party AI platforms rather than building solutions internally. Evaluating a vendor's security posture through detailed questionnaires covering encryption standards, incident history, employee background checks, frequency of penetration testing, and disaster recovery plans helps identify potential risks before procurement decisions are finalized.

For example, a fintech startup comparing two RPA vendors might find one holds ISO 27001 certification with quarterly third-party audits plus SOC 2 reports readily available, while the other offers basic encryption without formalized risk assessments or documented response procedures—an important factor influencing selection.

An actionable checklist for embedding security into AI automation includes:

- Enforcing strong encryption protocols across all sensitive data flows
- Defining strict access controls aligned with least privilege principles
- Selecting deployment models compliant with regional data residency laws
- Building comprehensive audit trails covering automated decisions
- Incorporating privacy-by-design throughout development cycles
- Preparing incident response playbooks tailored to AI-related threats
- Conducting regular vulnerability assessments

including supply chain components

- Rigorously vetting vendors for security certifications and proven track records

Successfully weaving these elements together requires ongoing collaboration among IT security teams, compliance officers, legal advisors, developers, and business leaders. Rather than a one-time project milestone, it becomes a continuous discipline that evolves alongside emerging threats.

Failing to prioritize these imperatives invites not only regulatory penalties but also operational disruptions—for example, an attacker exploiting weak API authentication could manipulate inventory automations causing stockouts during peak sales periods or expose sensitive financial customer data leading to lawsuits.

embedding robust security frameworks alongside strict compliance measures forms the backbone of trustworthy AI-powered automation deployments. This foundation enables sustainable growth while effectively managing risk within today's complex business environments.

Pilot testing and iteration

Pilot testing plays a pivotal role in the automation strategy lifecycle, bridging the gap between theoretical planning and practical implementation. Skipping or rushing this phase risks missing critical nuances that only surface in real-world conditions—such as unpredictable interactions among AI algorithms, legacy systems, and end-users. The primary purpose of pilot testing is to validate design assumptions while identifying hidden gaps in functionality or integration.

A common method is to create a controlled environment —a sandbox—that closely replicates production without exposing live data or disrupting ongoing operations. Take this example, an e-commerce company deploying AI-driven inventory forecasting might run simulations using anonymized sales data from the previous quarter. This approach enables safe evaluation of predictive accuracy, system responsiveness, and downstream impacts on supply chain workflows.

Defining clear success criteria during the pilot is essential. These may include quantitative targets like maintaining forecast error rates below a specific threshold or qualitative feedback from end-users regarding usability and trustworthiness of automation outputs. Real-time dashboards tracking key performance indicators (KPIs), such as transaction processing times or alert frequencies, help detect deviations early and maintain visibility into system behavior.

Pilot findings naturally lead to iterative improvements. For example, if the AI model consistently underestimates demand for certain product categories during promotions, the next step might involve retraining with augmented datasets emphasizing seasonality or adjusting feature weighting algorithms. Such iterations highlight why rigid "big bang" deployments seldom succeed in complex AI automation projects.

Engaging stakeholders throughout this process helps reduce resistance ahead of full-scale rollout. Hands-on demonstrations showcasing incremental improvements build confidence among operational teams who will rely on these tools daily. Involving customer service representatives in chatbot pilot tests, for example, provides valuable insights that refine conversational flows and uncover edge cases missed during initial scripting.

Documentation should evolve alongside development cycles. Recording each change—including its rationale, impact assessment, and any unintended consequences—creates a vital audit trail useful for compliance reviews and future troubleshooting. Take this example, documenting adjustments to data preprocessing clarifies how raw inputs translate into automated decisions.

Maintaining feedback loops between technical teams and business units strengthens alignment with strategic goals. An agile approach—deploying small batches of enhancements followed by user testing—accelerates learning compared to lengthy development cycles detached from actual use. This dynamic also guards against overengineering features that add complexity without clear benefits.

Consider a mid-sized logistics firm piloting AI-powered route optimization algorithms. Initial tests reduced delivery times by only 5%, falling short of expectations. Analysts identified that the algorithm failed to account for traffic anomalies during holiday weekends. By integrating localized event data and rerunning simulations, performance improved by 15%, demonstrating the value of iterative refinement during pilots.

Neglecting adequate resources for pilot testing often leads to costly post-deployment fixes or project abandonment. Conversely, treating pilots as learning platforms turns uncertainty into actionable knowledge and fosters a culture open to continuous improvement rather than viewing it as an abstract ideal.

For organizations subject to regulatory scrutiny, pilots offer an added benefit: they provide a safe space to demonstrate compliance readiness before wide-scale automation deployment. Testing security measures like access controls and encryption within limited environments helps uncover vulnerabilities without risking production breaches.

An effective pilot test plan typically includes:

- Clear objectives aligned with business outcomes
- Defined scope limiting system components and user groups
- Data governance policies ensuring privacy and compliance
- Pre-established performance benchmarks
- Mechanisms for gathering quantitative metrics and qualitative feedback
- Scheduled iteration cycles for timely adjustments
- Transparent communication channels engaging all stakeholders

Addressing unforeseen challenges during pilots also sharpens risk management strategies—whether identifying integration bottlenecks between AI modules and ERP systems or recognizing knowledge gaps requiring targeted training.

 comprehensive pilot testing paired with disciplined iteration separates successful AI automation initiatives from those that falter amid complexity and uncertainty. It transforms ambitious visions into practical solutions tailored to real-world demands and equips organizations to adapt quickly as conditions change or new opportunities arise.

Ensuring alignment with business goals

Aligning AI-powered automation with core business goals is not just beneficial—it's critical. No matter how advanced the technology, automation initiatives risk becoming costly distractions if they don't directly support strategic objectives. When properly aligned, every algorithm deployed and workflow redesigned contributes measurable value, moving the organization closer to its mission.

Begin by revisiting your company's key performance indicators (KPIs). For example, if customer satisfaction is a top priority, automation should focus on reducing response times or personalizing interactions. If cost reduction drives your strategy, target repetitive manual tasks—like invoice processing or routine data entry—that consume valuable labor without adding strategic value. The rationale behind each automation effort must be unmistakably clear.

A useful technique is to develop a business-automation matrix. Place strategic priorities such as revenue growth, operational efficiency, or regulatory compliance along one axis and potential automation projects along the other. Assign impact scores reflecting how directly each initiative advances these priorities. This objective mapping helps prioritize projects and allocate resources where they will generate the greatest return.

Take, for instance, a mid-sized insurance company aiming to speed up claim processing while maintaining accuracy. Their automation plan included two key workflows: document digitization through OCR and an AI-driven fraud detection system. Digitization accelerated data capture, improving cycle times and customer satisfaction—clearly aligned with their goals. Meanwhile, fraud detection enhanced risk management and compliance. Both initiatives connected tightly to business outcomes rather than existing as isolated technology experiments.

Keep in mind that alignment is an ongoing process. As business goals evolve and market conditions shift, regular checkpoints are essential for automation teams to collaborate with business leaders and reassess priorities. Embedding these reviews into quarterly evaluations or agile sprint retrospectives maintains tight feedback loops that keep efforts focused.

Another frequently overlooked aspect is integrating

technical metrics with business KPIs. For example, a machine learning model might achieve 95% accuracy predicting customer churn but fail to boost retention because follow-up actions aren't automated or integrated into CRM systems effectively. Success criteria should therefore measure not only technical performance but also real impact on sales, loyalty, or cost savings.

Effective communication plays a vital role in this integration. Translating technical jargon into clear language allows stakeholders—from finance to marketing—to understand how automation supports their objectives. Tailored dashboards that present both high-level business impacts and underlying system health can bridge these perspectives efficiently.

Security and compliance requirements also shape alignment decisions deeply. Automations that speed up transactions but create gaps in audit trails can backfire in regulated industries like finance or healthcare. Designing workflows that balance efficiency with regulatory obligations demands early involvement from legal and compliance teams alongside IT.

Ownership of automated processes should rest within relevant business units rather than solely with IT departments or external vendors. When product managers or operations leads feel accountable for outcomes, they are more likely to drive continuous improvement and keep alignment front and center.

Consider a retail chain automating inventory replenishment across hundreds of stores. Instead of centralizing control under IT alone, regional supply managers were assigned as process owners responsible for monitoring AI forecasts against actual sales trends. This decentralized ownership enabled rapid adjustments when discrepancies arose due to local market differences—a crucial factor in aligning automation outputs with real-world needs.

During project planning, incorporating "business value checkpoints" alongside technical milestones helps maintain strategic focus throughout development cycles. Cross-functional reviews might prompt marketing insights to refine customer segmentation algorithms or alert finance teams to budget overruns requiring scope adjustments.

Alignment doesn't end at deployment; it must extend through maintenance and scaling phases as well. A well-aligned AI solution includes mechanisms for ongoing measurement against evolving business goals and triggers intervention if performance drifts—whether through automated alerts or scheduled audits.

To put these principles into practice:

1. Define Clear Business Objectives: Establish precise goals linked to measurable KPIs before scoping any automation project.

2. Map Automation Opportunities: Use matrices or scoring systems to prioritize initiatives based on direct impact.

3. Establish Cross-Functional Collaboration: Engage stakeholders from all affected departments early.

4. Create Integrated Metrics Dashboards: Combine technical data with business outcomes in accessible formats.

5. Assign Process Ownership Within Business Units: Promote accountability beyond IT teams.

6. Plan Regular Review Cycles: Reassess alignment frequently as goals evolve.

7. Balance Efficiency With Compliance: Involve legal teams during design phases.

8. Embed Business Value Checkpoints: Align development sprints with strategic validation points.

When disconnected from strategy, automation becomes a costly collection of siloed tools; when tightly aligned, it transforms into an engine driving competitive advantage and sustained growth.

the challenge lies not only in selecting which tasks AI should handle but in ensuring those tasks translate into meaningful progress on your company's roadmap—a distinction that separates successful implementations from mere technological curiosities cluttering dashboards without delivering real results.

Communication and training for stakeholders

Effective communication and thorough training are essential to the success of AI-powered automation initiatives. Without them, even the most advanced tools can be underused or misapplied, which diminishes their benefits and frustrates stakeholders. Often, business leaders underestimate the importance of translating technical capabilities into practical knowledge that resonates with diverse teams.

The first step is to identify all stakeholder groups affected by the automation project—executives, managers, frontline employees, IT specialists, and external partners. Each group has unique concerns and informational needs. Executives tend to focus on strategic outcomes and return on investment; operational teams are concerned with changes to daily workflows; IT professionals prioritize system stability and integration; compliance officers monitor regulatory adherence. A single, uniform message rarely meets these varied expectations.

Developing tailored communication plans helps ensure

messages connect meaningfully with each audience. For example, when introducing an AI-driven invoice processing system to finance staff, emphasize how it minimizes manual entry errors and frees up time for analytical work rather than presenting it as a complex algorithmic change. Conversely, technical teams require more in-depth information about model training data quality or API integrations to effectively support and troubleshoot the system.

Interactive workshops provide valuable opportunities for information sharing and building buy-in. Hands-on sessions allow employees to explore new tools in a controlled setting before a full rollout. Demonstrations paired with real-world scenarios—such as showing a chatbot accurately triaging customer queries or an automated report generating within minutes—help demystify AI in ways that slide decks alone cannot.

Training should not end after onboarding; ongoing learning programs are necessary to keep pace with evolving AI functionalities. As automation tools receive updates introducing new features or workflows, neglecting continuous education can create skill gaps that erode efficiency gains over time. Microlearning modules—short videos or quizzes delivered digitally—offer convenient ways for employees to refresh their skills without disrupting their schedules.

Equally important is establishing clear feedback mechanisms so users can report issues or suggest improvements promptly. These might include dedicated Slack channels, regular check-in meetings, or anonymous surveys. Such two-way communication not only surfaces challenges early but also fosters trust that user input influences system development rather than being ignored.

Transparent reporting on automation performance

addresses another key need. Stakeholders want evidence of progress aligned with previously defined business goals—whether faster processing times, reduced error rates, or higher customer satisfaction scores. Role-specific dashboards can highlight relevant metrics without overwhelming recipients with unnecessary data.

Take this example, a marketing manager's dashboard might showcase lead conversion improvements following the deployment of AI-powered segmentation tools, while a CFO's view focuses on cost savings from automated expense approvals. Aligning reported results with stakeholder priorities helps sustain enthusiasm well beyond initial implementation.

Training should also address common misconceptions about AI automation to ease fears of job displacement or loss of control. Sharing success stories from similar organizations humanizes technology adoption and highlights opportunities for upskilling instead of obsolescence.

Consider a mid-sized logistics firm implementing route-optimization algorithms: drivers were initially skeptical about technology dictating their schedules. Management responded by involving them early in testing sessions and providing scenario-based training illustrating how AI reduces fatigue through smarter scheduling rather than enforcing rigid mandates. This approach transformed resistance into advocacy as drivers recognized personal benefits alongside organizational efficiency gains.

Leadership plays a crucial role in reinforcing communication standards around AI adoption. Visible endorsement from executives who articulate clear visions encourages alignment across departments while setting expectations for transparency and collaboration.

To embed these practices systematically:

1. Map Stakeholder Groups: Identify who needs what information at each stage.

2. Customize Messaging: Tailor language and detail depth to audience expertise.

3. Implement Hands-On Training: Use realistic use cases in interactive formats.

4. Provide Continuous Learning: Schedule periodic refreshers aligned with updates.

5. Create Feedback Loops: Establish multiple channels for user input.

6. Develop Role-Based Dashboards: Present pertinent KPIs clearly.

7. Address Fears Proactively: Educate on AI's augmentative—not replacement—role.

8. Secure Leadership Buy-In: Encourage visible advocacy and support from the top down.

Neglecting structured communication and training risks fragmented adoption where pockets of success coexist alongside confusion and disengagement—a costly outcome that undermines the organization-wide benefits expected from AI-powered automation projects.

effective dialogue paired with adaptive education transforms skeptical observers into informed collaborators who not only use tools competently but actively contribute to continuous improvement cycles essential for long-term success in any transformative endeavor driven by artificial intelligence technologies.

CHAPTER 7:
IMPLEMENTING
AI SOLUTIONS

Tool selection and procurement

C hoosing the right AI tools and managing procurement effectively are crucial to the success of any automation initiative. The market offers a vast array of options, each promising transformative capabilities but differing greatly in suitability, scalability, and total cost of ownership. Organizations often falter by making hasty decisions based on hype or superficial feature comparisons instead of conducting thorough evaluations aligned with their strategic goals.

Begin by clearly defining your automation objectives. Are you looking to reduce manual invoice processing errors, enhance customer support response times, or optimize supply chain logistics? Being specific helps narrow down the tool options considerably. For example, a mid-sized retailer aiming to automate customer inquiries would likely prioritize natural language processing (NLP) chatbots integrated with CRM platforms over investing in complex machine vision solutions designed for manufacturing quality control.

Vendor research should extend beyond marketing materials. Request product demos tailored to your business scenarios to reveal potential limitations—perhaps a chatbot struggles with multilingual queries, or an RPA platform lacks connectors for your existing ERP system. Simulating real workflows during demonstrations can provide valuable insight into how well a tool handles typical exceptions or irregular inputs.

Assessing integration capabilities is equally vital. Tools that operate as isolated silos lose value over time. Look for APIs, SDKs, or middleware compatibility that enables seamless connection with your current infrastructure—whether databases, cloud services, or enterprise software suites like SAP or Salesforce. Take this example, UiPath's RPA platform is favored partly because it supports extensive integrations, making it suitable when automation spans multiple departments.

Cost considerations go far beyond initial licensing fees. Factor in implementation expenses such as customization, consulting support, ongoing maintenance, and potential downtime during rollout. Compare subscription models versus perpetual licenses and examine how pricing scales with increased usage. Creating a spreadsheet model to evaluate these variables often uncovers significant differences in total cost across vendors.

Security and compliance must never be afterthoughts. Automation frequently involves sensitive data—personal customer information or financial records—that are subject to regulations like GDPR or HIPAA. Before finalizing procurement, verify security certifications and inquire about data residency policies; vendors unwilling to provide clear answers introduce risks that may outweigh short-term benefits.

Running a pilot phase before full procurement helps mitigate many uncertainties. Choose a low-risk but impactful process —such as automating order status updates—to test the tool's effectiveness and user acceptance in controlled conditions. Documenting performance metrics like time saved or error reduction builds quantitative evidence to justify scaling up investments.

A checklist can guide thorough tool selection:

- Does the solution align closely with defined business objectives?

- Can it integrate smoothly with existing systems via standard APIs?

- Are demo scenarios reflective of real workflows and exceptions?

- What are the comprehensive costs over a 3–5 year period?

- How strong are security features and compliance assurances?

- Is vendor support responsive and experienced in your industry?

When negotiating contracts, pay close attention to service level agreements (SLAs) that guarantee uptime and support response times critical for operational continuity. Flexibility clauses allowing phased rollouts or contract adjustments help manage unforeseen challenges.

Consider the experience of one fintech company that initially adopted an AI-driven fraud detection platform boasting advanced algorithms but lacking integration with their legacy transaction system. This mismatch led to months of costly patchwork development before they switched to a more compatible solution offering modular API access. This example underscores that compatibility outweighs bells and whistles every time.

Procurement also demands internal alignment; involve IT early to assess technical feasibility while engaging finance teams to approve budgets based on long-term returns rather than short-term costs alone. Effective communication across departments bridges silos and paves the way for smoother implementation.

Once tools are selected and contracts secured, detailed deployment planning follows—mapping timelines, assigning roles from project managers to end-user trainers, and preparing fallback plans should unexpected issues arise during integration.

effective AI tool selection combines strategic clarity with rigorous due diligence—balancing technical fit, economic viability, security assurance, and vendor partnership quality —to establish a foundation that maximizes return on automation investments from day one onward.

Integration into existing systems

Integrating AI solutions into existing business systems is often the most challenging aspect of automation projects. Few companies operate in greenfield environments; instead, they rely on legacy software, databases, and workflows shaped over many years. The goal is to embed new AI capabilities within these established ecosystems smoothly, avoiding disruption to core operations or the creation of data silos.

A good starting point is conducting a thorough technical audit of your current infrastructure. Identify all critical systems—ERP platforms like SAP or Oracle, customer databases, cloud services, and internal communication tools —and understand how data moves among them. Pinpoint bottlenecks and manual handoffs that could benefit from automation. For example, a manufacturing company automating quality control with AI-powered vision must ensure seamless access to production line sensors and integration of results back into inventory management systems.

API availability greatly influences integration complexity. Modern AI tools usually provide RESTful APIs or SDKs to communicate with other applications. However, older enterprise systems may lack these interfaces or rely on proprietary protocols requiring middleware adapters. If your CRM runs on an outdated platform without native API support, integrating an AI chatbot might involve building custom connectors or employing Robotic Process Automation (RPA) to simulate user interactions as a workaround.

Data compatibility is equally crucial. Inconsistent schemas or disparate formats can quickly degrade automation accuracy. Establishing data normalization pipelines that convert inputs into standardized formats is essential before feeding data into AI models. Take this example, retail companies often need to harmonize product information scattered across spreadsheets, databases, and third-party feeds to train effective recommendation engines.

Security concerns intensify during integration since sensitive data flows more frequently across new channels. Implementing robust encryption for data in transit and at rest, applying role-based access controls, and regularly auditing logs are critical steps to detect unauthorized access early. Compliance with regulations like GDPR adds further complexity, demanding careful handling of personally identifiable information (PII).

Adopting an incremental rollout strategy can mitigate risks. Instead of a full-scale system overhaul—which risks prolonged downtime—start with non-critical modules or run new AI features in parallel with existing processes, allowing fallbacks if issues arise. For example, a financial services firm might pilot an AI-driven document classification tool alongside manual workflows before gradually increasing its usage.

Cross-functional collaboration plays a vital role in successful integration. IT teams need to work closely with business units to align technical possibilities with operational realities. When embedding AI-driven demand forecasting into supply chain software, procurement officers' insights ensure that predictive outputs reflect practical ordering cycles rather than purely statistical trends detached from supplier constraints.

Testing is paramount after integration. Automated regression tests should confirm that existing workflows continue functioning while new features perform correctly under real-world conditions—including handling exceptions like incomplete inputs or network interruptions. Monitoring dashboards that track latency and error rates help catch performance issues before users are affected.

Middleware platforms such as MuleSoft or Apache Kafka can further streamline integration by acting as centralized hubs for data transformation and message routing between diverse systems. This reduces the complexity of point-to-point connections and supports scalability when expanding AI capabilities across departments.

Consider a mid-sized logistics firm that integrated an AI-powered route optimization engine into its legacy fleet management system using middleware connectors rather than direct API calls. This approach saved months of redevelopment effort while enabling rapid feature deployment across regional hubs.

Change management should not be overlooked during integration efforts. Employees accustomed to familiar interfaces may resist new tools embedded in daily workflows unless they receive proper training and involvement in the design process. Hands-on workshops demonstrating how automation reduces repetitive tasks encourage adoption and surface hidden process nuances developers might otherwise miss.

Comprehensive documentation supports smooth integration as well—detailed records of system architectures, interface specifications, encountered error codes, and troubleshooting guides help resolve issues long after the initial deployment team moves on.

successful integration balances technical rigor with pragmatic flexibility—leveraging APIs where possible while innovating around legacy constraints through solutions like RPA or middleware intermediaries—to embed AI deeply within the existing business fabric without disruption.

Walkthrough Example: Integrating an AI Chatbot into a Legacy CRM

Imagine a sales team using an outdated CRM without API support, relying on desktop client software for tracking leads and customer communications. Introducing an NLP-powered chatbot to automate initial inquiries requires creative bridging:

1. Assessment: Confirm the CRM version lacks direct programmatic access; no RESTful API available.

2. Solution Design: Deploy RPA bots programmed to mimic user input—opening CRM windows and entering responses based on chatbot output.

3. Data Flow: Customer messages arrive via a website chat widget and are processed by the NLP engine.

4. Automation Trigger: For qualifying queries (e.g., pricing requests), the chatbot passes structured information to RPA bots.

5. Execution: RPA bots enter lead details into the CRM interface just as human agents would.

6. Feedback Loop: Confirmation messages return through the chatbot; exceptions are flagged for human follow-up.

7. Monitoring: Track RPA success rates against manual inputs; log errors such as unexpected screen changes.

8. Iteration: Refine bot scripts based on feedback from sales reps identifying edge cases missed initially.

This approach avoids costly CRM upgrades while delivering valuable automation—demonstrating how understanding system limitations guides practical integration choices without disrupting business continuity.

Integration requires patience but offers lasting benefits when executed thoughtfully: smoother workflows emerge naturally rather than being forced onto brittle infrastructures prone to failure under pressure—a lesson CIOs who have witnessed botched rollouts know well when automating forward-looking enterprises amidst legacy complexity.

Upskilling employees

Upskilling employees is essential when integrating AI solutions into business processes. Without a workforce equipped to understand and leverage these new tools, automation initiatives risk falling short or encountering resistance. While technology advances rapidly, human skills often lag behind, creating a gap that companies must address proactively. Training goes beyond simply teaching new software; it involves fostering a mindset comfortable with AI's decision-making processes and inherent limitations.

Begin by assessing the current skill sets within your team against those needed for effective AI adoption.

Take this example, a marketing department adopting AI-driven campaign analytics may require training focused on interpreting machine learning outputs instead of traditional spreadsheet metrics. Conducting a skills gap analysis helps target training efforts precisely, avoiding generic sessions that could overwhelm or disengage employees.

Practical workshops provide immersive learning experiences. Hands-on sessions where employees interact directly with AI dashboards or build simple automation scripts can reduce apprehension and encourage ownership. For example, in a customer service center introducing chatbot support, frontline agents might simulate conversations with the bot to learn how to interpret responses and identify when manual intervention is necessary. These role-playing exercises highlight both the strengths and limitations of automation, preparing staff for hybrid workflows.

Tailoring upskilling programs to specific roles is crucial. Technical teams may need in-depth training on AI model tuning or data preprocessing, while business users benefit more from understanding how AI insights translate into actionable decisions. Offering modular courses aligned with job functions and career goals increases motivation and enhances knowledge retention.

Leveraging e-learning platforms helps scale training across distributed teams. Platforms such as Coursera, Udacity, or internal Learning Management Systems can host curated AI content—from natural language processing basics to ethical considerations in automation. Supplementing these resources with live Q&A sessions or expert-moderated discussion forums addresses practical application challenges and deepens understanding.

Consider the example of a mid-sized financial services firm deploying AI-powered fraud detection software. The compliance team initially struggled to interpret alerts generated by machine learning models due to unfamiliar terminology and probabilistic outcomes. By creating an internal certification program focused on "AI literacy" tailored specifically for compliance officers, the company boosted confidence in automated alerts and reduced false positives requiring manual review by 30%.

Incentivizing continuous learning through recognition programs or linking career advancement to AI competencies encourages employees not only to participate in training but also to apply their knowledge actively. Gamified elements like badges for completed modules or internal hackathons challenging teams to develop automation ideas help embed learning into the corporate culture.

Beyond formal education, fostering cross-functional mentorship between technical experts and operational staff bridges communication gaps that can otherwise derail AI projects. When data scientists explain model limitations directly to sales personnel, it helps manage expectations around automation outcomes while uncovering domain-specific nuances often overlooked during development.

Upskilling is not a one-time event; it requires ongoing commitment as AI technologies evolve rapidly. Establishing feedback loops where employees share experiences with automated systems allows emerging skill needs to surface early, enabling timely updates to training materials before issues arise.

Avoid overwhelming users with technical jargon at the outset. Focus initially on practical applications relevant to daily tasks—how an AI tool saves time or improves accuracy—rather than abstract algorithmic details. Gradually introducing more complex topics supports deeper engagement without alienating non-technical audiences.

Informal learning channels also play an important

role. Peer-to-peer knowledge sharing groups and internal newsletters highlighting success stories involving AI tools create relatable examples that inspire broader acceptance throughout the organization.

upskilling employees creates a virtuous cycle: better-trained teams use AI more effectively, generating measurable business results that justify continued investment in talent development. This foundation is critical for sustainable automation success in any enterprise embracing digital transformation.

Developing internal expertise

Developing internal expertise is fundamental to achieving lasting success with AI-powered automation. While upskilling broadens general capabilities, cultivating specialists who possess deep knowledge of both the technology and the business context allows organizations to innovate and resolve challenges more effectively. These internal experts serve as vital links between vendors, IT teams, and operational units, reducing dependence on external consultants and enabling agile responses to evolving automation needs.

Begin by identifying employees who show aptitude in areas such as data analysis, programming, or systems thinking. These individuals often demonstrate curiosity about new tools and a willingness to explore beyond their usual responsibilities. Support their growth through targeted development plans that blend formal education —like certifications in machine learning or data science —with hands-on project experience. For example, an operations analyst proficient in Excel might transition into an automation engineer role by learning Python scripting focused on optimizing workflows.

Structured mentorship programs play a crucial role in building expertise. Pairing junior staff with experienced data scientists or AI architects during pilot projects accelerates skill development and fosters the cross-disciplinary understanding essential for successful AI adoption. A global logistics company, for instance, reduced deployment times by 40% by embedding AI specialists within regional teams, allowing solutions to be tailored locally rather than imposed from above.

Establishing a dedicated Center of Excellence (CoE) for AI and automation further strengthens internal capabilities. Such hubs centralize resources, set standards, and curate best practices across departments. They often serve as innovation incubators—experimenting with emerging algorithms and testing new tools before broader implementation. A healthcare provider leveraged its CoE to develop proprietary predictive models for patient readmission risk, significantly enhancing care while lowering costs.

Alongside technical skills, internal experts must develop strong communication abilities and stakeholder management. Training should include workshops on storytelling with data and change management, preparing experts to advocate for AI initiatives effectively. When experts can translate complex model outputs into clear, actionable insights that resonate with executives and frontline managers alike, adoption challenges decrease markedly.

Real-world application solidifies knowledge better than theory alone. Encourage staff to lead small-scale projects addressing concrete business problems using tools like RPA platforms or cloud-based machine learning services such as AWS SageMaker or Google Vertex AI. Documenting these projects internally builds valuable institutional knowledge while boosting team confidence.

Fostering a culture that embraces experimentation—even

when it involves failure—is equally important. Iterative learning is critical in the fast-evolving AI landscape. For example, an internal team at a retail firm developed an AI-driven inventory forecasting prototype that initially underperformed but improved significantly after several refinement cycles incorporating frontline feedback.

Investing in proprietary tools and customization also enhances internal strength. Off-the-shelf solutions often need adaptation to fit unique workflows, so having experts capable of modifying codebases or configuring APIs ensures smoother integration without overreliance on vendor support.

Keeping pace with emerging trends helps maintain relevant expertise. Regular participation in industry conferences like NeurIPS or Gartner's Data & Analytics Summit exposes teams to cutting-edge research and practical applications beyond immediate business needs, sparking ideas that may yield future competitive advantages.

Finally, recognizing and rewarding internal expertise fosters ongoing growth. Formal career paths that highlight specialization in AI automation help retain talent in a competitive market for skilled professionals.

By developing internal expertise, organizations evolve from passive technology users into proactive innovators who harness AI strategically rather than reactively—a shift essential for unlocking sustained financial benefits from automation initiatives.

Continuous monitoring and adjustment

Continuous monitoring and adjustment are essential to the success of any AI-powered automation initiative. Deployment marks just the beginning; the ever-changing nature of business environments and AI models requires ongoing oversight to sustain effectiveness, identify emerging issues, and respond to evolving needs.

Start by defining clear performance metrics aligned with your automation goals. These might include reductions in processing time, error rates, user adoption levels, or cost savings—whichever best reflect your initial objectives. For example, an e-commerce company automating order fulfillment might track daily average order processing time and inventory accuracy. Establishing such key performance indicators (KPIs) creates a baseline for evaluating changes over time.

To make this data accessible, set up dashboards using tools like Power BI, Tableau, or cloud-native platforms such as AWS CloudWatch or Google Cloud Monitoring. Visualizing real-time information allows stakeholders—from executives to frontline operators—to quickly grasp system health without sifting through raw logs. A dashboard highlighting spikes in failed automated invoice processing, for instance, signals a need for prompt investigation before customers or vendors are affected.

Equally important are alerting mechanisms that trigger notifications when key thresholds are breached. For example, if an AI-driven customer support chatbot's resolution rate falls below 85%, an alert can prompt the team to review conversation transcripts and retrain models as needed, ensuring swift corrective action.

Monitoring extends beyond performance metrics to include auditing the quality of data feeding into AI systems. The adage "garbage in, garbage out" holds especially true in automation. Regular validation routines should confirm that datasets are complete, consistent, and up-to-date—particularly when sourced from multiple systems or transformed through complex pipelines. In financial firms automating fraud detection, for example, stale or inconsistent transaction data can significantly degrade model accuracy.

Adjustment cycles often involve retraining or fine-tuning machine learning models as new data emerges or business contexts shift. This process requires robust version control and rollback procedures to avoid introducing errors during updates. Tools like MLflow or Kubeflow support lifecycle management by tracking model parameters and performance over time.

Feedback from end-users interacting daily with automated workflows is another invaluable component. Frontline employees frequently identify subtle issues machines overlook: unexpected edge cases, clunky interfaces, or bottlenecks that hinder efficiency gains. Establishing formal channels—such as surveys, suggestion boxes, or periodic focus groups—ensures these insights are captured systematically.

Take this example, warehouse staff at a logistics company observed that an AI-driven sorting robot occasionally mishandled fragile packages during peak hours—a detail invisible in aggregated sensor data but obvious on-site. Incorporating their feedback led to retraining with adjusted weight sensitivity settings and improved task scheduling algorithms.

Monitoring must also address compliance as regulations around AI use and data privacy evolve rapidly worldwide (consider GDPR updates). Continuous auditing verifies that automated processes adhere to legal requirements and ethical guidelines established during the strategy phase.

Documenting every adjustment is critical for transparency and institutional memory. Versioned release notes explaining why changes were made and their effects help future teams understand decisions without repeating past mistakes.

From a technical perspective, integrating automation monitoring with existing IT Service Management (ITSM) tools streamlines incident response workflows. Linking anomaly detection alerts from a robotic process automation (RPA) bot directly into Jira tickets accelerates troubleshooting while maintaining audit trails vital for postmortem analyses.

Investing in continuous monitoring pays dividends by enabling early detection of issues that could cause costly downtime or reputational damage. It also supports proactive improvements that keep automation aligned with shifting business priorities. For example, routine health checks at a multinational bank uncovered model drift caused by unexpected market volatility; timely intervention prevented millions in fraudulent transactions from slipping through undetected.

Sustaining this vigilance often requires dedicated roles— AI Ops specialists who blend technical skills with domain knowledge—and sometimes Managed Services when internal resources are limited but responsiveness remains critical.

viewing automation solutions as living systems rather than static installations shifts success metrics away from "set it and forget it" toward adaptive excellence capable of maintaining competitive advantages over time.

Ongoing investment in robust monitoring infrastructure not only protects current benefits but also enables organizations to seize emerging opportunities through agile iterations—transforming automated processes into engines of continuous innovation rather than mere cost-cutting tools.

Data collection and analysis

Data collection and analysis are fundamental to any AI-powered automation system, directly shaping its accuracy, adaptability, and overall business impact. Without dependable data fueling AI models, automation workflows risk becoming unreliable guesses rather than informed actions. To maximize effectiveness, organizations must adopt a strategic approach to gathering and interpreting data that truly reflects real-world conditions and business goals.

The process begins with identifying the data sources relevant to your automated workflows. These sources might include internal transactional databases, CRM systems, ERP logs, or external feeds such as market data and social media streams. Take this example, a retail company automating inventory replenishment could draw from point-of-sale systems, supplier delivery schedules, and warehouse stock counts. Selecting the right sources provides a comprehensive view of the factors influencing automated decisions.

After pinpointing data origins, it's important to decide how often and at what level of detail data should be collected. Some processes require real-time streaming—for example, fraud detection algorithms that analyze transactions as they occur—while others may function effectively with daily or weekly batch updates. This choice influences system architecture: real-time needs often call for event-driven pipelines built with tools like Apache Kafka or AWS Kinesis, whereas batch processing can be managed through scheduled ETL jobs using orchestrators such as Airflow.

Ensuring data quality during collection is critical. Anomalies like missing values, duplicates, or inconsistent formats can undermine model performance or lead to flawed automation outcomes. Automated validation scripts help detect irregularities early; for example, a financial firm's invoice automation might include checks on date validity, numeric ranges, and vendor ID consistency before passing data downstream.

Equally important is the strategy for storing collected data. Centralized data lakes offer flexibility for diverse datasets but can become difficult to manage without strong governance. In contrast, relational databases simplify querying structured data but may struggle with scalability when handling unstructured or high-volume AI workloads. Many organizations adopt hybrid solutions: Netflix, for example, combines Amazon S3 data lakes with query engines like Presto to balance scalability and performance.

Once data is collected and stored, transformation prepares raw inputs into usable formats through cleaning, normalization, and enrichment. Data pipelines frequently leverage frameworks such as Apache Spark or Python's Pandas library for efficient manipulation. Consider merging customer interaction logs with demographic details to enrich predictive models that power personalized marketing automation.

The next phase involves extracting actionable insights through statistical analysis and machine learning techniques. Exploratory data analysis (EDA) uncovers patterns—like seasonal sales fluctuations or recurring supply chain delays—that inform automation rules or model features. Visualizations created with tools such as Tableau or Matplotlib help communicate these findings clearly to both technical teams and business stakeholders.

For example, a simple Python script using Pandas can analyze customer churn probability based on subscription length:

```python
import pandas as pd

data = pd.read_csv('customer_data.csv')

churn_rate        =        data.groupby('subscription_length')['churned'].mean()
```

```
print(churn_rate)
```
` ` `

This calculation segments churn rates by subscription duration, providing insight to guide targeted retention efforts embedded within automated CRM workflows.

Beyond descriptive statistics, predictive analytics powered by supervised learning algorithms—like random forests or gradient boosting machines—enable forecasting future outcomes. Training these models involves splitting datasets into training and testing sets to assess accuracy before deployment. Techniques such as cross-validation help prevent overfitting, ensuring models generalize well beyond historical data.

Integrating continuous feedback loops allows live operational data to refine analytical models through retraining or recalibration. Take this example, an AI chatbot's conversation transcripts can feed natural language processing models that improve intent recognition over time. Implementing automated pipelines with ML Ops tools like TensorFlow Extended (TFX) supports this ongoing cycle of enhancement.

Data privacy and regulatory compliance add essential layers of complexity. Adherence to standards like GDPR requires implementing anonymization methods, secure access controls, and audit trails throughout the pipeline. Privacy-preserving techniques such as differential privacy enable organizations to derive insights without compromising individual-level information—an especially vital consideration in sensitive fields like healthcare and finance.

Real-world examples highlight the benefits of robust data practices: a logistics company that incorporated weather patterns and traffic data into AI-driven demand forecasting reduced stockouts by 30%, while a multinational bank improved fraud detection accuracy by combining transactional metadata with behavioral analytics collected continuously.

At its core, effective data collection paired with advanced analysis transforms raw inputs into informed actions that drive operational efficiency and smarter decision-making within automated systems. Neglecting this foundation risks rendering automation brittle or obsolete amid evolving market conditions—a costly misstep in dynamic industries where agility is paramount.

Success demands investment not only in technology but also in skilled professionals who bridge domain expertise and advanced analytics. Data engineers build dependable pipelines; data scientists develop predictive models; business analysts interpret insights—together turning static data into a dynamic engine of AI-powered business value.

Overcoming resistance to change

Resistance to change is one of the greatest challenges in AI automation projects. It often emerges subtly—whether from employees concerned about job security, managers doubtful of new workflows, or a company culture deeply rooted in established routines. More often than not, resistance stems less from the technology itself and more from fear of the unknown or a perceived loss of control. Understanding these underlying emotions is essential before launching any technical implementation.

Begin by pinpointing where resistance arises within your organization. Are frontline staff worried about being replaced? Does middle management fear losing decision-making authority? Or are IT teams feeling overwhelmed by integration demands? Tools like anonymous surveys or candid focus groups can help gather honest insights. For example, a mid-sized logistics company discovered that warehouse operators feared automation would make their roles obsolete; addressing these concerns early prevented sabotage and smoothed the rollout.

Clear and consistent communication plays a vital role in easing anxieties. Explaining not just what automation replaces but how it empowers employees can shift perspectives. At a financial services firm, showing how AI took over repetitive data entry allowed analysts to focus on complex risk assessments, turning fear into opportunity. Using multiple channels—team meetings, newsletters, informal check-ins—to share these messages helps build trust over time.

Involving employees early transforms skeptics into advocates. Instead of imposing AI tools from the top down, engaging key users in pilot phases or design workshops uncovers workflow details developers might overlook and fosters ownership that accelerates adoption. Take this example, a healthcare provider automating appointment scheduling invited receptionists to co-create system rules, which reduced friction and improved accuracy during deployment.

Training addresses both skill gaps and confidence. Offering hands-on sessions tailored to different roles prevents staff from feeling overwhelmed by unfamiliar technology. An e-commerce company, for example, separated training for customer support agents using AI chatbots from sessions for IT specialists managing backend systems—this targeted approach enhanced engagement and relevance.

Resistance sometimes takes the form of passive inertia rather than outright opposition. In these cases, embedding small wins builds momentum. Automating simple tasks —like email sorting or report generation—and publicly highlighting time savings encourages adoption. Positive reinforcement creates social proof; when employees see colleagues benefiting without downsides, skepticism naturally fades.

Leadership endorsement is indispensable. Executives must visibly champion AI initiatives, consistently linking them to broader business goals and reinforcing their strategic value. One manufacturing CEO held Q&A sessions emphasizing AI's role in improving safety rather than cutting jobs—a message that positively reshaped company attitudes.

Monitoring adoption metrics helps uncover lingering resistance. Tracking tool usage, error rates, or helpdesk tickets reveals friction points needing additional support or process tweaks. Establishing feedback loops where employees can voice challenges fosters continuous improvement rather than top-down enforcement.

Sometimes, organizational culture must evolve before automation can thrive. Moving away from rigid hierarchies toward agile mindsets means promoting psychological safety—encouraging experimentation without fear of blame —and rewarding innovation at all levels.

To overcome resistance effectively:

1. Map stakeholders: Identify who will be affected and anticipate their concerns.

2. Tailor communication: Align messages with each group's priorities.

3. Involve users early: Facilitate workshops or pilots that gather real input.

4. Invest in training: Provide role-specific skill development opportunities.

5. Celebrate quick wins: Transparently showcase benefits to all staff.

6. Lead from the top: Ensure executive sponsorship is visible and engaged.

7. Measure and adapt: Use data insights to address ongoing challenges.

Ignoring resistance risks derailing even the most advanced AI projects because human factors ultimately determine success.

From my consulting experience: one retail chain struggled for months with low adoption until frontline cashiers were involved in redesigning checkout automation. Empowered this way, adoption surged beyond expectations within weeks.

Successfully navigating change requires as much empathy as expertise—a commitment to listening deeply while guiding decisively toward innovations that benefit both people and business outcomes alike.

CHAPTER 8: AI IN CUSTOMER RELATIONSHIP MANAGEMENT (CRM)

Personalization of customer interactions

Customer relationships have undergone a profound transformation thanks to AI-powered personalization, shifting the focus from broad audience targeting to engaging individuals on a uniquely tailored level. Today's personalization goes well beyond traditional segmentation by dynamically adapting interactions based on specific customer preferences, behaviors, and contexts. This is made possible through AI algorithms that analyze vast datasets to uncover subtle patterns that might escape human detection. Take this example, Netflix's recommendation engine doesn't simply categorize users by favorite genres; it also considers factors like viewing times, device usage, and even moments when users pause or rewind content to deliver highly personalized suggestions. This level of precision fosters stronger engagement and loyalty by making customers feel truly understood.

In practice, businesses implement AI-driven personalization using customer data platforms (CDPs) that unify inputs from CRM systems, social media activity, purchase histories, and browsing behavior. Imagine a retail company personalizing its email marketing campaigns: the system could combine recent purchase frequency with browsing patterns to predict the best timing and content—for example, sending a flash sale offer on running shoes to an avid jogger who has recently browsed sneakers but not made a purchase. Setting up such campaigns involves several key steps: first, aggregating diverse data streams into a single platform; second, training machine learning models to identify signals of purchase intent; and third, automating email triggers based on model predictions. Tools like Python's scikit-learn or TensorFlow support model training, while marketing automation platforms such as HubSpot or Marketo manage campaign execution.

To illustrate this concept, consider a simple Python example using scikit-learn for customer segmentation—a foundational step in personalization:

```python
import pandas as pd

from sklearn.cluster import KMeans


\#\# Sample customer data: annual spending on electronics and apparel

data = 'customer_id': [1, 2, 3, 4, 5],

'electronics_spend': [2000, 5000, 3000, 7000, 1200],
```

```
'apparel_spend': [1500, 3000, 2000, 4000, 800]
df = pd.DataFrame(data)

\#\# Feature matrix for clustering
X = df[['electronics_spend', 'apparel_spend']]

\#\# Create KMeans model with two clusters
kmeans = KMeans(n_clusters=2)
df['segment'] = kmeans.fit_predict(X)

print(df)
` ` `
```

This code groups customers based on similar spending habits—segments that marketing teams can then target with tailored offers. For example, customers who spend heavily on electronics might receive promotions for new gadgets, while those focused on apparel get fashion-related deals. The next logical step is connecting these segments with dynamic content engines that personalize messaging in real time.

Personalization also extends beyond marketing emails and product recommendations to conversational interfaces like chatbots and virtual assistants. These AI-driven tools employ natural language processing (NLP) to understand user intent and respond accordingly. Consider a telecom company chatbot that recalls a customer's previous billing complaints and proactively offers tailored solutions or account adjustments during the conversation. This approach creates a seamless experience that feels genuinely attentive rather than scripted.

On the operational front, delivering personalized interactions requires robust infrastructure: reliable data pipelines for real-time ingestion; privacy-compliant storage solutions; fast inference engines; and tightly integrated front-end channels such as websites or mobile apps. Overcoming challenges like data silos or inconsistent identifiers across systems is essential to build the comprehensive customer views necessary for effective personalization.

Privacy concerns add another layer of complexity. Customers expect transparency about how their data is used and want control over what information is collected or shared. Complying with regulations such as GDPR means implementing clear consent management processes and maintaining audit trails for automated decisions impacting customers.

A notable example comes from Marriott International in the hospitality sector. Their AI system analyzes booking histories, feedback scores, and social media sentiment to tailor offers—from room upgrades to dining recommendations—based on each guest's unique preferences. This personalized approach strengthens brand loyalty and drives repeat bookings in an intensely competitive market.

AI-driven personalization goes far beyond surface-level customization; it reshapes how businesses interpret customer needs across channels and moments of interaction. When done well, it builds trust by anticipating desires without feeling intrusive—a delicate balance maintained through ongoing refinement using engagement metrics like click-through rates and conversion rates.

To build your own personalized interaction workflows:

1. Aggregate multi-source customer data with

attention to quality and timeliness.

2. Choose suitable AI models: clustering for segmentation or predictive models for purchase likelihood.

3. Train these models using historical behavior combined with demographic information.

4. Integrate models into marketing platforms or conversational agents for dynamic response generation.

5. Continuously monitor performance and update models as new patterns emerge.

6. Ensure strict adherence to privacy laws by embedding consent management throughout all data processes.

By harnessing AI-powered personalization effectively, businesses can not only increase revenue but also significantly enhance customer satisfaction—an essential advantage in today's competitive landscape where attention is scarce but expectations are high. Understanding these mechanisms equips organizations to move beyond one-size-fits-all approaches toward genuinely individualized customer journeys that resonate deeply and deliver measurable results.

Predictive analytics for CRM

Predictive analytics has fundamentally shifted customer relationship management (CRM) from a reactive practice into a proactive strategy. Rather than waiting for customers to take action or respond, businesses can now anticipate their needs, preferences, and behaviors by analyzing both historical and real-time data. This proactive approach enables more timely and targeted engagement, often leading to increased sales and stronger customer loyalty.

Consider an online retailer using predictive models to forecast customer churn. By monitoring indicators such as declining purchase frequency, browsing without buying, or reduced engagement with marketing emails, the model assigns a churn risk score to each customer. The CRM system then automatically launches personalized retention campaigns—like discount offers, exclusive previews, or tailored product recommendations—to re-engage at-risk customers before they leave. This preemptive tactic helps protect substantial revenue that might otherwise be lost.

Developing predictive models generally involves several key stages: data collection, feature engineering, model selection and training, evaluation, and deployment. To illustrate this process with a practical example, here's a simple logistic regression model built using Python's scikit-learn library to predict customer churn based on transactional and behavioral data:

```python
import pandas as pd

from sklearn.model_selection import train_test_split

from sklearn.linear_model import LogisticRegression

from sklearn.metrics import classification_report


\#\# Sample dataset: features include number of purchases, days since last purchase, and email engagement score

data = 'customer_id': [101, 102, 103, 104, 105],

'num_purchases': [5, 2, 0, 8, 1],

'days_since_last_purchase': [10, 45, 90, 5, 60],

'email_engagement': [0.8, 0.3, 0.1, 0.9, 0.2],
```

```
'churned': [0, 1, 1, 0, 1] \# Target variable: 1 means churned

df = pd.DataFrame(data)

X = df[['num_purchases', 'days_since_last_purchase',
'email_engagement']]
y = df['churned']

\#\# Split data into training and testing sets
X_train, X_test, y_train,y_test =
train_test_split(X,y,test_size=0.4)

\#\# Train logistic regression model
model = LogisticRegression()
model.fit(X_train,y_train)

\#\# Predict on test set
y_pred = model.predict(X_test)

print(classification_report(y_test,y_pred))
` ` `
```

This example highlights the core workflow: selecting meaningful predictors linked to customer behavior and training a model to classify whether customers are likely to churn. The classification report provides precision and recall metrics that help assess the model's accuracy—essential for targeting campaigns effectively without wasting resources.

Once validated—whether on small samples as shown here or on much larger datasets in practice—these predictive models integrate directly into CRM platforms via APIs or built-in analytics modules. Solutions like Salesforce Einstein Analytics or Microsoft Dynamics AI blend machine learning with extensive CRM data infrastructure to automate prediction-driven actions seamlessly.

Predictive analytics also plays a vital role in lead scoring, especially within B2B sales environments where identifying high-potential prospects quickly can make a significant difference. By analyzing firmographic data (such as industry size and location), past interactions (like webinar attendance), and behavioral signals (including downloads or demo requests), AI models rank leads by their likelihood of converting into customers. This allows sales teams to prioritize outreach efforts based on data rather than intuition or generic lists.

Beyond scoring individual leads or predicting churn risk, predictive analytics can forecast broader trends such as seasonality effects on buying patterns or customer lifetime value (CLV). CLV estimates future revenue from each customer by analyzing historical purchase frequency and average order size—figures that predictive models continuously refine with fresh data.

For example, if you manage subscription services for software users, a predictive CLV model could segment your audience based on expected revenue contribution over the next year. Marketing teams can then allocate communication budgets more efficiently instead of distributing uniform advertising across all users regardless of their potential value.

Implementing predictive analytics demands careful attention to data quality. Models rely heavily on accurate inputs; missing values or outdated records can skew predictions dangerously. Rigorous preprocessing—such as removing duplicates, normalizing scales, and encoding categorical variables—should be embedded within automated pipelines that feed CRM systems reliably.

Ethical considerations are equally important since these predictions influence how customers are treated—in pricing strategies or support prioritization. Biases in training data may lead to unfair outcomes if left unchecked. Transparency about model functioning and regular audits must complement technical measures to ensure responsible deployment.

A practical workflow might look like this:

1. Collect diverse datasets including transaction history, user behavior metrics (clicks, time spent), and demographics.

2. Define target outcomes such as churn status or lead conversion.

3. Engineer features capturing meaningful signals (e.g., recency-frequency-monetary value metrics).

4. Choose appropriate algorithms—from interpretable logistic regression to powerful gradient boosting machines.

5. Use train/test splits with cross-validation to ensure model robustness.

6. Deploy models within CRM platforms enabling automated triggers based on predicted scores.

7. Monitor ongoing performance relative to business KPIs and recalibrate as needed.

8. Maintain ethical oversight ensuring fairness and transparency throughout the process.

When applied thoughtfully following these steps—as

many companies have demonstrated—predictive analytics transforms CRM from static record-keeping into dynamic decision-making engines that drive sustainable growth.

Building on these predictive insights naturally leads into automating customer support interactions. AI-powered chatbots can respond dynamically with solutions before issues escalate—a step beyond prediction itself toward conversational automation strategies that further enhance the customer experience.

Automating customer support

Automating customer support has transformed from a simple cost-saving measure into a strategic imperative for businesses seeking to provide consistent, high-quality service around the clock. Unlike traditional call centers staffed solely by humans, AI-powered systems can instantly handle routine inquiries, allowing human agents to concentrate on more complex or sensitive issues. This shift not only boosts efficiency but also leads to measurable improvements in customer satisfaction.

Take, for example, a mid-sized e-commerce company that routinely fields questions about order status, return policies, product details, and troubleshooting. These repetitive queries are ideal candidates for chatbot automation. By integrating an AI chatbot with the company's CRM and order management systems, customers can receive real-time updates without waiting on hold. When a customer asks, "Where is my order?" the bot quickly pulls shipping information from backend databases and provides an immediate response.

Implementing automated support typically follows a clear progression:

1. Analyze historical support tickets or call logs to identify common customer inquiries.

2. Categorize these inquiries by complexity—distinguishing simple FAQs from issues needing human intervention.

3. Choose or build an AI chatbot platform with natural language understanding (NLU) tailored to industry-specific terminology.

4. Integrate the chatbot with essential databases such as product catalogs, order tracking, and billing systems.

5. Design conversational flows that anticipate follow-up questions and include seamless escalation paths to human agents.

6. Train the chatbot on real conversation transcripts and continuously refine it through feedback.

7. Launch as a hybrid model where humans oversee interactions and step in when necessary.

8. Track metrics like resolution time, customer satisfaction scores (CSAT), and deflection rates—the share of queries resolved without human involvement.

Shopify's use of automated support illustrates this well. Their AI assistant handles over 60% of routine questions related to account setup, billing, and app usage, significantly cutting wait times while enhancing merchants' confidence in self-service options.

Beyond text-based chatbots, voice assistants are gaining traction in sectors like banking and telecommunications, where many customers prefer verbal communication. Equipped with speech recognition and sentiment analysis, these voice bots can guide callers through troubleshooting or appointment scheduling without human assistance.

On the technical side, frameworks such as Google

Dialogflow and Microsoft Bot Framework offer built-in NLU capabilities alongside connectors for backend integration. Consider this simplified Python example demonstrating webhook handling for intent detection within a Dialogflow environment:

```python
from flask import Flask, request, jsonify

app = Flask(__name__)

@app.route('/webhook', methods=['POST'])
def webhook():
data = request.get_json()
intent = data['queryResult']['intent']['displayName']
parameters = data['queryResult'].get('parameters', )

if intent == 'OrderStatus':
order_id = parameters.get('order_id')
\#\# Mock function to fetch status
status = get_order_status(order_id)
response_text = f"Your order order_id is currently status.
else:
response_text = "Sorry, I didn't understand your request.

return jsonify('fulfillmentText': response_text)
```

```
def get_order_status(order_id):

\#\# In practice, fetch from database or API

mock_statuses = '12345': 'in transit', '67890': 'delivered'

return mock_statuses.get(order_id, 'being processed')


if __name__ == '__main__':

app.run(port=5000)
` ` `
```

This minimal setup shows how user intents trigger responses linked dynamically to backend data—a fundamental capability of automated support systems.

However, automation requires careful balance. Overly rigid scripts or failure to grasp nuanced queries risk frustrating customers rather than helping them. Continuous training on emerging conversation patterns and effective fallback mechanisms—like prompt transfers to human agents—are essential safeguards.

Complementing automation with customer sentiment monitoring further enhances support quality. Natural language processing models analyze tone or keywords signaling dissatisfaction; when negative sentiment is detected, supervisors receive alerts to intervene before issues escalate. Take this example, a telecommunications provider reduced average handling times by 30% after deploying chatbots alongside sentiment analysis tools that prioritize urgent calls.

Data privacy also demands careful attention. Automated agents often handle sensitive personal information during interactions, so transparent disclosure policies and robust encryption are vital to comply with regulations such as GDPR and CCPA.

Automation's benefits extend beyond reactive support into proactive outreach. AI can identify customers likely to encounter problems by analyzing usage patterns or service disruptions recorded in operational systems. Automated notifications or guided self-help resources can then reduce incoming tickets altogether. For example, a SaaS provider might automatically send troubleshooting tips upon detecting unusual login activity or a drop in usage—a subtle nudge that prevents frustration without requiring direct contact.

Enhancing customer retention

Enhancing customer retention through AI-powered automation focuses on creating consistent, meaningful engagement that anticipates customer needs before they are expressed. Successful retention depends on understanding behaviors, preferences, and pain points—areas where AI shines by analyzing complex data to drive targeted actions.

Take a subscription-based streaming service as an example. Rather than waiting for subscribers to cancel or disengage, AI algorithms monitor viewing habits, frequency, and content preferences to identify early signs of churn. When the data reveals reduced usage—such as fewer weekly sessions or abrupt stops after certain episodes—the system launches personalized retention efforts. These may include tailored recommendations, limited-time offers, or direct outreach via email or in-app notifications designed to reignite interest.

A practical method involves combining predictive analytics with marketing automation platforms. It starts with collecting historical customer interaction data: purchase history, support tickets, browsing patterns. Machine learning models then score each customer's risk of churn.

Following this, customers are segmented by risk level and behavior profiles, enabling customized retention workflows.

Take this example:

1. High-risk customers receive immediate attention through exclusive discounts or VIP event invitations.

2. Moderate-risk segments get informative newsletters highlighting new features or benefits.

3. Low-risk users stay engaged via routine value-added communications.

This approach requires seamless integration between AI models and CRM systems to automate outreach efficiently while tracking response metrics in real time.

Retail loyalty programs provide a concrete example of AI-driven personalization in action. While retailers have traditionally relied on point accumulation and generic promotions, automation now enables sending individualized coupons based on recent purchases or browsing behavior. This targeted strategy significantly boosts redemption rates compared to broad campaigns.

To illustrate prioritizing customers for retention efforts using scoring, consider this simple Excel formula applied in an e-commerce context:

| Customer ID | Last Purchase (days ago) | Average Purchase Value | Churn Risk Score |

| 1001 | 45 | 150 | =IF(B2>30, 0.8, 0.2)*C2/200 |

| 1002 | 10 | 300 | =IF(B3>30, 0.8, 0.2)*C3/200 |

| 1003 | 60 | 75 | =IF(B4>30, 0.8, 0.2)*C4/200 |

This formula assigns higher churn risk scores to customers who haven't purchased recently (more than 30 days ago), while factoring in average spend to prioritize high-value at-risk customers.

On the technology front, platforms like Salesforce Einstein and HubSpot's AI capabilities offer built-in predictive scoring models that integrate smoothly into existing sales and marketing pipelines—reducing manual data handling while enhancing retention strategies.

Beyond scoring and segmentation, automated follow-up sequences triggered by specific customer behaviors add another layer of effectiveness. For example, a SaaS platform might detect when a user hasn't logged in for two weeks and automatically send an email with tips tailored to their last-used features. If engagement remains low after several days, the system could escalate outreach with a phone call.

Automation also supports continuous learning loops where feedback from retention campaigns refines AI predictions over time, improving personalization accuracy.

However, effective retention isn't just about incentives or nudges; it requires delivering relevant experiences consistently across all channels. This means unifying data from mobile apps, websites, social media interactions, and even offline touchpoints into a comprehensive customer view that informs every automated action.

Data privacy plays a critical role here since sensitive personal information underpins these predictive models and personalized outreach efforts. Transparency about how data is collected and used must be embedded in automation design—customers increasingly expect control over their information.

Practically speaking, businesses should implement clear opt-in mechanisms within automated workflows alongside easy-to-access preference management portals integrated directly into communication channels.

One often overlooked but powerful tactic involves proactive

service interventions powered by AI monitoring operational systems for anomalies impacting customers—such as shipping delays or service outages—and automatically notifying affected users with apologies and compensation offers before complaints arise.

For example, telecommunications providers use automated systems to detect network degradation and send SMS alerts accompanied by temporary discounts or added perks without requiring any effort from customers—strengthening trust even during disruptions.

AI-driven automation transforms customer retention from reactive problem-solving into strategic foresight supported by data intelligence and seamless execution across multiple platforms—turning satisfied customers into loyal advocates without overburdening internal resources.

CRM tools and platforms

The landscape of CRM tools has transformed rapidly alongside advances in AI, offering businesses a wide array of options designed to automate and enhance customer relationship management. No longer mere digital Rolodexes or simple contact managers, today's platforms integrate sophisticated AI-driven features such as predictive analytics, sentiment analysis, automated workflows, and multi-channel communication. This evolution creates seamless interfaces where sales, marketing, and support teams operate with greater efficiency and precision.

Salesforce stands out as a leader in this space, with its Einstein AI layer embedding machine learning directly into the CRM workflow. Einstein automatically scores leads based on their likelihood to convert, recommends optimal next steps for sales reps, and even analyzes email tone to gauge customer sentiment. Take this example, if a lead's engagement suddenly drops off, Einstein can trigger alerts or launch tailored outreach sequences without human intervention—saving time and ensuring no opportunity slips away.

HubSpot offers another compelling example with its AI-powered Marketing Hub. It automates lead nurturing by dynamically adjusting email campaigns according to user behavior. If a prospect opens an email but doesn't click on the offer, HubSpot can schedule follow-up messages with content customized to that individual's interests. Additionally, HubSpot's chatbots qualify leads in real time on websites and route promising prospects instantly to sales teams, reducing manual workload while accelerating pipeline velocity.

For smaller businesses or those with tighter IT budgets, Zoho CRM provides a robust yet accessible solution featuring Zia, its built-in AI assistant. Zia analyzes historical deal data to predict the likelihood of closing new opportunities, flags anomalies in sales trends, and supports voice-enabled commands for quick information access during calls or meetings. Its seamless integration with other Zoho products enables end-to-end automation across finance, marketing, and customer service functions.

A key strength shared by these platforms is their ability to centralize customer data from multiple touchpoints— including websites, social media channels, mobile apps, and offline interactions—into unified profiles. Microsoft Dynamics 365 excels here by combining CRM with enterprise resource planning (ERP) capabilities and embedding AI modules that identify patterns like churn risk or upsell potential within these consolidated datasets.

To illustrate how automation can streamline processes, consider setting up lead scoring within Salesforce Einstein:

1. Define Criteria: Determine attributes that influence lead quality such as industry type, company size, and previous engagement.

2. Input Historical Data: Upload past leads along with outcomes (won or lost deals) to train the model.

3. Train Model: Use Einstein's machine learning functions to find correlations between attributes and conversion rates.

4. Deploy Score: Assign each new lead a score automatically based on the model's predictions.

5. Automate Actions: Create workflows where leads exceeding a certain score trigger immediate outreach notifications or are auto-assigned to top-performing reps.

6. Monitor & Refine: Continuously evaluate the model's accuracy using dashboards tracking conversion rates against scores and adjust criteria as needed.

This approach not only speeds up prioritization but also reduces subjective bias often inherent in manual scoring.

Beyond general CRMs, specialized platforms like Zendesk and Freshworks focus on automating customer support through AI-enhanced ticketing systems. Zendesk's Answer Bot leverages natural language processing (NLP) to interpret incoming requests and either suggests relevant knowledge base articles or routes tickets appropriately—reducing response times while maintaining customer satisfaction.

Integration capabilities further differentiate leading CRM tools. Many offer open APIs and pre-built connectors that synchronize with marketing automation platforms (like Marketo), e-commerce systems (such as Shopify), or communication tools (including Slack). This interoperability enables businesses to build customized automation ecosystems tailored precisely to their operational needs instead of relying solely on default features.

Choosing the right AI-driven CRM platform can be daunting given the variety available; however, focusing on key factors helps narrow options effectively:

- Scalability: Can it handle growing data volumes without slowing down?

- Customization: Does it support tailoring workflows and dashboards to specific business requirements?

- AI Sophistication: Are predictive analytics, NLP capabilities, and automation robust enough for your needs?

- User Experience: Is the interface intuitive enough for quick team adoption?

- Integration Ecosystem: How easily does it connect with existing tools?

- Security & Compliance: Does it meet relevant data protection standards?

Testing trial versions alongside gathering input from stakeholders often uncovers practical insights beyond what specs alone reveal.

Sometimes, organizations build proprietary CRM automation systems using open-source frameworks like Rasa for conversational AI or TensorFlow for custom predictive models. While resource-intensive, this approach offers precise alignment with unique customer journeys—a competitive advantage in highly specialized markets.

modern CRM tools have moved far beyond static databases by embedding AI at their core—transforming them into dynamic engines that actively drive engagement strategies. Selecting the right platform involves balancing advanced functionality against usability and cost while ensuring alignment with broader business goals.

The true value lies in integrating these intelligent systems seamlessly into daily operations so teams can spend less time on administrative tasks and more time nurturing meaningful relationships—boosting retention rates and lifetime customer value without needing proportional increases in headcount.

Leveraging chatbots and virtual assistants

Chatbots and virtual assistants have become essential in automating customer interactions, fundamentally changing how businesses connect with their audiences. Unlike traditional scripted replies, today's chatbots leverage natural language processing (NLP) to better understand queries, enabling smooth, conversational exchanges that feel more human than robotic. For example, Amtrak's "Ask Julie" handles thousands of daily inquiries with over 80% customer satisfaction. This chatbot goes beyond answering routine questions—it can book tickets, provide travel updates, and manage cancellations—freeing human agents to address more complex issues.

Successful implementation begins by identifying the most common customer pain points. An e-commerce company, for instance, might find that 40% of support requests involve order tracking and returns. Focusing on these areas first delivers quick efficiency gains. Setting up a chatbot with platforms like Dialogflow or Microsoft Bot Framework involves defining intents (user goals), entities (key data such as order numbers), and training phrases to cover diverse ways customers express themselves.

Consider a simple order status chatbot built with Dialogflow:

1. Create Intents: Define an intent like "Check Order Status" with training phrases such as "Where is my order?", "Track my package," or "Order delivery status."

2. Set Entities: Establish an entity called "order_number" to capture tracking IDs from user input.

3. Fulfillment Setup: Connect the chatbot backend to your order management system API so it can retrieve real-time order status when provided with an order number.

4. Test Interactions: Use the Dialogflow console to simulate conversations and refine responses based on unexpected inputs.

5. Deploy: Integrate the chatbot into your website, mobile app, or messaging platforms like Facebook Messenger or WhatsApp.

Virtual assistants extend this automation by combining proactive outreach with contextual awareness. Bank of America's Erica illustrates this well—it not only responds to user requests but also suggests bill payments before due dates, alerts customers about unusual transactions, and offers budgeting advice tailored from spending patterns. These assistants rely on machine learning models that evolve continuously based on user behavior, increasing their relevance over time.

Operationally, chatbots and virtual assistants bring tangible benefits. Response times drop sharply—customers rarely wait more than seconds during business hours—and scalability improves dramatically since bots don't tire or need breaks. This makes handling seasonal spikes in inquiries manageable without increasing staff while maintaining service quality.

However, challenges remain. Natural language understanding isn't flawless; ambiguous or complex questions can confuse bots unless fallback flows are carefully designed to direct users to human agents when necessary. Crafting conversational scripts requires balancing thoroughness with brevity—overloading users with irrelevant prompts can frustrate rather than help.

Security is another critical consideration. When chatbots process sensitive data like payment information or personal details, robust encryption and compliance with regulations such as GDPR are essential to protect user privacy and prevent breaches.

Integration capabilities also differentiate effective chatbot platforms. Many organizations use middleware tools like Zapier or custom APIs to connect chatbots with CRM systems such as Salesforce, ensuring every interaction enriches customer profiles automatically—enabling marketers to track engagement history and tailor future campaigns more precisely.

Voice-enabled virtual assistants are gaining traction in business settings as well. Amazon Alexa for Business, for example, allows voice commands in conference rooms for scheduling or accessing information hands-free—a subtle yet powerful way to expand AI assistance beyond text-based interactions.

As conversational AI tools evolve rapidly, companies must weigh the trade-offs between off-the-shelf solutions that offer ease of use and bespoke bots tailored to unique workflows but requiring more development effort. Regardless of the approach, success depends on continuous monitoring through analytics dashboards that track completion rates, collecting user satisfaction scores via post-interaction surveys, and analyzing chat transcripts to uncover improvement opportunities.

chatbots and virtual assistants are transforming customer service from a reactive function into a proactive partnership where automation amplifies human efforts rather than replacing them—speeding up response times while preserving the personalized experiences vital for brand loyalty in today's competitive landscape.

Measuring performance and customer satisfaction

Measuring performance and customer satisfaction in AI-enhanced customer relationship management (CRM) systems requires a balanced approach that integrates both quantitative metrics and qualitative insights. While traditional KPIs like first response time and ticket resolution rates remain important, AI introduces new dimensions of complexity and opportunity. For example, tracking chatbot conversation completion rates—how often a bot resolves inquiries without human intervention—provides immediate insight into the effectiveness of automation. An 85% independent resolution rate signals operational efficiency; lower rates suggest a need to revisit training data or dialogue design.

Take an e-commerce retailer using an AI-powered CRM as an illustration. They might monitor average handle time (AHT), customer satisfaction scores (CSAT), and net promoter scores (NPS), layering in AI-specific indicators such as intent recognition accuracy. This metric reflects how well the system understands customer queries. Low intent recognition accuracy can lead to declines in CSAT or increased escalations to human agents. Take this example, if a question about "refund status" is misinterpreted, the resulting unhelpful response can erode customer trust.

Beyond these numbers, sentiment analysis tools use natural language processing (NLP) to scan chat logs and emails, automatically detecting negative emotions or signs of frustration. Such analysis can reveal issues that standard surveys might miss. Imagine customers repeatedly expressing confusion over return policies during chat interactions—while CSAT scores remain steady, sentiment trends highlight underlying dissatisfaction before it escalates into formal complaints. Many companies integrate these insights into dashboards that correlate sentiment shifts with operational changes like bot updates or policy revisions.

To maintain effective oversight, organizations can adopt step-by-step monitoring frameworks:

1. Define Key Metrics: Focus on core indicators such as response times, resolution rates, fallback frequency (when bots transfer to humans), and satisfaction scores.

2. Set Benchmarks: Use historical data from before AI implementation to establish baselines for comparison.

3. Implement Real-Time Dashboards: Employ tools like Power BI or Tableau connected to CRM data for live tracking.

4. Collect Qualitative Feedback: Use brief post-interaction surveys to gauge customers' perceptions of clarity and helpfulness.

5. Analyze Chat Transcripts: Regularly review conversations flagged by sentiment analysis or low completion rates.

6. Iterate Improvements: Refine chatbot training datasets and adjust workflows based on observed patterns.

For example, a telecom company deploying an AI virtual assistant for billing inquiries initially saw a 5% drop in CSAT. Examining chat transcripts revealed the bot struggled with nuanced questions about payment plans. The team responded by expanding training phrases and introducing improved fallback protocols that directed uncertain queries to human agents. Within three months, CSAT not only recovered but increased by 8%, demonstrating how measurement informed targeted refinements.

Incorporating customer effort score (CES) adds another valuable dimension by measuring how easy it is for customers to resolve issues through AI channels compared to traditional support lines. Even marginal reductions in effort contribute meaningfully to loyalty and retention.

It's equally important to monitor internal user satisfaction among employees who interact with AI tools. Help desk agents relying on AI-generated suggestions may experience frustration if those recommendations are inaccurate or intrusive, which can negatively impact overall service quality despite technological advances. Combining surveys with usage analytics helps uncover these challenges.

Ethical considerations also come into play: transparency about data collection fosters trust in how customer feedback is handled. Clearly communicating that chats may be analyzed anonymously for quality purposes helps alleviate privacy concerns.

balancing automation metrics with human judgment remains crucial. While data guides decisions, frontline intuition often detects emerging trends before they appear in the numbers.

A robust measurement framework transforms raw data into actionable insights, enabling continuous improvement that enhances both operational performance and customer experience alongside evolving AI capabilities. Without this discipline, automation risks becoming a black box rather than a strategic asset driving lasting business value.

Customer data privacy concerns

Customer data privacy is among the most sensitive and strictly regulated facets of AI-driven customer relationship management. As AI systems process vast amounts of personal information—names, addresses, purchase histories, and behavioral patterns—the stakes increase dramatically. Privacy concerns extend beyond mere compliance with regulations like GDPR or CCPA; they touch the fundamental trust customers place in a brand. Any mishandling or unauthorized exposure of data can result in severe reputational damage and legal penalties, ultimately negating the benefits gained through automation.

A significant challenge arises from data aggregation practices. AI's effectiveness depends on large datasets to enhance accuracy, but merging information from diverse sources—CRM platforms, social media, transactional logs— can unintentionally reveal details customers never intended to share across channels. For example, an AI-driven marketing tool might combine purchase behavior with location data to personalize offers, yet if access controls are insufficient, it could expose sensitive habits. Addressing this requires rigorous data segmentation and anonymization techniques. Methods such as differential privacy introduce controlled noise into datasets, enabling useful analytics while protecting individual identities.

Third-party vendors and cloud services, integral to many AI solutions, present another practical concern. Outsourcing AI infrastructure means entrusting customer data to external parties, which expands the risk of breaches. While contracts can mandate strict security measures and audit rights, enforcing these consistently remains a challenge. To reduce exposure during transmission and storage, some organizations adopt end-to-end encryption and tokenization. Take this example, a financial services company using cloud-based AI for fraud detection encrypts customer transaction records with internally managed keys rather than relying solely on provider safeguards.

Transparency is also essential when addressing privacy issues. Customers expect clear communication about what data is collected, how it will be used, and their options for consent or opting out. Automated consent management integrated into AI workflows helps businesses maintain compliance while respecting user preferences dynamically. Consider an e-commerce site that prompts users at checkout to approve personalized recommendations based on browsing history—capturing explicit permission rather than hiding it within lengthy privacy policies.

Data retention policies further complicate privacy management. AI models require ongoing training with fresh data to stay effective, but retaining personal information indefinitely violates many regulations and best practices. Automated deletion schedules aligned with legal requirements prevent unnecessary data accumulation while balancing operational needs. A practical strategy might involve archiving older customer records in encrypted cold storage for audit purposes before securely purging them after a predetermined period.

Bias and discrimination represent another critical dimension tied closely to privacy concerns. Improperly curated datasets containing sensitive attributes like race or gender risk violating fairness mandates or anti-discrimination laws when such information is revealed or misused. Privacy-enhancing machine learning techniques can obscure or exclude protected attributes while still supporting accurate predictions—a subtle yet powerful safeguard against unfair outcomes.

Auditing mechanisms are vital for ensuring compliance within complex AI environments handling customer data. Automated logging tracks who accesses specific information and when, creating tamper-evident trails that support forensic analysis during incidents or regulatory reviews. For example, an enterprise deploying chatbot support may encrypt every conversation's metadata with timestamps designed to detect unauthorized access swiftly.

Achieving privacy by design involves embedding protective measures throughout every stage—from initial data collection to model training, deployment, and user interaction—rather than treating privacy as an afterthought added post-implementation. Conducting privacy impact assessments early on helps identify vulnerabilities unique to specific business contexts and guides tailored mitigation strategies.

Consider the example of a global retailer deploying an AI recommendation engine across regions with varying privacy laws. Their approach involved region-specific data handling protocols automatically enforced by middleware controlling data flows according to jurisdictional requirements. This solution ensured seamless compliance without sacrificing personalization quality—a balance many organizations find challenging.

safeguarding customer privacy in AI-powered CRM requires continuous vigilance instead of one-time fixes. As technology evolves rapidly, new threats emerge alongside innovative protection methods such as federated learning —which trains models locally on user devices without transmitting raw data centrally—and homomorphic encryption that enables computations on encrypted inputs.

For businesses seeking not only compliance but also lasting trust through responsible AI use, integrating robust privacy practices transforms customer relationships from mere transactions into partnerships grounded in respect and transparency. Without such commitment, the promise of intelligent automation risks being overshadowed by eroded confidence—damage no algorithm can easily repair.

CHAPTER 9: SUPPLY CHAIN AND LOGISTICS AUTOMATION

Inventory management automation

I nventory management automation transforms the traditional challenge of juggling stock levels, orders, and deliveries into a streamlined, nearly seamless process. Unlike manual methods or basic spreadsheets, AI-driven inventory solutions continuously track real-time data from various sources—warehouse sensors, sales channels, and supplier feeds—to maintain optimal stock levels without human intervention. This proactive approach helps prevent costly overstocking or stockouts that can disrupt sales or inflate carrying costs.

Take, for example, a mid-sized e-commerce business facing fluctuating demand across its product range. By adopting an AI inventory platform with predictive analytics, the system can analyze historical sales data alongside external factors such as seasonality, promotions, and market trends. If it anticipates a surge in demand for winter apparel based on weather forecasts and past patterns, the platform automatically alerts procurement teams to increase orders accordingly. This shift from guessing stock needs manually to relying on automated predictions can save tens of thousands of dollars annually.

Practical implementations often involve software like NetSuite or TradeGecko integrated with machine learning modules that dynamically update reorder points. Instead of relying on static thresholds—such as reordering when inventory drops below 100 units—the system recalculates safe minimums daily based on current turnover rates. This adaptability accounts for sudden disruptions like supplier delays or unexpected bulk orders without requiring constant manual adjustments.

Inventory automation also benefits from technologies like RFID combined with AI-powered vision systems for precise asset tracking within warehouses. Take this example, a logistics company equipped its storage facilities with smart cameras and RFID readers connected to an AI engine capable of identifying misplaced items or potential bottlenecks in picking routes. When a product is scanned outside its designated zone or flagged as missing during routine checks, alerts prompt immediate correction before errors escalate into fulfillment delays.

For those interested in building a basic inventory forecasting model using Python, this snippet demonstrates how the statsmodels library's ARIMA (AutoRegressive Integrated Moving Average) method can be applied:

```python
import pandas as pd

from statsmodels.tsa.arima.model import ARIMA
```

```
import matplotlib.pyplot as plt

\#\# Load historical sales data (date indexed)
data    =    pd.read_csv('sales_data.csv',    index_col='date',
parse_dates=True)
sales = data['units_sold']

\#\# Fit ARIMA model (order parameters chosen based on
AIC minimization)
model = ARIMA(sales, order=(5,1,0))
model_fit = model.fit()

\#\# Forecast next 30 days
forecast = model_fit.forecast(steps=30)

\#\# Visualize results
plt.plot(sales[-60:], label='Historical Sales')
plt.plot(forecast, label='Forecasted Sales', color='red')
plt.legend()
plt.show()
` ` `
```

This script reads daily sales figures and forecasts future demand trends essential for automating reorder schedules. While simpler than commercial platforms, it illustrates how predictive inventory management can begin with open-source tools tailored to specific datasets.

From a financial perspective, automating inventory reduces tied-up capital by lowering safety stock levels without increasing shortage risks. Research by McKinsey shows that companies implementing advanced inventory automation typically cut working capital requirements by 20-30%, which is particularly advantageous for startups and SMEs where cash flow constraints limit growth.

Beyond cost savings, operational agility also improves significantly. Integrating inventory systems directly with suppliers via APIs enables automatic triggering of purchase orders once thresholds are reached—shortening procurement cycles from days to hours. For example, manufacturers connected through Electronic Data Interchange (EDI) can receive near-instantaneous updates on order statuses, ensuring full transparency across the supply chain.

Despite these benefits, challenges remain if data quality or organizational readiness are neglected. Incomplete SKU records or inconsistent barcode scanning can feed flawed inputs into AI models, leading to poor stocking decisions. Addressing this requires thorough auditing of existing inventory data before deployment and investing in staff training on new technologies.

Scalability is another important consideration: solutions effective for one warehouse may struggle across multiple locations with varying demand patterns and logistical constraints. Employing modular AI architectures allows tailoring algorithms to each site while maintaining centralized oversight—a crucial balance for rapidly expanding companies or those managing diverse product lines.

automating inventory management combines predictive intelligence with disciplined operations—freeing human resources from routine monitoring so they can focus on strategic initiatives such as supplier negotiations or market analysis. As technologies evolve with advances in edge computing and IoT sensor networks, the depth and speed of insights will only increase.

Inventory automation serves as a foundational element within broader AI-powered business workflows—not only reducing costs but also enhancing responsiveness and resilience across entire value chains. Organizations that fail to adopt these capabilities risk falling behind competitors who treat smarter stock control as essential rather than optional.

The natural next step is to integrate these automated processes seamlessly with other supply chain functions —from demand forecasting to logistics optimization— to unlock compounded efficiency gains beyond isolated improvements.

Predictive demand forecasting

Predictive demand forecasting advances inventory management by leveraging AI to anticipate future customer needs with remarkable accuracy. Unlike reactive stock replenishment, which responds only after demand changes, predictive models draw on a rich mix of historical sales data, market trends, seasonal patterns, and external factors like economic indicators or social media sentiment. This comprehensive analysis enables businesses to forecast demand precisely enough to optimize procurement, reduce waste, and enhance customer satisfaction.

Take, for example, a retailer focused on consumer electronics. Traditional forecasting might depend heavily on last year's holiday sales to set stock levels. While straightforward, this method often misses sudden shifts —such as a competitor's product launch or supply chain disruptions—that can dramatically affect demand. By contrast, AI-driven forecasting allows the retailer to adjust orders dynamically in near real-time. Machine learning algorithms can spot emerging trends, like a surge in interest for wireless earbuds following a viral social media campaign, and recommend increasing inventory accordingly.

A practical technique involves time-series forecasting augmented with external regressors. Facebook's open-source Prophet library is one tool that simplifies incorporating events like holidays or promotions into demand predictions:

```python
from fbprophet import Prophet

import pandas as pd


\#\# Load sales data with 'ds' (date) and 'y' (units sold) columns

df = pd.read_csv('sales_data.csv')


\#\# Define custom holidays/promotions

holidays = pd.DataFrame(

'holiday': 'promo',

'ds': pd.to_datetime(['2024-11-25', '2024-12-10']),

'lower_window': 0,

'upper_window': 1,

)


model = Prophet(holidays=holidays)

model.fit(df)
```

```
\#\# Forecast for next 60 days

future = model.make_future_dataframe(periods=60)

forecast = model.predict(future)


\#\# Visualize forecast components

model.plot_components(forecast)
` ` `
```

This snippet integrates key sales-driving events into the forecast, helping businesses prepare inventory for demand spikes tied to promotions or holidays—factors often missed by simpler models.

Beyond structured data, incorporating unstructured sources such as news feeds or weather reports adds another dimension of sophistication. Take this example, agricultural suppliers use AI models that factor in rainfall and temperature forecasts to predict regional demand for fertilizers and seeds, enabling a more nuanced and responsive supply chain.

Retail giant Walmart reportedly combines point-of-sale data with macroeconomic trends and localized weather forecasts in its predictive analytics to fine-tune stocking decisions across thousands of stores. This capability to anticipate regional demand variations has significantly reduced overstock costs while preventing out-of-stock situations during peak seasons.

Implementing predictive models within existing enterprise resource planning (ERP) systems presents challenges but offers substantial rewards. Success requires clean historical data pipelines, ongoing model retraining to keep pace with shifting market conditions, and close collaboration among sales, marketing, and supply chain teams.

One common hurdle is "data drift," where evolving consumer behaviors alter the relationships the model has learned, leading to forecast inaccuracies if left unchecked. Automated alerts that trigger when prediction errors exceed set thresholds help maintain model effectiveness over time.

Operationally, blending predictive insights with automated procurement workflows creates a seamless process. Generating purchase orders based on forecasted demand—rather than solely current inventory levels—smooths supply chain fluctuations and minimizes costly last-minute rush orders.

The financial benefits are clear: companies using predictive demand forecasting often report inventory carrying cost reductions exceeding 25%, alongside order fulfillment improvements surpassing 95%. These gains translate directly into higher revenue retention and more efficient capital use.

Still, it's important to treat AI-generated forecasts as informed guidance rather than absolute truths. Human oversight remains essential to contextualize model outputs against real-world events that data alone cannot capture—such as geopolitical disruptions affecting logistics or sudden supplier bankruptcies.

successful adoption depends on combining technical rigor with organizational readiness. Teams must grasp the assumptions behind predictive models and build trust through iterative validation cycles.

By transforming forecasting from guesswork into a strategic asset, this approach aligns supply chains closely with market realities—providing an indispensable advantage in today's fast-paced business landscape.

Real-time tracking systems

Real-time tracking systems have transformed supply chain visibility by delivering continuous, up-to-the-minute information about the location and status of goods in transit. Unlike traditional batch updates, which can leave critical gaps, these systems use IoT sensors, GPS devices, and cloud platforms to provide detailed insights accessible anytime and anywhere. This constant flow of data empowers businesses to react promptly to disruptions— whether rerouting shipments, adjusting delivery schedules, or proactively communicating delays.

Take, for example, a mid-sized logistics company managing hundreds of shipments daily across various routes. Before adopting real-time tracking, their reliance on manual status checks and phone calls led to delays and inaccuracies. After implementing GPS trackers on vehicles and RFID tags on pallets—combined with a centralized dashboard aggregating all this data—the operations team gained unprecedented visibility. If a truck encounters unexpected traffic congestion, dispatchers receive instant alerts and can quickly coordinate alternative routes to meet delivery commitments.

Essentially of these systems are hardware components like GPS modules embedded in transport vehicles or cargo containers, along with IoT sensors monitoring environmental factors such as temperature or humidity— essential for perishable or sensitive products. Data from these devices streams through cellular or satellite networks into cloud-hosted applications where it's processed and visualized.

Typically, implementations combine lightweight communication protocols such as MQTT with cloud services like AWS IoT Core or Azure IoT Hub to support scalable data ingestion and real-time analytics. Take this example, a simple Python script using the paho-mqtt client can listen for GPS tracker messages:

```python
import paho.mqtt.client as mqtt

\#\# Callback when a message is received
def on_message(client, userdata, message):
payload = message.payload.decode()
print(f"Received data: payload")
\#\# Further processing: parse GPS coordinates, timestamp, etc.

client = mqtt.Client("tracker_listener")
client.connect("mqtt.broker.address", 1883)
client.subscribe("fleet/vehicle123/location")

client.on_message = on_message
client.loop_forever()
```

This listener captures live location updates sent by a vehicle's GPS tracker. In production environments, such data typically flows into databases or stream-processing pipelines like Apache Kafka for aggregation and alerting in real time.

User interfaces then display this information on interactive maps featuring dynamic overlays that indicate estimated arrival times (ETAs), route deviations, or temperature alerts for sensitive cargo. Dashboards often integrate GIS tools such as Mapbox or Google Maps API to provide intuitive tracking views accessible via desktop or mobile apps.

One significant challenge is managing the vast volumes of data generated by fleets operating worldwide. Optimizing storage often involves tiered databases where recent data remains immediately accessible while older records move to cost-effective archives. Additionally, edge computing can preprocess sensor data locally to reduce bandwidth consumption by filtering redundant updates before sending them to the cloud.

Integrating real-time tracking with enterprise resource planning (ERP) or transportation management systems (TMS) further enhances operational efficiency. Directly linking shipment statuses to order workflows automates customer notifications and triggers inventory updates upon delivery confirmation.

For example, DHL utilizes advanced IoT tracking combined with AI-driven analytics to continuously monitor shipments. Their system detects anomalies such as unauthorized route changes or unexpected temperature spikes inside pharmaceutical containers. These immediate alerts enable timely interventions that reduce spoilage risks and bolster customer trust through transparent communication.

Given the sensitive nature of shipment data, security is critical. Encrypted communication channels (TLS/SSL), device authentication mechanisms, and strict access controls safeguard against tampering or unauthorized access to tracking information.

The return on investment from deploying real-time tracking manifests in multiple ways: reduced freight costs through optimized routing, minimized detention fees thanks to accurate ETAs at loading docks, and improved customer satisfaction due to proactive order updates. Take this example, a major food distributor reported a 15% decrease in delivery delays after implementing sensor-based real-time monitoring combined with automated exception handling workflows.

Despite these benefits, some organizations face challenges during initial deployment. Integrating diverse devices across different carriers requires standardized protocols and thorough testing to ensure interoperability.

embracing real-time tracking transforms supply chains from reactive networks into predictive ecosystems capable of swiftly adapting to changing conditions. This enhanced visibility also sets the stage for further automation—such as AI-powered demand forecasting or autonomous vehicle coordination—that continues driving operational excellence forward.

Optimizing logistics routes

Optimizing logistics routes stands out as one of the most impactful ways AI-powered automation enhances supply chain management. The objective is clear: reduce transit times, lower fuel consumption, and boost delivery reliability by identifying the most efficient paths through complex transportation networks. Achieving this, however, involves juggling numerous constraints—traffic patterns, vehicle capacities, delivery windows, road restrictions, and even weather conditions.

In the past, route planning relied on manual scheduling or static algorithms that struggled to adapt to changing circumstances. Today's AI-driven solutions integrate real-time data from GPS trackers and traffic sensors with advanced optimization techniques such as genetic algorithms, simulated annealing, or reinforcement learning. This combination enables dynamic route adjustments that respond instantly to evolving conditions. Take this example, UPS's proprietary ORION system (On-Road Integrated Optimization and Navigation) reportedly saves millions of miles each year by recalculating routes based on traffic delays and customer preferences.

An effective logistics route optimizer typically begins by ingesting a variety of data inputs:

- Vehicle fleet characteristics (capacity, speed profiles)

- Delivery locations with priorities and time constraints

- Traffic forecasts or live congestion updates

- Regulatory restrictions (e.g., no-truck zones)

- Driver work-hour limitations

These factors feed into a mathematical model known as the Vehicle Routing Problem (VRP), a classical NP-hard challenge in operations research. Because exact solutions are computationally prohibitive for large fleets, heuristics and approximation methods are employed to find near-optimal routes efficiently.

To illustrate the core concept programmatically, consider this simple Python example using Google's OR-Tools library:

```python
from ortools.constraint_solver import pywrapcp

from ortools.constraint_solver import routing_enums_pb2


def create_distance_callback(dist_matrix):

def distance_callback(from_index, to_index):

return dist_matrix[from_index][to_index]

return distance_callback


distance_matrix = [
```

```
[0, 9, 6, 4, 7],

[9, 0, 3, 8, 5],

[6, 3, 0, 7, 4],

[4, 8, 7, 0, 6],

[7, 5, 4, 6, 0]

]


manager                                              =
pywrapcp.RoutingIndexManager(len(distance_matrix), 1, 0)

routing = pywrapcp.RoutingModel(manager)


distance_callback                                    =
create_distance_callback(distance_matrix)

transit_callback_index                               =
routing.RegisterTransitCallback(distance_callback)


routing.SetArcCostEvaluatorOfAllVehicles(transit_callback_
index)


search_parameters                                    =
pywrapcp.DefaultRoutingSearchParameters()

search_parameters.first_solution_strategy = (

routing_enums_pb2.FirstSolutionStrategy.PATH_CHEAPEST
_ARC)


solution                                             =
routing.SolveWithParameters(search_parameters)
```

```
if solution:

index = routing.Start(0)

route_plan = []

while not routing.IsEnd(index):

route_plan.append(manager.IndexToNode(index))

index = solution.Value(routing.NextVar(index))

route_plan.append(manager.IndexToNode(index))

print("Optimized route:", route_plan)

else:

print("No solution found!")
```
` ` `

While simplified, this code demonstrates how to define distances between stops and let the solver determine a minimal-cost path. Real-world systems extend this logic by incorporating live traffic feeds or historical congestion data to continuously reoptimize routes during operations.

One especially challenging area is last-mile delivery in congested urban environments where tight time windows make manual scheduling nearly impossible. AI models analyze delivery density patterns to cluster nearby packages into efficient runs that respect constraints like package size or temperature sensitivity. For example, Amazon's AI-based routing reportedly increased driver productivity significantly while reducing carbon emissions through fewer miles traveled.

Complexities multiply when integrating multi-modal transport—such as combining trucks with drones or autonomous vehicles—or when unpredictability spikes during peak seasons or due to incidents like accidents or road closures. Advanced platforms use predictive analytics powered by machine learning models trained on years of historical traffic data alongside real-time sensor inputs to anticipate bottlenecks before they occur.

A multinational retailer illustrates this approach by cross-referencing weather forecasts with shipment urgency scores. When severe storms threaten usual routes within hours, the system proactively reroutes shipments through safer corridors. This anticipatory automation minimizes late deliveries and lowers damage risks for sensitive goods.

Beyond operational efficiency, AI-enabled route optimization can integrate directly with cost accounting systems for transparent cost attribution per shipment or vehicle run. This insight allows managers to identify underperforming routes or vehicles needing maintenance before breakdowns happen—a subtle yet powerful layer of intelligence often absent without automation.

Security also plays a critical role when transmitting live location data across distributed networks. Encryption protocols combined with role-based access controls ensure only authorized personnel can modify critical logistics parameters—safeguarding against sabotage attempts that could disrupt supply chains.

 successful logistics optimization enhances more than just financial metrics; it builds trust through reliable delivery windows and enables scalable growth without proportional overhead increases. As fleets expand and networks grow more intricate, automated route planning becomes essential for competitive survival rather than optional.

At its core, optimizing logistics routes transcends merely finding the shortest path—it weaves together diverse datasets into adaptive plans that balance cost efficiency with service excellence amid ever-shifting conditions.

With increasingly accessible technology powering this transformation, businesses that start now can expect tangible returns within months instead of years.

Supplier relationship management

Supplier relationship management (SRM) has shifted from a primarily transactional function to a strategic advantage, largely driven by AI-powered automation. Traditionally, managing supplier interactions involved manually tracking contracts, performance metrics, and communications—a process prone to delays, misinterpretations, and missed opportunities. Today, AI-driven SRM platforms revolutionize this approach by analyzing vast datasets drawn from procurement history, market trends, and supplier capabilities, delivering actionable insights in real time.

Take, for example, a mid-sized manufacturing company facing frequent supply delays that jeopardize on-time delivery. Rather than relying on spreadsheets and sporadic communication, their procurement team adopted an AI-enabled SRM tool. This system continuously monitors supplier lead times alongside order volumes and external factors such as geopolitical risks or fluctuations in raw material prices. By flagging potential disruptions weeks in advance, it suggests alternative suppliers or points for renegotiation based on past negotiation outcomes and current market conditions—saving thousands of dollars in expedited shipping fees alone.

AI also streamlines supplier evaluation through automated scorecards that assess multiple dimensions including quality consistency, delivery punctuality, compliance adherence, and cost competitiveness. Take this example, a retailer uses machine learning models to scan supplier invoices for anomalies that might indicate billing errors or fraud attempts. These models improve their accuracy over time by learning from confirmed discrepancies, significantly reducing financial leakage without increasing manual audit efforts.

Setting up such automated scoring systems starts with consolidating diverse data sources. Structured data like purchase order fulfillment rates can be combined with unstructured inputs such as email exchanges or contract documents. Natural language processing (NLP) tools help extract relevant clauses or detect sentiment from communication logs, identifying early signs of dissatisfaction or risk. The following Python snippet demonstrates how sentiment analysis can be applied to supplier email responses:

```python
import nltk

from nltk.sentiment.vader import SentimentIntensityAnalyzer


\#\# Sample email texts from suppliers

emails = [

We will unfortunately be delayed due to unforeseen circumstances.",

All orders will be shipped ahead of schedule.",

There are issues with raw material availability affecting delivery.

]


nltk.download('vader_lexicon')

sia = SentimentIntensityAnalyzer()
```

```
for idx, email in enumerate(emails):

sentiment = sia.polarity_scores(email)

print(f"Email idx + 1 sentiment scores: sentiment")
` ` `
```

By integrating sentiment scores with quantitative metrics, procurement managers can prioritize communications and address concerns proactively before they escalate.

Beyond evaluation, AI enhances contract lifecycle management by automating document generation, compliance verification, and renewal reminders. A global technology firm, for example, employs robotic process automation (RPA) bots that review supplier contracts in real time against evolving regulatory requirements. These bots flag clauses needing revision and alert legal teams well before contract expiration dates—reducing bottlenecks and ensuring continuous compliance across jurisdictions.

Supplier collaboration benefits as well from AI-driven platforms designed to increase transparency and foster mutual performance improvement. Dashboards equipped with predictive analytics offer suppliers insight into upcoming demand spikes or product launches, helping them optimize capacity planning. Coupled with real-time feedback loops powered by IoT sensors monitoring shipment conditions or production efficiency, these systems transform suppliers from reactive vendors into proactive partners.

In the automotive industry—where just-in-time inventory is critical—a leading car manufacturer's AI-based SRM platform integrates sensor data from supplier factories and logistics providers to anticipate bottlenecks before they disrupt assembly lines. When deviations occur, such as delays in component quality testing, the platform automatically triggers contingency workflows involving alternate suppliers or expedited freight options.

Ensuring data integrity is fundamental to effective AI implementation in SRM. Harmonizing disparate supplier datasets demands robust master data management strategies supported by automation tools capable of detecting inconsistencies or duplicates early. To avoid "garbage in, garbage out" scenarios—where poor-quality data leads to faulty decisions—regular audits enhanced with AI-driven anomaly detection quickly highlight questionable entries for human review.

As environmental sustainability gains prominence, evaluating vendors beyond cost becomes standard practice. Automated tracking of supplier carbon footprints through integration with external databases enables companies to enforce green procurement policies systematically without excessive manual effort.

From an implementation standpoint, integrating AI-driven SRM solutions with legacy ERP systems often poses challenges. Middleware platforms offering APIs can bridge old and new technologies, allowing phased rollouts that preserve business continuity. Pilot projects targeting specific supplier segments or regions facilitate iterative refinement of automation parameters before full-scale deployment.

Measuring the return on investment for AI-enhanced SRM extends beyond immediate cost savings to include risk mitigation and improved supply chain agility. For example, a pharmaceutical company avoided costly production halts worth millions by identifying regulatory non-compliance early through automated contract reviews—highlighting the strategic value of these technologies beyond mere expense reduction.

Building trust remains essential throughout this transformation. Transparent algorithms that explain decision-making processes help increase acceptance among procurement teams and suppliers alike. Customizable dashboards tailored to user roles ensure relevant information surfaces without overwhelming stakeholders.

Today, effective supplier relationship management empowered by AI is no longer optional—it is a competitive imperative for businesses seeking resilience and efficiency at scale. By blending predictive foresight, operational rigor, and collaborative spirit grounded in actionable intelligence extracted from complex data ecosystems, organizations can forge stronger partnerships while confidently navigating today's volatile supply chains.

Through thoughtful application of technologies—from sentiment analysis and automated scorecards to contract lifecycle bots—companies unlock new levels of supplier collaboration and supply chain agility essential for long-term success.

Automation in warehousing

Warehousing plays a pivotal role in supply chain management, where the effectiveness of storing, retrieving, and distributing goods directly impacts overall operational success. Automation in this space goes beyond simple mechanization by incorporating AI-driven systems that optimize inventory handling, reduce errors, and speed up throughput. A prime example is the use of Autonomous Mobile Robots (AMRs), which move freely around warehouse floors, adapting to changing layouts and shifting task priorities without following fixed paths.

Take, for instance, a mid-sized e-commerce fulfillment center deploying AMRs for picking tasks. Instead of relying on traditional conveyor belts or manual pickers navigating long aisles, these robots receive real-time instructions through AI-powered warehouse management systems (WMS). These systems account for factors like order urgency, robot battery life, and aisle congestion. The process often begins with order batching—grouping orders by item proximity to minimize travel distances. Then, AMRs are dispatched to collect items sequentially, with their routes continuously refined by machine learning algorithms that analyze traffic patterns. This approach can reduce pick times by nearly 30% while lowering error rates thanks to automated scanning and item verification.

Beyond robotics, AI also enhances storage optimization by examining historical data on product turnover and seasonality. For example, an algorithm might forecast demand spikes for specific SKUs weeks ahead. Warehouse slotting can then adjust automatically—fast-moving items are relocated closer to packing stations, while slower-selling SKUs move to less accessible racks. This dynamic arrangement further reduces picker travel time and maximizes the efficient use of limited warehouse space.

To begin implementing automation, start by mapping your current warehouse layout and workflows. Identify bottlenecks: Are certain aisles frequently congested? Do pickers spend excessive time searching for misplaced items? From there, consider technologies that suit your operation's scale and complexity:

- Barcode scanners integrated with handheld devices enhance accuracy during manual picking.

- Automated Storage and Retrieval Systems (AS/RS) optimize high-density inventory storage in compact areas.

- AI-powered WMS dynamically manage inventory levels and allocate tasks.

- Vision-guided robotic arms assist with sorting irregular or fragile products.

A practical pilot might involve outfitting one aisle with

AMRs while keeping manual operations elsewhere. Track key performance indicators such as picks per hour, order accuracy, and labor costs before expanding automation further. Employee training is essential to ensure operators safely interact with autonomous systems and effectively interpret AI-generated insights.

A noteworthy example comes from a global retailer whose warehouse automation reduced order processing times from 48 hours to under 12 during peak seasons—achieved without increasing headcount. Their success was driven by integrating AI-based forecasting tools with robotic picking systems that adapted in real time to changing demand.

Maintenance is another critical aspect; predictive analytics can monitor sensor data from robot motors or conveyor belts to anticipate equipment failures. Proactive scheduling of downtime helps avoid costly disruptions.

automation in warehousing transforms not only physical workflows but also decision-making processes—shifting the focus from reactive problem-solving toward proactive optimization powered by data insights. Embracing this shift enables businesses to meet rising customer expectations while controlling costs amid increasingly complex supply chains.

Enhancing supply chain resilience

Supply chains today contend with a volatile mix of disruptions—from natural disasters and geopolitical tensions to sudden shifts in consumer demand. Building resilience within this complex network requires more than traditional contingency plans; it demands AI-driven automation that anticipates challenges, adapts quickly, and sustains operations under pressure. True resilience means not just recovering after disruptions, but proactively minimizing risks and maintaining smooth workflows.

Predictive analytics powered by machine learning offers a

powerful tool in this effort. By analyzing vast datasets —ranging from weather forecasts and supplier reliability scores to transportation delays and social media signals reflecting market sentiment—these models help supply chain managers identify potential bottlenecks before they occur. For example, an AI system might detect an increased likelihood of port congestion due to a combination of forecasted storms and recent shipping delays. Armed with this foresight, companies can strategically reroute shipments or adjust inventory levels to mitigate impact.

DHL provides a practical illustration of this approach. Their AI-enhanced risk management tools aggregate real-time data from multiple global sources to alert logistics teams about emerging threats such as labor strikes or customs slowdowns. Instead of reacting after problems arise, the team gains crucial lead time to implement alternative plans —switching carriers or prioritizing urgent orders—which has reduced their average disruption response time from days to hours.

Inventory optimization also plays a vital role in strengthening resilience. AI models continuously assess stock levels across distribution centers against fluctuating demand forecasts, dynamically adjusting safety stock thresholds and reorder points. This balance helps avoid costly overstocking while protecting against shortages caused by unexpected demand spikes or supply interruptions. Implementing this process typically involves:

1. Collecting historical sales data segmented by SKU and geography.

2. Integrating external variables such as supplier lead times and transportation reliability.

3. Training machine learning models (for example, random forest regressors) to predict short-term demand fluctuations.

4. Setting automated alerts for inventory approaching critical levels.

5. Establishing warehouse management system rules to trigger expedited replenishment or alternative sourcing.

The value extends beyond forecasting accuracy to automation's ability to execute decisions swiftly—whether reallocating stock between warehouses via autonomous vehicles or adjusting delivery routes in real time.

Route optimization further enhances resilience by enabling fleets to respond dynamically to changing conditions. AI algorithms analyze factors like traffic patterns, fuel costs, vehicle capacities, and delivery windows to continuously recalibrate optimal routes. UPS's ORION system exemplifies this, reportedly saving millions of miles annually through efficient driver rerouting that balances customer service with environmental objectives.

A typical integration might involve:

- Aggregating GPS data streams from fleet vehicles.

- Applying graph-based algorithms that minimize total distance traveled while respecting constraints such as time windows and vehicle load.

- Utilizing reinforcement learning techniques that refine routing based on historical driver performance and traffic trends.

- Feeding route adjustments directly into driver communication apps for seamless updates.

Beyond logistics and inventory, supplier diversification informed by AI insights contributes significantly to resilience. Machine learning tools assess supplier risk factors —including financial stability, geopolitical exposure, and historical delivery performance—to guide sourcing strategy adjustments.

Take this example, a multinational electronics manufacturer uses AI dashboards monitoring over 500 global suppliers. When political instability disrupted raw material supplies in one region, the system identified alternative suppliers elsewhere within hours rather than weeks, enabling swift response.

Embedding such resilience is not without challenges. Data silos across departments can limit visibility; legacy IT systems may lack flexibility; and organizational culture might resist rapid changes prompted by AI recommendations. Overcoming these obstacles often requires adopting integrated platforms that unify disparate data streams under centralized analytics, alongside securing executive support to build trust in automated decision-making.

leveraging AI-powered automation transforms supply chain management from reactive firefighting into strategic foresight combined with agile execution. Organizations equipped with these capabilities can better withstand shocks —reducing downtime costs while maintaining customer satisfaction—and gain a competitive edge in unpredictable markets.

The goal is clear: develop supply chains that do more than survive disruptions—they adapt dynamically, ensuring reliable operations amid uncertainty. Achieving this depends on thoughtful integration of intelligent automation technologies woven deeply into every layer of supply chain management.

Data-driven decision making

Data-driven decision making forms the foundation of effective AI-powered automation in supply chain and logistics. When decisions rely on reliable, timely data rather than intuition or incomplete reports, businesses gain the agility needed to navigate complexity and volatility. Achieving this, however, requires not only the right infrastructure to collect data at scale but also sophisticated analytics that transform raw information into actionable insights.

The process begins with comprehensive data integration. Supply chains generate a vast array of data types—from transactional records and sensor outputs to market trends and social media signals. Bringing these disparate sources together on a unified platform is essential. For example, a retailer might combine point-of-sale data with supplier delivery logs, inventory levels, and external factors like weather or economic indicators. This integrated perspective allows decision-makers to uncover correlations that remain hidden within siloed datasets.

Consider Walmart's logistics operations as an illustrative case. Their system continuously collects millions of data points across stores, warehouses, trucks, and suppliers. This consolidated dataset feeds machine learning models that predict stockouts with impressive accuracy. When a potential shortage arises in real time, automated alerts prompt inventory reallocation or expedited shipments— sometimes without human intervention—ensuring shelves stay stocked and customers satisfied.

Beyond prediction, prescriptive analytics adds another dimension by recommending optimal actions. Imagine demand suddenly surging for a product due to viral social media attention. Prescriptive models assess factors such as supplier lead times, transportation capacity, and costs before suggesting prioritized shipping routes or alternative suppliers. This helps rapid response while controlling expenses.

Implementing these capabilities often involves tools like Python's pandas library paired with optimization packages such as PuLP or Google OR-Tools. A typical workflow might look like this:

- Load historical shipment data into pandas DataFrames.

- Apply clustering algorithms (e.g., K-means) to segment delivery locations by proximity and order volume.

- Formulate an optimization problem minimizing total transportation costs subject to vehicle capacity constraints.

- Solve it using PuLP to generate route assignments.

- Visualize results with mapping libraries like Folium to provide actionable driver instructions.

This practical example reflects industry practices where automated routing adjustments save both time and fuel, demonstrating how advanced analytics drive tangible operational gains.

Visualization also plays a crucial role. Business intelligence dashboards powered by tools such as Tableau or Power BI offer supply chain managers intuitive displays of key performance indicators (KPIs). Real-time heat maps highlight delayed shipments or inventory shortages, drawing immediate attention to problem areas. Interactive filters allow users to drill down by region, product category, or supplier reliability scores, speeding up root-cause analysis.

Still, relying on data-driven systems brings challenges around data quality and governance. Inaccurate or outdated information can result in flawed decisions that ripple through the supply chain—exacerbating delays or increasing costs instead of reducing them. Embedding regular audits and automated validation routines within data pipelines is necessary to detect anomalies early.

Another challenge lies in balancing automation with human judgment. While AI excels at processing complex numerical scenarios, experienced managers contribute contextual insights—such as geopolitical risks or contractual nuances —that algorithms might miss. The most successful organizations adopt hybrid frameworks where machine recommendations are reviewed by experts before execution.

Ethical considerations are also important when analytics inform supplier evaluations. Transparency about how risk scores are calculated helps prevent unintended biases that could unfairly disadvantage smaller vendors or those from emerging markets—a concern underscored by recent research on algorithmic fairness.

Looking ahead, integrating real-time IoT sensor data promises even finer-grained monitoring of supply chain conditions—from temperature controls in cold chains to vibration alerts indicating potential transit damage. AI systems capable of ingesting these continuous streams will enhance decision-making further by proactively flagging risks before they escalate into costly disruptions.

embedding data-driven decision making within supply chain automation transforms raw information into strategic advantage. Whether through predictive insights anticipating demand shifts or prescriptive solutions optimizing routes and supplier choices, organizations that leverage this capability position themselves for unmatched responsiveness and resilience.

What you should know is clear: rich datasets combined with advanced analytical tools empower smarter—not just faster —decisions, enabling supply chains that evolve proactively alongside shifting realities rather than reacting after the fact.

CHAPTER 10: AI FOR MARKETING AUTOMATION

Segmentation and targeting

Segmentation and targeting are fundamental to effective AI-driven marketing automation, allowing businesses to deliver the right message to the right audience at the right time. While traditional marketing often depended on broad demographics or guesswork, AI enhances this approach by analyzing vast datasets —such as behavioral patterns, purchase histories, and online interactions—to identify micro-segments that were previously unnoticed.

Take an e-commerce platform aiming to boost conversion rates for its summer collection. Instead of sending a generic email to its entire subscriber list, AI can segment customers based on recent browsing behavior, previous seasonal purchases, and geographic factors related to climate. For example, shoppers in coastal areas might receive promotions for beachwear, while urban customers see ads for casual city outfits. This kind of precision increases relevance and drives higher customer engagement.

From a technical perspective, marketers often use clustering algorithms like K-means or hierarchical clustering to group users based on multiple attributes—age, income, device usage, engagement frequency, and more. Python's scikit-learn library is a popular choice for building these models. The following code snippet demonstrates how to create customer segments using purchase frequency and average order value:

```python
from sklearn.cluster import KMeans

import pandas as pd


data = pd.DataFrame(

'purchase_frequency': [5, 1, 3, 8, 2],

'avg_order_value': [100, 20, 50, 200, 30]

)


kmeans = KMeans(n_clusters=2)

kmeans.fit(data)


data['segment'] = kmeans.labels_

print(data)
```

This process separates high-value frequent buyers from occasional shoppers, enabling marketers to tailor campaigns specifically for each group's preferences.

Targeting then applies these segments through personalized

content delivered across multiple channels—email, social media ads, search engines. Programmatic advertising platforms use AI-driven bidding strategies to optimize ad spend dynamically. Take this example, Google Ads employs machine learning models that continuously analyze user signals and adjust bids in real time to maximize ROI. These systems also predict conversion likelihood and allocate budget accordingly.

A notable example is Netflix's recommendation engine. It segments viewers not only by genre preferences but also by factors like viewing time and session length. These insights support targeted promotions—for instance, nudging users with new episodes of their favorite shows—which helps improve retention rates.

To implement segmentation and targeting effectively, follow these steps:

1. Collect rich data: Aggregate customer touchpoints from CRM systems, website analytics, and social media interactions.

2. Clean and preprocess data: Remove duplicates, normalize values, and handle missing entries to ensure model accuracy.

3. Select segmentation criteria: Identify key features that influence buying behavior and align with business goals.

4. Build clustering models: Utilize machine learning tools such as scikit-learn or TensorFlow.

5. Validate segments: Assess whether segments show meaningful differences in customer response or sales performance.

6. Deploy targeted campaigns: Integrate with marketing automation platforms like HubSpot or

Marketo.

7. Measure performance: Monitor KPIs including click-through rates (CTR), conversion rates, and customer lifetime value (CLV).

It's important to balance algorithmic insights with domain expertise. Human judgment remains vital in interpreting data nuances and identifying outliers that models might overlook.

Ethical considerations also come into play. Overly narrow targeting can alienate audiences or create filter bubbles where customers are exposed only to familiar content. Transparency about data use and compliance with privacy regulations such as GDPR help maintain brand trust.

Real-world examples highlight these benefits: one retailer achieved a 35% sales increase after applying AI-driven segmentation combined with personalized discount offers tailored by segment profiles. Another company reduced its cost per acquisition by 20% by shifting budget from generic ads toward high-potential micro-segments identified through behavioral modeling.

At its core, effective segmentation paired with precise targeting moves marketing away from shotgun tactics toward smarter resource allocation—resulting in measurable growth without unnecessary spending.

By leveraging AI to dissect your customer base beyond surface-level data and linking those insights to targeted outreach, businesses can transform engagement into revenue with impressive efficiency.

Content creation and curation

Content creation and curation have become fundamental to AI-driven marketing automation, transforming how businesses develop and manage messaging across multiple channels. Moving beyond traditional methods that depended heavily on manual effort and intuition, AI now enables dynamic content generation tailored to specific audiences, optimizing both relevance and timing.

Take, for example, a global fashion brand launching a seasonal campaign. Instead of relying on generic messages, AI-powered platforms analyze user preferences, browsing history, and social media behavior to generate personalized content variations. These might include email subject lines optimized for higher open rates or social media posts scheduled to coincide with peak engagement times in different regions. This ability to scale customization without burdening creative teams significantly streamlines marketing workflows.

At the heart of this innovation lies natural language generation (NLG), a branch of AI focused on producing human-like text from data inputs. Advanced models like OpenAI's GPT series or Hugging Face transformers have made sophisticated language tools accessible for drafting product descriptions, blog posts, and ad copy with minimal human intervention. Marketers can provide key product features and tone guidelines to these systems and iteratively refine the outputs to suit their needs.

Take this example, imagine creating ten variations of a promotional email targeting different demographics —millennials interested in eco-friendly products versus baby boomers drawn to classic styles. Using Python's transformers library, this process can be automated efficiently:

```python
from transformers import pipeline


generator = pipeline('text-generation', model='gpt-2')
```

```
prompts = [

Write an eco-friendly fashion promo for millennials:",

Write a classic style promo for baby boomers:

]


for prompt in prompts:

result    =    generator(prompt,    max_length=100,
num_return_sequences=3)

print(f"Prompt: prompt")

for idx, text in enumerate(result):

print(f"Variation idx+1: text['generated_text']")
` ` `
```

This example demonstrates how multiple content versions can be generated quickly for A/B testing or multichannel campaigns.

Curation works hand-in-hand with creation by automating the selection and distribution of relevant third-party content alongside original materials. AI algorithms scan news sources, blogs, and social feeds to identify trending topics that align with brand messaging. Platforms such as Curata and Anders Pink employ machine learning to refine these selections continuously based on engagement data.

In practice, a tech company might combine curated articles about emerging cybersecurity threats with its own whitepapers to position itself as an industry thought leader. Integrated scheduling tools then ensure timely posting across platforms like LinkedIn or Twitter without requiring manual oversight.

Bridging creation and curation calls for robust workflow orchestration. Marketing automation suites like HubSpot and Marketo offer APIs that link NLG services with content repositories and publishing calendars. Automating these pipelines drastically reduces turnaround times while maintaining quality through editorial review checkpoints embedded in the process.

Still, challenges remain. Relying too heavily on automated generation can result in generic or off-brand messages if not carefully managed. Human editors play a critical role in providing strategic oversight and contextual judgment —especially when dealing with sensitive topics or complex products.

Ethical considerations also come into play. Transparency about AI-generated content fosters trust among increasingly discerning audiences. For example, The Washington Post openly acknowledges its use of AI assistants for certain reports, setting a standard for responsible communication.

Measuring success involves more than just output volume; engagement metrics such as clicks and shares, conversion rates linked to specific content variants, and sentiment analysis all feed into ongoing refinement. Machine learning models themselves can evolve by incorporating feedback from these key performance indicators.

One retail client reported cutting its content production cycle from weeks to days after adopting an AI-driven creative engine paired with smart curation workflows—achieving a 25% increase in customer interaction metrics within three months.

 integrating AI into content creation and curation enables marketers not only to scale their efforts but also to sharpen messaging precision. This approach transforms raw data into compelling stories that resonate deeply with diverse audience segments while freeing human talent to focus on strategic innovation and higher-level creativity.

Social media automation tools

Social media automation tools have transformed the way businesses maintain an active and engaging presence across multiple platforms, eliminating the constant resource drain associated with manual posting. By handling routine scheduling tasks, these tools enable marketers to precisely time and target content based on audience behavior. Platforms like Hootsuite and Buffer allow users to queue posts weeks in advance, tailor messages for each channel, and monitor engagement metrics—all from a centralized dashboard.

What sets advanced social media automation apart is its use of AI-driven insights to optimize content delivery. For example, Sprout Social leverages machine learning algorithms to suggest the best posting times by analyzing audience activity and platform trends. A LinkedIn post scheduled for 10 a.m. might perform better at 2 p.m., while Instagram content often sees higher engagement during evening hours. This level of fine-tuning reduces guesswork and significantly enhances return on investment.

Beyond timing, automation increasingly incorporates sentiment analysis within its workflows. Tools scan comments and reactions in real time, flagging negative feedback or emerging topics that require immediate attention. Identifying a customer complaint early on Twitter, for instance, allows brands to respond promptly—preventing escalation and protecting their reputation.

For organizations managing multiple brands or campaigns simultaneously, features like bulk uploading and template libraries save valuable time. A marketing manager at a mid-sized consumer electronics company shared how batch uploads combined with AI-generated caption suggestions cut social media campaign preparation from days to just hours, streamlining efforts across diverse product lines.

To illustrate foundational automation, consider this simple Python script using the Tweepy library to schedule tweets via Twitter's API:

```python
import tweepy

import schedule

import time


\#\# Authenticate with Twitter API

auth = tweepy.OAuth1UserHandler('consumer_key', 'consumer_secret', 'access_token', 'access_token_secret')

api = tweepy.API(auth)


def post_tweet(message):

try:

api.update_status(message)

print(f"Tweet posted: message")

except Exception as e:

print(f"Error posting tweet: e")


\#\# Schedule tweets

schedule.every().day.at("09:00").do(post_tweet, message="Good morning! Check out our latest products.")

schedule.every().day.at("15:00").do(post_tweet, message="Don't miss our special offer this week!")
```

```
while True:

schedule.run_pending()

time.sleep(60)

` ` `
```

While straightforward, this example demonstrates automated posting of pre-written messages at set times. Scaling this approach involves integrating AI components that analyze trending hashtags or dynamically generate content ideas based on live data streams.

Another important trend is balancing cross-platform consistency with channel-specific customization. Automation suites often provide unified content calendars where marketers can visualize scheduled posts across Facebook, Instagram, LinkedIn, TikTok, and more—while automatically adapting format and tone for each platform. LinkedIn copy tends to be professional; Instagram captions lean into storytelling and hashtags; Twitter favors brevity and immediacy.

Some platforms also extend automation into influencer marketing by tracking collaborators' posting schedules and engagement metrics automatically. This capability helps brands adjust campaigns in real time without manual oversight or missed opportunities.

Despite its benefits, social media automation has pitfalls when overused or applied without human judgment. Automated responses can sound robotic or fail to capture contextual nuances—especially during crises or rapidly changing conversations online. Brands like Wendy's exemplify how combining automated scheduling with a personable social media team maintains authenticity while scaling output.

Privacy considerations are equally important. As users grow more wary of extensive data collection, transparency about what information drives targeted posts or ad placements within these tools becomes essential.

Measuring success requires more than follower counts or likes; it calls for sophisticated analytics dashboards that link conversion rates to specific posts or automated sequences. Some platforms integrate directly with CRM systems to connect social engagement data with sales figures, enabling comprehensive attribution modeling.

Companies adopting social media automation often report significant efficiency gains but emphasize the need for agility —remaining ready to intervene manually when tone shifts or unexpected events arise. Striking this balance transforms automation from a mere convenience into a powerful driver of growth within today's digital marketing landscape.

Lead scoring and conversion analysis

Lead scoring and conversion analysis are essential for transforming marketing efforts into measurable revenue. Generating leads alone is insufficient; businesses must understand which prospects are most likely to convert in order to allocate resources efficiently. AI-powered automation elevates this process from manual estimation to data-driven accuracy, constantly enhancing how leads are assessed and nurtured.

Traditional lead scoring typically depends on fixed criteria such as job title, company size, or engagement frequency. While these factors provide a baseline, they often miss the subtle behaviors that indicate true buying intent. AI changes this by analyzing extensive datasets—including web activity, email interactions, and social media signals—to uncover patterns that humans might overlook. For example, machine learning models can assign dynamic scores that adjust in real time as prospects download whitepapers, attend webinars, or repeatedly visit pricing pages.

Take a SaaS company using an AI-driven lead scoring system integrated with their CRM. Each inbound lead begins with a baseline score based on demographic fit. Every interaction thereafter feeds into a predictive model trained on historical sales data. The system might identify that prospects who schedule product demos within two days of receiving a follow-up email have a 70% higher chance of converting. So, those leads automatically rise in priority for sales reps.

Achieving this requires connecting multiple data sources —website analytics platforms like Google Analytics or Mixpanel; marketing automation tools such as HubSpot or Marketo; and CRM systems like Salesforce or Zoho. The key is creating unified customer profiles that continuously supply input to scoring algorithms without gaps or delays.

From a practical perspective, implementing AI-powered lead scoring involves several critical steps:

1. Define Conversion Goals: Specify what counts as conversion—demo requests, trial sign-ups, purchases—to tailor the scoring model accordingly.

2. Gather Historical Data: Compile past lead interactions and outcomes to train machine learning models effectively.

3. Select Features: Choose relevant behavioral indicators (page visits, email opens), firmographic data (industry, company size), and engagement recency.

4. Choose Algorithms: Begin with interpretable methods like logistic regression, progressing to more complex models such as gradient boosting or neural networks if appropriate.

5. Train & Validate Models: Employ cross-validation

to prevent overfitting and ensure reliable predictions.

6. Integrate with CRM: Automate score updates and trigger alerts for sales teams based on defined thresholds.

Below is a simplified Python example using scikit-learn to build a logistic regression model for lead scoring with synthetic data:

```python
import pandas as pd

from sklearn.model_selection import train_test_split

from sklearn.linear_model import LogisticRegression

from sklearn.metrics import classification_report


\#\# Sample dataset with features: 'email_opens', 'web_visits', 'demo_requested'

data = pd.DataFrame(

'email_opens': [5, 2, 8, 1, 7],

'web_visits': [10, 4, 15, 3, 12],

'demo_requested': [1, 0, 1, 0, 1],

'converted': [1, 0, 1, 0, 1]

)


X = data[['email_opens', 'web_visits', 'demo_requested']]

y = data['converted']
```

```
X_train,        X_test,        y_train,        y_test        =
train_test_split(X,y,test_size=0.4)

model = LogisticRegression()

model.fit(X_train,y_train)

predictions = model.predict(X_test)

print(classification_report(y_test,predictions))
` ` `
```

This basic example illustrates building predictive models from historical behaviors to generate actionable lead scores. In production environments, this process scales with additional features and real-time data streams.

Conversion analysis complements lead scoring by monitoring how prospects progress through the sales funnel after initial contact. AI-powered dashboards reveal drop-off points and bottlenecks dynamically rather than relying solely on static monthly or quarterly reports.

For example, an e-commerce company might find that visitors who click personalized recommendation emails but don't complete checkout tend to abandon carts due to slow page load times—a factor machine learning models correlate with lost conversions in prior campaigns. Equipped with this insight, automated workflows can launch retargeting ads or trigger chatbots offering discounts precisely when shoppers hesitate.

Integration between marketing automation platforms and analytics tools is vital in this context:

- Combining Google Analytics Enhanced Ecommerce

with AI services like Google Cloud AutoML enables detailed attribution modeling.

- AI-driven funnel visualization tools uncover hidden customer journeys beyond simple linear paths.

- Automated A/B testing frameworks accelerate landing page optimization through conversion feedback loops powered by algorithmic insights.

However, it's important to recognize that not all conversions carry equal value across segments. Incorporating weighted lead scores based on deal size or long-term customer lifetime value further refines prioritization.

A cautionary example comes from an online education provider that initially automated lead nurturing solely on generic engagement metrics but neglected student readiness levels. This approach wasted effort chasing cold leads while warm prospects slipped away until manual adjustments corrected the strategy.

In summary, applying AI-driven lead scoring alongside advanced conversion analysis turns raw marketing data into strategic intelligence. Businesses gain sharper focus on high-potential opportunities while continuously enhancing campaign effectiveness through iterative feedback grounded in real user behavior rather than assumptions. The financial benefits extend beyond increased sales volume to optimized use of human resources—focusing effort where it truly matters: closing deals instead of pursuing unlikely prospects.

Performance analytics and reporting

Performance analytics and reporting are fundamental to effective AI-powered marketing automation, turning raw campaign data into strategic insights that directly impact business results. Without precise measurement, even the most advanced AI-driven marketing efforts risk missing alignment with broader objectives. Analytics uncover what's working well while highlighting underperforming segments or tactics in need of adjustment.

A practical way to leverage these insights is through real-time dashboards that consolidate metrics from various channels—social media, email, paid ads, and website traffic—into a unified view. Tools like Google Data Studio, Tableau, or Power BI can integrate seamlessly with AI platforms to visualize key performance indicators (KPIs) such as click-through rates, cost per acquisition, and customer lifetime value. For example, a retailer running Facebook and Instagram ad campaigns might automate daily data pulls on spend and conversions, enabling continuous ROI monitoring rather than relying on delayed manual reports.

Beyond visualization, machine learning algorithms can uncover subtle patterns within performance data that may escape human analysis. Clustering methods segment audiences by engagement behaviors, revealing niche groups that respond differently to messaging or timing. Imagine an AI model identifying a demographic that engages more with video ads during weekend evenings; marketing automation can then adjust ad schedules and content delivery dynamically. This type of optimization not only enhances efficiency but also personalizes customer interactions at scale.

Consider a B2B software company using AI-driven attribution modeling. Traditional models often credit only the last touchpoint before conversion, overlooking the complex paths prospects take across multiple channels. An AI-powered system employs probabilistic modeling to distribute credit among various touchpoints—email opens, webinar attendance, whitepaper downloads—offering a more nuanced view of what truly drives sales. These insights guide budget shifts toward high-impact channels and refine content strategies based on actual influence rather than assumptions.

To implement such analytics effectively, organizations can follow these actionable steps:

1. Define Relevant KPIs: Align metrics with campaign goals like brand awareness, lead generation, or revenue growth.

2. Integrate Data Sources: Use APIs or connectors to combine CRM records, ad platform data, and website analytics for a holistic perspective.

3. Automate Data Cleaning: Utilize scripts or tools (e.g., Python's Pandas) to handle missing values, remove duplicates, and normalize datasets for accurate modeling.

4. Apply Machine Learning Models: Deploy supervised learning for predictive insights or unsupervised techniques like clustering for audience segmentation.

5. Build Interactive Dashboards: Create user-friendly visualizations that highlight trends and anomalies to support timely decision-making.

6. Schedule Regular Reviews: Establish routines for analyzing reports to track progress and adapt strategies dynamically.

The following Python snippet illustrates basic data cleaning using Pandas:

```python
import pandas as pd


\#\# Load dataset from CSV

data = pd.read_csv('marketing_data.csv')
```

```
\#\# Remove duplicates
data.drop_duplicates(inplace=True)

\#\# Fill missing values with zeros for numerical columns
numeric_cols = ['clicks', 'impressions', 'conversions']
for col in numeric_cols:
data[col].fillna(0, inplace=True)

\#\# Normalize 'cost' column between 0 and 1
data['cost_normalized'] = (data['cost'] - data['cost'].min()) / (data['cost'].max() - data['cost'].min())

print(data.head())
```
```

This preprocessing ensures downstream AI models work with consistent and reliable data.

Automating reporting also fosters transparency among stakeholders. Automatically generated summaries and alerts keep marketing teams informed about campaign milestones or performance issues without waiting for manual updates. Take this example, Slack integrations can notify managers immediately if the cost per lead surpasses set thresholds, enabling swift corrective action before budgets escalate uncontrollably.

It's equally important to balance analytic complexity with clear communication tailored to diverse audiences. Executives often prefer high-level KPIs in concise scorecards, while analysts need detailed datasets for deeper exploration.
```

Segmenting reports accordingly improves engagement and decision-making across the organization.

Organizations should also beware of "vanity metrics" — such as likes or impressions — that don't directly correlate with business impact. Prioritizing outcome-driven measurement encourages teams to link their efforts to tangible financial results like conversion rates or revenue per channel.

performance analytics and reporting empower businesses not only to track how well their AI-powered marketing performs but also to iterate intelligently on strategies that drive sustained growth. The ability to translate complex data into actionable knowledge is where automation delivers its greatest value—enabling smarter decisions faster at every stage of the customer journey.

Cross-channel marketing strategies

Cross-channel marketing strategies leverage AI to synchronize campaigns across multiple platforms, crafting cohesive customer experiences that boost engagement and conversions. Rather than running isolated efforts on social media, email, or paid ads, integrated automation ensures messaging aligns precisely with each customer's position in their journey. This synchronization goes beyond simply sharing the same content everywhere; it involves dynamic adjustments informed by real-time data and behavioral insights.

For example, an AI system might notice a prospect engaging with an email newsletter and then tailor subsequent social media ads to highlight products or content relevant to that interaction. This creates a seamless, personalized narrative —avoiding repetition or disjointed messaging. AI-powered Customer Data Platforms (CDPs) like Segment or Tealium play a key role here by unifying customer profiles across channels. These platforms collect data from web visits, app usage, purchase history, and offline interactions, providing marketers with a single source of truth.

To build effective cross-channel strategies, begin by mapping typical customer touchpoints for your business. Break these into key stages—awareness, consideration, decision—and identify which channels dominate each phase. Next, assess your current campaign tools: Do they support API integrations? Can they share data in real time? Without this technical foundation, cross-channel automation will remain fragmented.

A practical approach might involve the following steps:

1. Centralize Customer Data: Combine inputs from CRM systems, website analytics, social platforms, and offline sources into one platform.

2. Define Unified Customer Journeys: Establish rules or AI models that detect when a user moves between channels or devices.

3. Develop Adaptive Content: Create modular messaging assets that AI can adjust based on channel constraints and user preferences.

4. Automate Orchestration: Use marketing automation suites (like HubSpot or Marketo) enhanced with AI to trigger context-aware messages.

5. Monitor Cross-Channel KPIs: Track conversions across channels and use attribution models that capture multi-touch paths.

Consider a retailer launching a holiday promotion across Facebook Ads, Google Search campaigns, email blasts, and SMS alerts. An AI-driven system continuously analyzes engagement signals: if email open rates drop within certain segments but search queries rise for specific products, the system reallocates budget toward paid search while refreshing email content to regain interest—all without manual input.

Maintaining a consistent brand voice across platforms is equally important. Take this example, chatbots handling post-click conversations on Facebook Messenger should reflect the tone used in earlier promotional emails—a subtlety often overlooked but vital for building trust.

Cross-channel marketing also gains from predictive analytics layered on top of orchestration engines. These algorithms forecast optimal timing and channel combinations based on historical user behavior, allowing marketers to anticipate when prospects are most receptive rather than merely react after engagement occurs.

Below is a simplified Python example illustrating how one might prepare datasets for such predictive modeling using scikit-learn:

```python
import pandas as pd

from sklearn.model_selection import train_test_split

from sklearn.preprocessing import LabelEncoder

from sklearn.ensemble import RandomForestClassifier


\#\# Sample dataset with user interactions across channels

data = pd.read_csv('user_engagement.csv')


\#\# Encoding categorical variables like channel type

le = LabelEncoder()

data['channel_encoded'] = le.fit_transform(data['channel'])
```

```
\#\# Features could include time spent on site, prior
purchases, channel engaged

features    =    data[['time_on_site',    'prior_purchases',
'channel_encoded']]

target = data['conversion']  \# Binary: 1 if converted after
interaction


\#\# Split data for training model

X_train, X_test, y_train, y_test = train_test_split(features,
target,

test_size=0.2,

random_state=42)


\#\# Train a random forest classifier to predict conversion
likelihood

model = RandomForestClassifier(n_estimators=100)

model.fit(X_train, y_train)


\#\# Predict conversion probabilities for new interactions

predictions = model.predict_proba(X_test)[:,1]


print(predictions[:5])
```
` ` `

This snippet demonstrates how historical channel
interactions feed predictive models that guide automated
decisions about where and when to focus marketing efforts

next.

Measurement plays a pivotal role as well—not all channels contribute equally, nor do customers respond uniformly over time. Cross-channel attribution models such as Shapley values or Markov chains help break down complex journeys into actionable insights. This helps marketers to refine strategies iteratively rather than relying solely on simplistic last-click metrics.

At the same time, it's important to guard against over-automation risks. Hyper-personalization must respect privacy boundaries and avoid overwhelming audiences with redundant messaging simply because multiple channels are involved.

successful cross-channel marketing demands both technical sophistication and a nuanced understanding of customer psychology. When applied thoughtfully, AI-powered automation transforms fragmented marketing pushes into orchestrated symphonies of engagement— driving sustainable business growth over time.

Ethical considerations in AI marketing

Ethical considerations in AI marketing are often overlooked, yet they form a vital foundation for sustainable business practices. Unlike traditional marketing, AI-driven strategies analyze vast amounts of personal data to deliver highly personalized experiences. This approach immediately raises important questions about consent, transparency, and respect for user privacy. Without clear ethical guidelines, companies risk eroding customer trust and potentially violating regulations such as GDPR or CCPA.

For example, targeted advertising platforms sometimes infer sensitive information like health conditions or financial status. If handled carelessly, these insights can perpetuate discrimination or lead to manipulative tactics. In 2019, a major social media platform faced criticism when its ad targeting algorithm excluded certain demographic groups from housing ads. Such incidents highlight how automated systems can unintentionally reinforce biases embedded in historical data or developer assumptions.

To avoid these pitfalls, ethical AI marketing requires explicit frameworks emphasizing fairness and accountability. Transparency plays a central role: customers should know when AI influences the content they see and have meaningful control over their data. This might involve clear opt-in choices and straightforward explanations of how their information shapes marketing messages. Brands like Patagonia exemplify this approach by openly discussing their data policies and avoiding invasive targeting, demonstrating that ethical commitment can strengthen brand loyalty.

Algorithmic bias presents another significant challenge. Machine learning models trained on skewed datasets may prioritize certain customer profiles while marginalizing others without intent. Tools like IBM's AI Fairness 360 toolkit provide practical methods to detect and mitigate bias before campaigns launch. These include testing models on diverse datasets and incorporating fairness metrics throughout training.

Ethical marketing also extends beyond legal compliance to consider the psychological effects of AI automation. Over-personalization can feel intrusive if it crosses into predictive behavior manipulation—nudging customers toward purchases in ways they neither expect nor fully understand. Behavioral economist Richard Thaler's concept of "nudging" illustrates how subtle cues influence decisions; when amplified by AI at scale, these effects become even more powerful. Marketers must tread carefully here, as aggressive tactics risk consumer backlash and reputational damage.

Consider a retail chain that uses AI to dynamically adjust prices based on individual browsing histories. While this may boost short-term sales, customers who later discover unfair pricing could feel alienated. The key lies in balancing personalization with respect—offering consumers agency while delivering relevant content.

Integrating ethics systematically involves establishing governance structures that oversee AI marketing initiatives. Multidisciplinary teams—comprising legal experts, ethicists, technologists, and marketers—should collaborate from project inception through deployment and monitoring. Clear ethical guidelines covering data sourcing, algorithmic transparency, user consent, and bias mitigation are essential components.

Practical steps toward ethical AI marketing include:

1. Conducting Data Audits: Regularly review datasets for representativeness and privacy concerns.

2. Implementing Explainable AI: Use models whose decision-making processes can be interpreted by humans.

3. Establishing User Controls: Provide easy-to-use tools enabling customers to adjust personalization settings or opt out.

4. Monitoring Campaign Outcomes: Track not only ROI but also potential negative impacts on specific groups.

5. Training Teams: Educate marketing staff about ethical principles alongside technical skills.

Companies leveraging platforms like Google Ads or Facebook Ads must carefully scrutinize automated bidding strategies that optimize for conversions but might disproportionately target vulnerable populations. Incorporating fairness checks during campaign setup helps mitigate such risks.

Take this example, an e-commerce business using dynamic product recommendations could analyze engagement metrics segmented by demographic variables to detect exclusion patterns early—adjusting algorithms accordingly to ensure inclusivity.

The following Python example demonstrates how fairness metrics might be evaluated in customer segmentation models:

```python
from sklearn.metrics import confusion_matrix

import numpy as np


\#\# Assume y_true is true labels (e.g., purchase made or not)

\#\# y_pred are predictions from recommendation model

\#\# group is a sensitive attribute (e.g., gender: 0=male, 1=female)


def demographic_parity(y_true, y_pred, group):
positive_rate_group0 = np.mean(y_pred[group == 0])

positive_rate_group1 = np.mean(y_pred[group == 1])

return abs(positive_rate_group0 - positive_rate_group1)


\#\# Example data arrays

y_true = np.array([1,0,1,0,1,0])

y_pred = np.array([1,0,0,0,1,1])

group = np.array([0,0,1,1,0,1])
```

dp_diff = demographic_parity(y_true,y_pred,group)

print(f"Demographic parity difference: dp_diff:.2f")

` ` `

This snippet calculates the difference in positive prediction rates between groups—a straightforward indicator revealing potential bias in recommendations.

Ethics in AI marketing go beyond regulatory requirements; they build competitive advantage by fostering trust at a time when consumers increasingly demand responsible data use. As Accenture's CEO put it: "Transparency isn't optional anymore; it's foundational." Companies that embrace ethical marketing position themselves for long-term loyalty and resilience.

embedding ethics into AI marketing means recognizing the human behind every data point—not treating users as mere conversion statistics but as stakeholders deserving respect and clarity throughout their journey with your brand.

Case studies: Successful AI marketing campaigns

AI-powered campaigns have revolutionized marketing strategies across industries, reshaping how brands engage audiences and optimize outcomes. For example, a global sportswear brand combined AI-driven segmentation with predictive analytics to personalize marketing messages for millions of customers. Instead of generic email blasts, their system analyzed past purchase behavior, browsing habits, and social media interactions to deliver tailored offers at the most effective times. This approach led to a 30% increase in click-through rates and a 20% boost in conversions within six months—results that traditional methods struggled to achieve.

Similarly, a mid-sized e-commerce retailer specializing

in home decor implemented AI-powered chatbots using natural language processing to handle customer inquiries around the clock. Beyond answering frequently asked questions, the chatbot recommended complementary products based on real-time preferences. This automation cut customer service response times from hours to seconds and created upsell opportunities. Within the first quarter after deployment, sales driven through chatbot interactions accounted for nearly 15% of monthly revenue.

In the financial sector, an investment firm leveraged machine learning algorithms to analyze market sentiment and predict client interests for targeted communications. By processing extensive news feeds, social media chatter, and economic indicators, their AI system generated personalized newsletters highlighting relevant investment options tailored to individual risk profiles. This resulted in a 40% improvement in open rates and measurable gains in client retention.

The hospitality industry offers another example where a major hotel chain automated social media advertising budget allocation using AI. Their platform dynamically adjusted spending across Facebook, Instagram, and Google Ads based on real-time campaign performance alongside seasonal trends and regional events. This continuous rebalancing ensured funds were directed toward the highest-performing ads without manual intervention. The chain reported a 25% reduction in cost per acquisition accompanied by increased bookings during peak periods.

Smaller businesses have also found success with AI-driven marketing. A local bookstore used AI tools to analyze customer purchase histories and web browsing patterns, then automatically curated weekly personalized newsletters featuring new releases aligned with reader interests. Though modest in scale, this effort doubled email engagement rates and significantly boosted foot traffic.

What these cases share is the intelligent use of data combined with automation that frees marketing teams from repetitive tasks while delivering highly relevant customer experiences. Yet success depends on ongoing testing and refinement rather than a "set-it-and-forget-it" approach. Take this example, the sportswear brand continuously updated its segmentation models to reflect seasonal shifts and emerging trends detected by AI.

The technical backbone supporting these achievements typically involves integrating multiple tools: customer data platforms (CDPs), predictive machine learning models, natural language processing engines for chatbots or content generation, and automated bidding algorithms for ad placements. To illustrate, consider how an e-commerce company might build a lead scoring model using Python's scikit-learn library:

```python
import pandas as pd

from sklearn.model_selection import train_test_split

from sklearn.ensemble import RandomForestClassifier

from sklearn.metrics import classification_report


\#\# Load dataset: customer behavior features + target (purchase: 1=yes, 0=no)

data = pd.read_csv('customer_data.csv')


X = data.drop('purchase', axis=1)

y = data['purchase']
```

```
\#\# Split into training and testing sets

X_train, X_test, y_train, y_test =
train_test_split(X,y,test_size=0.3, random_state=42)


\#\# Initialize Random Forest classifier

model = RandomForestClassifier(n_estimators=100,
random_state=42)


\#\# Train model

model.fit(X_train,y_train)


\#\# Predict on test set

y_pred = model.predict(X_test)


\#\# Evaluate performance

print(classification_report(y_test,y_pred))
` ` `
```

This model predicts whether a customer is likely to purchase based on behaviors such as site visits, time spent per page, previous purchases, and demographics. Marketing teams can then prioritize high-probability leads for personalized outreach or special offers.

Beyond lead scoring, dynamic content generation powered by natural language processing is increasingly common in campaigns aiming for personalization at scale. Some platforms use GPT-based APIs to automatically generate email subject lines or social media captions tailored to audience segments while maintaining consistent brand voice—a combination of human creativity enhanced by AI efficiency.

More advanced still are reinforcement learning approaches where algorithms continuously optimize messaging based on real-time feedback within campaigns—a technique pioneered by platforms like Google Ads' Smart Bidding system.

While these technologies are powerful individually or combined into suites of tools, campaign success ultimately depends on aligning AI capabilities with business objectives and rigorous measurement practices. Marketers must define clear KPIs—such as click-through rate (CTR), conversion rate (CVR), cost per acquisition (CPA), or customer lifetime value (CLV)—to objectively assess ROI.

One retailer exemplified this integration through an AI-powered multichannel campaign launched around last year's Black Friday sales:

- Segmented customers by purchase frequency and average order value using clustering algorithms.

- Developed personalized discount offers based on predicted price sensitivity.

- Automated delivery of tailored emails paired with retargeting ads via programmatic platforms.

- Monitored conversions and spend efficiency through real-time dashboards.

- Adjusted campaign parameters daily based on performance data to optimize resource allocation.

This strategy generated a sales increase exceeding projections by nearly 35% while cutting wasted ad spend by over 20%. Such precision would be impossible without embedding AI-driven insights directly into campaign execution workflows.

In summary, successful AI marketing campaigns rest not only on advanced technology but also pragmatic implementation—built on quality data pipelines, thoughtful model development, continuous feedback loops, and close collaboration between marketers and data scientists. When these elements come together effectively, businesses unlock efficiencies that translate into revenue growth while enhancing customer experiences at scale.

As marketing expert Seth Godin puts it: "Marketing is no longer about the stuff you make but about the stories you tell." Today's stories are increasingly co-created with AI— tools that help marketers craft narratives finely tuned to individual preferences without sacrificing authenticity or brand integrity.

Developing personalized customer journeys

Developing personalized customer journeys with AI goes beyond simple segmentation; it involves integrating data points, behavior patterns, and predictive insights to create experiences that feel uniquely tailored to each individual. Today, such customization is essential, as customers increasingly expect interactions that anticipate their needs rather than merely respond to them.

The process begins with integrating customer data from multiple sources. Businesses typically gather information from CRM systems, website analytics, purchase histories, social media engagement, and even offline touchpoints like in-store visits. Combining these diverse inputs into a unified customer profile enables AI models to gain a comprehensive understanding of preferences and behaviors. For example, a retail company might merge browsing data revealing interest in hiking gear with previous purchases of running shoes to suggest complementary items like hydration packs or trail maps—guiding customers thoughtfully without resorting to intrusive sales tactics.

Next, it's important to map out the key journey stages—awareness, consideration, purchase, and retention—and determine which touchpoints are best suited for automation. AI-powered tools analyze historical conversion funnels to identify where customers tend to drop off or engage more deeply. If data shows that many users abandon their carts after reviewing return policies, the system could trigger personalized emails addressing return concerns or offer live chat support tailored to those products.

Maintaining relevance at each stage depends on creating dynamic content. Natural language generation (NLG) engines allow marketers to automatically craft messages that reflect real-time context—such as weather conditions, local events, or inventory changes—and adapt tone based on customer sentiment analysis. Take this example, an AI-driven email campaign for a cosmetics brand might personalize product recommendations while adjusting phrasing depending on whether the recipient has left positive reviews or expressed dissatisfaction. These subtle nuances can significantly boost engagement rates.

Setting up such personalized journeys typically starts with choosing a platform capable of multichannel orchestration. Solutions like Adobe Experience Platform or Salesforce Marketing Cloud include built-in AI features for journey analytics and content personalization. After integrating your data sources, define customer segments based on behavioral patterns—for example, "frequent purchasers," "window shoppers," or "seasonal buyers." Then configure triggers and rules: if a frequent purchaser browses new arrivals but doesn't make a purchase within three days, an automated SMS offering an exclusive preview might be sent.

Measuring success hinges on establishing clear KPIs aligned with business objectives—such as click-through rates on personalized messages, conversion lifts among targeted segments, or increases in average order value after campaigns. Regular A/B testing should be integral to the process; experimenting with messaging variants alongside timing and channel preferences ensures strategies resonate across different audiences.

An advanced approach involves predictive journey modeling using machine learning algorithms that forecast next-best actions by analyzing millions of interaction patterns. Netflix's recommendation engine exemplifies this by suggesting content based on viewing history combined with real-time behavioral signals like pause frequency or rewinds —creating an experience that feels intuitive rather than formulaic.

However, it's crucial to avoid over-automation that leads to generic or robotic interactions. Maintaining brand voice consistency while leveraging AI's speed requires human oversight in crafting templates and reviewing generated content regularly. Personalization at scale shouldn't come at the expense of empathy or storytelling authenticity—a balance captured well by Ann Handley's advice: "Don't bore people; make it personal."

From a technical perspective, implementing personalization workflows benefits from a modular architecture—separating data ingestion, model training, decision logic, and delivery channels—so each component can evolve independently as AI capabilities improve. For example, updating the recommendation engine shouldn't necessitate reworking email templates; instead, new models can be plugged into existing APIs for seamless upgrades.

Finally, privacy regulations like GDPR and CCPA must be carefully considered when designing journeys involving sensitive data. Integrating explicit consent management frameworks from the outset helps avoid backlash from regulators and customers alike.

At its core, developing AI-powered personalized customer journeys transforms raw data into meaningful narratives that guide prospects smoothly through every phase of engagement. The combination of predictive analytics, dynamic content generation, and strategic orchestration creates experiences that not only convert but also foster lasting loyalty through relevance and responsiveness—a true competitive advantage in today's marketplace.

CHAPTER 11: FINANCE AND ACCOUNTING AUTOMATION

Automated financial reporting

Automated financial reporting is revolutionizing traditional accounting by transforming repetitive manual tasks into efficient digital workflows. Instead of waiting weeks to compile monthly reports, finance teams can now generate real-time financial statements with just a few clicks. This shift not only minimizes errors from manual data entry but also speeds up decision-making, enabling companies to respond swiftly to market changes.

Take, for example, a mid-sized company using AI-driven platforms like Workiva or BlackLine. These tools seamlessly integrate with enterprise resource planning (ERP) systems and bank feeds to automatically gather transactional data. Rather than having accountants manually reconcile accounts, the software identifies discrepancies and anomalies for review. If an unexpected expense appears twice, the system triggers an alert, prompting investigation before the error affects financial summaries.

Setting up automated reporting begins by defining which reports are needed—such as balance sheets, profit and loss statements, or cash flow summaries—and how often they should be updated. Next, data sources must be connected, typically linking ERP modules like SAP or Oracle Financials with external inputs such as payroll systems or vendor invoices. Data validation rules are applied to ensure inputs meet expected formats, catching irregularities early in the process.

Consider a practical scenario: an accountant configures a monthly revenue report that pulls sales figures from multiple regions. The AI engine consolidates data daily from CRM sales pipelines and point-of-sale systems, updating dashboards automatically. If the system detects a sudden revenue drop in one region, it flags this immediately for management review, eliminating the need to wait for end-of-month analysis.

Excel remains a valuable tool within this automated ecosystem when combined with AI features like Power Query and Power Pivot. Power Query can import transaction records from various CSV files or databases into a single workbook and refresh the data on a set schedule. Meanwhile, DAX formulas in Power Pivot enable creation of calculated columns—such as year-over-year growth rates—offering a flexible yet automated approach without requiring full ERP deployment.

A straightforward example of using Excel's Power Query for automated reporting includes these steps:

1. Open Excel and navigate to the Data tab.

2. Select "Get Data" > "From File" > "From Folder."

3. Choose the folder containing daily sales CSV files.

4. Allow Power Query to consolidate all files into one table.

5. Apply transformations like removing duplicates or adjusting date formats.

6. Load the output into a worksheet.

7. Create PivotTables summarizing sales by product category or region.

8. Refresh the query daily to update the report dynamically.

This integration cuts down hours spent gathering scattered data while providing timely insights.

Beyond internal reporting, AI-driven platforms can automate compliance documentation by embedding regulatory requirements into workflows. Take this example, generating Sarbanes-Oxley (SOX) compliance reports becomes more manageable as automated controls verify necessary checks and systematically document exceptions.

Machine learning models add another layer of sophistication by uncovering patterns that might escape human notice —for example, predicting cash flow shortages based on historical payment behavior combined with current receivables aging. Such foresight allows treasury teams to proactively adjust borrowing strategies rather than scrambling at month-end.

However, automation's benefits come with important caveats. It demands thorough initial setup and ongoing oversight to avoid "garbage in, garbage out" scenarios. Maintaining data integrity is crucial since even advanced AI cannot compensate for poorly structured input data or inconsistent accounting policies across departments.

Consulting firms like Deloitte highlight that successful

implementation depends on close collaboration between finance professionals and IT specialists to align technical capabilities with business needs effectively.

automated financial reporting redefines the finance function —not merely as a bookkeeping task but as an agile strategic partner delivering actionable intelligence quickly and reliably. Embracing these technologies unlocks significant time savings while enhancing competitive advantage through improved financial transparency and control.

Fraud detection and prevention

Fraud detection and prevention have become essential elements of AI-powered automation in finance and accounting. The sheer complexity and volume of daily transactions make traditional manual oversight inadequate for identifying sophisticated fraudulent schemes. AI systems, equipped with anomaly detection algorithms, can analyze millions of records and recognize patterns that deviate from normal behavior—often long before human auditors would spot them. Take this example, machine learning models trained on historical transaction data can flag suspicious activities such as duplicate invoices, unusual payment amounts, or irregular vendor behavior.

Take the example of a mid-sized enterprise that implemented an AI-driven fraud detection system to monitor its accounts payable. This system continuously analyzed transaction metadata—timestamps, payment amounts, vendor history—and applied clustering techniques to define what 'normal' looked like for each supplier relationship. When the model detected an outlier, such as a sudden spike in invoice frequency from a rarely used vendor or payments made outside regular business hours, it immediately triggered alerts for review. So, the company reduced fraudulent losses by 40% within the first year.

Beyond basic anomaly detection, modern fraud prevention

also leverages advanced natural language processing (NLP) to analyze unstructured data sources like emails, contracts, or customer communications. For example, sentiment analysis can identify potential coercion or social engineering attempts by highlighting language patterns consistent with phishing scams. Integrating an NLP module into an existing email monitoring system might involve several steps: extracting email content related to financial transactions, preprocessing the text by removing stop words and normalizing terms, applying a sentiment classifier trained on labeled phishing and legitimate emails, and scoring each message to set thresholds that trigger alerts for suspicious content. This multilayered strategy strengthens protection not only at the transaction level but also across communication channels vulnerable to exploitation.

Automated fraud detection systems often incorporate real-time risk scoring engines that assign risk values to transactions based on weighted criteria such as geolocation inconsistencies, IP address anomalies, device fingerprinting data, and user behavioral analytics. Take this example, a financial institution might use a risk scoring algorithm where payments originating from unusual countries or unfamiliar devices attract heightened scrutiny before approval. An example formula could be:

Risk Score = (Transaction Amount Factor × 0.4) + (Geolocation Anomaly Factor × 0.3) + (Device Risk Factor × 0.2) + (Behavioral Anomaly Factor × 0.1).

Transactions exceeding a predetermined threshold may be held for manual review or automatically blocked, effectively reducing fraud exposure while maintaining workflow efficiency.

To illustrate, consider this simplified Python snippet demonstrating an anomaly detection model using the Isolation Forest algorithm—a popular choice for identifying outliers in high-dimensional data:

```python
from sklearn.ensemble import IsolationForest
import pandas as pd

\#\# Sample transaction data: amount, time_delta (seconds between transactions), vendor_id encoded numerically
data = pd.DataFrame(
'amount': [1000, 1050, 990, 50000, 1020],
'time_delta': [60, 55, 70, 10, 65],
'vendor_id': [1, 1, 1, 2, 1]
)

model = IsolationForest(contamination=0.1)
model.fit(data)

data['anomaly_score'] = model.decision_function(data)
data['anomaly'] = model.predict(data)

\#\# -1 indicates anomaly
print(data)
```

In this example, the transaction with an amount of 50,000 combined with a short time delta is likely flagged as anomalous (-1), signaling potential fraud or error warranting further investigation.

Automation also streamlines invoice processing by reducing manual entry errors and introducing multi-layered verification through AI-based optical character recognition (OCR). A typical workflow involves scanning invoices with OCR tools to extract structured fields—vendor name, invoice number, total amount—and cross-referencing these against purchase orders and contract terms stored in enterprise resource planning (ERP) systems. Any discrepancies such as mismatched amounts or unrecognized vendors automatically halt payment workflows pending human validation.

Fraud prevention extends beyond detection; it also aims to deter fraudulent behavior through enhanced transparency and audit trails enabled by automation platforms. Blockchain technology is gaining traction here by providing immutable ledgers that securely store transaction histories accessible for audits without risk of tampering. By combining AI's predictive power with blockchain's transparency features, businesses can significantly strengthen their internal controls.

Despite technological advances, human oversight remains indispensable in fraud management frameworks. AI excels at flagging anomalies but cannot replace expert judgment —it equips finance teams with prioritized cases requiring attention rather than overwhelming them with false positives or routine reviews.

Deloitte's experience offers an insightful example: after deploying AI-driven fraud analytics tools across numerous client engagements worldwide, they observed a marked decline in lost revenue but emphasized the ongoing need for employee training to interpret AI findings contextually rather than relying blindly on "black-box" outputs.

AI-driven automation transforms finance departments from reactive auditors into proactive guardians of organizational integrity—a critical shift in today's fast-paced digital economy where speed and accuracy are paramount yet risks continue to evolve rapidly.

Invoice processing automation

Invoice processing automation has become a fundamental driver of efficiency in finance and accounting departments. Traditional methods often involve manual data entry, prone to errors and delays that strain resources and disrupt cash flow. By automating invoice handling, organizations can speed up operations and significantly reduce human mistakes, allowing staff to focus on more strategic activities.

The process typically begins with document capture, where Optical Character Recognition (OCR) technology plays a key role. OCR converts scanned paper invoices or digital PDFs into machine-readable data. Modern OCR engines go beyond simple text extraction by interpreting context to identify essential fields such as vendor names, invoice numbers, dates, line items, and totals. Tools like ABBYY FlexiCapture and Kofax leverage AI-driven pattern recognition to adapt to various invoice formats without requiring extensive manual template setup.

Once extracted, the data undergoes validation against predefined business rules and records stored within Enterprise Resource Planning (ERP) systems or procurement databases. Take this example, if an invoice from "Acme Supplies" for)15,000 references purchase order number 45321, the system verifies the existence of that PO and confirms the amount matches agreed terms. Any discrepancies—like unmatched POs or price variances—trigger exception workflows that route the invoice to designated personnel for review rather than halting the entire payment process. This targeted intervention helps avoid bottlenecks while maintaining compliance.

Invoice matching is another critical step often automated

using three-way matching techniques that compare invoice details with purchase orders and receiving reports. To illustrate, imagine three Excel tables: Invoices, Purchase Orders, and Goods Received. An automated script or robotic process automation (RPA) bot can cross-reference these daily to flag inconsistencies such as missing deliveries or overbilling. Consider this simplified Python snippet demonstrating such reconciliation:

```python
import pandas as pd

\#\# Sample dataframes
invoices = pd.DataFrame('invoice_id': [1], 'po_number': [1001], 'amount': [5000])

purchase_orders = pd.DataFrame('po_number': [1001], 'approved_amount': [5000])

receiving_reports = pd.DataFrame('po_number': [1001], 'received_amount': [4800])


\#\# Merge datasets on PO number
merged = invoices.merge(purchase_orders, on='po_number').merge(receiving_reports, on='po_number')


\#\# Check discrepancies
merged['match'] = merged.apply(lambda row: row['amount'] == row['approved_amount'] == row['received_amount'], axis=1)


print(merged[['invoice_id', 'match']])
```

` ` `

Here, the 'match' column indicates whether amounts are perfectly aligned; a true value means no issues, while false flags potential payment holds.

Beyond accuracy in matching, many automation platforms incorporate machine learning models trained to detect patterns of fraud or errors in invoices based on historical data. For example, if a vendor repeatedly submits invoices with slight overcharges just below approval thresholds, anomaly detection algorithms can spot these suspicious trends early. Such insights empower companies to strengthen controls without resorting to exhaustive manual audits.

In practical deployments, Robotic Process Automation tools like UiPath or Automation Anywhere are often combined with AI-powered OCR engines to automate the entire cycle end-to-end. Bots may download incoming invoices from emails or vendor portals overnight, extract data via OCR APIs, validate entries against ERP records through API calls or database queries, execute matching logic as described above, route exceptions via email notifications to finance managers for review, and ultimately submit approved payments automatically through integrated financial software.

A global manufacturing firm provides a compelling example: after implementing such automation, it cut average invoice processing time from 10 days to under 48 hours while reducing manual input errors by 85%. This accelerated turnaround enhanced vendor relationships through timely payments and improved audit readiness thanks to detailed digital trails.

Despite these gains, managing exceptions remains a critical focus—the "last mile" where human judgment is indispensable. Not all anomalies represent errors; some reflect legitimate contract modifications or delivery delays requiring nuanced decisions beyond what algorithms can determine.

Security is paramount throughout the process since invoices contain sensitive financial information and personally identifiable data. Encryption during transmission and storage, coupled with strict access controls, helps prevent breaches. Automated audit logs generated at each step also provide transparency needed for regulatory compliance with frameworks such as Sarbanes-Oxley (SOX) or GDPR depending on jurisdiction.

In summary, automating invoice processing transforms a labor-intensive bottleneck into a streamlined workflow defined by speed, accuracy, and control—essential elements of operational excellence in modern finance functions. By combining OCR-powered extraction with intelligent validation rules and machine learning-driven anomaly detection, companies can confidently scale transaction volumes while reducing costs and improving vendor satisfaction simultaneously.

Budget forecasting and analytics

Budget forecasting and analytics are fundamental to leveraging AI-powered automation in finance. Unlike traditional budgeting methods that depend heavily on static spreadsheets and historical data, automated forecasting employs dynamic models that integrate real-time inputs. This approach enables businesses to anticipate changes with greater accuracy. The impact goes beyond speed—it transforms how companies allocate resources, manage risks, and align financial plans with operational realities.

At the heart of automated budget forecasting is predictive analytics, a branch of AI that examines patterns and trends across diverse datasets to forecast future financial outcomes.

For example, an AI model might combine sales data, market trends, seasonal fluctuations, and external influences such as currency exchange rates or commodity prices to create a detailed budget projection. This level of granularity allows finance teams to move from broad estimates to precise scenario planning.

Take the case of a retail chain looking to optimize quarterly budgets for multiple stores. Traditional approaches often involve manually aggregating sales forecasts, which can overlook subtle trends at individual locations. By adopting an AI-driven solution—like Microsoft Azure's Machine Learning Studio or IBM Watson Analytics—the company can analyze point-of-sale data alongside marketing campaign performance and inventory levels. The system then generates customized budget recommendations for each store while flagging areas of potential overspending or underspending.

A straightforward Python example demonstrates how time series forecasting can support budget planning using Facebook's Prophet library:

```python
```python

from prophet import Prophet

import pandas as pd


\#\# Load historical monthly revenue data

data = pd.read_csv('monthly_revenue.csv')  \# columns: ds (date), y (revenue)


model = Prophet()

model.fit(data)
```
```

```
\#\# Create future dataframe for next 6 months
future = model.make_future_dataframe(periods=6, freq='M')

\#\# Predict future revenue
forecast = model.predict(future)

print(forecast[['ds', 'yhat', 'yhat_lower', 'yhat_upper']].tail(6))
` ` `
```

This output provides forecasted revenue figures (yhat) along with confidence intervals (yhat_lower and yhat_upper), helping budget officers set flexible targets instead of relying on fixed numbers that might miss unexpected shifts.

Visualization tools are essential for interpreting these forecasts effectively. Platforms like Tableau or Power BI integrate seamlessly with AI outputs to present interactive dashboards that track variances between actual and predicted budgets over time. These visual insights enable swift adjustments; for instance, if a forecast indicates declining sales in a product category next quarter, marketing resources can be reallocated proactively.

One common challenge is integrating disparate data sources —such as ERP systems, CRM databases, and market research —and maintaining data quality for accurate predictions. Automated data cleansing routines using scripts or platforms like Alteryx help standardize formats and address missing values, preventing distorted forecasts that could mislead budgeting decisions.

Scenario analysis adds another valuable dimension. AI models facilitate rapid what-if simulations reflecting different business conditions like economic downturns or supply chain disruptions. Finance teams can explore multiple scenarios without rebuilding complex spreadsheets each time. For example, Monte Carlo simulations coded in R enable generation of probability distributions illustrating possible outcomes:

```r
library(mc2d)


set.seed(123)

simulations <- mcstoc(rnorm, mean=1000000, sd=50000)
\# simulate sales revenue

summary(simulations)

hist(simulations)
```

This method provides decision-makers with a clearer understanding of potential revenue ranges rather than relying on single-point estimates—a crucial advantage amid uncertainty.

Beyond forecasting numbers alone, automated analytics deepen insights by linking budgets to key performance indicators such as customer acquisition costs or inventory turnover rates. Identifying correlations—for example, how increased marketing spend might boost sales but also raise customer churn if messaging misses the mark—allows finance leaders to fine-tune budgets more strategically.

Organizations embracing these techniques often report substantial improvements. A mid-sized manufacturing firm implementing AI-driven budget forecasting reduced variance from 15% to under 5%, enhancing cash flow management and investment timing with a direct positive impact on profitability.

Still, human oversight remains vital. While AI delivers powerful forecasting tools, contextual judgment ensures decisions stay grounded in reality. Budget models require regular reviews to detect drift as markets evolve, and assumptions embedded in algorithms must be validated against new data over time.

Automated budget forecasting transforms finance teams from reactive number crunchers into proactive strategic partners within their organizations—converting raw data into actionable foresight with clarity and agility unmatched by manual processes alone. Mastering these approaches elevates financial planning from guesswork to a reliable discipline rooted in continuous learning and adaptation.

Compliance and regulatory reporting

Regulatory compliance and reporting are fundamental pillars of the finance sector, particularly as AI-driven automation transforms traditional workflows. The challenge lies not only in meeting stringent financial regulations but also in adapting to evolving standards that differ across jurisdictions. While automation streamlines data collection and reporting processes, it also requires careful oversight to maintain accuracy and ensure adherence.

Take, for example, the preparation of quarterly financial reports compliant with the Sarbanes-Oxley Act (SOX) in the United States or International Financial Reporting Standards (IFRS) globally. Manual compilation often involves cross-checking multiple sources, which can lead to delays and human errors. AI-powered platforms such as BlackLine or Workiva automate reconciliation and control testing, significantly shortening cycle times while preserving audit readiness. These tools continuously monitor transactions for anomalies or policy deviations, alerting compliance officers almost in real time.

To illustrate this approach, consider a Python script designed to validate transactional data against compliance rules before it enters reporting systems. The snippet below flags invoices missing critical fields or exceeding predefined thresholds:

```python
import pandas as pd

\#\# Load transaction dataset

transactions = pd.read_csv('transactions.csv')  \# columns: invoice_id, amount, approval_status

\#\# Define compliance checks

def validate_transaction(row):

if pd.isnull(row['invoice_id']):

return 'Missing Invoice ID'

if row['amount'] <= 0:

return 'Invalid Amount'

if row['approval_status'] != 'Approved':

return 'Unapproved Transaction'

return 'Valid'

\#\# Apply validation

transactions['validation_result']                  =
transactions.apply(validate_transaction, axis=1)
```

```
\#\# Extract non-compliant records

non_compliant                                    =
transactions[transactions['validation_result'] != 'Valid']


print(non_compliant)
` ` `
```

This output highlights records needing review prior to submission to regulatory bodies, helping to prevent costly penalties from overlooked mistakes. Scaling this process with rule-based engines or machine learning classifiers enables detection of more subtle issues, such as suspicious patterns that may indicate fraud.

Automation also simplifies mapping financial data to standardized taxonomies mandated by regulators. Take this example, XBRL (eXtensible Business Reporting Language) tagging is required for many filings. AI systems can automatically parse raw data and assign appropriate tags, eliminating manual tagging errors and inconsistencies. Tools like Fujitsu's Interstage XWand combine natural language processing with rule-based approaches to accelerate this task.

The true integration challenge extends beyond automating individual tasks—it requires maintaining end-to-end traceability from ERP inputs through AI validations to report generation platforms. Robust audit trails are essential; emerging solutions based on blockchain technology offer secure, immutable transaction histories that regulators can inspect without compromising data privacy.

Compliance also demands ongoing vigilance as legislation evolves. AI-driven monitoring tools ingest regulatory updates and compare them against company policies, flagging discrepancies that require action. This proactive approach shifts compliance from a reactive obligation into a strategic advantage.

Operationally, finance teams must align automation initiatives with governance frameworks that clearly define roles and responsibilities. Segregation of duties controls built into workflows ensure no single individual has unchecked authority; automation enforces these controls systematically rather than relying solely on periodic manual audits.

A practical example comes from Deloitte's deployment of AI-powered compliance tools in clients' financial close processes. They reported over a 40% reduction in reporting errors and halved cycle times thanks to improved data validation and automated control implementation.

Nevertheless, automation alone does not guarantee compliance success. Human expertise remains crucial for interpreting complex regulations and exercising judgment where AI may fall short. Ongoing training programs help finance professionals deepen their understanding of both technological capabilities and legal requirements—a combination that equips organizations to navigate dynamic regulatory environments effectively.

At its core, embedding regulatory reporting within AI-driven automation enhances accuracy and efficiency while reinforcing control environments vital for trustworthiness. Organizations adopting this integrated approach benefit from reduced operational risk and greater agility in responding to regulatory changes—foundations for sustainable financial management amid rising compliance demands.

Risk management enhancements

Risk management is central to financial operations, and AI-driven automation has become essential for enhancing defenses against evolving threats. Traditional risk assessment methods often struggled to handle vast datasets and detect subtle warning signs hidden within them. Automation addresses these challenges by enabling continuous, detailed analysis that updates dynamically as new data streams in.

Take credit risk evaluation as an example. Legacy models typically depended on static inputs such as credit scores or income statements, updated at best on a quarterly basis. In contrast, modern AI-powered platforms incorporate real-time transactional data, social signals, and alternative sources like utility payments or online behavior to generate a more refined risk profile. Banks using machine learning algorithms can now identify early signs of default with greater accuracy and speed than human analysts. These models are trained on historical patterns and then applied automatically to customers' changing profiles.

A practical illustration involves building a simple credit risk classifier using Python's scikit-learn library. The following script trains a logistic regression model on labeled borrower data to predict the likelihood of default based on key features:

```python
import pandas as pd

from sklearn.model_selection import train_test_split

from sklearn.linear_model import LogisticRegression

from sklearn.metrics import classification_report


\#\# Load dataset (columns: income, debt_ratio, credit_score, defaulted)

data = pd.read_csv('borrowers.csv')
```

```
\#\# Define features and target
X = data[['income', 'debt_ratio', 'credit_score']]
y = data['defaulted']

\#\# Split into train/test sets
X_train, X_test, y_train, y_test = train_test_split(X, y, test_size=0.3, random_state=42)

\#\# Train logistic regression model
model = LogisticRegression()
model.fit(X_train, y_train)

\#\# Predict and evaluate
y_pred = model.predict(X_test)
print(classification_report(y_test, y_pred))
` ` `
```

Models like this underpin automated alert systems that flag high-risk accounts for review or immediate action. When integrated into core banking platforms, they provide frontline staff with timely insights without the need for manual intervention.

Automation also enhances market risk management through advanced analytics that assess volatility and correlations across asset classes nearly in real time. AI algorithms can rapidly simulate thousands of scenarios; for example, Monte Carlo simulations augmented with neural networks enable traders and risk managers to stress-test portfolios under varying conditions with unprecedented speed.

Operational risk management benefits from AI as well by detecting anomalies that may signal fraud or process failures. Pattern recognition techniques analyze transaction flows and user behavior to spot deviations that might be missed by human monitors due to sheer volume or complexity. One effective method applies anomaly detection algorithms within payment systems to isolate suspicious transactions based on how much they deviate from normal patterns.

Here is a concise example using the Isolation Forest algorithm from scikit-learn to identify unusual transactions:

```python
from sklearn.ensemble import IsolationForest


\#\# Assume 'transactions' DataFrame with numerical features describing each transaction

features = transactions[['amount', 'transaction_time', 'merchant_id']]


\#\# Train Isolation Forest model for anomaly detection

iso_forest = IsolationForest(contamination=0.01)   \# Assuming 1% anomalies expected

iso_forest.fit(features)


\#\# Predict anomalies (-1 indicates anomaly)

transactions['anomaly_flag'] = iso_forest.predict(features)

anomalies = transactions[transactions['anomaly_flag'] == -1]
```

```
print(anomalies)
```
` ` `

This approach equips compliance teams with prioritized lists of suspicious activities while reducing false positives compared to traditional rule-based systems.

Automation also excels in dynamic regulatory reporting related to risk exposures. Dashboards that consolidate internal risk metrics alongside external market data in real time allow decision-makers to identify emerging threats promptly. These dashboards often feature visualizations powered by tools such as Power BI or Tableau connected directly to AI-analyzed databases.

Successfully embedding AI into risk frameworks requires clear governance protocols and ongoing validation of models to avoid blind spots or unintended biases. Regular backtesting against actual outcomes keeps predictive models calibrated—an especially critical discipline in financial contexts where errors carry significant costs.

Contingency planning gains from AI-powered scenario generation tools that forecast potential operational disruptions—from cyber-attacks to market shocks—and suggest mitigation strategies aligned with business continuity plans.

Real-world implementations demonstrate substantial benefits. For example, JP Morgan Chase's COiN platform automates contract reviews while strengthening fraud detection across loan portfolios, resulting in a 75% reduction in manual reviews alongside faster identification of risky agreements.

Despite these advances, relying solely on automation demands caution; overdependence without human oversight risks missing complex nuances or ethical considerations inherent in certain decisions. Skilled risk managers remain indispensable partners who interpret AI insights within broader strategic contexts.

At its core, AI-enhanced risk management shifts organizations from reactive responses toward proactive systems that continuously learn and adapt. This synergy between technology and expertise empowers businesses to safeguard assets more effectively amid volatile conditions while optimizing resource allocation across monitoring activities—laying the foundation for resilient financial operations capable of navigating complexity without sacrificing precision or speed.

Streamlining payroll processes

Payroll is frequently an overlooked bottleneck in business operations—complex, repetitive, and burdened by regulatory requirements. AI-powered automation is revolutionizing this critical function by significantly reducing processing time and minimizing costly errors. Traditional payroll workflows rely heavily on manual data entry from timesheets, calculating deductions, managing tax withholdings and benefits, and performing compliance checks—tasks that are highly suited for automation.

Take, for example, a mid-sized company managing hundreds of employees. Without automation, payroll specialists juggle spreadsheets and disconnected systems, often leading to delays or miscalculations that can hurt employee satisfaction and risk regulatory penalties. Automating payroll accelerates calculations while ensuring consistent compliance with ever-changing tax codes and labor laws.

AI-enhanced payroll platforms like Workday or ADP Workforce Now illustrate this transformation well. These systems use machine learning models to detect anomalies —such as unusual overtime hours or inconsistent benefit deductions—that might signal errors or fraud. When paired with robotic process automation (RPA), tasks like importing time-tracking data, running payroll calculations, generating pay stubs, and processing direct deposits become seamless and efficient.

For organizations seeking more customization, Python offers robust libraries to automate core payroll functions. The following simplified script demonstrates calculating salary with overtime and tax deductions:

```python
` ` `python

\#\# Sample payroll calculation script


def calculate_pay(hours_worked, hourly_rate):

standard_hours = 40

overtime_rate = 1.5 * hourly_rate


if hours_worked <= standard_hours:

gross_pay = hours_worked * hourly_rate

else:

overtime_hours = hours_worked - standard_hours

gross_pay    =    (standard_hours    *    hourly_rate)    +    (overtime_hours * overtime_rate)


\#\# Example tax brackets (simplified)

if gross_pay <= 1000:

tax = 0.1 * gross_pay

elif gross_pay <= 2000:
```

```
tax = 100 + 0.15 * (gross_pay - 1000)

else:

tax = 250 + 0.2 * (gross_pay - 2000)


net_pay = gross_pay - tax

return round(net_pay, 2)


\#\# Example usage

employee_hours = [38, 45, 50]

hourly_wage = 25


for hours in employee_hours:

pay = calculate_pay(hours, hourly_wage)

print(f'Hours Worked: hours, Net Pay: \(pay')
` ` `
```

This script captures essential logic for handling overtime premiums and progressive taxation without unnecessary complexity. Companies can build upon it by integrating attendance data or HR databases to achieve full-cycle payroll automation.

Beyond calculations, AI excels at generating detailed reports and compliance documentation automatically. Payroll managers benefit from dashboards powered by real-time data that monitor labor costs broken down by department or project, enabling more informed budgeting decisions. Take this example, identifying unexpected overtime spikes across teams can prompt adjustments to workload distribution.

AI also enhances exception handling. If an employee's

timesheet shows irregularities—like missing clock-ins or excessive leave requests—the system flags these issues for human review before payments are processed, reducing post-payday disputes.

Managing payroll in multinational corporations adds layers of complexity with currency conversions, local tax laws, and varying benefits schemes. AI-driven platforms maintain up-to-date regulatory databases worldwide and apply region-specific rules dynamically during payroll runs, eliminating the need for manual intervention.

Integrating payroll automation with other HR processes creates further efficiencies. Linking recruitment systems with automated onboarding ensures new hires are added promptly and accurately to payroll schedules, preventing duplication errors common when onboarding operates separately.

Of course, these advancements require rigorous security measures. Payroll data contains sensitive personal and financial information that demands strict access controls and encryption throughout processing pipelines.

Companies like Netflix have heavily invested in automating their global payroll using a mix of cloud services and custom AI tools. Their efforts have reduced administrative overhead by over 60% and nearly eliminated human error in pay calculations—a compelling example for others to follow.

streamlining payroll through AI doesn't just ease administrative burdens; it builds employee trust by ensuring compensation is accurate and timely—an essential foundation for workforce satisfaction and retention.

For businesses already using basic automation, the next frontier lies in predictive analytics. Forecasting staffing costs aligned with projected business activity helps prevent budget overruns before they occur.

In summary, applying AI-powered automation transforms payroll from a tedious back-office task into a strategic asset that boosts operational efficiency while safeguarding compliance—a clear win both financially and culturally for any organization.

AI tools for financial advisors

Financial advisors are increasingly embracing AI tools not merely as assistants but as strategic partners that enhance decision-making, client management, and portfolio optimization. These technologies enable advisors to craft personalized investment strategies with greater precision and efficiency, shifting the role from reactive advice toward proactive wealth management.

Natural language processing (NLP), for instance, allows AI-driven platforms to analyze vast amounts of unstructured data—such as market news, earnings call transcripts, and regulatory filings—and distill actionable insights in real time. This capability helps advisors stay ahead of market movements without manually sifting through information overload. Tools like Sentieo and AlphaSense, for example, scan thousands of documents daily, flagging developments relevant to clients' holdings or sectors of interest.

Beyond data analysis, AI enhances client segmentation and risk profiling with remarkable granularity. Traditional questionnaires often miss nuanced investor preferences or shifts in risk tolerance over time. Machine learning models can digest behavioral data—including transaction histories, communication patterns, and even social media sentiment —to create dynamic profiles that evolve alongside clients' goals and market conditions. An advisor using Salesforce's Einstein Analytics might receive timely alerts suggesting when a portfolio needs rebalancing or when new investment products better align with emerging objectives.

Portfolio construction also benefits significantly from AI

advancements. Robo-advisors have evolved from basic asset allocation engines into sophisticated hybrid systems that blend human judgment with algorithmic rigor. Platforms like BlackRock's Aladdin incorporate predictive analytics and scenario simulations to optimize diversification while accounting for macroeconomic variables, liquidity constraints, and tax implications. These systems can recommend tactical adjustments more swiftly than traditional manual reviews.

To illustrate this concept practically, consider the following Python snippet using the scikit-learn library to perform a basic risk classification on client data. The logistic regression model predicts risk profile based on hypothetical features representing volatility tolerance and investment horizon:

```python
from sklearn.linear_model import LogisticRegression

import numpy as np


\#\# Sample client features: [volatility_tolerance (0-1), investment_horizon (years)]

X = np.array([

[0.2, 1],  \# Low tolerance, short horizon

[0.8, 10],  \# High tolerance, long horizon

[0.5, 5],  \# Moderate tolerance and horizon

[0.9, 20],  \# Very high tolerance, very long horizon

])


\#\# Risk classes: 0 = Conservative, 1 = Aggressive

y = np.array([0, 1, 0, 1])
```

```
model = LogisticRegression()
model.fit(X, y)

\#\# Predict risk class for new client
new_client = np.array([[0.6, 7]])
predicted_risk = model.predict(new_client)
print("Predicted    risk    profile:",    "Aggressive"    if
predicted_risk[0] == 1 else "Conservative")
```
` ` `

While simplified here for demonstration purposes, real-world models incorporate dozens of features such as income stability, liquidity needs, tax status, and behavioral biases.

Client communication also receives a boost from AI chatbots and virtual assistants designed specifically for financial services. Solutions like Kasisto's KAI provide instant responses to routine inquiries—such as account balances or transaction histories—freeing advisors to focus on more complex interactions. These conversational agents can gather preliminary information before meetings and deliver personalized educational content tailored to clients' portfolios.

Risk management tools increasingly integrate machine learning–based anomaly detection to identify unusual trading activity or potential fraud quickly. For example, AI systems monitor transaction patterns across accounts and alert advisors when deviations suggest insider trading or money laundering attempts—critical safeguards in highly regulated environments.

On the compliance side, AI supports advisors in meeting

regulatory requirements such as Know Your Customer (KYC) and Anti-Money Laundering (AML). Automated document verification combined with pattern recognition reduces manual workload while improving accuracy and audit readiness.

Firms like Morgan Stanley report that AI adoption has boosted advisor productivity by up to 20%, enabling more focused client engagement rather than administrative drudgery. Their hybrid approach blends human expertise with AI-driven analytics to deliver both scale and personalization.

That said, caution remains essential. Overreliance on algorithms without human oversight can lead to misaligned recommendations—especially during volatile market conditions when historical data may not predict future outcomes accurately. Advisors must uphold ethical responsibility by validating AI-generated suggestions against their professional judgment.

Implementing these tools requires careful IT architecture planning. Secure APIs facilitating data exchange between CRM systems and AI platforms ensure seamless workflows without exposing sensitive client information. Robust cybersecurity measures are paramount given the heightened risks associated with financial data.

AI elevates financial advisory from a transactional service into a strategic partnership—amplifying analytical capabilities while preserving the human relationships essential for trust. Advisors who embrace this technology can offer deeper insights more quickly while managing compliance complexities effectively—delivering superior value that drives business growth in an increasingly competitive landscape.

CHAPTER 12:
HUMAN RESOURCES
AND RECRUITMENT

AI in candidate sourcing

Finding the right talent continues to be a significant challenge for businesses, and AI is transforming the way organizations source candidates. Rather than depending solely on manual resume reviews or traditional job boards, companies now leverage intelligent algorithms that quickly and accurately sift through vast pools of profiles to identify the best matches for job requirements.

AI-powered sourcing platforms like LinkedIn Talent Insights and HireVue's tools illustrate this shift. These systems analyze candidate data from multiple channels—not just resumes, but also social media activity, professional networks, and coding repositories such as GitHub. By employing natural language processing (NLP), they grasp nuanced skill descriptions and dynamically align them with job specifications. For example, an AI system can understand that terms like "data wrangling" and "data preprocessing" often represent overlapping skills, avoiding missed opportunities caused by rigid keyword searches.

Consider recruiting software engineers with expertise in Python and machine learning. Traditional sourcing methods might filter candidates based only on these keywords in resumes. In contrast, AI expands this search by evaluating candidate portfolios for relevant projects, contributions to open-source machine learning libraries, or participation in specialized online communities. This broader approach uncovers talent beyond standard applications.

Successful AI sourcing begins with clearly defined role requirements, as the quality of recommendations depends heavily on these input parameters. The platform then ingests candidate data from integrated databases and external sources. Behind the scenes, machine learning models score profiles based on technical skills, relevant experience, cultural fit indicators—such as endorsements or previous employers—and even predicted career trajectories.

Many sourcing platforms provide dashboards that allow recruiters to adjust filters in real time, such as increasing emphasis on leadership experience or narrowing geographic preferences. This iterative refinement helps recruiters fine-tune candidate pools without restarting the search process manually.

A common concern involves bias within these algorithms. If historical hiring data reflects demographic biases, AI can unintentionally perpetuate them. Addressing this requires deliberate strategies: training models on diverse datasets, incorporating fairness constraints during development, and regularly auditing outputs for unintended discrimination. Some companies, like Pymetrics, complement traditional metrics with behavioral science–based assessments to promote objective evaluations and a more level playing field.

Another emerging practice uses predictive analytics to identify passive candidates—those not actively applying but likely open to new opportunities based on digital footprints and career signals. This proactive method broadens recruitment reach beyond active job seekers.

An example AI sourcing workflow might include:

1. Inputting a detailed job description into the platform.

2. Scanning internal databases and external sources.

3. Automatically scoring candidate profiles across multiple dimensions.

4. Reviewing top-ranked candidates through an intuitive interface.

5. Sending personalized outreach emails generated by NLP engines.

6. Tracking responses and advancing interested candidates to automated pre-screening interviews.

By automating these repetitive yet essential tasks, AI frees recruiters from sifting through irrelevant resumes and allows them to focus on engaging high-potential candidates personally—improving both productivity and the candidate experience.

Still, human judgment remains vital throughout the process; AI serves as a powerful assistant rather than a replacement for nuanced decision-making involving interpersonal dynamics and cultural fit.

Organizations integrating AI into talent sourcing report significantly reduced time-to-hire—sometimes by 30% or more—while expanding access to diverse talent pools previously difficult to reach due to scale constraints.

embedding AI in talent acquisition shifts sourcing from a reactive task into a strategic advantage that closely aligns workforce capabilities with evolving business goals and market demands.

Automating screening and selection

Screening and selection are pivotal stages in recruitment, where AI automation can dramatically reduce manual effort while improving accuracy. Traditional approaches often involve painstaking resume reviews and lengthy interviews, but AI-powered screening tools quickly assess candidate suitability based on customized criteria, allowing recruiters to focus on more strategic activities. These tools leverage natural language processing (NLP), predictive analytics, and machine learning to evaluate qualifications, experience, and even subtle indicators of cultural fit embedded within candidate information.

Consider an AI system designed to screen resumes for a mid-level marketing manager role. Rather than simply searching for keywords, it interprets the context around phrases like "campaign management" or "ROI optimization," distinguishing between casual mentions and demonstrated expertise. This deeper understanding comes from NLP models trained on extensive datasets of job descriptions and profiles of successful hires, enabling nuanced scoring instead of simple yes-or-no matches. So, candidates who use unconventional phrasing or varied terminology receive fairer consideration.

A common method combines rule-based filters with machine learning classifiers. Initially, straightforward exclusion rules remove clearly unqualified applicants—such as those lacking required certifications or sufficient experience. Then, advanced models rank the remaining candidates based on predicted success factors derived from historical hiring outcomes and performance data. A typical workflow might look like this:

1. Input applicant resumes into the AI platform.

2. Apply exclusion rules to eliminate unqualified candidates.

3. Score remaining candidates according to skill relevance and depth of experience.

4. Factor in soft attributes like leadership potential or adaptability inferred from language patterns.

5. Present a prioritized shortlist for recruiter review.

This layered approach balances efficiency with quality control, ensuring AI complements rather than replaces human judgment.

Beyond resume analysis, video interview tools add another dimension by evaluating candidate responses through speech recognition and sentiment analysis. Platforms such as HireVue track facial expressions and vocal tone to gauge confidence or hesitation—though these capabilities raise important questions about bias and privacy. Careful implementation and transparent criteria are essential to uphold fairness when using such technologies.

Chatbots also play a role as virtual screeners by conducting initial candidate interactions. They ask standardized questions about availability, salary expectations, or technical skills, capturing responses in structured formats that facilitate automated evaluation. For example:

- Chatbot: "Do you have experience managing teams larger than five?"

- Candidate: "Yes, I led a team of seven for three years."

The system logs the answer and proceeds accordingly. This conversational style improves candidate engagement while streamlining early data collection.

Effective implementation begins with clearly defining job requirements and translating them into measurable attributes for the AI system. Vague or overly broad criteria risk overwhelming the pipeline with unqualified candidates or overlooking transferable skills. Continuous training— where recruiters provide feedback on mismatches or unexpected results—helps refine algorithms over time.

One useful practice is running AI-assisted screening alongside manual review over several hiring cycles. Comparing metrics such as time-to-hire, quality-of-hire (based on post-employment performance), and candidate diversity offers an objective way to assess the tool's impact.

Legal compliance remains a top priority throughout automation efforts. Decision-making processes must adhere to equal employment opportunity laws and avoid inadvertent discrimination related to gender, ethnicity, age, or other protected characteristics. Regular audits using fairness assessment tools help identify biases embedded in training data or algorithms.

In sum, automating screening and selection transforms recruitment into a more scalable, data-driven process that surfaces qualified talent more efficiently without sacrificing fairness—provided it is paired with ongoing oversight and refinement. What was once a manual bottleneck becomes an opportunity for precision and strategic focus within talent acquisition.

Enhancing employee engagement

Employee engagement has long been the defining factor that distinguishes thriving organizations from those merely surviving. AI-powered automation opens new possibilities to deepen this engagement by shifting focus away from routine tasks and toward meaningful human interactions. Traditional methods—such as surveys, town halls, and incentive programs—often lack real-time insight into employee sentiment and struggle to adapt quickly to changing workforce dynamics. AI addresses this gap by enabling continuous feedback loops and personalized interventions.

For example, platforms that combine natural language processing with pulse surveys and communication tools can analyze everyday interactions—emails, chat messages, even anonymous comments—instead of relying solely on quarterly or annual surveys. These systems detect patterns of disengagement or morale issues as they emerge. An AI tool might flag increased negative language within a team's Slack channel, prompting HR or management to investigate promptly. This real-time sentiment analysis transforms engagement from a reactive process into a proactive one.

AI also enhances recognition and rewards programs by automating personalized acknowledgments based on performance data and peer feedback. Imagine a sales team where each closed deal triggers tailored commendations delivered through internal social platforms. The system not only identifies top performers but also highlights individuals showing growth or collaboration, fostering a culture of appreciation that feels timely and genuine.

Gamification powered by AI analytics offers another practical example. By assigning points or badges for behaviors like meeting deadlines, contributing ideas, or assisting colleagues, organizations tap into intrinsic motivation drivers. Machine learning models dynamically adjust challenges according to individual progress and preferences, helping to prevent disengagement caused by monotony or excessive difficulty.

Employee well-being benefits as well. AI-driven wellness apps monitor work patterns and suggest breaks or mindfulness exercises when signs of burnout appear. Take this example, if calendar data reveals consecutive days packed with back-to-back meetings without downtime, the system encourages employees to engage in self-care activities and alerts managers to potential workload imbalances.

Training and development become more effective through personalized learning pathways curated by AI algorithms. Instead of generic modules, employees receive recommendations tailored to their skill gaps, career goals, and preferred learning styles. A customer service representative struggling with conflict resolution might be offered microlearning videos alongside simulated scenarios, continuously adapted based on ongoing performance assessments.

Despite these advantages, it is crucial to approach AI-driven engagement thoughtfully to avoid perceptions of surveillance or dehumanization. Transparency about data usage and opt-in participation maintain trust, while combining automated insights with empathetic human follow-up preserves the relational core essential for authentic engagement.

Consider an organization implementing an AI engagement platform integrated with Microsoft Teams chats and Outlook calendars. The system includes:

1. Daily extraction of textual communications and meeting schedules.

2. Sentiment analysis models trained on company-specific language nuances.

3. Dashboard alerts for HR highlighting teams experiencing declining morale.

4. Automated "kudos" generated from key achievements logged in the CRM.

5. Wellness prompts delivered via mobile app when high workload indicators arise.

6. Weekly learning content recommendations pushed

through the corporate LMS aligned with role-specific competencies.

Over six months, HR observes a 20% increase in voluntary wellness program participation alongside a 15% reduction in mid-quarter attrition rates among flagged teams.

By moving beyond superficial metrics, AI-driven engagement strategies foster authentic connection and sustained motivation at scale—a critical leap for maintaining competitive advantage in today's talent landscape.

Performance evaluation tools

Performance evaluation, a fundamental aspect of effective human resource management, experiences a significant evolution when enhanced by AI-powered automation. Traditional appraisal systems often struggle with biases, infrequent feedback, and administrative tasks that pull managers away from coaching and employee development. By automating these processes, AI not only streamlines evaluations but also introduces greater objectivity and continuous insight that were previously difficult to achieve.

Natural language processing (NLP) exemplifies this transformation by analyzing qualitative feedback gathered from diverse sources such as peer reviews, customer comments, and self-assessments. Rather than relying exclusively on annual performance reviews, AI aggregates unstructured data in real time to identify recurring themes like teamwork strengths, communication challenges, or leadership potential. Take this example, an AI system could sift through hundreds of 360-degree feedback responses to highlight consistent praise for problem-solving abilities while drawing attention to concerns about punctuality. This detailed perspective enables managers to create highly tailored development plans.

Incorporating quantitative data adds another layer of depth to performance evaluations. Metrics like sales figures, project completion rates, and customer satisfaction scores feed into machine learning models that establish personalized benchmarks. Consider a marketing analyst whose campaign success rates are evaluated against industry standards and historical performance; the AI tool adjusts goals dynamically based on current results instead of static targets set months earlier. This adaptability fosters growth that aligns closely with evolving business needs.

Automated scoring systems offer standardized ratings but also detect discrepancies warranting human review. For example, if an employee's quantitative metrics improve while sentiment analysis of peer feedback declines, the system flags this inconsistency for further examination. By combining numerical data with qualitative insights, organizations promote balanced and nuanced judgments rather than relying solely on numbers.

Beyond individual assessments, AI-driven predictive analytics support talent management by uncovering patterns across teams or departments. This helps organizations to anticipate turnover risks or identify high-potential employees ready for advancement. A retail chain, for example, implemented an AI-powered evaluation platform integrating sales data with engagement scores from internal surveys. So, managers received early alerts about key staff showing signs of disengagement, leading to timely interventions that reduced turnover by 12% within a year.

Successful implementation depends on integrating these tools seamlessly with existing HR information systems (HRIS) and communication platforms to maintain smooth data flow. One enterprise combined Workday with an AI plugin for continuous performance monitoring through a workflow that includes:

1. Automated collection of task completions and project milestones.

2. Real-time sentiment extraction from internal chats and email threads.

3. Dynamic dashboards accessible to employees and managers illustrating ongoing progress.

4. AI-generated personalized feedback suggestions delivered via mobile notifications.

5. Scheduled calibration sessions where human reviewers validate AI findings.

This hybrid model balances the efficiency of automation with essential human judgment, helping to preserve trust in the evaluation process.

Nonetheless, challenges remain in designing unbiased algorithms and maintaining transparency regarding data usage. Overreliance on automated scores without contextual understanding risks alienating employees or perpetuating biases embedded in historical data sets. Regular audits of AI models and involving diverse stakeholders in defining evaluation criteria are critical steps toward fairness.

For example, IBM's Watson Talent Insights platform uses anonymized data to reduce gender bias by focusing on competencies rather than subjective descriptors often tied to stereotypes. Such thoughtful applications show how AI can enhance both fairness and accuracy.

Integrating AI into performance evaluation ultimately equips organizations with actionable intelligence that moves beyond periodic reviews—enabling ongoing development conversations grounded in data rather than intuition alone. This shift opens opportunities to motivate employees more meaningfully while aligning their growth with strategic objectives without overwhelming HR teams with manual tasks.

To ensure successful adoption, clear communication about the benefits and limitations of these tools is essential to prevent resistance or misinterpretation. Training managers to interpret AI-generated reports helps maintain their role as facilitators rather than mere administrators of automated outputs.

When combined with prior advances in employee engagement—such as sentiment analysis and personalized learning pathways—automated performance evaluation completes a comprehensive feedback ecosystem that fosters continuous improvement at both individual and organizational levels. This integration boosts employee satisfaction and business agility alike, vital components for sustained success in today's rapidly changing technological landscape.

Predictive analytics for HR

Predictive analytics has become a powerful extension of AI in human resources, shifting the focus from traditional data collection to proactively shaping workforce strategies. Rather than reacting to spikes in turnover or performance issues after they occur, organizations can now anticipate these trends by analyzing patterns within diverse employee data sets. This approach combines historical HR metrics with real-time inputs such as engagement surveys, attendance records, and external labor market indicators to provide a comprehensive view.

For example, an organization noticing a gradual decline in team morale can use predictive models to identify links between management styles, workload distribution, and rising absenteeism before these problems escalate into formal complaints or resignations. A global consulting firm applied a predictive HR analytics platform that integrated employee feedback scores with project deadlines and overtime hours. The system flagged teams at risk of burnout weeks in advance, enabling managers to redistribute workloads and offer targeted support. This foresight not only preserves productivity but also helps reduce costly turnover.

The technical foundation often relies on machine learning algorithms trained on labeled datasets representing various HR outcomes—such as promotions, voluntary exits, and performance ratings. These models reveal which factors most strongly influence specific outcomes and assign probabilities accordingly. Take this example, a predictive model might determine that employees with low participation in development programs combined with frequent schedule changes have a 30% higher chance of leaving within six months. Equipped with this insight, HR teams can implement tailored interventions like personalized training or flexible scheduling.

Implementing predictive analytics typically involves several key steps:

1. Data consolidation: Collecting relevant information from multiple sources such as payroll systems, performance management tools, and employee engagement platforms.

2. Data cleaning and normalization: Addressing inconsistencies or missing data to ensure accuracy.

3. Feature selection: Identifying the most predictive variables using domain expertise and statistical analysis.

4. Model training: Applying algorithms like random forests or logistic regression to detect patterns.

5. Validation and tuning: Testing models against new data to prevent overfitting.

6. Integration into decision workflows: Delivering actionable insights through dashboards or alerts designed for HR professionals.

A practical example comes from retail chains using predictive analytics for workforce planning during seasonal peaks. By analyzing past sales cycles alongside employee availability and turnover rates, these companies can forecast staffing needs more accurately—avoiding both understaffing and overstaffing costs.

Despite these benefits, challenges remain in balancing predictive capabilities with ethical considerations. Privacy concerns necessitate anonymizing sensitive data whenever possible while preserving enough detail for meaningful analysis. Transparency about how predictions are generated is essential to building trust among employees who may be wary of automated evaluations affecting their career paths.

Importantly, predictive analytics should augment rather than replace human judgment and communication in talent management. Models may miss contextual nuances like sudden life events that temporarily impact an individual's engagement or performance.

Some organizations have addressed this by developing "what-if" simulation tools that allow HR managers to explore hypothetical scenarios before implementing policy changes suggested by analytics—for example, assessing how extending remote work options might influence retention across departments.

Today's tools, such as Workday People Analytics and SAP SuccessFactors, offer embedded predictive modules tailored for HR functions. These platforms often feature intuitive interfaces that visualize risk scores alongside recommended actions, enabling quick interpretation without requiring advanced data science skills.

adopting predictive analytics transforms reactive HR practices into proactive strategies aligned closely with business objectives. It empowers companies not only to retain top talent but also to develop workforce capabilities that adapt dynamically to evolving market demands.

While successful integration requires careful planning—from selecting appropriate KPIs to iterative validation—the rewards are significant: decisions grounded in data rather than guesswork improve organizational resilience and provide a competitive advantage in fast-changing environments where talent is critical.

By turning raw employee data into a strategic asset, predictive analytics equips leaders at all levels to forecast workforce trends confidently—offering a crucial edge in today's complex business landscape where human capital remains the most valuable resource.

Training and development automation

Automating training and development is transforming how organizations build skills and nurture talent at scale. Instead of relying on traditional classroom sessions or occasional workshops, AI-driven platforms create personalized learning paths that adapt continuously based on individual performance and engagement. This dynamic approach moves beyond the one-size-fits-all model, which often leaves employees either disengaged or overwhelmed.

Take, for example, a mid-sized tech company grappling with rapid product updates and an ongoing need for upskilling across teams. By implementing an AI-based Learning Management System (LMS), managers could automatically assign modular courses tailored to employees' prior assessments and specific role requirements. The system monitored quiz scores, time spent on each module, and even sentiment from feedback forms to pinpoint knowledge gaps in real time. If a software engineer struggled with a particular Python concept, the platform might recommend targeted microlearning videos or hands-on coding challenges until mastery was achieved. This iterative process encourages continuous improvement while relieving HR of manual tracking burdens.

From a technical perspective, these platforms use recommendation algorithms similar to those behind streaming services, but repurposed for professional growth. Collaborative filtering matches learners with content that peers with similar profiles have found helpful, while natural language processing analyzes open-ended feedback to fine-tune course materials. Many systems also incorporate gamification—such as badges and leaderboards—to boost motivation and create a sense of progression that feels engaging rather than obligatory.

Implementing an automated training program generally involves several key steps:

1. Needs assessment: Collecting insights from managers and employees about skill gaps and upcoming projects that require new capabilities.

2. Content curation: Selecting or developing modular learning resources compatible with the LMS's adaptive framework.

3. Platform configuration: Setting rules for course assignments based on roles, past performance, or certification needs.

4. Integration: Linking the LMS with HR systems to synchronize employee data and automate progress tracking.

5. Monitoring: Creating dashboards to track learner engagement and completion rates for timely interventions.

6. Feedback loops: Continuously gathering learner input to improve content relevance and delivery methods.

A practical illustration comes from a global retail chain that automated customer service training across hundreds of locations. Employees received personalized modules updated monthly according to insights from mystery shopper reports and customer satisfaction scores analyzed by AI. This strategy reduced onboarding time by 30% while significantly boosting service quality ratings.

Despite these benefits, automation carries risks if it becomes too impersonal or rigidly data-driven. Overreliance on algorithms can miss critical contextual factors such as individual career goals or soft skills like communication, leadership potential, and emotional intelligence—qualities essential for long-term success but difficult to quantify through metrics alone.

To address this, effective programs incorporate human touchpoints: mentor check-ins triggered by algorithmic alerts indicating stalled progress or low engagement; periodic workshops fostering peer interaction; and coaching sessions initiated by AI-identified developmental needs but delivered live by skilled facilitators.

Many leading vendors now offer hybrid solutions combining AI automation with curated human experiences—for example, LinkedIn Learning paired with live Q&A sessions or Coursera for Business supplemented by virtual instructor-led training (VILT). These blends provide flexibility without sacrificing the depth of personalization.

From an implementation standpoint, the following Python snippet shows a simple way to track learner progress using pandas, identifying employees who may need additional support based on average module completion below 70%:

```python
import pandas as pd

\#\# Sample dataset: Employee IDs with module completion percentages
data =
'EmployeeID': [101, 102, 103, 104],
'Module1_Completion': [80, 65, 90, 55],
'Module2_Completion': [75, 60, 85, 50],
'Module3_Completion': [90, 70, 95, 45]


df = pd.DataFrame(data)

\#\# Calculate average completion per employee
df['Avg_Completion']                     =                    df.loc[:,
'Module1_Completion':'Module3_Completion'].mean(axis=1)

\#\# Flag employees needing support (<70% average)
df['Needs_Support'] = df['Avg_Completion'] < 70

print(df[['EmployeeID', 'Avg_Completion', 'Needs_Support']])
```

This basic approach can be scaled within an LMS environment where real-time data streams replace static tables—enabling automated alerts to managers when intervention becomes necessary.

Automation also streamlines compliance training—mandatory modules like workplace safety or data privacy often require timely certifications across large workforces. By scheduling refresher courses automatically before deadlines and centrally tracking completions through AI-powered dashboards synced with regulatory calendars (e.g., GDPR), organizations reduce risk without manual effort.

automated training empowers organizations not only to keep pace with evolving skill demands but also to democratize learning access regardless of location or schedule—a crucial advantage in today's hybrid work environments.

Striking the right balance between intelligent automation and empathetic human involvement ensures development programs remain effective without feeling mechanical—a subtlety that separates successful initiatives from mere digital checklists masquerading as growth efforts.

When implemented thoughtfully and supported by robust analytics, training automation transforms workforce capability into a proactive asset rather than a reactive expense—preparing businesses to seize opportunities arising from technological change instead of falling behind them.

Onboarding process improvements

Onboarding processes have long been a bottleneck in workforce integration—often lengthy, paperwork-heavy, and inconsistent. AI automation is transforming this crucial phase by speeding up task completion, enhancing data accuracy, and customizing the experience to fit each new hire's role and needs.

Traditionally, a new employee arrives on day one with a stack of forms to fill out manually—tax documents, benefits enrollment, confidentiality agreements. This slows down productivity and increases the risk of errors. AI-powered onboarding platforms address these challenges by automating administrative tasks, pre-filling information when possible, and guiding employees through seamless digital workflows. Solutions like BambooHR or Workday's onboarding module incorporate AI-driven checklists and reminders to ensure every step is completed.

For example, BambooHR's onboarding automation kicks into gear as soon as a candidate accepts an offer. The system sends personalized welcome emails, generates e-signature requests for legal forms, schedules introductory meetings with relevant teams, and assigns mandatory training modules aligned with the new hire's responsibilities. This entire sequence runs without manual intervention but remains visible to HR through an intuitive dashboard. The result: significant time savings per hire and consistent compliance with company policies.

Setting up such a process typically involves mapping all essential onboarding activities—document submission, policy acknowledgments, equipment provisioning, team introductions—and configuring automated triggers tied to key milestones (like offer acceptance triggering document dispatch). Automated reminders prompt both new hires and managers at critical intervals such as day-one orientation or end-of-week check-ins. Post-onboarding feedback surveys then help measure effectiveness and continuously refine the workflow.

Beyond efficiency, AI enhances personalization during onboarding. Machine learning algorithms analyze role-specific competencies and historical employee success data to recommend tailored training paths or mentorship matches. Take this example, a software engineer might receive customized tutorials distinct from those assigned to a sales associate; the system dynamically adapts as it gathers more data over time.

Real-world results highlight benefits that extend beyond streamlined processes. One multinational company reduced its average time-to-productivity by 30% after deploying an AI-driven onboarding system featuring virtual assistants available 24/7 to answer FAQs about benefits or company policies—eliminating bottlenecks caused by limited HR availability during busy periods.

Automation also improves cross-departmental coordination. For example, integrating AI with asset management systems can automatically schedule hardware provisioning aligned with hiring dates while notifying IT teams well in advance.

The following Python snippet illustrates how simple automation logic can initiate such workflow orchestration:

```python
import datetime


\#\# Sample employee onboarding event

class OnboardingEvent:

def __init__(self, employee_name, start_date):

self.employee_name = employee_name

self.start_date = start_date


def send_welcome_email(self):

print(f"Welcome email sent to self.employee_name.")


def schedule_orientation(self):
```

```
        orientation_date        =        self.start_date        +
        datetime.timedelta(days=1)

        print(f"Orientation        scheduled        on
        orientation_date.strftime('%Y-%m-%d').")


def automate_onboarding(employee_name, start_date_str):

    start_date = datetime.datetime.strptime(start_date_str, '%Y-%m-%d')

    event = OnboardingEvent(employee_name, start_date)

    event.send_welcome_email()

    event.schedule_orientation()


\#\# Example usage:

automate_onboarding('Jane Doe', '2024-07-01')
` ` `
```

This code simulates sending a welcome email and scheduling orientation automatically based on the employee's name and start date—a simple foundation that can be expanded with API integrations into corporate communication tools like Slack or Microsoft Teams.

Additionally, chatbots embedded in onboarding portals handle repetitive questions instantly—about dress code or parking—freeing HR resources from routine inquiries.

Implementing automated onboarding does require careful change management. Organizations need transparency about data usage since sensitive personal information flows through automated systems. Clear communication regarding what data is collected and how it is processed fosters trust among new hires.

Importantly, automation should enhance—not replace—the human connections essential to effective onboarding. AI-powered calendaring tools can schedule virtual meet-and-greets that help newcomers build relationships early on, even in remote work environments.

In sum, AI-enhanced onboarding streamlines administrative tasks while boosting personalization and engagement from day one. Structured workflows supported by automation platforms reduce operational friction significantly yet preserve vital human elements through thoughtful scheduling and communication.

The overall impact? New employees ramp up faster with higher satisfaction scores—leading to improved retention rates and positively influencing organizational performance without compromising compliance or security standards.

Diversity and inclusion through AI

Diversity and inclusion initiatives have gained renewed momentum as businesses increasingly recognize the strategic advantage of embracing varied perspectives. AI automation plays a key role in advancing these efforts by helping to eliminate unconscious biases in recruitment and employee management, providing tools that identify and address systemic barriers.

Traditional hiring methods often fall prey to implicit biases, where recruiters—sometimes unintentionally—favor candidates who resemble current employees or fit familiar profiles. AI-driven recruitment platforms counteract this by scanning resumes and applications using predefined fairness criteria, deliberately ignoring demographic details such as gender, age, ethnicity, or educational background unless they are directly relevant. Solutions like HireVue and Pymetrics leverage machine learning to assess candidate skills through gamified tests or structured video interviews, reducing the influence of subjective human judgment.

Take this example, Pymetrics uses neuroscience-based games to evaluate cognitive and emotional traits. The resulting data enables algorithms to match applicants to roles based on competencies rather than resumes that may contain bias-triggering keywords. One company adopting Pymetrics reported a 25% increase in hiring women for technical roles, largely because the system prioritized aptitude over pedigree.

AI's impact extends beyond hiring. Workforce analytics platforms analyze organizational demographics to highlight underrepresented groups or disparities in promotion rates. Tableau's AI-enhanced dashboards allow HR teams to visualize representation gaps by department or role and monitor progress toward inclusion goals with clear, quantitative metrics.

Yet, automating inclusion efforts requires careful oversight. Because algorithms learn from historical data, they risk perpetuating existing biases—a challenge known as algorithmic bias. To guard against this, organizations must regularly audit AI systems for fairness using methods like disparate impact analysis or counterfactual testing.

Consider this simple Python example illustrating a basic fairness check on hiring scores:

```python
import pandas as pd


\#\# Sample candidate data with 'score' and 'group' columns
data = 'candidate_id': [1, 2, 3, 4],

'score': [85, 90, 75, 80],

'group': ['A', 'B', 'A', 'B']    \# Group A and B represent demographic groups
```

```
df = pd.DataFrame(data)

\#\# Calculate average scores per group
avg_scores = df.groupby('group')['score'].mean()
print("Average scores by group:")
print(avg_scores)

\#\# Basic fairness check: difference in average scores should
not exceed threshold
threshold = 5
difference = abs(avg_scores['A'] - avg_scores['B'])

if difference > threshold:
print("Warning: Potential bias detected between groups.")
else:
print("Scores appear balanced across groups.")
` ` `
```

This snippet compares average scores between demographic groups as a preliminary way to detect potential bias in automated decisions.

Beyond recruitment and analytics, AI fosters inclusive workplaces through sentiment analysis of employee feedback and real-time monitoring of communication channels to identify language that signals exclusion or harassment. Platforms like Culture Amp use natural language processing (NLP) to reveal subtle patterns in anonymous comments that might escape human notice due to their volume or nuance.

AI also enables more personalized learning and development by identifying diverse learning styles through assessments, ensuring equitable growth opportunities tailored to individual preferences.

Transparency is essential when deploying AI in personnel decisions. Clear communication about how data is used builds trust and reassures employees that automation supports fairness rather than obscuring discriminatory practices behind opaque algorithms.

Leaders who champion responsible AI adoption assemble multidisciplinary teams—including ethicists and legal experts—to continuously review and refine processes. Engaging employees through workshops on algorithmic literacy promotes open dialogue about both the benefits and limitations of automated diversity measures.

By combining human judgment with AI-powered analytics, organizations create an environment where biases surface quickly and are addressed proactively rather than being overlooked due to tradition or inertia.

 integrating AI into diversity and inclusion strategies drives measurable improvements—not only increasing representation but also enhancing innovation through broader perspectives. As Intel's CEO Pat Gelsinger remarked, "Diversity fuels creativity—and technology has the power to accelerate that transformation."

When thoughtfully incorporated into DEI efforts, automated tools position organizations not just as compliant entities but as pioneers building equitable workplaces ready for tomorrow's challenges. This commitment demands ongoing effort but yields profound rewards: fairer processes that foster stronger teams capable of sustaining business success.

CHAPTER 13: AI-DRIVEN INNOVATION AND PRODUCT DEVELOPMENT

Identifying market trends with AI

I dentifying market trends with AI revolutionizes the traditional, labor-intensive task of analyzing vast amounts of data, turning it into a swift, insight-driven process. Rather than depending on intuition or manual review, businesses can now use AI algorithms to uncover subtle patterns and emerging shifts in consumer behavior well ahead of competitors. These advanced capabilities are no longer exclusive to large corporations; cloud-based AI services provide scalable solutions accessible even to mid-sized companies aiming to stay competitive.

Natural language processing (NLP) is a prime example of this shift, excelling at extracting sentiment from sources like social media posts, product reviews, and news articles. By training models to analyze real-time feeds, companies gain near-instantaneous insights into consumer attitudes toward their brands or products. Take this example, a retail chain might set up an NLP system that continuously monitors Twitter mentions for sentiment related to a new clothing line. If negative sentiment rises sharply in a specific region, marketing or supply chain teams can quickly adjust campaigns or redistribute inventory to address the issue.

A practical way to start is by using Python's TextBlob library for basic sentiment analysis on Twitter data. First, authenticate with the Twitter API to collect relevant tweets about your product or sector, then run code like this:

```python
from textblob import TextBlob

import tweepy


\#\# Set up Twitter API client (assumes keys are set)

auth       =       tweepy.OAuth1UserHandler(consumer_key, consumer_secret, access_token, access_token_secret)

api = tweepy.API(auth)


\#\# Fetch recent tweets mentioning 'yourproduct'

tweets    =    api.search_tweets(q='yourproduct',    lang='en', count=100)


\#\# Analyze sentiment polarity (-1 negative, +1 positive)

sentiments = []

for tweet in tweets:

analysis = TextBlob(tweet.text)

sentiments.append(analysis.sentiment.polarity)
```

```python
average_sentiment = sum(sentiments) / len(sentiments)

print(f'Average sentiment score: average_sentiment:.2f')
```
` ` `

This output provides a quantified measure of public opinion—valuable intelligence for fine-tuning messaging or anticipating shifts in demand. Beyond social media, AI also analyzes transactional data and web traffic logs to reveal buying trends or seasonal patterns hidden within complex datasets.

To deepen understanding, machine learning models such as time-series forecasting project how these trends may evolve. Tools like Facebook's Prophet or LSTM networks in TensorFlow capture seasonality and external influences, delivering actionable forecasts rather than static snapshots. For example, a beverage company predicting summer sales spikes can improve accuracy by integrating historical sales data with weather information rather than relying on simple averages.

Here's a streamlined example using Prophet:

` ` `python

```python
from prophet import Prophet

import pandas as pd


\#\# Load historical sales data with columns 'ds' (date) and 'y' (sales)

df = pd.read_csv('sales_data.csv')


model = Prophet()
```

```python
model.fit(df)
```

```
\#\# Predict next 30 days
```

```python
future = model.make_future_dataframe(periods=30)
```

```python
forecast = model.predict(future)
```

```python
print(forecast[['ds', 'yhat', 'yhat_lower', 'yhat_upper']].tail())
```
` ` `

The forecasted values (yhat) enable supply chain planners to proactively adjust inventory levels—helping avoid costly stockouts or excess stock.

Another promising approach involves image recognition AI that detects emerging products on store shelves or e-commerce platforms faster than human observation allows. Companies like Amazon use computer vision to track competitors' merchandising strategies across thousands of SKUs daily. Smaller businesses can leverage open-source tools such as OpenCV combined with pre-trained models to monitor product placement or customer foot traffic via video feeds.

A simple prototype for object detection might look like this:

` ` `python

```python
import cv2
```

```
\#\# Load pre-trained MobileNet SSD model
```

```python
net = cv2.dnn.readNetFromCaffe('deploy.prototxt', 'mobilenet.caffemodel')
```

```python
image = cv2.imread('store_shelf.jpg')

(h, w) = image.shape[:2]


blob = cv2.dnn.blobFromImage(cv2.resize(image, (300, 300)), 0.007843,

(300, 300), 127.5)

net.setInput(blob)

detections = net.forward()


for i in range(detections.shape[2]):

confidence = detections[0, 0, i, 2]

if confidence > 0.6:

idx = int(detections[0, 0, i, 1])

box = detections[0, 0, i, 3:7] * [w, h, w, h]

(startX, startY, endX, endY) = box.astype("int")

label = f"Product idx: confidence * 100:.1f%

cv2.rectangle(image, (startX,startY), (endX,endY), (0,255,0), 2)

cv2.putText(image,label,(startX,startY-10),

cv2.FONT_HERSHEY_SIMPLEX,.5,(0,255,0),2)


cv2.imshow("Detected Products", image)

cv2.waitKey(0)

cv2.destroyAllWindows()
```

` ` `

Even with this straightforward setup, small retailers can automatically track product visibility trends and competitive positioning.

Real-world examples highlight AI's impact: Nike employs predictive analytics not only for sales forecasting but also for spotting fashion trends by analyzing Instagram images and user engagement worldwide—a blend of social listening and computer vision that enables rapid design adjustments.

While these tools offer powerful insights, they require careful tuning tailored to each business context. Seasonal variations differ; cultural nuances influence online discourse; camera angles affect image recognition accuracy. Investing time in training custom models and validating results against known benchmarks is essential.

Equally important is maintaining human oversight when interpreting AI-driven market insights. Data reveals behaviors but not underlying motivations; algorithms may overlook subtleties that experienced strategists understand intuitively.

Integrating these approaches effectively involves establishing feedback loops: regularly incorporate sales outcomes back into forecasting models and update NLP keyword sets as slang or industry jargon evolves. Combining multiple data sources—social sentiment alongside transactional spikes—in dashboards creates a richer view of market dynamics.

leveraging AI for market trend identification empowers businesses not just to react swiftly but to anticipate changes before they occur. This foresight supports smarter inventory management and targeted promotions driven by real-time data instead of guesswork—leading to more confident strategic decisions grounded in measurable evidence.

Starting this journey doesn't require heavy upfront investment: experimenting with public datasets and open APIs using example scripts builds internal capabilities while demonstrating early value. The ongoing digital advantage lies in transforming scattered signals from diverse channels into coherent strategies that optimize outcomes continuously as markets evolve right before your eyes.

Enhancing R&D processes

Enhancing research and development (R&D) with AI transforms innovation from a linear, often slow process into a dynamic, data-driven cycle. While traditional R&D can struggle to manage vast amounts of data and unpredictable results, AI algorithms excel at synthesizing complex datasets to uncover insights that might elude human analysis. This not only speeds up discovery but also sharpens focus on viable product features, reducing the costly trial-and-error phases common in development.

One clear advantage appears in automating literature reviews. For example, pharmaceutical companies face thousands of scientific papers daily, making manual review impractical. Natural language processing (NLP) tools can quickly scan, summarize, and categorize relevant research far faster than any human team. IBM Watson's AI has been used effectively to sift through biomedical literature, identifying potential drug candidates or flagging adverse interactions. Similarly, engineering disciplines benefit when patents and technical documents must be thoroughly examined before moving forward with new designs.

In practical terms, Python libraries like spaCy or NLTK enable text mining and entity recognition to extract key terms from research abstracts. Take this example:

```python
import spacy
```

```
from collections import Counter

nlp = spacy.load("en_core_web_sm")

documents = [
This study explores new materials for battery technology...",
Novel catalysts improve reaction rates in chemical synthesis...",
\#\# Add more abstracts here
]

all_tokens = []
for doc in documents:
processed = nlp(doc)
tokens = [token.lemma_ for token in processed if token.is_alpha and not token.is_stop]
all_tokens.extend(tokens)

common_terms = Counter(all_tokens).most_common(10)
print("Top key terms:", common_terms)
```

Extracting such keywords helps prioritize promising areas or identify gaps ripe for exploration.

Beyond literature reviews, AI supports experimental design by simulating outcomes before physical trials begin. Machine learning models can predict how changes in parameters

—like material composition or process conditions—affect results, guiding researchers toward the most fruitful experiments. This predictive approach conserves resources and shortens development timelines.

Materials science offers a concrete example: regression models trained on existing datasets forecast properties such as tensile strength or thermal conductivity based on composition. Using scikit-learn's RandomForestRegressor simplifies this task:

```python
from sklearn.ensemble import RandomForestRegressor

import pandas as pd


\#\# Sample dataset: columns for material components + target property

data = pd.read_csv('material_properties.csv')

X = data.drop('tensile_strength', axis=1)

y = data['tensile_strength']


model = RandomForestRegressor(n_estimators=100)

model.fit(X, y)


\#\# Predict tensile strength for a new composition

new_sample = [[0.3, 0.5, 0.2]] \# Example component ratios

predicted_strength = model.predict(new_sample)

print(f"Predicted tensile strength: predicted_strength[0]:.2f MPa")
```

Such models allow iterative refinement without needing physical tests after every change.

AI-driven image analysis further enhances R&D workflows by automating inspections of microscopic images or quality control photos to detect defects invisible to the human eye. Convolutional neural networks (CNNs), widely used in computer vision tasks, are increasingly integrated into lab equipment to provide real-time feedback during prototype manufacturing or biological assays.

For example, training a CNN on labeled defect images enables automatic classification during production:

```python
import tensorflow as tf

from tensorflow.keras.models import Sequential

from tensorflow.keras.layers import Conv2D, MaxPooling2D, Flatten, Dense


model = Sequential([

Conv2D(32, (3,3), activation='relu', input_shape=(64,64,3)),

MaxPooling2D((2,2)),

Flatten(),

Dense(64, activation='relu'),

Dense(2, activation='softmax')   \# Defect / No defect classification

])


model.compile(optimizer='adam', loss='categorical_crossentropy', metrics=['accuracy'])
```

```
\#\# Assume training_data and validation_data are prepared
image datasets

model.fit(training_data,                          epochs=10,
validation_data=validation_data)
```
` ` `

Integrating this technology accelerates feedback loops by identifying issues immediately rather than after batch completion.

Collaborative platforms augmented with AI are also reshaping how R&D teams interact across departments and geographies. By aggregating data inputs and suggesting connections between findings, these tools foster interdisciplinary innovation and help break down silos that often slow progress.

Knowledge graphs powered by AI exemplify this approach by mapping relationships among patents, publications, and internal reports—enabling teams to spot unexploited overlaps or adjacent technologies ripe for exploration.

While these advances streamline processes remarkably well, they require careful integration with domain expertise. Models trained without sufficient contextual grounding risk misleading conclusions; human judgment remains essential for interpreting AI recommendations effectively.

Organizations adopting AI in R&D often begin by automating repetitive data gathering tasks before scaling up predictive analytics or computer vision applications. Over time, this layered approach fosters a culture where experimentation is guided by robust insights rather than guesswork alone.

incorporating AI transforms R&D from a resource-heavy gamble into an evidence-based pursuit—accelerating product launches while cutting costs and enhancing quality assurance throughout development cycles.

As Fei-Fei Li insightfully observed: "The future of AI lies not just in automation but amplifying human creativity." This perspective resonates deeply within R&D—where machines handle complexity so humans can focus on the imaginative leaps that drive breakthroughs.

Collaboration and co-creation platforms

Collaboration and co-creation platforms empowered by AI are transforming how teams innovate together, often reaching beyond traditional organizational boundaries. These platforms go far beyond simple digital meeting rooms; they actively analyze contributions, suggest connections, and reveal patterns across diverse datasets and disciplines. For example, a global product development team working across multiple time zones can benefit from AI tools that surface relevant prior work, align task dependencies, and even predict potential bottlenecks before they occur.

Siemens provides a compelling example with its AI-driven collaboration hubs. Their platform integrates engineering documents, code repositories, and experimental data into a single cohesive environment. AI agents continuously scan this aggregated information to flag inconsistencies or propose alternative design approaches based on past successes. This approach significantly reduces redundant efforts and accelerates decision-making cycles.

Essentially of many such platforms lie technologies like knowledge graphs. These graphs visually and queryably represent entities—such as projects, patents, and personnel expertise—and the relationships between them. Take this example, a product manager might query the graph to identify engineers with experience in specific materials or processes relevant to a current challenge, helping to avoid costly misalignments caused by siloed knowledge.

To illustrate this concept in practice, consider how Python

libraries like NetworkX can build simple knowledge graphs for team collaboration:

```python
import networkx as nx

import matplotlib.pyplot as plt


G = nx.Graph()


\#\# Add nodes representing people and projects

G.add_node("Alice", role="Engineer")

G.add_node("Bob", role="Data Scientist")

G.add_node("Project X")

G.add_node("Project Y")


\#\# Add edges representing relationships or expertise

G.add_edge("Alice", "Project X", expertise="Materials")

G.add_edge("Bob", "Project X", expertise="AI Modeling")

G.add_edge("Alice", "Project Y", expertise="Testing")


\#\# Visualize the graph

pos = nx.spring_layout(G)

nx.draw(G, pos, with_labels=True, node_color='skyblue', edge_color='gray', node_size=2000)

edge_labels = nx.get_edge_attributes(G, 'expertise')

nx.draw_networkx_edge_labels(G,                              pos,
```

edge_labels=edge_labels)

plt.show()

``` ``` ``

This simple network visualization helps teams recognize overlaps in responsibilities and expertise—an essential advantage during phases like rapid prototyping when cross-functional input is critical.

Beyond static graphs, AI-powered collaboration tools leverage real-time language processing to enhance brainstorming sessions. Platforms such as Miro and Microsoft Teams increasingly embed smart assistants that transcribe meetings, automatically tag action items, and recommend relevant documents or experts based on conversation context. For example, an AI assistant might detect repeated discussion about "battery life optimization" during a design sprint and suggest related research papers or internal reports tagged with those keywords. This feature saves valuable time otherwise spent manually searching for information.

Co-creation now extends beyond internal teams to include customers and external partners within innovation ecosystems. LEGO Ideas exemplifies this by analyzing fan submissions using machine learning models trained on historical sales data and social sentiment analysis. This approach allows LEGO to identify promising designs early while fostering deep community engagement.

Implementing such collaborative systems requires careful attention to data integration and access controls. Security protocols must balance openness with confidentiality—especially when involving third parties. Combining role-based permissions with AI-driven anomaly detection ensures robust protection without hindering seamless communication.
```

From an organizational standpoint, fostering a culture that embraces AI-augmented collaboration involves more than deploying technology. Leadership must promote transparency and knowledge sharing while equipping employees to interpret AI-generated insights critically rather than follow them blindly.

It's important to remember that AI does not eliminate all collaboration challenges; human dynamics—such as trust issues and communication styles—still require deliberate management alongside technological solutions.

these platforms transform innovation workflows into dynamic ecosystems where information flows effortlessly across functions and borders. They enable businesses to iterate faster on ideas, uncover hidden opportunities through data synthesis, and harness collective intelligence more effectively than ever before.

As Alex "Sandy" Pentland from MIT's Human Dynamics Lab observes: "The future of innovation lies in combining human creativity with computational power through seamless collaboration." This synergy encapsulates the promise of AI-powered co-creation platforms—bridging gaps between minds while accelerating the journey from concept to market-ready products.

AI in product lifecycle management

AI is fundamentally transforming product lifecycle management (PLM), evolving it from rigid, linear models into dynamic, data-driven processes that adapt quickly to market changes and internal insights. Rather than progressing through isolated stages, AI weaves continuous feedback loops and predictive analytics throughout the lifecycle, enabling companies to monitor products from ideation to end-of-life with unmatched precision and foresight.

Take product design as an example. Traditional approaches often depend heavily on human intuition or limited historical data. In contrast, AI systems now process vast amounts of information—ranging from customer feedback and competitor analysis to supply chain constraints—and distill these into actionable design criteria. Autodesk's generative design tools illustrate this well: leveraging machine learning, they explore thousands of design variations aligned with specific goals like reducing weight or cutting material costs. The result isn't a single "best" option but a diverse portfolio of optimized designs that engineers can quickly assess.

This AI-driven approach extends seamlessly into manufacturing and quality control. Sensors embedded in production lines gather real-time data on machine performance and product integrity, while anomaly detection algorithms identify deviations moments before defects occur. This early warning system minimizes waste and avoids costly recalls. GE's Predix platform exemplifies this, continuously monitoring jet engine components during manufacturing and operation to enable predictive maintenance instead of reactive repairs.

Post-sale product tracking also benefits significantly from AI-enhanced PLM. When paired with Internet of Things (IoT) devices, AI analyzes usage patterns to anticipate maintenance needs or recommend personalized upgrades. Tesla's over-the-air software updates are a prime example—they continuously enhance vehicle functionality based on real-world data without the delays or expenses associated with traditional recalls or service visits.

To illustrate how an organization might implement AI across the PLM spectrum:

1. Data Aggregation: Collect cross-functional datasets, including R&D results, supplier metrics,

customer feedback, warranty claims, and sensor data from production lines.

2. Machine Learning Model Development: Build predictive models that estimate failure rates by combining historical defect records with current manufacturing conditions.

3. Generative Design Integration: Employ AI platforms like Autodesk Fusion 360 to create design alternatives optimized for key performance indicators such as durability or cost-effectiveness.

4. Real-Time Monitoring Deployment: Install IoT sensors feeding data into anomaly detection algorithms that catch defects early in production.

5. Post-Market Analytics: Use data from connected devices (e.g., smart appliances) to trigger predictive maintenance alerts and suggest feature upgrades tailored to users.

6. Feedback Loop Creation: Develop automated dashboards that relay insights back to designers and suppliers, fostering continuous improvement throughout the lifecycle.

The financial benefits are substantial. Reduced time-to-market combined with fewer recalls can significantly boost profit margins and enhance brand reputation. According to McKinsey, applying AI in product development alone has the potential to cut development costs by up to 30% while accelerating innovation cycles by 20–30%.

Yet adopting AI in PLM is not without challenges. Integrating legacy systems—often siloed and incompatible—requires careful planning. Additionally, fostering collaboration across traditionally separate teams such as engineering, manufacturing, and marketing is essential to avoid fragmented or underused insights. Without comprehensive data governance and stakeholder alignment, the full value of AI-driven intelligence may never be realized.

Siemens provides a notable example through its Digital Industries Software division, where the Teamcenter PLM platform incorporates AI modules for predictive analytics and change impact analysis. These tools assess how design changes ripple through the supply chain before resources are committed, helping prevent costly downstream disruptions.

Regulatory demands further underscore AI's value in PLM, especially in industries like aerospace and pharmaceuticals where strict compliance requires thorough traceability throughout the product lifecycle. AI automates documentation and generates detailed audit trails—from raw data inputs through final approvals—streamlining processes that were traditionally labor-intensive and prone to error.

AI-powered PLM transforms what was once a sequential checklist into an interconnected ecosystem energized by real-time intelligence. It empowers organizations not only to respond reactively but also to proactively shape product outcomes based on comprehensive data spanning conception to retirement.

As Gartner's Peter Sondergaard insightfully observes, "Information is the oil of the 21st century, and analytics is the combustion engine." By harnessing this energy within PLM, companies unlock new possibilities for innovation agility and operational excellence—without compromising compliance or quality at any stage of the product journey.

Customization and personalization of products

Customization and personalization have become essential differentiators in today's competitive markets, with AI playing a crucial role in scaling these strategies beyond traditional limits. Moving away from the one-size-fits-all approach of the past, AI enables businesses to tailor their offerings with remarkable precision—responding to individual preferences, usage patterns, and even anticipating future needs.

Take Amazon's AI-driven recommendation engine as an example. By analyzing browsing history, purchase behavior, and contextual factors such as seasonality or regional trends, the system creates an evolving profile that predicts what a customer might want next—often before they realize it themselves. This dynamic personalization not only increases conversion rates but also deepens customer engagement.

In product development, AI supports mass customization through technologies like generative design and modular architectures. Adidas's "Futurecraft" line illustrates this well: customers personalize sneaker designs online while AI algorithms optimize manufacturing parameters to enhance fit and performance. Behind the scenes, machine learning models analyze biomechanical data from user trials to predict which custom features improve comfort or durability. This blend of customer input and algorithmic refinement speeds up production without sacrificing quality.

To implement effective customization, companies should begin by acquiring detailed individual-level data. This includes behavioral information from digital interactions, IoT-enabled products, and CRM systems enriched with demographic insights. Machine learning models then segment customers into micro-groups—or even individual profiles—using clustering or collaborative filtering techniques.

Take this example, the following Python example demonstrates a simple recommendation system based on user-product interactions:

```python
import pandas as pd
```

```python
from sklearn.metrics.pairwise import cosine_similarity

\#\# Sample user-item interaction matrix
data = 'Product_A': [5, 3, 0, 1],
'Product_B': [4, 0, 0, 1],
'Product_C': [1, 1, 0, 5],
'Product_D': [0, 1, 5, 4]

user_ids = ['User1', 'User2', 'User3', 'User4']
df = pd.DataFrame(data, index=user_ids)

\#\# Compute cosine similarity between users
user_similarity = cosine_similarity(df)
user_similarity_df = pd.DataFrame(user_similarity, index=user_ids, columns=user_ids)

\#\# Recommend products for User3 based on similar users (User1 and User4)
similarity_users = user_similarity_df['User3'].sort_values(ascending=False)[1:3].index

products_watched_by_similar_users = df.loc[similar_users]

recommendations = products_watched_by_similar_users.mean().sort_values(ascending=False)
```

```
print("Recommended     Products     for     User3:",
recommendations)
```
```
```

This example uses collaborative filtering to suggest products by identifying users with similar preferences—a foundational method in personalization engines.

Beyond retail, AI-driven customization extends into manufacturing sectors like automotive and electronics. BMW applies AI to adjust vehicle interiors dynamically based on driver habits collected via sensors: seat positions adapt to recognized profiles while infotainment settings change according to time of day or route preferences. These automated adjustments enhance the user experience seamlessly without manual input.

AI also enables dynamic pricing tailored to personalized bundles or service packages. Industries such as airlines and hospitality have long used revenue management systems that adjust prices based on demand forecasts. Modern AI refines these models further by incorporating individual willingness-to-pay signals derived from purchase histories and online behaviors.

However, delivering effective personalization at scale requires overcoming common challenges like data silos embedded in legacy IT systems. Integrating disparate sources—CRM databases, IoT telemetry streams, marketing platforms—is essential to build comprehensive customer profiles that fuel AI algorithms in near real-time.

Privacy considerations add another important dimension. Transparent communication about data use and strict adherence to regulations such as GDPR are vital for maintaining customer trust while leveraging personal information responsibly.

Software platforms can simplify personalization workflows

significantly. Tools like Salesforce Einstein offer marketers intuitive drag-and-drop interfaces for building AI-powered customer journeys that deliver personalized content based on behavioral triggers—no heavy coding needed. Similarly, Shopify integrates machine learning apps that automate product recommendations directly within e-commerce storefronts.

A practical process for deploying AI-driven personalization might include:

1. Mapping Customer Touchpoints: Identify all channels—websites, apps, physical stores—where data can be collected.

2. Centralizing Data Storage: Use cloud-based data lakes or warehouses to securely aggregate information.

3. Applying Segmentation Algorithms: Employ clustering methods (e.g., k-means or hierarchical) to group customers by behavior or preference.

4. Developing Recommendation Engines: Implement collaborative or content-based filtering tuned for your industry.

5. Testing Personalization Impact: Run A/B tests comparing personalized offers against control groups to measure conversion improvements.

6. Continuous Iteration: Refine models regularly as consumer behaviors evolve over time.

Netflix offers a striking example of personalization's power: its early recommendation algorithm reportedly saved the company)1 billion annually by reducing churn through improved content suggestions—a clear demonstration of how effective customization drives both loyalty and financial performance.

AI-powered customization transforms products from static commodities into adaptive solutions aligned closely with consumer desires and operational realities alike. The true business advantage lies not just in meeting current expectations but anticipating them—and doing so efficiently at scale.

To borrow Jeff Bezos's metaphor: "We see our customers as invited guests to a party, and we are the hosts." With AI-driven personalization, each guest feels uniquely welcomed every time they engage—a critical factor for success in today's experience-driven economy.

Predictive maintenance and quality assurance

Predictive maintenance is among the most transformative applications of AI in product lifecycle management. Unlike traditional scheduled maintenance, which can result in unnecessary downtime or unexpected failures, predictive maintenance uses real-time data and machine learning to anticipate equipment issues before they arise. This proactive strategy not only reduces costs but also improves operational efficiency and enhances product reliability.

Imagine a manufacturing plant outfitted with IoT sensors that monitor vibration, temperature, and pressure on critical machinery. These sensors continuously feed data to an AI model trained to detect subtle anomalies signaling potential faults. Take this example, an increase in vibration frequency beyond a certain threshold might indicate bearing wear in motors. Instead of waiting for a breakdown that could halt the entire production line, the system issues maintenance alerts, enabling technicians to intervene precisely when needed.

A practical way to implement this approach is through time-series anomaly detection using an LSTM (Long Short-Term Memory) neural network, which excels at modeling sequential sensor data. The following simplified example demonstrates how historical sensor readings can train an LSTM model to predict normal operational values and flag deviations:

```python
``` python
import numpy as np

import pandas as pd

from tensorflow.keras.models import Sequential

from tensorflow.keras.layers import LSTM, Dense

from sklearn.preprocessing import MinMaxScaler


\#\# Load sample sensor data: 'timestamp' and 'vibration_level'

data = pd.read_csv('sensor_data.csv', parse_dates=['timestamp'])

values = data['vibration_level'].values.reshape(-1,1)


\#\# Scale data between 0 and 1 for neural network stability

scaler = MinMaxScaler(feature_range=(0,1))

scaled_values = scaler.fit_transform(values)


\#\# Prepare sequences for supervised learning

def create_sequences(data, seq_length=50):

X, y = [], []

for i in range(len(data)-seq_length):

X.append(data[i:i+seq_length])

y.append(data[i+seq_length])
```
```

```
return np.array(X), np.array(y)

X, y = create_sequences(scaled_values)

\#\# Split into train/test sets (80/20 split)
split = int(len(X)*0.8)
X_train, X_test = X[:split], X[split:]
y_train, y_test = y[:split], y[split:]

\#\# Build LSTM model
model = Sequential()
model.add(LSTM(50,                        activation='relu',
input_shape=(X_train.shape[1], 1)))
model.add(Dense(1))
model.compile(optimizer='adam', loss='mse')

\#\# Train model
model.fit(X_train, y_train, epochs=20, batch_size=32)

\#\# Predict on test set
y_pred = model.predict(X_test)

\#\# Calculate error and flag anomalies where error exceeds
threshold
errors = np.abs(y_test - y_pred.flatten())
```

```
threshold = np.mean(errors) + 3*np.std(errors)

anomalies = errors > threshold


print(f"Detected np.sum(anomalies) anomalies indicating potential failures.")
```
` ` `

This code illustrates the core workflow: ingesting time-series sensor data; training a predictive model; and detecting abnormal behavior that signals impending maintenance needs. While this example focuses on a single sensor type and a straightforward model, real-world systems typically incorporate multiple sensors and more sophisticated algorithms tailored to specific equipment.

Alongside predictive maintenance, quality assurance benefits significantly from AI-driven inspection and defect detection throughout production. Computer vision algorithms analyze images or video streams from assembly lines to identify imperfections that may be invisible or too subtle for human inspectors. For example, convolutional neural networks (CNNs) can rapidly classify surface defects on automotive parts or detect inconsistencies in semiconductor wafers with high accuracy.

Tesla's Gigafactory offers a compelling example: AI-powered cameras monitor battery cell assembly in real time. By combining high-resolution imaging with deep learning models trained on thousands of defect examples, the system achieves near-perfect detection rates—dramatically reducing faulty batteries reaching customers. This not only enhances safety but also cuts costly recalls.

For companies lacking extensive AI expertise or infrastructure, commercial platforms like Landing AI or Cognex provide plug-and-play visual inspection solutions.

These tools can be quickly trained on custom datasets and offer dashboards that track defect rates over time while enabling engineers to investigate specific failure modes without manual image analysis.

Beyond identifying defects after production starts, predictive quality assurance leverages process data to anticipate deviations before they occur. By analyzing parameters such as temperature fluctuations during molding or torque variations during assembly using machine learning models like random forests or gradient boosting machines, manufacturers receive early warnings that allow them to adjust processes proactively.

The following example shows how feature importance from a gradient boosting classifier can reveal which process variables most influence product quality:

```python
import pandas as pd

from sklearn.ensemble import GradientBoostingClassifier

from sklearn.model_selection import train_test_split


\#\# Load dataset: features are sensor/process parameters; target is pass/fail quality label

df = pd.read_csv('process_quality.csv')

X = df.drop('quality_label', axis=1)

y = df['quality_label']


X_train, X_test, y_train, y_test = train_test_split(X,y,test_size=0.2)
```

```
model = GradientBoostingClassifier()
model.fit(X_train,y_train)

importances = model.feature_importances_
features = X.columns

for feature, importance in zip(features, importances):
print(f"feature: importance:.3f")
` ` `
```

Interpreting these results helps engineers identify which process controls require tightening or which sensors need recalibration—shifting quality control from reactive inspection toward proactive optimization.

The financial benefits are significant: according to McKinsey research, predictive maintenance can reduce unplanned downtime by up to 50%, while automated quality inspection may cut defect rates by over 90%, substantially lowering waste and warranty claims.

However, challenges remain. Noisy sensor data can trigger false alarms, and integrating AI systems with legacy manufacturing execution systems (MES) often demands careful planning. Building robust data pipelines and establishing regular retraining cycles are essential to maintain model accuracy as conditions evolve—a detail sometimes overlooked in deployment.

AI's impact also reshapes workforce roles. Technicians increasingly become data interpreters who blend domain expertise with analytical insight; quality inspectors shift focus from manual checks toward supervising AI systems and investigating flagged anomalies.

By combining predictive maintenance with advanced quality assurance, manufacturers create a virtuous cycle: well-maintained machines produce fewer defects; fewer defects mean less rework and recall costs; both factors contribute directly to improved profitability while enhancing customer satisfaction through consistent product excellence.

At its core, AI transforms reactive upkeep and sporadic inspections into continuous intelligence-driven operations —a competitive advantage no modern manufacturer can afford to overlook.

Competitive analysis using AI

Competitive analysis powered by AI has transformed from a manual, labor-intensive task into a dynamic, data-driven process that allows businesses to anticipate market shifts and refine strategies rapidly. Traditional competitor research typically relied on periodic reports and static data snapshots, which quickly became outdated. In contrast, AI continuously scans diverse data sources—ranging from social media chatter to financial filings—and extracts actionable insights in real time, injecting much-needed agility into competitive intelligence.

Take the example of a mid-sized retailer striving to keep pace with evolving consumer preferences and emerging competitors. Instead of relying on monthly market reports, an AI-driven system can monitor competitor pricing, promotional campaigns, product launches, and customer sentiment on a daily basis. Natural language processing (NLP) algorithms sift through thousands of online reviews and social media posts, uncovering subtle shifts in brand perception that might otherwise go unnoticed. This continuous stream of intelligence enables the retailer to adjust marketing tactics promptly or fine-tune inventory before a competitor's new product affects demand.

Central to this approach is the automation of data gathering through techniques like web scraping and API integration. Python, for example, offers powerful libraries such as BeautifulSoup for parsing HTML content and Selenium for automating browser interactions when APIs are unavailable. The following code snippet demonstrates how to scrape competitor pricing data from an e-commerce site:

```python
import requests

from bs4 import BeautifulSoup


url    =    'https://www.example-competitor.com/category/
electronics'

headers = 'User-Agent': 'Mozilla/5.0'


response = requests.get(url, headers=headers)

soup = BeautifulSoup(response.text, 'html.parser')


products = soup.find_all('div', class_='product-item')

for product in products:

name = product.find('h2', class_='product-title').text.strip()

price = product.find('span', class_='price').text.strip()

print(f"Product: name | Price: price")
```

This code accesses a competitor's webpage, extracts product names and prices, and outputs them for further analysis. While it's important to consider the legal and ethical aspects of web scraping, such tools greatly reduce manual effort in maintaining up-to-date competitor databases.

Beyond collecting raw data, machine learning models can classify competitors along multiple dimensions—such as market share trends, innovation pace, and customer loyalty —using clustering or classification algorithms. Take this example, k-means clustering can segment competitors into groups that share similar attributes like pricing strategy or geographic focus:

```python
import pandas as pd

from sklearn.cluster import KMeans


\#\# Sample dataset: columns include market_share_pct, avg_price_usd, ad_spend_usd

df = pd.read_csv('competitor_metrics.csv')

features = df[['market_share_pct', 'avg_price_usd', 'ad_spend_usd']]


kmeans = KMeans(n_clusters=3, random_state=42)

df['cluster'] = kmeans.fit_predict(features)


print(df[['competitor_name', 'cluster']])
```

Interpreting these clusters helps decision-makers distinguish direct rivals from peripheral players or emerging disruptors that warrant strategic attention.

Sentiment analysis further enriches competitive insights by quantifying public perception across social media and review platforms. Pretrained NLP models like BERT or lighter approaches such as VADER sentiment scoring enable the measurement of consumer emotions toward brands:

```python
from vaderSentiment.vaderSentiment import SentimentIntensityAnalyzer

analyzer = SentimentIntensityAnalyzer()
reviews = [
Great product quality but slow delivery.",
Terrible customer support!",
Excellent value for money.
]

for review in reviews:
score = analyzer.polarity_scores(review)
print(f"Review: review: score")
```

Tracking these sentiment scores over time reveals reputation trends that influence market positioning.

One practical challenge lies in integrating various data types —numeric financial metrics, textual feedback, image-based ads—into unified dashboards that provide a holistic view of the competitive landscape. Modern business intelligence platforms like Tableau or Power BI facilitate embedding AI models and custom scripts to automate this synthesis. For example, incorporating Python scripts within Power BI allows real-time updates of competitor segmentation alongside traditional key performance indicators.

Companies that harness AI for competitive analysis gain early-warning capabilities against disruptive entrants and shifting consumer loyalties. Walmart, for instance, reportedly uses AI-powered analytics to dynamically adjust pricing based on competitor moves and local demand signals across thousands of stores simultaneously—a feat impossible without automation at scale.

Nevertheless, such sophistication requires rigorous model validation and ongoing tuning since market conditions evolve rapidly. Without careful attention to data quality—addressing incomplete scraping results or biased sentiment samples—insights can become misleading. Cross-validation and data augmentation techniques are essential safeguards.

Beyond analytics, AI-driven scenario simulations empower strategists to explore "what-if" questions: How would launching a new product line affect competitor responses? What if a rival slashes prices by 10%? Combining agent-based modeling with reinforcement learning makes it possible to simulate competitor behaviors and adaptive strategies under uncertainty.

AI transforms competitive analysis from a static snapshot into an ongoing conversation with the market ecosystem. This shift enables businesses to anticipate moves rather than react belatedly. As competitive landscapes grow increasingly complex and fast-paced, organizations equipped with intelligent automation gain not only insights but strategic foresight—a decisive advantage in sustaining long-term growth.

Cross-industry innovation case examples

Cross-industry innovation driven by AI is transforming how companies design products, services, and business models. Traditional boundaries between sectors are fading as AI-powered insights and automation tools facilitate knowledge sharing and collaborative breakthroughs across diverse fields.

Take the automotive industry's use of AI-driven image recognition and sensor fusion techniques originally developed for healthcare diagnostics. Self-driving cars depend on computer vision algorithms to interpret their surroundings—algorithms that trace their roots to medical imaging technologies used to detect tumors or fractures. This exchange accelerates innovation cycles: automakers apply advances from radiology to enhance object detection under challenging conditions like fog or nighttime driving. Conversely, healthcare benefits from autonomous vehicle navigation research, which informs the optimization of robotic surgery systems where precise motion control is critical.

In retail and agriculture, AI-powered demand forecasting models highlight a similar shared utility despite different applications. Retailers predict product demand fluctuations influenced by seasonality, promotions, and social trends using machine learning. Meanwhile, farmers employ comparable time-series forecasting techniques combined with satellite imagery to anticipate crop yields and adjust planting strategies. Though each domain adapts algorithms like Long Short-Term Memory (LSTM) networks to its unique data sets, both rely on core principles of pattern recognition and temporal correlation.

Financial services exemplify another wave of cross-industry innovation through natural language processing (NLP). Chatbots developed initially for telecom customer support have been repurposed by banks to handle routine inquiries, fraud alerts, and personalized financial advice at scale. The ability to understand nuanced human language and generate context-aware responses improves continuously through shared datasets and transfer learning. For example, an NLP model fine-tuned on healthcare call transcripts can better comprehend medical jargon when applied to insurance claims processing—demonstrating how cross-sector collaboration creates cyclical benefits.

Manufacturing also draws from aerospace engineering innovations in predictive maintenance powered by AI. Jet engines are equipped with thousands of sensors generating telemetry data; analyzing this information enables early fault detection to prevent catastrophic failures. Manufacturing plants apply the same anomaly detection algorithms to monitor industrial machinery vibrations or temperature fluctuations, scheduling maintenance proactively rather than reacting to breakdowns. This approach reduces downtime and extends equipment lifespan—clear advantages derived from aerospace advancements.

AI-driven personalization techniques pioneered by entertainment streaming platforms have similarly influenced marketing strategies in education technology (EdTech). Recommender systems that suggest movies or music based on user behavior inspire adaptive learning platforms that dynamically tailor content delivery according to student performance and engagement metrics. Python libraries such as Surprise or TensorFlow Recommenders offer reusable frameworks for building these systems:

```python
from surprise import Dataset, Reader, KNNBasic

\#\# Sample EdTech user-course rating data
data = Dataset.load_from_df(df[['user_id', 'course_id', 'rating']], Reader(rating_scale=(1, 5)))

trainset = data.build_full_trainset()
algo = KNNBasic()
```

```
algo.fit(trainset)

\#\# Predict rating for user 42 on course 101
pred = algo.predict(uid=42, iid=101)
print(f"Predicted rating: pred.est:.2f")
```
```

This example illustrates how a simple collaborative filtering model can predict learner preferences much like Netflix forecasts viewer choices—a technique directly borrowed from entertainment analytics.

Healthcare providers have integrated virtual assistants originally created for customer service into patient engagement platforms. These assistants help triage symptoms, schedule appointments, and provide medication reminders via voice or chat interfaces powered by AI frameworks such as Rasa or Dialogflow. The adaptability of these tools across industries highlights the economic value of modular AI components that can be rapidly customized.

AI's impact on environmental sustainability further showcases cross-industry innovation's potential. Energy companies use machine learning models trained on climate simulation data to optimize power grid management and forecast renewable resource availability like wind or solar output. Urban planners leverage similar geospatial analytics combined with transportation sector datasets to design smarter cities aimed at reducing congestion and emissions.

Successfully implementing such cross-industry solutions requires flexible technical architectures that embrace interoperability standards like RESTful APIs alongside containerization tools such as Docker or Kubernetes. These
```

enable diverse teams to integrate AI modules efficiently without reinventing the wheel each time. For example:

- A logistics company might incorporate a weather prediction API developed by agricultural researchers into its route optimization software.
- A financial firm could integrate sentiment analysis services trained on social media data into risk assessment workflows.

This modularity speeds deployment while ensuring scalability across various operational contexts.

Nevertheless, not all cross-industry adoptions proceed smoothly. Differences in data quality, regulatory environments, and domain-specific expertise often necessitate tailored adaptations rather than direct transfers of AI solutions. Privacy restrictions around patient data in healthcare limit how certain innovations translate into sectors without similar protections—and vice versa.

organizations that embrace cross-industry AI innovation gain competitive advantages by leveraging breakthroughs outside their immediate domain instead of starting from scratch—a strategy renowned strategist Rita McGrath calls "disruptive adjacency." This mindset expands problem-solving toolkits while fostering cultures that encourage experimentation beyond traditional silos.

Real-world examples abound: Siemens applies smart grid technologies inspired by telecommunications infrastructure; Amazon's logistics optimization draws heavily from manufacturing process automation; even fashion brands use predictive analytics techniques refined in finance for inventory planning.

By connecting disparate sectors through AI-driven automation, businesses unlock new efficiencies and discover novel revenue streams—transforming seemingly unrelated domains into fertile grounds for growth.

CHAPTER 14: LEGAL AND ETHICAL IMPLICATIONS OF AI AUTOMATION

Data privacy and security

Data privacy and security are fundamental to the success of any AI automation initiative in business. Without strong protections, the efficiency gains promised by AI can quickly unravel amid data breaches, leaks, or costly regulatory penalties. Organizations that handle sensitive information—such as customer records, financial data, and proprietary algorithms—must integrate stringent controls at every stage of AI deployment to safeguard their assets and maintain trust.

Take, for example, a global retail chain that implemented AI-powered recommendation engines to personalize marketing efforts. This system analyzed vast amounts of customer purchase histories and behavioral data to predict preferences and tailor offers. However, lacking encrypted storage and anonymization protocols, a security breach exposed millions of customer profiles. The fallout included significant reputational damage and expensive compliance investigations under GDPR. This case highlights how automation's value collapses when data security is treated as an afterthought rather than a core design principle.

Technically, protecting data begins with establishing secure ingestion pipelines. Data should be verified for integrity and processed within isolated environments to prevent contamination or unauthorized access. End-to-end encryption—both at rest and in transit—is essential. Take this example, when streaming real-time sales figures from point-of-sale systems to cloud-based AI analytics platforms, employing TLS (Transport Layer Security) protocols helps block interception by malicious actors.

Role-based access control (RBAC) is another practical measure that limits individuals' and systems' data access strictly to what they need for their functions. Cloud tools like AWS Identity and Access Management (IAM) enable granular permission management supporting AI workloads. Layering in multi-factor authentication (MFA) further protects against credential compromise—a frequent attack vector.

Legal requirements also shape how organizations collect and process personal data for AI models. Laws such as the California Consumer Privacy Act (CCPA) and Europe's GDPR impose strict rules around obtaining user consent, honoring opt-outs, and maintaining transparent audit trails documenting data usage. To comply, businesses must comprehensively map data flows to pinpoint where personal information enters AI pipelines. Automated data lineage tools play a vital role here by tracking data movements in real time and alerting teams to unauthorized transfers.

In healthcare, for example, providers using AI diagnostics must de-identify patient images and medical histories before feeding them into machine learning models to meet HIPAA standards in the U.S. Techniques like differential privacy add statistical noise to datasets, obscuring individual identities while preserving aggregate insights crucial for training.

These technical safeguards are most effective when combined with privacy-by-design principles throughout development lifecycles. Regular threat modeling exercises help teams anticipate potential attacks on AI environments —from adversarial input manipulation to insider threats seeking confidential data extraction.

Blockchain technologies also offer promising solutions by creating immutable audit trails for sensitive transactions involving AI-generated decisions or automated contract executions (smart contracts). Though integrating blockchain can increase complexity and costs, it enhances transparency—an increasingly important factor amid tightening global regulations.

Securing the models themselves is equally important. Attacks like model inversion can reconstruct sensitive training data from exposed outputs. Defenses such as federated learning help mitigate this risk by training models locally on devices rather than aggregating raw data centrally, sharing only model updates instead.

Beyond technical controls, organizational policies must align closely with security objectives. Clear incident response guidelines ensure rapid containment when breaches occur, limiting damage through predefined internal and external communication channels.

Third-party cybersecurity audits validate compliance with industry standards such as ISO 27001 or SOC 2 Type II certifications, providing stakeholders with assurance about maturity levels in managing sensitive AI operations.

The constantly evolving cyber threat landscape demands ongoing vigilance; yesterday's defenses may not suffice tomorrow against new attack vectors targeting emerging components like edge devices or IoT sensors feeding automation workflows.

securing data privacy within AI-driven automation is not a one-time task but an enduring commitment woven into enterprise culture. As cybersecurity expert Bruce Schneier famously said: "Security is not a product but a process." Organizations embracing this mindset will better protect their competitive advantage while building trust with customers increasingly concerned about how their information powers artificial intelligence advancements.

Success depends on harmonizing technological safeguards with legal frameworks and human oversight; neglecting any one element exposes businesses to risks that could negate the transformative benefits automation offers.

Intellectual property issues

Intellectual property (IP) challenges have surged to the forefront as AI-powered automation transforms business innovation. Unlike traditional inventions, AI-generated outputs blur the lines of authorship and ownership, complicating how companies protect their proprietary advancements. For businesses that rely heavily on AI—whether for product design, content creation, or algorithm development—grasping the nuances of IP law is essential to maintaining a competitive edge.

Take, for example, a software firm that uses generative AI to produce novel code snippets or design assets. A critical question emerges: who owns these creations—the company deploying the AI, the developers who built the AI model, or the AI system itself? Most legal frameworks do not recognize machines as inventors or authors, so ownership typically defaults to human creators or organizations commissioning the work. However, this becomes less clear when multiple parties contribute data, models, and expertise collaboratively.

Patent protection presents particular challenges. Patents traditionally require clear identification of an inventor along with proof of novelty and non-obviousness. When a machine learning algorithm autonomously generates solutions without direct human input, patent offices face difficulties in granting rights. Take this example, in 2020, the U.S. Patent and Trademark Office rejected a patent application that named an AI system as the inventor—a decision upheld by courts affirming that only natural persons qualify as inventors under current law.

From a practical perspective, companies must draft contracts that clearly establish IP ownership for AI-generated outputs from the outset. Licensing agreements should spell out how models trained on proprietary datasets may be used and who retains rights over derivative works. For example, a media company outsourcing content generation via AI platforms needs assurances that all resulting assets can be assigned back to them without restrictions imposed by the technology provider.

Trade secrets add another layer of protection but also bring complexities. When AI systems learn from large volumes of confidential data, safeguarding secrecy requires strong access controls and monitoring. Consider a financial institution developing an AI-driven risk assessment tool based on sensitive client information—without rigorous data handling protocols, competitors might reverse-engineer proprietary methodologies, undermining the firm's IP value.

Open-source AI frameworks further complicate IP management. While leveraging open-source components can speed development and reduce costs, it also introduces licensing obligations that may limit commercial use or require disclosure of derivative works. Businesses must carefully audit these dependencies to avoid inadvertent violations that could lead to costly disputes or loss of trade secrets.

Copyright law raises additional questions about protection for AI-generated creative content like text, music, or artwork. Jurisdictions vary widely—for example, the U.K.'s Copyright Act allows protection for computer-generated works without a human author if sufficient human input guides creation; many others require demonstrable human originality. Given this uncertainty, companies often adopt cautious policies when monetizing such assets, relying on agreements that assign copyright interests to human operators overseeing or curating outputs.

Emerging legal frameworks are beginning to address these issues more directly. The European Union's proposed Artificial Intelligence Act includes obligations around transparency and accountability in automated decision-making but stops short of defining ownership rules for AI-created IP. Nonetheless, regulatory momentum suggests businesses should prepare for evolving compliance demands that may require documenting contributions from humans versus machines.

Strategically, incorporating IP considerations early in automation initiatives helps prevent conflicts that could delay deployment or lead to litigation. During an AI-driven product development cycle, close collaboration between legal teams and engineers can clarify patentability prospects and data rights before significant investments are made—avoiding costly retrofits later on.

Technology solutions also support IP management within automated workflows. Blockchain platforms enable immutable timestamping of model versions and provenance tracking, creating transparent chains of custody valuable for defending ownership claims. Similarly, digital watermarking can embed identifiable markers into AI-generated content to assert copyright.

The commercial stakes are high: companies pioneering proprietary AI technologies risk losing market advantage if their inventions lack adequate protection or if weak contractual safeguards expose them to misuse. Conversely, overly aggressive IP enforcement may stifle collaboration critical to advancing complex AI ecosystems across industries.

Balancing these competing interests calls for nuanced policies tailored to sector-specific realities—for instance, pharmaceuticals operate under stringent patent regimes distinct from those governing software innovations or creative media generated by AI algorithms.

addressing intellectual property challenges in AI-powered automation requires proactive governance combining legal expertise with technical understanding. Businesses must build multidisciplinary teams capable of anticipating issues rather than reacting after infringement claims or regulatory scrutiny arise.

In this context, securing IP rights goes beyond mere compliance; it becomes a strategic enabler that unlocks value from automated innovation pipelines while minimizing risks tied to ambiguous ownership and unauthorized use. Only then can companies fully harness AI's transformative potential without relinquishing control over their most valuable intangible assets.

Regulatory compliance challenges

Regulatory compliance presents one of the most complex challenges when integrating AI-powered automation into business processes. Unlike traditional software deployments, AI systems add layers of difficulty due to their adaptive nature, reliance on vast datasets, and potential for opaque decision-making. Industries such as finance and healthcare, which operate under strict regulations regarding data handling, reporting accuracy, and auditability, often face conflicts with AI's inherent black-box tendencies.

Take the GDPR in Europe as an example. This regulation prioritizes personal data protection and user consent. AI models trained on extensive datasets must ensure full compliance with these mandates. However, because many machine learning algorithms continuously evolve based on new data inputs, maintaining a clear, auditable trail of how personal information is processed becomes challenging. Take this example, a healthcare provider using AI to support patient diagnoses had to address the need to document how each prediction aligned with patient consent and data access policies. To meet this requirement, they implemented additional logging mechanisms designed specifically to track data provenance—something that traditional software rarely necessitates.

Beyond data privacy, regulators also demand transparency in automated decision-making. The financial sector's Know Your Customer (KYC) regulations highlight this need. When an AI system flags suspicious transactions or denies services based on risk assessments, regulators require clear explanations: why the decision was made, on what grounds, and how it can be challenged. This creates a demand for interpretability frameworks that can complement black-box models. Tools like SHAP (SHapley Additive exPlanations) and LIME (Local Interpretable Model-agnostic Explanations) are commonly employed to provide such insights. While effective, integrating these tools increases development complexity and requires specialized expertise within organizations.

A practical way to manage regulatory compliance begins with early-stage risk mapping. Developing a matrix that aligns automated tasks with relevant legal frameworks— such as HIPAA for healthcare data, SOX for financial controls, or PCI DSS for payment security—helps identify potential pitfalls. Involving legal teams to regularly validate this matrix is essential as automation scales or changes. For example, during an AI-driven invoice processing project at a multinational retailer, the compliance group conducted monthly reviews of regulatory updates and collaborated closely with developers to embed real-time compliance checks within the automation pipeline.

Another key component is establishing automated audit trails. Rather than relying on manual documentation prone to errors and gaps, AI workflows should be designed to log decisions at every critical step. Timestamped records detailing model versions, input datasets, applied feature transformations, and output decisions simplify audits later on. Coupled with secure storage solutions featuring encryption and access controls, these logs create a verifiable chain of accountability.

Implementations often involve integrating governance tools like Apache Atlas or commercial platforms such as Collibra. These help catalog datasets and algorithms while tracking their lineage—an invaluable asset when responding to regulatory inquiries about model behavior or dataset composition months after deployment.

Keeping up with evolving regulations is equally important. Compliance today does not guarantee compliance tomorrow. Automated monitoring systems that periodically scan regulatory repositories or government updates via APIs can alert stakeholders to relevant changes impacting AI operations. Taking a proactive approach like this significantly reduces risk compared to reactive audits.

Addressing regulatory demands also requires balancing performance optimization with compliance constraints. Organizations might restrict certain model types due to explainability concerns or limit data usage to avoid privacy issues—even if this means sacrificing some accuracy or efficiency gains. Take this example, credit scoring algorithms governed by the Equal Credit Opportunity Act often favor simpler decision trees over complex neural networks because regulators can more easily scrutinize the former.

Global expansion adds another layer of complexity: conflicting regulations across jurisdictions require adaptable compliance strategies. Building modular AI components that can be adjusted for each region's rules is more effective than creating monolithic solutions tailored to a single market.

embedding regulatory compliance into AI automation is an ongoing operational discipline rather than a one-time hurdle. It demands collaboration between technical teams, legal experts, and business units alike. Organizations that invest in robust governance frameworks not only avoid costly penalties but also build trust with customers and regulators—turning compliance from a burdensome obligation into a strategic advantage.

To summarize the approach:

1. Catalog all applicable regulations for your industry and assign responsibility for each.

2. Map automation workflows against these regulations to identify risks.

3. Implement comprehensive logging within AI systems—capture inputs, outputs, model versions, and decision rationales.

4. Choose explainability tools suited to your models' complexity and integrate them into evaluation processes.

5. Establish regular review cycles involving both technical and legal teams.

6. Use governance platforms to manage metadata and consolidate audit trails.

7. Deploy automated alerts linked to regulatory update feeds.

8. Provide ongoing staff training focused on AI-related compliance protocols.

9. Develop fallback procedures for pausing automation when compliance issues arise.

10. Document all processes meticulously in preparation for external audits.

By following these steps thoughtfully and anticipating future changes, organizations can ensure that regulatory compliance supports—and never hinders—their AI-driven transformation efforts.

Ethical AI framework

Ethical considerations must be a foundational part of AI automation strategies, not an afterthought, especially given the risk of unintended consequences that can undermine trust or cause harm. An ethical AI framework acts as a guiding compass throughout the design, deployment, and ongoing management of AI systems in business settings. By providing clear principles and actionable guidelines, it helps balance innovation with responsibility.

Central to such frameworks is accountability. Every automated decision that impacts stakeholders—whether customers, employees, or partners—requires a clearly defined chain of responsibility. Assigning ownership of AI outcomes ensures that when problems arise, there is clarity about who assesses risks and enforces corrective measures. For example, if a retail company's AI-driven pricing tool unintentionally discriminates against certain customer groups due to biased training data, accountability protocols determine how quickly the issue is detected, who investigates its root causes, and what remediation steps follow.

Complementing accountability is transparency, which calls on businesses to openly communicate how their AI systems operate in meaningful ways. Transparency goes beyond sharing technical documentation; it involves explaining in accessible language what data is used, how decisions are made, and what limitations exist. Take this example, banks using AI to evaluate loan applications should provide applicants with clear explanations if their requests are denied. While tools that generate model interpretability reports can aid this effort, they must be paired with communication strategies tailored to non-technical audiences.

Fairness remains one of the most complex pillars to uphold. Biases embedded in training data or skewed sample populations can lead to discriminatory outcomes unless actively addressed. A common example is historical hiring data favoring certain demographics, which then biases automated candidate screening tools. To combat this, organizations deploy bias detection algorithms that flag disparities in model outputs across different groups. Additionally, diverse development teams help surface potential blind spots during design.

Privacy protection extends beyond mere compliance; it requires embedding privacy-by-design principles from the outset. Limiting data collection to what is strictly necessary and applying techniques such as differential privacy or federated learning reduce exposure risks while preserving utility. For example, a healthcare provider using AI for patient monitoring might anonymize data streams so that individual identities cannot be reconstructed even if datasets are compromised.

Robust security measures safeguard both the integrity of AI models and the confidentiality of underlying data. With adversarial attacks becoming more sophisticated—aimed at manipulating inputs or extracting sensitive information —it's vital to implement multi-layered defenses like encryption in transit and at rest, role-based access controls, and continuous security audits to protect automation pipelines from exploitation.

An ethical framework also emphasizes ongoing monitoring and evaluation rather than one-time validation before deployment. Since automated systems evolve as they process new data or adapt to changing conditions, continuous oversight is essential for detecting emerging risks or declines in fairness and accuracy over time.

Incorporating stakeholder engagement adds practical value by creating vital feedback loops that foster refinement and build trust. This might involve surveys following interactions with customer service chatbots or employee focus groups evaluating automated performance reviews.

Some organizations formalize this approach by establishing ethics committees composed of cross-functional members —legal experts, ethicists, technologists—who review automation projects at critical stages. These bodies provide structured assessments of ethical implications and recommend adjustments aligned with corporate values.

Microsoft's responsible AI governance offers a concrete example: their six principles—fairness; reliability and safety; privacy and security; inclusiveness; transparency; accountability—are brought to life through internal toolkits for bias detection and explainability alongside mandatory training programs for engineers developing AI products.

To effectively implement an ethical AI framework:

1. Define core ethical principles that reflect your organization's mission and societal expectations.

2. Develop policies outlining acceptable uses of AI within business processes.

3. Integrate fairness audits into model development cycles using quantitative metrics such as disparate impact ratio or equal opportunity difference.

4. Establish transparency protocols featuring user-facing disclosures supported by comprehensive internal documentation.

5. Apply privacy-preserving techniques tailored to your specific data context.

6. Set up continuous monitoring systems to track performance drift or emerging biases after deployment.

7. Create channels for stakeholder input with clear paths for escalating concerns.

8. Train all relevant staff on ethical standards pertinent to their roles.

9. Form interdisciplinary governance teams empowered to pause or revise projects when ethical issues arise.

10. Regularly review frameworks against evolving industry norms and regulatory requirements.

Ethics is not static; it evolves alongside technological advances and societal values. Organizations investing time now in structured frameworks position themselves not merely as compliant entities but as trusted leaders who leverage automation responsibly—a competitive advantage increasingly valued by customers and partners worldwide.

The road ahead demands vigilance against complacency; embedding ethics deeply within automation workflows transforms risk management into strategic stewardship that fosters sustainable growth in an era dominated by intelligent machines.

Bias and fairness in AI

Bias and fairness remain among the most persistent and complex challenges in AI-powered automation. Although algorithms are often presented as objective decision-makers, they inherently reflect the data they are trained on— and that data frequently carries the weight of historical inequalities and systemic prejudices. For example, an AI model developed using hiring data from a company with a history of favoring certain demographics will likely reproduce those biases unless explicitly corrected. This is not just theoretical: Amazon's widely reported abandonment of a recruitment tool in 2018 demonstrated how unchecked bias can infiltrate automated decisions with tangible, real-world consequences.

Tackling bias starts with a careful examination of training datasets. Raw data rarely arrives neutral; it often mirrors societal inequities, underrepresenting marginalized groups or encoding subtle stereotypes. Take credit scoring as an example: if past loan approvals favored urban applicants over rural ones, an AI system trained on such data could unfairly disadvantage rural customers. Addressing this requires techniques like re-sampling to balance datasets or augmenting underrepresented classes, crucial steps before any modeling begins.

However, cleaning data alone is not enough. Fairness must be integrated into both model evaluation metrics and deployment strategies. Various quantitative fairness measures have emerged to guide this process—such as disparate impact ratio, equal opportunity difference, and demographic parity—each offering a way to detect unfair treatment across defined groups. Take this example, equal opportunity difference ensures equal true positive rates among subpopulations, which is vital in areas like medical diagnosis where missing positive cases in one group can have life-threatening consequences.

Putting these fairness metrics into practice involves iterative testing during model development. Data scientists use bias detection tools that highlight performance disparities and generate reports pinpointing where models fall short. Open-source frameworks like IBM's AI Fairness 360 and Microsoft's Fairlearn enable these audits to be integrated programmatically into existing workflows, reducing reliance on intuition alone.

Beyond numerical analysis lies a deeper challenge: making ethical judgments about which definitions of fairness best align with an organization's values and regulatory landscape. Different contexts require different priorities; demographic parity might be suitable in hiring to promote proportional representation but less appropriate in credit scoring, where risk profiles demand a more nuanced approach. These decisions call for collaboration among technical teams, legal advisors, and diversity experts to avoid simplistic "one-size-fits-all" solutions.

The composition of AI development teams also significantly affects fairness outcomes. Homogeneous groups may unintentionally overlook biases due to shared blind spots, while diverse teams bring varied perspectives that help anticipate unintended consequences or edge cases impacting underrepresented users. Google's "AI Principles" highlight inclusivity as a cornerstone of responsible innovation, underscoring how organizational culture shapes the technology created.

Fairness enforcement must continue beyond deployment because models evolve over time as new data streams in— a phenomenon known as concept drift—that can introduce new biases previously unnoticed. Continuous auditing frameworks establish thresholds for acceptable variance and trigger reviews when disparities emerge. For example, a financial institution might monitor loan approval rates by ethnicity quarterly to detect shifts caused by changes in applicant pools or economic conditions.

Sometimes technical solutions need to be complemented by human oversight mechanisms—"human-in-the-loop" processes—to address situations where automated decisions produce questionable outcomes requiring nuanced judgment. In customer service chatbots handling sensitive complaints, escalation pathways ensure problematic interactions reach trained personnel instead of relying solely on rigid algorithms lacking empathy.

Real-world examples illustrate proactive bias management:

- A European bank implemented an AI-driven credit scoring system with built-in demographic analysis modules that identified disproportionate declines among minority applicants early on; adjustments were then made to both training data and decision thresholds.

- Mayo Clinic researchers incorporated fairness constraints targeting reduced false negatives across gender groups when developing an AI tool for detecting heart disease.

- Uber's self-driving division introduced diverse scenario simulations—including unusual pedestrian behaviors from various cultures during training phases—to prevent culturally biased safety gaps.

Organizations seeking to minimize bias can take practical steps:

1. Conduct comprehensive audits of datasets focusing on representation balance and historical context.

2. Choose fairness metrics relevant to their specific use cases, involving cross-disciplinary

stakeholders.

3. Embed bias detection tools within model pipelines for automated, ongoing evaluation.

4. Build diverse teams by actively recruiting varied expertise.

5. Establish review boards or ethics committees empowered to halt deployments if unacceptable bias is detected.

6. Train employees at all levels to recognize signs of bias and report concerns.

7. Design systems that allow human override in high-stakes decisions.

8. Maintain transparent communication with customers about algorithmic fairness efforts and limitations.

ensuring fairness is not a one-time checkbox but an ongoing commitment requiring technical rigor paired with organizational accountability and cultural sensitivity. This balance is essential for maintaining trust among customers and regulators while unlocking AI automation's full potential without causing unintended harm or exclusion.

As Fei-Fei Li aptly noted, "The future of AI depends not just on what it can do technically but on who it serves." Embedding fairness throughout the development lifecycle ensures automated systems uplift all stakeholders equitably rather than perpetuate existing divides hidden behind mathematical complexity. The challenge is formidable—but so is the reward: equitable AI automation that drives broad-based success grounded in trustworthiness and social responsibility alike.

Transparency and explainability

Transparency and explainability are essential for building

trust and accountability in AI-powered automation. While AI systems excel at processing vast amounts of data and identifying complex patterns beyond human capability, their inherent complexity often obscures how specific decisions or recommendations are made. This "black box" nature raises significant concerns: without clear insight into a model's reasoning, organizations risk deploying solutions that may unintentionally harm stakeholders or violate compliance standards.

Take, for example, a loan approval algorithm denying credit to an applicant without providing a clear rationale. Both customers and regulators expect explanations that justify such automated outcomes. Transparency involves revealing not only the inputs and outputs but also the underlying logic and assumptions driving the AI system's decisions. Explainability goes a step further by presenting this information in an accessible manner, enabling non-technical audiences to understand, question, and make informed decisions based on the AI's behavior.

Achieving transparency requires rigorous documentation throughout the AI lifecycle. This includes tracking data provenance, criteria for feature selection, model parameters, and training procedures. Maintaining a detailed audit trail allows stakeholders to trace why certain variables influenced outcomes more heavily than others. Practical tools like model cards offer standardized templates summarizing these aspects concisely, facilitating clear communication both within organizations and to external parties.

On the technical side, explainable AI (XAI) methods help translate complex model behaviors into human-understandable terms. Techniques such as SHAP (SHapley Additive exPlanations) assign quantitative values to features by estimating each input's contribution to individual predictions. Take this example, in a customer churn prediction model, SHAP can highlight factors like recent service outages or billing disputes that disproportionately increase risk scores for certain users. Visual aids like bar charts or heatmaps further bridge the gap between raw data processing and actionable insights.

Another approach involves surrogate models—simpler algorithms trained to approximate the original model's behavior within specific contexts. For example, if a neural network forecasts inventory demand but offers little interpretability, a decision tree built on its outputs can provide clearer "if-then" rules for supply chain managers assessing stock replenishment. Although surrogate models may sacrifice some precision, they enhance understanding where transparency matters more than exactness.

Explainability is also gaining prominence in regulatory frameworks. The European Union's General Data Protection Regulation (GDPR), for instance, grants individuals the right to meaningful explanations of automated decisions affecting them. Failure to comply risks legal penalties and reputational damage, making explainability a critical component embedded from system design rather than an afterthought.

Balancing transparency with proprietary concerns presents additional challenges. Organizations often protect their algorithms as trade secrets; revealing too much detail could undermine competitive advantage or expose vulnerabilities exploitable by malicious actors—such as fraudsters adapting tactics once detection logic is known. Techniques like differential privacy and federated learning offer ways to limit data exposure while preserving interpretability benefits.

Transparency also requires cultural change within organizations. Encouraging openness about AI limitations —rather than overstating capabilities—sets realistic expectations among users and leadership alike. When employees understand why automation produces certain results and recognize potential failure points, they are better equipped to complement technology with human judgment instead of relying on it unquestioningly.

Several practical steps can enhance explainability:

1. Choosing inherently interpretable models when possible (e.g., linear regression or rule-based classifiers).

2. Integrating XAI frameworks early in model development.

3. Creating user-centric explanation dashboards tailored to diverse roles—from data scientists examining algorithm mechanics to frontline staff needing quick summaries.

4. Conducting regular audits to ensure explanations remain valid as models retrain on new data.

5. Training teams in communication techniques that demystify AI jargon without sacrificing accuracy.

6. Establishing feedback loops allowing end-users to flag confusing or unsatisfactory explanations for continuous improvement.

Consider Amazon's Alexa voice assistant: its developers regularly analyze how responses are generated by natural language processing modules and provide confidence scores indicating reliability levels to engineers refining interaction quality over time.

When organizations combine transparency with fairness efforts, they build durable trust foundations essential not only for regulatory compliance but also for long-term success with AI automation initiatives that impact people's daily lives.

ensuring transparency is less about fully unraveling every line of code—which becomes impractical with deep learning architectures—and more about crafting understandable narratives around AI behavior that empower users and stakeholders to engage critically rather than passively accept outputs.

As Cynthia Rudin, an expert in interpretable machine learning, often reminds us: "In high-stakes decisions, interpretable models should be used whenever possible instead of black-box models." Her insight underscores that clarity is not merely desirable but sometimes indispensable depending on context.

In this way, transparency combined with explainability transforms opaque automated processes into collaborative tools that support nuanced human decision-making rather than replacing it blindly—aligning technological innovation with ethical responsibility throughout business operations employing AI automation solutions.

Responsible AI deployment practices

Responsible AI deployment practices are fundamental to sustainable and ethical automation in business environments. Once transparency and explainability are established, organizations naturally turn their attention to implementing AI systems in ways that uphold integrity, fairness, and stakeholder trust. This means embedding responsibility throughout every phase—from design and development to deployment and ongoing management.

Take, for example, AI models used in credit scoring or hiring decisions. Without stringent controls, these systems can unintentionally perpetuate biases present in historical data or amplify discriminatory effects. Addressing this requires rigorous bias detection and mitigation strategies. Before launching a recruitment automation tool, developers should perform fairness audits comparing outcomes across demographic groups. Practical resources like IBM's AI Fairness 360 offer libraries to measure metrics such as disparate impact and equal opportunity difference, enabling objective assessments.

Responsibility extends beyond fairness to encompass data governance, particularly given the sensitive nature of personal information processed by many AI applications. Organizations must adhere to strict data minimization principles—collecting only what is necessary—and comply with regulations such as GDPR and CCPA. Techniques like anonymization and pseudonymization help protect privacy while still allowing meaningful analysis. Take this example, a healthcare provider deploying AI diagnostic tools might separate patient identifiers from medical data, safeguarding confidentiality without compromising model performance.

Robust validation protocols are also essential for responsible deployment. Testing models on diverse datasets helps prevent overfitting and reduces the risk of failure when scaling to real-world conditions. A financial institution implementing fraud detection algorithms might simulate seasonal transaction patterns to evaluate system resilience under varying scenarios. Importantly, monitoring continues after launch: continuous evaluation ensures that retrained models or those incorporating new data maintain performance standards. Automated alerts can flag issues such as performance degradation or bias drift, enabling timely human intervention.

Stakeholder involvement throughout the AI lifecycle is another key component. Cross-functional collaboration among data scientists, legal experts, ethicists, and end-users brings diverse perspectives that help identify potential blind spots. For example, engaging frontline customer service representatives during chatbot development can uncover practical usability challenges or ethical concerns that technical teams might overlook. Documenting decision-making processes and underlying assumptions enhances accountability—a practice often formalized within model risk management frameworks aligned with industry standards like ISO/IEC 38507 on IT governance.

Clear communication plays a vital role both internally and externally. Transparent documentation detailing system capabilities, limitations, and intended use cases empowers users to engage critically rather than blindly accept automated outcomes. Take this example, an insurance company deploying an AI claims-processing tool should provide accessible explanations about how evaluations are made and offer customers avenues to contest decisions if necessary. Employee training sessions further support this by helping staff interpret model outputs effectively and maintain a complementary role alongside technology.

Security considerations are tightly integrated into responsible AI deployment strategies as well. Protecting systems against adversarial attacks—where malicious actors manipulate inputs to deceive models—is increasingly important. Measures such as input validation, anomaly detection layers, and secure update mechanisms reduce vulnerabilities. A retail firm using AI-driven inventory forecasting must guard against manipulation that could generate false demand signals and disrupt supply chains.

Finally, fostering a culture of ethical reflection around AI adoption is crucial. Encouraging open dialogue about moral implications helps prevent complacency and drives innovation guided by human values rather than efficiency alone. Tim O'Reilly's insight captures this well: "Technology is neither good nor evil; it's a tool for amplifying human intent." Responsible AI deployment ensures that this intent aligns with fairness, privacy, and respect for all stakeholders involved.

Practical steps for embedding responsibility include:

1. Integrating bias testing and mitigation tools early in development

2. Establishing comprehensive data governance policies

3. Designing continuous monitoring systems with clear escalation protocols

4. Involving diverse stakeholders across functions throughout all phases

5. Providing transparent documentation tailored to varied audiences

6. Implementing robust cybersecurity measures around AI assets

7. Promoting organizational ethics training focused on AI impacts

By committing deliberately to these practices, businesses can protect their reputations while harnessing the benefits of automation—a balance that is increasingly critical amid evolving regulations and heightened societal expectations.

Responsible AI deployment is not a one-time checklist but an ongoing commitment requiring agility as technologies evolve and social norms shift—ensuring automation enhances human decision-making without compromising the ethical foundations essential for long-term success.

CHAPTER 15: MEASURING SUCCESS IN AI-POWERED AUTOMATION

Defining success metrics

S uccess in AI-powered automation depends on defining and measuring the right metrics. Without clear benchmarks, even the most advanced systems can fail to reach their full business potential. Establishing success metrics means aligning automation goals with specific, quantifiable outcomes that truly matter to the organization. For example, when automating invoice processing, key indicators might include reductions in processing time, error rates, and cost per invoice. These metrics offer concrete checkpoints rather than vague notions of "improvement."

It's important to differentiate between leading and lagging indicators when setting these metrics. Leading indicators predict future performance—such as user adoption rates or system uptime—while lagging indicators confirm results already achieved, like revenue growth linked to faster sales cycles or reduced customer churn after implementing an AI-driven CRM. A balanced mix of both ensures automation delivers value now and remains effective over time.

Consider predictive maintenance automation in manufacturing as a practical illustration. Success is often measured by reductions in equipment downtime and maintenance costs. Yet leading indicators like anomaly detection accuracy or the speed of identifying potential failures are just as crucial. Monitoring these allows teams to act proactively rather than simply recording issues after they occur.

Turning broad business objectives into actionable metrics also requires detailed data collection. Take a customer support chatbot: overall satisfaction scores provide a useful snapshot but don't tell the whole story. Examining first-contact resolution rates, average handling times for escalated inquiries, and where users drop off during conversations reveals where the bot performs well and where improvements are needed.

When multiple departments are involved—such as IT operations, finance, and customer service—defining shared success criteria helps avoid siloed assessments that may conflict. Collaborative workshops can clarify primary goals and secondary benefits across teams. Take this example:

- IT may prioritize system stability with uptime targets above 99.9%
- Finance might focus on reducing operational expenses by 20%
- Customer service could aim to increase Net Promoter Scores (NPS) by 10 points

This alignment creates a unified dashboard for tracking

progress and encourages cross-team accountability.

Once metrics are established, automated tracking integrated with existing data pipelines or business intelligence tools like Power BI or Tableau becomes essential. Dashboards that refresh with near-real-time data enable quick identification of trends—for example, triggering a weekly alert if error rates exceed a threshold allows for prompt investigation rather than delayed damage control.

To illustrate quantitatively evaluating AI-driven automation, imagine automating marketing campaign segmentation using clustering algorithms in Python. The process might involve:

1. Defining the key metric: improvement in click-through rate (CTR) over previous manual segmentation

2. Establishing a baseline CTR from historical campaign data—say 2%

3. Running the AI-driven segmentation and executing the campaign

4. Collecting post-campaign CTR data from analytics

5. Comparing new CTR against the baseline to calculate lift percentage

6. Monitoring secondary KPIs like conversion and bounce rates for a fuller picture

A simple Python snippet to calculate CTR lift could look like this:

```python
\#\# Historical manual campaign data

manual_clicks = 200

manual_impressions = 10000
```

```
\#\# Automated campaign data

auto_clicks = 300

auto_impressions = 12000


manual_ctr = manual_clicks / manual_impressions  \# 0.02 or 2%

auto_ctr = auto_clicks / auto_impressions        \# 0.025 or 2.5%


ctr_lift_percentage = ((auto_ctr - manual_ctr) / manual_ctr) * 100


print(f"CTR Lift: ctr_lift_percentage:.2f%")

\#\# Output: CTR Lift: 25.00%
```

This straightforward calculation demonstrates tangible improvement driven by AI automation.

However, no single metric tells the whole story. Measuring something inevitably shapes behavior but can also distort priorities if too narrowly focused—a concept known as Goodhart's Law ("When a measure becomes a target, it ceases to be a good measure"). Combining quantitative KPIs with qualitative feedback provides a richer understanding of success.

Periodic reassessment of success metrics is equally important as business needs evolve or AI capabilities advance. Take this example, a finance team automating expense approvals might begin by tracking time savings but later incorporate fraud detection accuracy as new threats emerge.

Benchmarking against industry standards adds another useful perspective—for example, comparing automated claims processing times in insurance or defect rates after AI inspection in electronics manufacturing helps contextualize internal performance relative to peers.

Finally, transparent communication of these success measures across all organizational levels builds trust in automation efforts and fosters a culture of continuous improvement.

Defining clear success metrics goes beyond numbers; it shapes how organizations recognize value from automation and guides decision-making that maximizes financial impact without losing sight of quality and stakeholder satisfaction over time.

Monitoring KPIs over time

Tracking KPIs continuously transforms raw data into actionable insights, enabling organizations to respond swiftly to both opportunities and challenges. Relying solely on static snapshots captured at project milestones misses the subtle performance fluctuations that can reveal emerging trends or hidden issues. Take this example, a sudden drop in an automated customer service bot's resolution rate might signal a problematic update that requires immediate rollback or patching. Without ongoing monitoring, such warning signs often go unnoticed until customer complaints surge.

Setting up automated KPI tracking systems goes beyond simply connecting metrics to dashboards. It requires careful configuration of alert thresholds, data validation rules, and contextual analytics to differentiate normal variability from real problems. Consider an AI-driven invoice processing tool: occasional minor delays are acceptable, but persistent slowdowns beyond a defined threshold should trigger alerts for investigation. Establishing these thresholds depends on understanding typical process baselines and tolerances, which evolve as the business grows and becomes more complex.

To implement continuous KPI monitoring effectively, teams often leverage Business Intelligence (BI) tools integrated with automation platforms. Solutions like Power BI, Tableau, or Looker can ingest real-time data streams from AI systems while applying trend analysis, anomaly detection, and predictive modeling. Embedding time-series analyses alongside core KPIs can reveal seasonal patterns—for example, certain automated processes slowing down during month-end closes or holiday periods—allowing teams to proactively allocate resources or adjust workflows.

Monitoring numbers is only part of the picture; interpreting them demands domain expertise and cross-functional communication. An AI fraud detection algorithm might automatically flag a rise in false positives, but deciding whether to tighten detection rules or retrain the model requires collaboration among data scientists, fraud analysts, and finance managers. Regular review sessions—whether weekly stand-ups or monthly deep dives—help maintain alignment on KPI trends and necessary actions.

Take an AI-enabled supply chain forecasting system as an example: daily forecasts continuously update using machine learning models that incorporate incoming sales data along with external factors like weather or market conditions. KPI monitoring here focuses on forecast accuracy compared against actual demand. A drop from 95% accuracy to 80% over several weeks should prompt an investigation into data quality issues or model drift rather than acceptance of declining performance.

Automating periodic health checks is another practical approach. For example, a Python script can extract KPIs from

APIs at regular intervals and calculate rolling averages or moving standard deviations to smooth out noise:

```python
import requests

import pandas as pd


\#\# Sample API endpoint returning daily KPI data as JSON

response       =       requests.get("https://api.company.com/automation_kpis")

data = response.json()


df = pd.DataFrame(data['daily_metrics'])


\#\# Calculate 7-day rolling average of error rates

df['error_rate_rolling_avg']                          = df['error_rate'].rolling(window=7).mean()


\#\# Identify days where error rate spikes above threshold

spikes = df[df['error_rate'] > 0.05]


print("Days with high error rates:")

print(spikes[['date', 'error_rate']])
```

Such automation allows teams to focus on investigating anomalies rather than manually crunching data.

Visualizing KPIs over time with line graphs, heatmaps, or sparklines further aids quick interpretation. Take this example, a heatmap highlighting daily throughput rates for automated document processing can reveal whether bottlenecks occur at specific times of day or for particular document types.

One common challenge is "alert fatigue," where excessive notifications desensitize teams and critical warnings get overlooked. To counter this, alert thresholds should be regularly reviewed and refined based on actual impact rather than theoretical limits. Combining multiple metrics into composite scores—such as merging uptime percentages with error rate trends into a single "system health" index—helps simplify monitoring without sacrificing nuance.

Effective KPI monitoring also incorporates qualitative feedback alongside quantitative data. Frontline employee insights about usability issues or unintended consequences of AI tools often precede measurable declines in system efficiency. Tracking user-reported problems through support channels provides valuable context that numbers alone may miss.

Transparency across departments benefits all stakeholders, provided role-based access controls protect data privacy and security compliance. Embedding narrative commentary or annotations within dashboards helps contextualize unexpected spikes or dips, turning raw metrics into meaningful stories that resonate with decision-makers.

continuous KPI monitoring sustains AI automation success by enabling iterative refinement rather than one-off implementation. This discipline transforms automation from a static project into a dynamic ecosystem that responds to evolving business realities—a crucial factor in achieving long-term financial returns and operational resilience.

Continuous improvement strategies

Continuous improvement is essential for sustaining AI-powered automation over the long term. Once key performance indicators (KPIs) are monitored and data begins to reveal meaningful patterns, attention naturally turns to the iterative refinement of workflows, models, and processes. Unlike traditional one-off projects, automation requires constant adaptation to evolving business conditions, emerging user needs, and technological advances. This ongoing evolution is what distinguishes successful AI initiatives from those that stagnate or become obsolete.

A practical way to foster continuous improvement is by establishing structured feedback loops. Teams should gather insights from diverse sources: automated system metrics, frontline user reports, stakeholder evaluations, and customer feedback when relevant. Take this example, a customer service chatbot might track conversation drop-offs or flag negative sentiment through natural language processing tools. Meanwhile, support agents can report recurring issues the bot struggles to handle effectively. By combining quantitative data with qualitative observations, organizations develop a more comprehensive understanding of system performance.

To manage these feedback loops efficiently, it's important to use agile tools designed for rapid response. Project management platforms like Jira or Trello, integrated with AI monitoring dashboards, enable teams to quickly identify problems and prioritize fixes. Imagine a sales forecasting AI missing seasonal fluctuations caused by unexpected market shifts; an alert system tied to ticketing software can immediately notify data scientists to retrain or fine-tune the model. Without such integration, critical issues may go unnoticed for too long.

Model retraining plays a crucial role in continuous improvement cycles. Machine learning models can degrade over time due to concept drift—the gradual shift in underlying data distributions. For example, a recommendation engine trained on last year's product catalog may underperform when new products are introduced or consumer preferences change. Regularly scheduled retraining using recent data helps counteract this decline, though it must be balanced against computational costs and potential disruption.

Version control systems tailored for AI development further support iterative refinement while maintaining governance standards. Tools like MLflow or DVC track different model versions alongside their training datasets and hyperparameters, allowing teams to revert to previous iterations if newer models perform poorly in production. This safeguards business continuity while encouraging experimentation.

Beyond technical adjustments, process improvements often arise from cross-functional collaboration within continuous improvement frameworks such as Kaizen or Six Sigma adapted for AI environments. Periodic retrospectives involving data engineers, business analysts, and end users can reveal bottlenecks not apparent through metrics alone —such as misaligned workflows or communication gaps between departments regarding automation capabilities.

A real-world example highlights these concepts: a logistics company deploying an AI-powered route optimization tool observed increasing delivery delays despite initial gains. Analysis showed that unexpected local events causing traffic congestion led to inaccurate estimated arrival times. By incorporating real-time traffic feeds alongside historical data and coordinating closely between dispatchers and analysts during retraining cycles, the company significantly improved prediction accuracy and responsiveness.

To put continuous improvement into practice effectively:

1. Establish clear review intervals—weekly for critical systems; monthly or quarterly for less volatile

processes.

2. Automate data collection pipelines to minimize manual effort.

3. Prioritize issues based on impact severity rather than sheer volume.

4. Document changes thoroughly to facilitate knowledge transfer.

5. Cultivate a culture that values experimentation and embraces change.

This approach recognizes that perfection at launch is rare but attainable through disciplined evolution of AI solutions closely aligned with business objectives.

From a financial perspective, iterative enhancement directly boosts ROI by increasing accuracy, reducing waste and errors, and enhancing both customer satisfaction and employee productivity—reasons why executives prioritize agility within AI governance frameworks today.

By embedding continuous improvement practices into automation strategies, organizations ensure their AI systems remain adaptive rather than rigid—transforming them into living assets that grow smarter alongside the enterprise instead of becoming costly relics of yesterday's technology decisions.

Benchmarking against industry standards

Benchmarking AI-powered automation against industry standards is essential for maintaining competitiveness and identifying both strengths and areas needing improvement. Without a reliable frame of reference, internal metrics can lack context, making it challenging to prioritize enhancements or justify further investment. By establishing a clear benchmarking framework, businesses can gauge their automation maturity relative to peers, enabling informed decisions grounded in real-world performance.

A practical first step is selecting benchmarks that align closely with your business objectives and operational domain. For example, a financial services firm automating fraud detection might measure detection rates, false positives, and processing speed against industry KPIs published by regulators or trade associations. Meanwhile, a retail company focusing on inventory automation could track stock turnover ratios and fulfillment accuracy compared to sector averages. These benchmarks serve as concrete indicators rooted in industry realities—not just aspirational targets.

Effective benchmarking depends on gathering standardized data from both internal and external sources. Internally, organizations can use dashboards that consolidate AI system outputs alongside traditional operational metrics. Externally, subscription services or consortiums often provide anonymized aggregate data for side-by-side comparison. Take this example, Gartner's Market Guide for Robotic Process Automation offers performance insights from multiple enterprises, helping calibrate expectations around speed and scalability.

Consider a mid-sized logistics provider employing AI for predictive demand forecasting. After initial deployment, their forecast accuracy was about 75%. When compared to an industry benchmark of 85% accuracy reported by leading competitors, they identified a clear gap warranting model refinement and improved data quality. Without this comparison, the 75% might have appeared sufficient— masking opportunities for greater efficiency.

Benchmarking also extends beyond performance metrics to include qualitative factors like governance maturity and ethical AI practices. Frameworks such as the European Commission's AI Ethics Guidelines provide standards for transparency, fairness, and accountability. Organizations adopting these criteria can assess their compliance relative to peers—a factor increasingly influencing customer trust and regulatory favor.

To create effective benchmarks:

1. Define measurement categories directly tied to business value (e.g., processing speed, error rate, customer satisfaction).

2. Identify credible data sources combining internal analytics with trusted external reports.

3. Normalize data for apples-to-apples comparisons— adjusting for scale, geography, or product lines.

4. Set realistic target ranges based on industry leaders while considering your current capabilities.

5. Regularly update benchmarks to reflect technological advances and shifting market conditions.

While quantitative targets are important, interpreting results requires understanding underlying factors such as workforce skills or legacy system constraints that influence outcomes beyond raw numbers alone.

Integrating benchmarking into continuous improvement cycles amplifies its benefits. Dashboards with dynamic benchmarking widgets enable stakeholders to track progress against peers in real time, helping prioritize resources toward automation projects with the highest relative gains rather than isolated internal successes.

For example, a healthcare provider using AI-driven patient scheduling compared appointment fill rates —a key efficiency metric—with national benchmarks from healthcare quality organizations. Identifying underperformance led them to refine scheduling algorithms and enhance patient communication via automated reminders. Over six months, fill rates improved by 12%, narrowing the gap with industry leaders while boosting patient satisfaction.

Similarly, manufacturing firms leveraging robotic process automation (RPA) monitor cycle times and defect rates through benchmarking to guide technology upgrades and operator training—improving throughput without sacrificing quality.

A common pitfall is focusing solely on raw scores without analyzing the causes behind performance differences. Take this example, an e-commerce platform might outperform competitors in delivery speed due to geographic advantages rather than superior AI optimization; misreading this could result in misguided investments.

Establishing robust benchmarking practices requires not only technical tools but also organizational commitment to transparency and honest self-assessment—a cultural challenge that yields sustained competitive advantage.

Financially, companies that actively benchmark tend to realize faster ROI on automation initiatives by identifying inefficiencies earlier and setting realistic expectations. This approach reduces costly trial-and-error often encountered when deploying AI solutions in isolation.

In summary, pragmatic next steps include:

- Developing a tailored benchmarking framework encompassing quantitative KPIs and qualitative governance standards.

- Integrating benchmarking insights into regular management reviews to maintain focus on measurable progress.

- Using external data judiciously—verifying source credibility before drawing conclusions.

- Balancing ambition with realism: setting stretch goals inspired by top performers but grounded in organizational context.

- Fostering cross-functional collaboration so insights translate into actionable improvements across technology, operations, and strategy.

By systematically benchmarking AI-powered automation against industry standards, organizations transform it from an experimental novelty into a strategic asset that drives sustained growth and operational excellence within a competitive landscape.

Feedback loops for refinement

Feedback loops are fundamental to effective AI-powered automation, turning static systems into adaptive engines that continuously learn and improve. Without a structured feedback mechanism, automation risks stagnation, missing chances for refinement and failing to adjust to changing operational conditions. Embedding cycles of data collection, analysis, and actionable insights directly into workflows enables dynamic adjustments that boost accuracy, efficiency, and relevance over time.

Take a customer service chatbot handling routine inquiries as an example. Its initial response accuracy might be around 80%, but without feedback from user interactions—such as failed queries or low satisfaction ratings—the bot cannot evolve. Introducing a feedback loop that flags problematic conversations allows developers to retrain natural language processing models on misunderstood intents or update scripted replies. This iterative process leads to higher resolution rates and an improved customer experience that scales with use.

Creating an effective feedback loop begins with identifying key metrics aligned with your automation goals. Take this example, when automating invoice processing, tracking error rates in data extraction or exceptions flagged by human reviewers provides measurable signals for adjustment. Collecting these metrics continuously through dashboards or automated reports helps stakeholders monitor performance trends instead of relying on periodic snapshots.

Next is designing the data flow architecture that supports feedback collection. This often means integrating AI tools with centralized logging systems where event data is aggregated and tagged by relevance. Consider robotic process automation (RPA) managing order fulfillment: every exception—like mismatched product codes or delayed shipments—should be captured and routed back to analysts for root cause assessment. Over time, these insights drive rule refinements or trigger machine learning retraining to reduce errors.

Automating feedback capture itself can speed up responsiveness. Embedding sentiment analysis in customer emails, for example, can automatically flag dissatisfaction levels after interactions without manual review delays. Similarly, anomaly detection algorithms monitoring operational metrics can alert teams proactively about declining automation outcomes before they escalate into major issues.

A practical illustration comes from a multinational logistics company that combined AI-driven route optimization with real-time driver feedback. Drivers reported unanticipated roadblocks or inefficiencies via a mobile app integrated with the routing system's analytics engine. This dual input enabled the AI model not only to optimize routes based on historical traffic patterns but also to adjust dynamically based on drivers' daily reports—improving delivery punctuality by nearly 15% within six months.

Feedback loops also help balance human oversight with machine autonomy—a crucial factor in high-stakes fields like healthcare or finance where blind trust in automation carries risks. Regular review sessions analyzing flagged anomalies maintain transparency and guide gradual expansion of AI decision-making as confidence grows.

From a technical standpoint, implementing these loops often involves combining multiple tools: monitoring platforms like Prometheus or Grafana for infrastructure health; business intelligence suites such as Power BI or Tableau for visualizing KPIs; and orchestration tools like Apache Airflow to automate data pipeline refreshes feeding retraining workflows. Such integrations require collaboration among data scientists, engineers, and domain experts to align technical capabilities with practical needs.

Not all feedback leads immediately to improvements; prioritization is essential when resources are limited. Using impact-versus-effort matrices helps focus refinement efforts on changes likely to yield significant returns relative to complexity. For example, adjusting an OCR model's sensitivity may substantially reduce invoice scanning errors at low development cost compared to redesigning entire workflows.

Transparency about how feedback drives changes builds trust among those affected by automation shifts—whether frontline employees adapting their processes or customers experiencing updated services. Documenting updates and sharing rationales through newsletters or internal portals reduces resistance and encourages constructive input for future cycles.

It's important to avoid common pitfalls as well. Over-relying on quantitative KPIs without qualitative context can mislead teams—for instance, optimizing response speed while overlooking customer satisfaction nuances captured only through open-ended survey comments. Combining numeric indicators with narrative feedback offers a richer foundation for informed decisions.

Embedding organizational routines around feedback loops establishes continuous improvement as a cultural norm rather than an afterthought. Scheduled retrospectives reviewing automation performance foster accountability and spark ideas for incremental innovation that cumulatively transform operations beyond initial expectations.

robust feedback mechanisms transform AI-powered automation from static deployments into living systems—responsive not only to predefined rules but also evolving business landscapes and user needs—ensuring sustained value well beyond rollout milestones.

Case studies: Measuring success

Real-world examples often provide the clearest insight into how success metrics translate into tangible business outcomes. Different organizations have applied measurement frameworks to validate and optimize their AI-powered automation initiatives, revealing key lessons along the way.

Take, for instance, a mid-sized e-commerce company that automated its order fulfillment using robotic process automation (RPA) combined with AI-driven demand forecasting. Initially, the company tracked basic KPIs like order processing time and error rates. After six months, dashboards showed a 30% reduction in processing time, but error rates stubbornly plateaued around 4%. Digging deeper, the team added customer return rates and complaint volumes to their monitoring system. This broader perspective revealed that while speed had improved, quality control bottlenecks persisted—specifically in packaging verification. In response, they integrated computer vision AI to scan packages before shipment, which reduced errors by 60%. This example highlights the importance of selecting multidimensional KPIs aligned with overall business goals rather than focusing on isolated operational metrics.

A financial services firm provides another perspective on measuring success beyond surface-level gains. They implemented an AI-based fraud detection system designed to flag suspicious transactions in real time. At first, success was measured primarily by detection rate—the percentage of fraudulent attempts identified. However, false positives created excessive workload for compliance officers and frustrated customers with unnecessary transaction holds. To address this, the team introduced precision and recall metrics, tracking not only how many frauds were detected but also how accurately flagged cases reflected true fraud versus false alarms. Iterative model tuning improved precision from 70% to 92%, cutting false positives nearly in half without sacrificing overall detection effectiveness.

Healthcare offers yet another compelling case involving AI automation measurement. A hospital system deployed natural language processing (NLP) tools to automate medical transcription and coding for billing purposes. Initial success was measured by speed alone—transcription time dropped by 50%. However, an increase in claim denials due to coding inaccuracies prompted the organization to broaden their KPIs to include accuracy alongside billing cycle duration and denial rates. They identified gaps in the AI's understanding of complex clinical terminology and retrained NLP models with specialized datasets. This targeted approach reduced denial rates by 25%, substantially improving revenue cycle efficiency.

Looking at a larger scale, a global logistics provider illustrates how integrating feedback loops supports continuous measurement and adjustment. Their AI-driven route optimization system collects granular data on delivery times, fuel consumption, driver feedback, and traffic anomalies across thousands of daily shipments worldwide. Rather than relying solely on aggregate performance summaries, their analytics platform segments data by region, vehicle type, and driver behavior patterns. This granularity enabled rapid identification of emerging issues —for example, a sudden rise in delays linked to a specific urban area led to quick route recalibrations based on historical trends and live traffic feeds. The result was improved punctuality alongside measurable fuel savings of approximately 12%, directly reducing operational costs.

These cases collectively reflect an evolving sophistication in defining what "success" means within AI automation projects—moving beyond simplistic output measurements toward holistic evaluations encompassing quality, user experience, cost-efficiency, and strategic alignment.

A practical approach to building your own measurement framework begins with identifying key performance indicators closely tied to your business objectives. Examples include:

- Accuracy Metrics: Error rates in data entry or recognition tasks (e.g., OCR accuracy for invoice processing).

- Speed Metrics: Reduction in process cycle times or increases in throughput.

- Financial Metrics: Cost savings realized or incremental revenue generated.

- User Experience: Customer satisfaction scores or employee engagement levels influenced by automation.

- Compliance Metrics: Number of regulatory exceptions flagged or audit readiness indicators.

After selecting relevant KPIs, establish baseline values through initial manual tracking or pilot tests before full automation rollout—providing benchmarks against which improvements can be measured.

Where possible, incorporate automated dashboards using tools like Power BI or Tableau that pull real-time data from your AI systems alongside traditional operational databases. Configuring alerts for KPI deviations enables prompt intervention rather than waiting for monthly reports.

For example, consider a simple Excel-based template adapted for monitoring invoice processing automation:

Metric	Baseline Value	Current Value	% Change	Target Value	Status
Invoice Processing Time (min)	15	10	-33%	<12	On Track
Data Extraction Accuracy (%)	85	92	+8%	>95	Needs Improvement
Exception Rate (%)	7	3	-57%	<2	At Risk
Human Review Workload (hrs/wk)	20	12	-40%	<10	On Track

This snapshot helps teams identify areas needing attention while celebrating progress.

Beyond quantitative data, layering qualitative feedback such as frontline employee surveys about workflow changes or customer comments related to service speed post-automation enriches insights and guides nuanced adjustments.

Establishing comprehensive success measurement practices requires collaboration across departments—from data analysts designing dashboards; operations managers interpreting trends; IT teams ensuring reliable data flows; through executive leadership aligning metrics with strategic vision.

Success stories consistently emphasize that transparency around these measures fosters trust during organizational change and builds momentum toward further innovation cycles.

Monitoring alone isn't sufficient without embedding mechanisms for continuous improvement based on findings. Schedule regular review meetings focused on KPI trends paired with actionable next steps: Are errors increasing? Does a dip in customer satisfaction coincide with recent software updates? How does employee feedback align with performance dashboards?

Strong feedback loops connect measurement results back into development roadmaps or process redesign efforts—a dynamic interplay essential for sustained value creation rather than one-off wins.

When multiple stakeholders share clear visibility into meaningful success metrics regularly—from developers fine-tuning algorithms to executives tracking ROI—the entire organization aligns around AI-powered automation's impact on business goals.

measuring success is less about fixed numbers at a point in time and more about creating living systems that respond intelligently as conditions evolve. Combining hard data with human insight produces outcomes no single approach alone could achieve effectively.

These case studies demonstrate that thoughtful metric selection coupled with rigorous monitoring transforms AI deployments from uncertain experiments into predictable growth drivers—empowering companies to make informed decisions grounded firmly in evidence rather than hope or hype.

Reporting automation achievements

Reporting automation achievements involves more than presenting numbers; it requires telling a clear, compelling story that resonates with diverse stakeholders. Raw data alone rarely captures the strategic value AI-powered automation delivers unless it is framed within the context of business goals and operational realities. Executives focus on how initiatives impact revenue, risk, or customer experience, while frontline managers look for practical insights to optimize workflows.

Take the example of a financial services firm automating invoice processing. Instead of simply reporting a 35% reduction in processing time, their report also highlighted declines in error rates, outcomes from compliance audits, and shifts in employee workload. Visual aids like before-and-after process maps alongside KPI trend charts helped make these improvements concrete and relatable. This layered approach transformed what might have been dry statistics into a vivid narrative of operational excellence.

Tailoring dashboards to specific audiences further enhances communication. A C-suite summary dashboard emphasizes high-level metrics such as cost savings, ROI, and risk mitigation, while departmental dashboards focus on detailed task metrics like exception resolution times or the ratio of automated to manual transactions. Tools like Microsoft Power BI and Tableau enable interactive reports that refresh in real time, promoting transparency and building trust throughout the organization.

Incorporating qualitative feedback alongside quantitative data adds valuable depth. Employee surveys on experiences with new automation tools or customer satisfaction scores reflecting service speed changes enrich the story behind the numbers. Take this example, in a retail case study, blending sales growth figures with frontline staff testimonials helped leadership appreciate both measurable results and human factors driving success.

Contextualizing achievements within broader strategic objectives prevents them from feeling like isolated wins. Linking automation milestones to long-term goals—such as scalability or advancing digital transformation maturity —demonstrates their ongoing relevance. For example, reducing manual data entry errors can be connected to faster customer onboarding times, highlighting how operational improvements support competitive advantage.

Common pitfalls include overloading reports with technical jargon or excessive detail that distracts from key messages. Clear, concise language combined with visual storytelling —charts, infographics, annotated screenshots—helps distill complex information effectively. Avoid dumping raw data; instead curate insights that enable informed decision-making.

Effective reporting doesn't end with distribution. Scheduling review sessions to openly discuss findings encourages dialogue and continuous improvement. These conversations align expectations across teams and allow timely adjustments if results stray from targets.

When AI automation spans multiple departments or regions, establishing standardized reporting frameworks becomes crucial. Consistent metric definitions and regular reporting cadences reduce confusion and enable internal benchmarking over time. Examples include monthly KPI scorecards, quarterly strategic impact summaries, and ad hoc deep-dives into specific projects. This layered approach ensures stakeholders receive relevant information at appropriate intervals without being overwhelmed.

Equally important is documenting lessons learned alongside successes. Transparently reporting setbacks reveals risks and informs future deployments better than glossing over challenges. This honesty builds credibility and signals a commitment to thorough evaluation rather than mere promotion.

From a technical perspective, integrating reporting pipelines directly with AI platforms improves data accuracy and timeliness. Automating extraction of performance logs or error rates minimizes manual effort and common mistakes seen in spreadsheet-based tracking.

For example, combining an RPA tool like UiPath with Power BI can streamline reporting on invoice automation results. UiPath robots export execution logs daily to a shared database, while Power BI connects live to this source to update dashboards automatically—offering near real-time visibility into throughput volumes, exception handling times, and robot utilization rates.

Choosing clear visualizations enhances understanding: bar charts for comparing before-and-after values, line graphs for trends such as error rate declines, and pie charts for breakdowns like percentages of automated tasks. Interactive filters allow users to explore data by region, process step, or user group as needed.

successful reporting transforms AI automation projects from opaque operations into transparent engines of measurable value across the organization. This transparency is vital for sustaining momentum well beyond initial implementation.

Crafting compelling reports blends solid data with storytelling finesse—when done effectively, it elevates AI initiatives from technical experiments to strategic assets valued at every level of the business hierarchy.

CHAPTER 16: OVERCOMING CHALLENGES IN AI IMPLEMENTATION

Handling data quality issues

Data quality remains one of the most persistent and challenging obstacles in AI automation projects. Even the most advanced algorithms struggle without clean, consistent, and comprehensive data, often producing unreliable or misleading results. Organizations frequently underestimate the effort required to prepare their data before feeding it into AI systems. Incomplete records, conflicting entries, and outdated information can all distort analytics and predictions.

Take, for example, a mid-sized retailer attempting to implement demand forecasting automation. Their initial forecasts missed the mark because their sales data contained duplicates, inconsistent product codes, and missing timestamps. To address this, the team undertook a meticulous data cleansing process that combined automated scripts with manual reviews. They standardized product identifiers through defined rules and filled gaps using interpolation based on historical trends. This foundation improved forecast accuracy by 25%, demonstrating that high-quality data is essential—not optional.

Effective handling of these challenges begins with a thorough audit of existing datasets. It's important to catalog all relevant sources—such as CRM systems, ERP databases, spreadsheets, and third-party feeds—and assess their reliability. Profiling tools like Python's pandas library can help identify null values, outliers, or unusual distributions through functions such as dataframe.describe() and dataframe.info(). Take this example:

```python
import pandas as pd


df = pd.read_csv('sales_data.csv')

print(df.info())

print(df.describe())

print(df.isnull().sum())
```

This initial analysis highlights where data is incomplete or anomalous. Cleaning then involves filling missing values with appropriate substitutes—mean or median for numeric fields, mode for categorical ones—removing duplicates using dataframe.drop_duplicates(), and correcting inconsistencies with mapping tables or regular expressions.

Automating validation checks within data ingestion workflows—such as ETL pipelines—helps catch errors early rather than after modeling begins. Platforms like Apache NiFi or Talend enable enforcement of schema validation rules and immediate flagging of exceptions.

Consider customer contact records used in marketing automation as a practical example. Addresses might appear in multiple formats; some use abbreviations like "St." instead of "Street," while others lack postal codes altogether. Standardizing address formats using tools like Google's Address Validation API ensures consistency before these records feed AI models targeting regional campaigns.

Yet cleaning alone isn't enough. Because data environments are dynamic, ongoing monitoring is crucial to detect new errors or shifts in format over time. Dashboards tracking metrics such as completeness rate, error frequency, and update latency provide early warning signals when intervention is needed.

Equally important is addressing biases embedded in datasets. Poor-quality data isn't just about technical errors —it can perpetuate unfair outcomes if left unchecked. For example, recruitment AI trained on historical hiring data may inherit gender or racial biases unless carefully audited and balanced using techniques like re-sampling or synthetic augmentation.

When legacy systems are involved—a common scenario— extracting data can become complicated by incompatible formats or limited access protocols. In such cases, creating custom connectors or using middleware solutions helps bridge these gaps without compromising data integrity.

A layered approach that combines automated tools with human oversight tends to be most effective. While scripts accelerate routine cleaning tasks, domain experts are essential for reviewing edge cases that algorithms might miss—a hybrid model balancing efficiency with contextual insight.

Organizations that emphasize data governance from the outset typically experience fewer issues during AI deployments. Clearly defined ownership responsibilities for data stewardship ensure ongoing accuracy and compliance —a critical factor in regulated industries like healthcare or finance where errors carry legal consequences.

In summary, tackling data quality challenges requires a disciplined process: thoroughly auditing sources; applying targeted cleaning; embedding validation into pipelines; continuously monitoring key metrics; mitigating bias risks; navigating legacy system complexities; and maintaining human oversight throughout. Without this solid foundation, AI-powered automation risks delivering flawed insights that undermine business goals rather than accelerate them.

The old adage still holds true: garbage in equals garbage out—but today it also means lost opportunity and potential reputational damage when decisions rely on faulty information streams. Thoughtful stewardship of data quality transforms raw inputs into trusted assets that power successful automation across industries and functions alike.

Managing legacy systems

Legacy systems often form both the backbone and the bottleneck for organizations pursuing AI-powered automation. These older software and hardware infrastructures weren't designed to support today's fast-paced technological advances, creating compatibility challenges that can delay or complicate integration efforts. Replacing legacy systems outright is rarely practical, given the high costs, operational risks, and concerns about maintaining data continuity.

A practical starting point is to conduct a comprehensive audit of the existing legacy environment. This involves cataloging all software applications, databases, middleware, and hardware components to understand their strengths and limitations. Take this example, a financial services firm might discover its core banking system runs on COBOL mainframes—renowned for reliability but difficult to integrate with modern platforms. This mapping process highlights where interfaces can be built or which components require modernization.

With a clear picture of the infrastructure, organizations can explore middleware or API gateways as effective bridging solutions. Middleware serves as an interpreter between legacy systems and AI tools by translating data formats and protocols into compatible forms. For example, a manufacturing company using an older ERP system might implement an API layer that exposes necessary data endpoints without altering the legacy codebase. This setup allows AI algorithms to access data for tasks like predictive maintenance without disrupting day-to-day operations.

Adopting a phased modernization strategy rather than a wholesale replacement can also ease the transition. Breaking down the legacy environment into modules and prioritizing those with the greatest automation impact helps manage risk while delivering early results. A customer service department, for example, could integrate AI-driven chatbots connected via APIs to its CRM module before extending automation into back-office finance systems. Incremental progress builds momentum and justifies further investment.

Virtualization or containerization can provide additional flexibility by encapsulating legacy applications within modern environments that enhance scalability and security. Technologies like Docker enable organizations to isolate old systems, making updates and connections to cloud-based AI services more manageable. A retail chain with distributed point-of-sale terminals might virtualize these components to centralize control and facilitate AI-powered inventory analytics across multiple locations.

Data quality often poses challenges when integrating

legacy systems because outdated structures may produce inconsistent or incomplete information. Implementing robust ETL (Extract, Transform, Load) pipelines helps cleanse and normalize data before feeding it into AI models. For example, an insurance company automating claims processing might use Python scripts with pandas to detect missing fields or outliers in records drawn from various legacy databases:

```python
import pandas as pd

\#\# Load legacy claims data
claims_data = pd.read_csv('legacy_claims.csv')

\#\# Identify missing values
missing_values = claims_data.isnull().sum()

print("Missing values per column:", missing_values)

\#\# Drop rows with critical missing fields
cleaned_data = claims_data.dropna(subset=['claim_id', 'policy_number', 'claim_amount'])

\#\# Save cleaned dataset for AI consumption
cleaned_data.to_csv('cleaned_claims.csv', index=False)
```

Beyond technology, managing organizational culture around legacy systems is critical for successful AI

431

adoption. Employees accustomed to traditional workflows may resist change due to concerns over job security or loss of familiarity with established tools. Transparent communication emphasizing how automation complements rather than replaces their roles can alleviate anxiety. Offering training programs that develop hybrid skills—combining domain expertise with new technology fluency—also supports a smoother transition.

Compliance considerations are equally important since some legacy systems contain sensitive or proprietary data regulated by standards such as GDPR or HIPAA. Integration plans must incorporate compliance measures from the outset; automated logging should track access during AI processing stages, while encryption safeguards data transfer between old and new platforms.

Consider a healthcare provider relying on decades-old patient record software unable to natively interface with modern natural language processing tools designed to summarize medical histories automatically. The solution combined an API facade wrapping the legacy database with a secure ETL process extracting anonymized text snippets for NLP analysis—all conducted under strict audit trails required by healthcare regulations.

managing legacy systems is less about discarding proven assets and more about designing thoughtful coexistence strategies that enable gradual transformation toward full automation maturity. By blending technical creativity with pragmatic project management, organizations can evolve these foundational systems instead of allowing them to become obstacles—turning potential liabilities into powerful enablers of efficiency.

The real challenge lies not only in technology but in harmonizing old and new worlds functionally and culturally to unlock meaningful business value from AI-powered automation initiatives already reshaping many industries today.

Addressing skill gaps in the workforce

Addressing skill gaps within the workforce becomes a critical challenge once legacy systems are mapped and integration pathways established. Without the right talent capable of leveraging AI-powered tools, even the most advanced automation strategies risk falling short. Unlike traditional IT deployments, adopting AI requires a hybrid skill set that combines domain expertise with data literacy, coding skills, and the ability to critically evaluate algorithmic outputs.

Many organizations underestimate the extent of reskilling needed. It goes beyond teaching employees to use new software; it involves fostering a deep understanding of AI's capabilities and limitations so workers can interpret results, spot anomalies, and troubleshoot effectively. Consider a logistics company implementing predictive analytics for route optimization. Truck dispatchers who previously relied on experience and manual planning must now engage with real-time data dashboards and model-driven recommendations. Their training focuses on critically assessing these suggestions rather than following them blindly.

A practical strategy is to develop layered training programs tailored to different roles. Entry-level staff might start with foundational AI literacy—learning what machine learning is and how automation changes workflows—while technical teams delve into topics like model parameters, data preprocessing, or API integrations. For example, a multinational retailer combined modular e-learning courses with hands-on workshops where employees could experiment with automation tools under supervision. This approach boosted adoption rates and reduced resistance by building confidence in navigating new technologies.

Mentorship also plays a key role in bridging skill gaps. Pairing AI-savvy employees with those less familiar encourages peer-to-peer knowledge sharing often missed in formal sessions. Cross-functional collaboration further breaks down silos: data scientists gain operational insights, while frontline workers provide context that enhances algorithm performance.

Closing skill gaps extends beyond internal efforts. Strategic partnerships with educational institutions or specialized training providers can supplement in-house programs. Some companies sponsor certifications in data science or AI ethics to systematically raise workforce competence. Others leverage vendor-led boot camps tied directly to AI deployments—immersive, hands-on experiences aligned with real business challenges.

Measuring progress during upskilling initiatives is as important as executing them. While course completion rates offer a basic indicator, they don't fully capture proficiency or behavioral change. More effective are scenario-based assessments that simulate real-world tasks—such as troubleshooting automation failures, adjusting processes based on AI insights, or designing workflow tweaks using low-code tools. These exercises reveal whether employees can apply their knowledge practically.

Beyond technical skills, soft skills gain renewed importance amid automation transformations. Adaptability, problem-solving under uncertainty, and effective communication help teams navigate evolving roles and maintain alignment between human judgment and automated outputs. Take this example, customer service agents working alongside chatbots benefit from coaching on empathy and escalation protocols when AI cannot handle complex queries.

Skill development also intersects closely with organizational culture—a factor sometimes overlooked in the rush to adopt new technology. Cultivating psychological safety where employees feel comfortable experimenting without fear of repercussions accelerates learning and innovation adoption. Leaders should encourage curiosity-driven exploration and celebrate incremental successes to sustain momentum.

Budgeting for continuous education is equally essential. Training isn't a one-time effort; as AI models evolve or new tools emerge, refresher courses prevent skills from becoming obsolete.

For example, imagine an accounting department implementing robotic process automation (RPA) for invoice processing. Initial training might cover bot management dashboards and exception handling—determining who intervenes when invoices fail automated checks. Over time, staff develop deeper analytical skills to identify patterns in exceptions and suggest adjustments to bot logic or upstream processes that reduce failures altogether.

closing workforce skill gaps demands strategic planning across multiple dimensions: role-specific curricula, experiential learning opportunities, mentorship programs, external certification partnerships, proficiency assessments focused on practical application, and a culture that encourages experimentation and continuous improvement.

The payoff is significant: empowered employees not only ensure smooth AI system operation but also actively refine automation workflows through their unique insights—a dynamic that drives sustainable business transformation far beyond initial implementation.

Avoiding scope creep

Scope creep in AI automation projects poses a subtle yet pervasive threat. It often begins innocently—with the addition of a single feature or a minor tweak to an algorithm —but can quickly escalate into uncontrolled growth that strains budgets, delays delivery, and jeopardizes overall project goals. While scope creep is a well-known challenge in traditional software development, AI initiatives face distinct risks due to their experimental nature and evolving requirements.

A primary factor driving scope creep is unclear or shifting objectives. Early enthusiasm frequently leads stakeholders to layer on additional use cases without fully considering resource limitations or timeline impacts. Take this example, a mid-sized retailer implementing AI for demand forecasting might start with the straightforward goal of optimizing inventory levels. However, over time, requests can multiply —from integrating supplier data streams to automating pricing strategies—without a thorough reassessment of feasibility. Without clear boundaries, teams struggle to prioritize and end up juggling too many moving parts.

To address this, projects should begin with rigorous scope definition during kickoff. Establishing clear success criteria tied directly to business outcomes helps anchor the team's efforts and provides an objective framework for evaluating new requests. For example, specifying a target like "reduce stockouts by 15% within six months" offers measurable focus, unlike vague aims such as "improve supply chain efficiency." Documenting deliverables and timelines upfront also helps set realistic expectations.

Implementing formal change management processes is equally critical in controlling scope expansion. Any proposed adjustments—whether adding data sources or increasing model complexity—should undergo structured review to assess impacts on resources, risks, and schedules. Project managers can use standardized change request templates requiring justification aligned with strategic goals and an estimate of additional effort involved.

Breaking development into modular phases or sprints offers

another effective tactic. This agile-inspired approach allows teams to deliver incremental value without becoming overwhelmed by complexity. After each sprint, stakeholders review progress and decide whether to incorporate further features or shift focus based on empirical results rather than assumptions.

Clear communication also plays a vital role. Regular updates keep stakeholders informed about the trade-offs associated with scope changes. When decision-makers understand the costs—such as longer model training or extra validation cycles—they are more likely to weigh additions carefully before approving them.

On the technical side, avoiding overengineering is essential. AI projects can be tempted by cutting-edge techniques that add complexity but yield diminishing returns compared to simpler alternatives. For example, chasing the latest deep learning architecture when a straightforward regression model suffices for certain forecasting tasks leads to unnecessary delays and wasted effort.

Data availability presents another common constraint. Ambitious plans that assume access to large, clean datasets often stumble if such data is unavailable or requires extensive preparation outside the project's scope. Conducting early, realistic assessments of data readiness helps prevent costly detours later on.

Collaboratively mapping out "must-have" versus "nice-to-have" features with business users and technical teams further clarifies priorities. This exercise highlights which components drive real value and which enhancements can be deferred or dropped if resources become tight.

Tracking adherence to scope boundaries benefits from project management tools that log changes alongside the original plan, creating a living document reflecting commitments throughout execution rather than static initial proposals.

External pressures can also fuel scope creep. Vendors pitching additional modules or consultants suggesting broader applications before foundational goals are met warrant careful scrutiny through internal governance committees. This safeguards against unchecked expansion driven more by sales incentives than operational needs.

The consequences of unchecked scope creep extend beyond project delays; they contribute to staff burnout as teams face mounting workloads under constant pressure for rapid results. Morale suffers when milestones slip repeatedly because priorities shift midstream without clear rationale.

Preventing this requires disciplined leadership willing to say no when necessary and committed to maintaining focus on agreed-upon objectives—even if it means postponing appealing but nonessential features.

controlling scope isn't about rigidity but purposeful focus: ensuring every added component serves the core business aim efficiently without derailing schedules or inflating costs unnecessarily.

For example, during an AI-driven customer service automation rollout at a financial institution, leaders limited the initial deployment strictly to chatbots handling routine inquiries. More complex case triage was introduced months later based on performance metrics from phase one. This staged approach contained risk while delivering tangible improvements early enough to build momentum and stakeholder trust without overextending resources prematurely.

In sum, maintaining disciplined boundaries around project scope protects investments in AI-powered automation by aligning efforts firmly with strategic priorities—avoiding distractions that dilute impact and erode confidence among teams driving innovation forward.

Contingency planning for failures

Failures are an inherent part of AI-powered automation projects, no matter how carefully they are planned. What distinguishes successful initiatives from costly setbacks is robust contingency planning. Preparing for failure isn't pessimism; it's a practical approach that ensures resilience and continuity when unexpected challenges arise.

Take, for example, a mid-sized logistics company deploying AI for route optimization. Early in the rollout, their system crashed due to unforeseen data inconsistencies from third-party sources. Without contingency measures, operations stalled for days, leading to missed deliveries and dissatisfied customers. Fortunately, the company had implemented fallback protocols—such as reverting to manual routing and alerting dispatch teams—that minimized disruption while engineers addressed the issue.

Creating effective contingency plans begins with identifying potential failure points throughout the AI workflow: data ingestion, model training, deployment environments, and integration layers. Each stage requires targeted risk assessments evaluating both likelihood and impact. Data pipelines may be vulnerable to corrupted files or missing records; training processes can face issues like overfitting or model drift; deployment might suffer latency or downtime.

After mapping these risks, it's essential to design redundant systems capable of automatically detecting faults or enabling swift manual overrides. Take this example, monitoring dashboards with real-time alerts can flag anomalies such as sudden drops in prediction accuracy or processing throughput. These tools empower technical teams to respond promptly before minor glitches escalate.

Fail-safe mechanisms also extend to version control for models and codebases. Archiving stable versions allows quick rollbacks if updates degrade performance. Consider an AI-driven credit scoring tool: if a new model iteration incorrectly flags too many applicants as high risk due to shifting data patterns, reverting to a previously validated version prevents financial loss and regulatory issues.

Communication planning plays a critical role during failures as well. Stakeholders need timely updates outlining the problem's nature, scope, and recovery timeline. Transparent communication builds trust both internally among staff and externally with clients or partners who depend on uninterrupted service.

Regularly simulating failure scenarios through drills uncovers vulnerabilities that theoretical plans might miss. These "fire drills" recreate outages or data corruption events in controlled settings, allowing teams to rehearse responses under pressure. This practice develops muscle memory and reveals gaps in tooling or documentation.

Allocating resources specifically for contingencies is equally important. Setting aside budget reserves for emergency fixes ensures organizations aren't caught off guard mid-project or post-launch. These funds cover rapid hiring of specialists, temporary infrastructure scaling, or third-party vendor support without disrupting overall finances.

Contingency plans should remain flexible rather than rigid scripts because AI systems operate within complex ecosystems affected by shifting external factors like regulatory changes or market dynamics. For example, during the COVID-19 pandemic, companies with adaptive AI-driven supply chain automation were better positioned to respond to wildly fluctuating demand patterns than those relying on static plans.

Finally, embedding lessons learned from failures into continuous improvement cycles transforms setbacks into growth opportunities. Postmortem analyses identify root causes that inform refinements—from enhanced data validation checks to improved user training materials.

A practical approach includes:

1. Risk Mapping: Identify components prone to failure (data sources, algorithms, infrastructure).

2. Redundancy Design: Develop backup workflows such as manual overrides or alternative data inputs.

3. Monitoring Setup: Implement dashboards with anomaly detection and alerting capabilities.

4. Version Control: Maintain archived stable models and codebases for quick rollback.

5. Communication Protocols: Define roles and responsibilities for incident reporting internally and externally.

6. Simulations: Conduct periodic drills replicating likely failure scenarios.

7. Budget Allocation: Reserve funds specifically for emergency response efforts.

8. Adaptive Strategies: Build flexibility into plans anticipating environmental changes.

9. Postmortem Reviews: Perform thorough analyses after incidents to update procedures accordingly.

Contingency planning transforms AI automation projects from fragile experiments into resilient assets that can withstand inevitable disruptions while safeguarding business continuity and stakeholder confidence.

Failing to prepare truly means preparing to fail—especially when complex AI systems touch core business functions where downtime directly impacts revenue and reputation.

Far from slowing progress, these proactive measures accelerate sustainable adoption by mitigating risks that otherwise cause costly delays and erode trust among users who depend on automated intelligence daily—helping organizations remain agile without vulnerability when unexpected challenges arise.

Balancing cost constraints

Balancing cost constraints is one of the most challenging yet essential aspects of implementing AI-powered automation. While budgets are limited, the promise of AI can be tempting, leading many to underestimate the full financial commitment involved. Beyond initial expenses like software licenses or hardware purchases, ongoing costs—such as data storage, model retraining, maintenance, and staff training —need to be considered from the outset. Overlooking these factors can quickly turn a seemingly affordable project into a costly burden.

To manage expenses effectively, it helps to break down costs into clear categories: upfront investments, recurring operational costs, and indirect expenditures. For example, a retail company using AI for inventory forecasting might face upfront costs related to purchasing cloud computing credits and integrating APIs with existing ERP systems. Recurring expenses would include data engineers maintaining pipelines and updating models to capture seasonal trends. Indirect costs could involve training supply chain managers to interpret AI-driven insights or dealing with downtime during system upgrades.

Hidden fees within vendor contracts are another common pitfall. Charges for additional users, premium support tiers, or surges in data volume can add up unexpectedly. Negotiating transparent terms that anticipate scaling needs helps prevent sudden financial surprises. Requesting detailed, multi-year cost projections from vendors—and comparing these across different providers—supports more informed decision-making.

Calculating return on investment (ROI) is crucial but often overly optimistic when focused solely on direct cost savings or productivity gains. It's important to also factor in less tangible benefits such as faster decision-making, fewer errors, and improved customer satisfaction. Take this example, an AI chatbot might reduce customer service labor hours by 30%, while simultaneously enhancing brand perception through instant responses—an effect that's harder to quantify but equally valuable.

Adopting staged rollouts through pilot programs can limit initial expenditure while validating concepts. Smaller-scale tests reveal unexpected costs before committing to full deployment. A healthcare provider, for example, might start by automating appointment scheduling in a single department to gauge integration challenges and user acceptance before expanding organization-wide.

Budget planning should also include contingency reserves for unforeseen expenses like data quality issues or compliance audits triggered by regulatory changes. Automation projects often require iterative adjustments after launch; having financial flexibility ensures continuous improvement without halting progress.

While it may be tempting to jump on the latest cutting-edge tools immediately, balancing innovation with caution is vital. Open-source AI frameworks such as TensorFlow or PyTorch can lower licensing fees but often require more internal expertise. On the other hand, turnkey SaaS platforms offer faster implementation at a higher price. Decision-makers must weigh the benefits of immediate convenience against long-term scalability and total cost of ownership.

A practical strategy involves maintaining a dynamic cost model that maps each expense category against expected benefits over time and updates regularly as new data becomes available. This living document promotes transparent communication with stakeholders and helps prioritize investments that align with strategic goals.

Amazon's early approach to warehouse robotics illustrates this balance well. They managed high capital expenditures by gradually increasing robot deployment alongside human workers rather than replacing them outright overnight. This phased approach enabled steady ROI realization while controlling upfront cash outflows.

Additionally, organizations should monitor key financial KPIs beyond simple budget adherence—metrics such as cost per automated transaction or savings generated per dollar spent on AI infrastructure offer actionable insights into project performance.

balancing cost constraints is not about indiscriminately cutting budgets but about optimizing spending to maximize value delivered. Efficiency gains from AI automation often justify higher initial investments when managed with realistic forecasts and flexible planning.

Striking this balance ensures automation initiatives not only launch successfully but maintain financial momentum throughout phases of growth, refinement, and scaling—transforming cost concerns from obstacles into strategic advantages.

Building stakeholder support

Building stakeholder support is essential for the successful deployment of AI-powered automation. Even when initiatives are technically sound and financially promising, they can falter without buy-in from key players—executives, department heads, frontline employees, and external partners alike. Resistance often arises from uncertainty about AI's impact on job roles, fears of losing control, or skepticism toward promised benefits. Overcoming these concerns requires transparent communication, active involvement, and practical demonstrations.

Engaging early champions within the organization can be particularly effective. These individuals, who understand both the technology and its strategic value, serve as bridges between technical teams and business units. They translate complex jargon into tangible outcomes that resonate with different stakeholder groups. For example, a marketing director enthusiastic about predictive analytics might influence colleagues by sharing pilot results that improved campaign targeting accuracy by 25%. Such real-world evidence tends to dispel doubt more effectively than theoretical promises.

Building trust also means openly acknowledging risks and limitations rather than glossing over them. Interactive workshops where teams can raise questions and explore scenarios help demystify AI's role. Take this example, a manufacturing company faced operator concerns about automation replacing jobs. In response, management organized hands-on sessions demonstrating how AI could augment quality control tasks instead of eliminating positions. This approach fostered collaboration and significantly reduced resistance.

Tailoring communication strategies is equally important because stakeholders vary in their familiarity with AI and their priorities. Executives often focus on ROI and strategic alignment, so concise reports highlighting cost savings, efficiency gains, or competitive advantages resonate better than detailed technical explanations. In contrast, IT teams need comprehensive integration plans and timelines to assess feasibility. Providing separate briefing materials for different audiences prevents overwhelming or alienating anyone.

Transparency also extends to data privacy and security. Stakeholders seek assurance that data governance meets compliance standards. Sharing governance frameworks and audit processes builds confidence that automation will not introduce unacceptable risks. A financial services firm exemplified this by publishing its AI ethics policy internally alongside an incident response plan for data breaches—a move that reassured both compliance officers and frontline staff.

Incentivizing participation goes beyond monetary rewards. Recognition programs that spotlight employees contributing to successful automation pilots motivate broader involvement. Gamified training modules around new AI tools add an element of fun while accelerating skill adoption. These tactics help overcome the inertia often accompanying large-scale change.

A step-by-step approach to fostering stakeholder support might include:

1. Stakeholder mapping: Identifying all parties affected by automation efforts, including indirect influencers.

2. Needs assessment: Understanding each group's concerns, priorities, and informational gaps.

3. Customized messaging: Developing targeted communications addressing specific questions or objections.

4. Pilot involvement: Inviting representatives from key departments to participate in test phases.

5. Feedback loops: Establishing regular channels for ongoing dialogue and adjustments based on input.

6. Training & enablement: Providing accessible learning resources tailored to different roles.

7. Recognition & rewards: Celebrating milestones and individual contributions visibly.

For example, when a mid-sized logistics firm introduced AI-driven route optimization software, they began by convening cross-functional meetings with drivers, dispatchers, IT staff, and executives to discuss expected changes. A phased rollout incorporated driver feedback on interface usability before full deployment, improving adoption rates and uncovering operational tweaks that enhanced overall system effectiveness.

Ignoring stakeholder dynamics can lead to costly delays or even project abandonment. Studies indicate that nearly 70% of digital transformation initiatives fail due to people-related factors rather than technological challenges—highlighting the importance of proactive engagement.

building stakeholder support is less about top-down resistance management and more about cultivating shared ownership of AI's transformative potential. When individuals feel heard, valued, and empowered throughout the process, automation shifts from being a disruptive threat into a collaborative opportunity—setting the stage for sustained success across the organization.

CHAPTER 17:
FUTURE TRENDS
IN AI AND
AUTOMATION

The rise of intelligent automation

Intelligent automation represents a fundamental shift in how businesses combine artificial intelligence with traditional automation. Unlike basic rule-based systems that follow predefined instructions, intelligent automation integrates AI technologies—such as machine learning, natural language understanding, and cognitive reasoning—with robotic process automation (RPA). This fusion creates systems that not only handle repetitive tasks but also learn from data patterns, adapt to exceptions, and make decisions based on context.

Invoice processing exemplifies a common application of automation. While traditional RPA can extract invoice details and input them into accounting systems, it often falters when facing irregular formats or errors. Intelligent automation platforms address these challenges by incorporating AI-powered optical character recognition (OCR) and anomaly detection algorithms. These tools identify inconsistencies and flag questionable entries without human intervention. Over time, the system improves by learning from user corrections, significantly reducing the need for manual review.

Building such solutions involves layering multiple technologies. The process begins with mapping workflows to pinpoint repeatable tasks. Then, machine learning models are integrated to interpret unstructured data like emails or scanned documents. Finally, RPA bots carry out the defined actions but can call upon AI components when complex situations arise. This hybrid design not only speeds up operations but also enhances accuracy and compliance.

In customer service centers, intelligent automation blends chatbots with sentiment analysis tools to elevate user interactions. Rather than relying on scripted responses, these chatbots grasp subtle language cues and emotions expressed by callers or online users. They promptly escalate urgent complaints to human agents while autonomously handling simpler inquiries—improving customer satisfaction and optimizing resource use.

Organizations adopting intelligent automation often experience notable productivity improvements alongside reduced operational risks. For example, a global bank applied this approach to loan application processing. Previously, manual checks took days and were susceptible to errors. After implementation, processing times dropped to hours while embedded AI enhanced fraud detection—demonstrating how agility and security can advance hand in hand.

Designing intelligent automation architectures requires careful attention to scalability and integration challenges. AI models demand continuous training with fresh data, making robust data pipelines essential. Additionally, legacy systems may lack the APIs needed for seamless real-time data exchange; addressing these issues early helps avoid costly setbacks later.

The impact on the workforce is equally important. Employees shift from performing routine tasks to managing exceptions and refining system performance through feedback loops. This transition calls for focused upskilling programs that foster collaboration between humans and machines rather than fueling fears of replacement.

Emerging low-code platforms are democratizing access to intelligent automation by enabling business users to create workflows without deep technical skills. Tools like Microsoft Power Automate's AI Builder allow analysts to develop custom form processing or prediction models that integrate directly into daily operations with minimal coding.

Consider a mid-sized retailer struggling with inventory shrinkage caused by inaccurate and delayed manual stock audits. By implementing intelligent automation that combines computer vision cameras scanning shelves with predictive analytics forecasting demand spikes based on sales trends and external factors like weather or local events, the retailer reduced stockouts by 30% and cut auditing labor costs in half within six months.

intelligent automation moves beyond simple task repetition toward dynamic systems capable of reasoning across complex information environments—making processes more resilient and adaptable amid uncertainty. Organizations embracing this next-generation capability position themselves for competitive advantage through operational excellence paired with faster decision-making.

However, technology alone is not enough. Establishing governance structures that promote transparency around AI-driven decisions builds trust both internally and externally. Regular audits of model bias or drift ensure fairness over time—a principle emphasized by experts like Andrew Ng, who advocates for "human-in-the-loop" frameworks as vital safeguards.

At its core, intelligent automation is more than an upgrade; it is a transformative force reshaping workflows across industries—from fraud prevention in finance to diagnostics in healthcare—and paving the way for smarter enterprises equipped to meet tomorrow's complex challenges today.

Augmented workforce models

Augmented workforce models are transforming the relationship between human labor and artificial intelligence in business operations. Instead of replacing employees, these models focus on collaboration—harnessing AI's analytical capabilities to enhance human decision-making, creativity, and efficiency. The aim is to empower workers with smarter tools, turning routine tasks into opportunities for higher-value contributions.

Consider a financial advisory firm that uses AI-driven analytics to process vast amounts of market data. Advisors no longer spend hours manually analyzing trends; AI delivers real-time insights and risk signals. This allows advisors to concentrate on interpreting the data within the context of each client and designing personalized strategies. By dividing responsibilities this way, human expertise is elevated while reducing errors caused by cognitive overload.

Building such augmented environments means integrating AI seamlessly into existing workflows to complement employee skills. Examples include natural language processing tools that distill lengthy documents into key points or intelligent scheduling assistants that predict workload peaks and optimize calendars. In healthcare, radiologists use AI image recognition software to highlight suspicious areas in scans but retain final diagnostic authority. The AI serves as a second pair of eyes—improving accuracy and turnaround times without replacing human judgment.

The effectiveness of augmented workforce models depends heavily on organizational culture and training. Employees need to trust AI outputs and understand their role in providing feedback that refines these systems. Transparent interfaces where users can question AI recommendations and offer corrections help avoid frustration or blind acceptance. Google's approach with its AI-assisted coding tool, Copilot, exemplifies this mindset by encouraging developers to treat suggestions as aids while maintaining critical judgment.

Challenges do arise, particularly around skill gaps and resistance. Some employees may feel threatened or overwhelmed when interacting daily with unfamiliar AI systems. Addressing this requires targeted upskilling programs that focus not only on technical skills but also on adaptability and problem-solving within hybrid workflows. For example, a multinational logistics company launched an internal academy teaching staff how to interpret AI-driven forecasts alongside traditional metrics, which eased adoption and boosted productivity.

The technology supporting augmented workforces often involves embedding AI APIs within enterprise software suites. Salesforce Einstein, for instance, integrates predictive lead scoring directly into sales CRM dashboards, enabling representatives to prioritize outreach based on conversion likelihood without switching platforms. Similarly, Microsoft Teams incorporates AI transcription and meeting highlights that help teams quickly recap discussions—saving time otherwise spent reviewing notes.

A more integrated example comes from an insurance claims department that introduced an intelligent assistant to review claim documents and flag inconsistencies before human evaluation. Processing times dropped by nearly 40%, but more importantly, adjusters could focus on complex cases requiring negotiation or empathy—areas where machines still fall short. This shift not only enhances throughput but also fosters greater job satisfaction.

Still, augmented models carry risks. Overreliance on AI suggestions can dull critical thinking if organizations fail to promote active engagement with the technology's outputs. Maintaining a "human-in-the-loop" approach ensures employees remain central decision-makers rather than passive automation recipients. Clear policies must define accountability when AI errs, accompanied by regular audits for algorithmic bias or outdated data.

Strategically, designing augmented workforce initiatives begins by identifying pain points where manual effort limits scalability or quality. From there, organizations can pinpoint which AI functions will best augment those areas—for example, deploying conversational agents to handle routine customer inquiries, freeing representatives for interactions that require emotional intelligence.

Pilots offer a practical way to test these solutions with minimal risk, gathering user feedback and refining usability before full deployment. Monitoring both user engagement and business KPIs helps leaders determine whether augmentation truly enhances productivity or unintentionally creates friction.

Even small businesses can benefit without heavy investment in custom AI solutions. Platforms like Zapier enable employees to build automated workflows—such as routing email requests into task management systems while prompting human intervention at key points—through simple interfaces.

augmented workforce models challenge the outdated man-versus-machine mindset by fostering synergy instead of competition. They enable smarter allocation of cognitive resources, freeing humans from repetitive tasks so creativity and judgment can flourish within digitally enhanced ecosystems ready for tomorrow's complexities.

AI and emerging markets

Emerging markets are rapidly becoming fertile ground for AI adoption, reshaping their economic landscapes in ways that challenge traditional development models. Unlike established economies burdened by entrenched infrastructure and legacy systems, many emerging regions are leapfrogging older technologies to embrace AI-powered automation as a driver of accelerated growth. This shift is far from theoretical—real-world applications span sectors from agriculture to financial services, each tailored to local needs and conditions.

Consider mobile money platforms in sub-Saharan Africa. Companies like M-Pesa have integrated AI algorithms to detect fraud patterns and optimize transaction routing in real time. These systems operate effectively despite limited physical banking infrastructure, a longstanding barrier in the region. By combining AI with widespread mobile networks, financial inclusion has surged, granting millions access to credit, insurance, and savings tools that were previously out of reach.

In India's agricultural sector, AI-driven crop monitoring tools assist farmers in forecasting weather impacts and disease outbreaks. Startups employ drone imagery alongside machine learning models to evaluate soil quality and plant health. This data enables smallholders to optimize inputs like fertilizers and water, boosting yields without increasing costs. Importantly, this technology is accessible not only to large enterprises but also to small-scale farmers through affordable sensor kits and smartphone apps, helping to close knowledge gaps common in rural areas.

While emerging markets face challenges distinct from developed countries—such as fragmented data sources, infrastructural bottlenecks, and regulatory uncertainty—these obstacles can become opportunities when addressed with adaptive AI solutions designed for low-resource environments. For example, natural language processing (NLP)-powered chatbots handle customer service inquiries across multiple local languages in Southeast Asia, where literacy levels vary widely. This innovation lowers barriers for consumers engaging with government services or telecom providers.

AI is also making significant inroads within microfinance institutions serving unbanked populations worldwide. Traditional loan approval processes relied on extensive paperwork and manual verification, often slow and prone to human error or bias. Today's AI models assess creditworthiness more inclusively by analyzing alternative data points like mobile phone usage or social media activity. This approach not only increases loan approval rates but also reduces default risks by capturing behavioral nuances beyond conventional credit scores.

These examples highlight an important reality: successful AI implementation in emerging markets requires customization rather than off-the-shelf adoption. Developers must consider local languages, cultural norms, and infrastructure constraints while ensuring affordability and scalability. Machine learning algorithms trained on North American data, for instance, may perform poorly in African contexts unless carefully adapted with relevant local datasets.

The pace of AI adoption benefits from growing smartphone penetration and improving internet connectivity, driven largely by investments in 4G networks and expanding fiber optic infrastructure. According to GSMA's Mobile Economy report 2023, internet usage grew over 10% annually across many emerging economies between 2018 and 2023. This enhanced connectivity forms the backbone for cloud-based AI services and real-time data analytics critical for automation workflows.

Beyond commercial applications, governments increasingly recognize AI's potential to improve public service delivery —from predictive maintenance of utilities to automated tax collection systems that detect anomalies indicative of evasion. Rwanda's use of drone delivery logistics combined with AI route optimization exemplifies this trend, significantly reducing delivery times for medical supplies across remote regions while lowering operational costs.

At the same time, rapid AI growth raises ethical concerns around data privacy, algorithmic fairness, and workforce displacement—issues often overshadowed by enthusiasm for innovation. Many emerging markets lack robust legal frameworks governing digital rights and data ownership, creating risks of exploitation or bias unless addressed proactively.

Multinational corporations also shape how AI unfolds in these economies by tailoring automation tools to support local partners and distribution networks instead of imposing standardized solutions. For example, a global consumer goods firm might deploy AI-driven demand forecasting customized for informal markets and inconsistent supply chains typical of many emerging retail environments.

For businesses seeking expansion through automation initiatives in emerging markets, understanding these nuanced dynamics is essential. A one-size-fits-all strategy risks failure or missed opportunities; instead, collaboration with local stakeholders and iterative pilot programs prove invaluable. Incorporating human-in-the-loop systems helps ensure automated decisions remain accountable while adapting intelligently over time.

Practical steps include starting with detailed audits that focus on resource constraints unique to target regions —such as unreliable power or variable internet speeds —and designing lightweight AI applications capable of offline functionality where necessary. Modular architectures allow gradual scaling as infrastructure improves without overwhelming existing operations.

To illustrate: an e-commerce platform entering Southeast Asia might first deploy an AI-powered chatbot that manages order inquiries asynchronously via popular local messaging apps like WhatsApp or LINE before investing in full-scale warehouse robotics requiring stable power grids and advanced logistics networks.

While challenges persist—chiefly inconsistent data quality— advanced techniques like federated learning enable models to train on decentralized datasets without compromising sensitive information or requiring continuous internet access. This approach suits emerging markets grappling with fragmented data sources spread across multiple jurisdictions or cautious about sharing proprietary information.

Looking ahead, the combination of affordable edge computing hardware with AI opens new possibilities for empowering small businesses outside urban centers. Devices equipped with inference capabilities can run pre-trained models locally on smartphones or microcontrollers, enabling instant decision-making without reliance on the cloud.

The transformation unfolding across emerging markets underscores a broader truth: technology deployment must embrace contextual intelligence—not just technical prowess —to unlock sustainable business value through automation. Leaders who approach these complexities pragmatically will not only tap new revenue streams but also foster economic resilience within communities often sidelined by globalization.

tailoring AI-powered automation strategies to the specific socioeconomic fabric of emerging economies turns challenges into competitive advantages—a lesson that resonates well beyond any single region where resource disparities persist.

Integration of AI with 5G

The arrival of 5G networks is transforming the landscape for AI-powered automation by dramatically increasing data transmission speeds and reducing latency to unprecedented levels. This enhanced connectivity enables AI applications to function closer to real time, allowing businesses to deploy more advanced and responsive automation workflows. For example, in a manufacturing facility equipped with AI-driven sensors monitoring equipment health, 5G allows these sensors to instantly send vast amounts of data to cloud analytics platforms or edge devices. This rapid data flow supports predictive maintenance decisions that minimize downtime without waiting for delayed uploads.

What distinguishes 5G further is its capacity to support an immense number of connected devices—up to a million per square kilometer—far surpassing the thousands manageable under 4G. This density unlocks new opportunities for businesses heavily reliant on the Internet of Things (IoT). Warehouses with thousands of smart assets, such as autonomous guided vehicles and temperature-controlled storage units, can now coordinate seamlessly. AI algorithms analyze streaming data at scale, and the near-instant communication enabled by 5G reduces lag, enhancing operational efficiency and optimizing resource allocation.

Real-world examples illustrate these advantages clearly. Logistics companies, for instance, benefit from AI-powered route optimization that integrates real-time traffic and weather data feeds. Thanks to 5G, GPS trackers and vehicle sensors continuously stream detailed telemetry, enabling AI systems to reroute drivers dynamically and avoid delays or hazards immediately instead of relying on periodic updates. This leads to faster deliveries and lower fuel consumption—a direct cost saving born from the synergy between AI and 5G.

Customer-facing applications also reap significant benefits. Retailers deploying AI chatbots within mobile apps can offer richer interactions because 5G supports high-definition video streaming with minimal delay. Imagine a virtual shopping assistant using AI-powered augmented reality (AR) that lets customers try on products virtually without frustrating buffering or lag. Such immersive experiences depend on the low latency and high throughput that only widespread 5G adoption can provide.

From a technical perspective, 5G's bandwidth improvements make it far more feasible to combine AI models with edge computing infrastructure. Edge devices located near data sources—whether factories, retail outlets, or handheld devices—can execute inference tasks locally while smoothly synchronizing model updates with central servers. This hybrid approach reduces reliance on cloud connectivity, lowers data transfer costs, and enhances privacy by limiting exposure of raw data.

Consider the following Python snippet illustrating a simple client-server interaction optimized for edge computing environments powered by 5G:

```python
import socket

import json


\#\# Client-side: Edge device sends sensor data
```

```python
def send_sensor_data(data):

client_socket = socket.socket(socket.AF_INET, socket.SOCK_STREAM)

client_socket.connect(('server_ip', 8080))

serialized_data = json.dumps(data).encode('utf-8')

client_socket.sendall(serialized_data)

response = client_socket.recv(1024)

client_socket.close()

return response.decode('utf-8')


\#\# Example sensor reading

sensor_data =

'temperature': 22.4,

'vibration': 0.003,

'timestamp': '2024-06-01T10:15:00Z'



result = send_sensor_data(sensor_data)

print(f"Server response: result")
```
` ` `

In this simplified scenario, the edge device transmits real-time sensor readings over the network with minimal delay —a process made efficient and reliable by robust 5G connectivity that supports continuous streaming without bottlenecks.

The integration of AI with 5G also paves the way for

new business models centered around "AI as a Service" deployed at scale across distributed environments. Telecom operators are already exploring partnerships to embed AI capabilities directly into their networks, offering enterprises tailored automation solutions that leverage both high-speed connectivity and powerful analytics hosted at the network edge.

This convergence introduces complexity in system design as well. Network slicing—a unique feature of 5G—enables operators to allocate dedicated virtual segments for critical applications requiring guaranteed performance levels. For companies automating safety-critical processes like industrial robotics or autonomous vehicles, ultra-reliable low-latency communication is essential. Configuring these slices alongside AI workloads demands close collaboration among IT teams, telecom providers, and solution architects.

Security considerations evolve in parallel. The increased velocity of data heightens exposure if safeguards do not keep pace. Encryption protocols must support real-time encrypted streams across numerous devices while complying with regulations such as GDPR and CCPA. Implementing secure multi-party computation or federated learning frameworks becomes more practical over 5G infrastructures where distributed nodes collaborate in training AI models without centralizing sensitive datasets.

A practical example comes from healthcare services using remote patient monitoring systems enhanced by AI diagnostics running on edge devices connected via 5G networks. These systems alert clinicians immediately upon detecting anomalies like irregular heartbeats or oxygen level drops—decisions that depend heavily on near-zero latency communication channels combined with intelligent data processing close to the source.

For businesses aiming to harness this integration effectively, success depends not on chasing technology trends but on rigorously redesigning end-to-end workflows to fully exploit what this combination uniquely offers—not just faster data transmission but smarter decisions delivered precisely when they matter most.

This shift transforms automation projects from periodic batch jobs or delayed reporting into continuous streams of actionable insights that drive operational agility across every level—from supply chain responsiveness to personalized customer experiences.

Unlocking full value requires assessing existing infrastructure readiness alongside strategic investments in network-enabled AI platforms designed for flexibility and scalability. Organizations should identify critical touchpoints where increased throughput or ultra-low latency remove bottlenecks while balancing costs against measurable performance gains.

the fusion of AI technologies with next-generation wireless networks forms the foundation for truly intelligent automation ecosystems capable of redefining competitive advantage worldwide. The impact goes beyond incremental improvements; it signals a new era where connectivity fuels continuous learning loops powering adaptive systems that anticipate challenges before they arise and respond autonomously at unprecedented speeds.

Approached thoughtfully, this convergence delivers tangible benefits: streamlined operations, enhanced customer satisfaction through responsive services, reduced overhead from predictive maintenance avoidance—and greater market agility driven by smarter use of ever-expanding data streams flowing seamlessly through integrated AI-5G architectures.

Decentralized AI: Blockchain and edge AI

Decentralized AI is transforming automation systems by

distributing computation and decision-making across a network instead of relying on a central server. This approach reduces bottlenecks, enhances privacy, and improves resilience by eliminating single points of failure. Central to this transformation is blockchain technology, originally developed for secure digital ledgers, which provides an immutable record of transactions. This capability enables validation and auditing of AI operations within decentralized environments.

In supply chain management, for example, rather than a centralized AI system managing inventory data, multiple nodes—such as manufacturers, distributors, and retailers—share encrypted data on a blockchain ledger. Smart contracts automate verification tasks like quality checks or delivery confirmations without intermediaries. Decentralized AI algorithms then analyze this distributed data locally at each node, minimizing latency and reducing the risk of tampering. This setup fosters trust among participants who might not fully trust each other but rely on the transparency offered by the blockchain framework.

Complementing decentralization, edge AI pushes inference and learning closer to data sources like sensors or user devices. Instead of continuously sending raw data to cloud centers—which can be expensive and raise privacy concerns—edge devices process information locally using lightweight AI models optimized for limited hardware. In smart factories, for instance, cameras equipped with edge AI detect anomalies on assembly lines in real time, enabling immediate corrective actions without delays introduced by cloud dependencies.

Adopting decentralized AI requires rethinking traditional centralized workflows. Developers must create algorithms resilient to intermittent connectivity and diverse device capabilities. Federated learning exemplifies this approach by enabling multiple edge devices to collaboratively train shared models without exchanging raw datasets. Each device updates its local model with private data and only transmits encrypted gradients or weights for aggregation on a coordinating server or blockchain network.

The following Python example illustrates federated averaging, a core concept in federated learning:

```python
import numpy as np

\#\# Simulate local model updates from 3 edge devices
local_models = [
np.array([0.2, 0.4, 0.6]),
np.array([0.25, 0.35, 0.65]),
np.array([0.22, 0.38, 0.63])
]

def federated_average(models):
return np.mean(models, axis=0)

global_model = federated_average(local_models)
print("Updated global model parameters:", global_model)
```

This snippet demonstrates how model parameters from distributed sources can be merged into an updated global state without exposing underlying data—a privacy-preserving technique essential for sectors like healthcare or finance.

Blockchain integration further ensures that all model updates are transparently recorded and verifiable by participating nodes while preventing unauthorized changes through cryptographic signatures and consensus protocols such as Proof of Stake or Practical Byzantine Fault Tolerance (PBFT). Companies like Ocean Protocol leverage these technologies to create secure data-sharing marketplaces where contributors maintain control over access while benefiting from decentralized AI-powered analytics.

Despite these advantages, challenges remain. Decentralized networks often face scalability issues due to consensus overheads; balancing computational loads across heterogeneous edge devices can be complex; governance frameworks must evolve to clarify responsibility in distributed decision-making; and legal compliance is complicated when datasets span multiple jurisdictions with varying regulations.

Still, the benefits are significant: enhanced security through reduced attack surfaces since there's no central repository vulnerable to hacks; increased fault tolerance as systems continue operating even if some nodes fail; and more equitable access by democratizing AI capabilities beyond large cloud providers.

In retail applications, blockchain-backed decentralized AI empowers consumers by giving them ownership over their personal shopping preferences stored locally on their smartphones rather than in centralized databases vulnerable to breaches or misuse—a response to growing demands for privacy and transparency.

The fusion of decentralized AI with edge computing creates ecosystems capable of dynamic adaptation at scale without sacrificing control or security—a fundamental shift away from the traditional cloud-centric automation strategies that have long dominated enterprise IT.

Organizations interested in these architectures should start by assessing their existing workflows for suitability: Are critical decisions latency-sensitive enough to benefit from edge inference? Do partners require trustless interactions that blockchain smart contracts could enable? What computational constraints exist across networked devices?

Pilot projects might deploy lightweight edge models in targeted areas alongside permissioned blockchains that govern participant actions—balancing performance with regulatory compliance and auditability.

decentralized AI anchored by blockchain represents a pivotal advancement toward intelligent systems that are not only faster but inherently more resilient and trustworthy— qualities essential as automation becomes deeply integrated into complex inter-organizational processes spanning global markets.

This evolution is not just about distributing workloads; it redefines who controls data flows and decision-making within automated ecosystems—empowering businesses with transparency while maintaining agility and scale.

Emerging standards and governance

As AI-powered automation becomes increasingly integrated into business operations worldwide, emerging standards and governance frameworks are playing a vital role. Without clear guidelines, organizations confront not only technical challenges but also legal and ethical uncertainties that can erode trust and hinder scalability. In response, regulatory bodies and industry consortia are developing structured approaches for responsible AI deployment. However, these frameworks are still evolving rapidly, reflecting ongoing technological advances and shifting societal expectations.

International organizations like the International Organization for Standardization (ISO) have made significant strides in this area. For example, ISO/IEC 22989 and ISO/IEC 23053 establish terminology, concepts, and frameworks to create a common language around AI systems. This helps reduce ambiguity when businesses design, audit, or certify automated processes. These standards emphasize transparency and explainability—foundations essential for effective governance. A manufacturing company deploying AI-driven quality control tools, for instance, must align with these standards to ensure that system decisions can be audited and clearly understood by regulators or compliance teams.

Alongside these broad frameworks, industry-specific guidelines address unique sector demands. In finance, the Basel Committee on Banking Supervision enforces strict model risk management protocols for AI applications such as credit scoring and fraud detection. These measures aim to prevent biased outcomes while mitigating systemic risks linked to opaque algorithmic models. Practically, banks implement continuous validation workflows where automated decisions undergo regular human review, supported by secure logs that maintain full traceability.

Governance also extends beyond regulatory compliance to embrace ethical principles like fairness, accountability, and privacy protection. The European Union's Ethics Guidelines for Trustworthy AI outline seven core requirements: human agency and oversight; technical robustness; privacy and data governance; transparency; diversity, non-discrimination, and fairness; societal well-being; and accountability. Companies integrating AI in customer-facing roles—such as chatbots handling sensitive information—must embed these principles from the outset to protect reputation and meet regulatory expectations.

Turning principles into practice involves operationalizing standards through concrete tools and processes. Model cards and datasheets have emerged as effective means of documenting an AI model's intended uses, performance across demographic groups, training data origins, and known limitations. For example, a healthcare startup deploying an AI diagnostic assistant can use a model card to help clinicians grasp the system's strengths and weaknesses —promoting informed trust rather than blind reliance.

Beyond documentation, auditing procedures are essential. Internal audit teams are expanding their expertise to include algorithmic risk assessments that evaluate potential biases, detect data drift over time, or identify vulnerabilities to adversarial attacks. Automated testing suites simulate edge cases while compliance dashboards monitor adherence to policies in real time. An e-commerce company automating product recommendations might track click-through rates across user demographics to spot early signs of unintended discrimination.

Importantly, governance frameworks emphasize involvement across multiple stakeholder levels—from engineers building models to executives guiding strategic decisions—and extend even to customers whose data fuels AI systems. Transparency tools such as consent management platforms empower users with granular control over how their personal information is utilized within automated processes. This layered approach fosters a culture where accountability is distributed rather than concentrated solely within technology teams.

Yet standardization faces challenges adapting to the rapid pace of innovation. Emerging paradigms like generative AI complicate explainability due to their inherent complexity and unpredictability. Jurisdictions also vary widely in regulatory approaches: the European Union's General Data Protection Regulation (GDPR) contrasts with the more sector-specific U.S. framework enforced by agencies like the Federal Trade Commission (FTC). This fragmentation compels multinational organizations to design flexible governance architectures capable of localization without sacrificing overall coherence.

Consider a global logistics provider using AI-driven route optimization tools that adjust dynamically based on traffic patterns and weather forecasts. To comply with diverse national laws, the company might implement modular consent workflows tailored per region while maintaining a centralized risk management framework monitored via cloud-based dashboards aligned with ISO standards for data security and privacy.

In addition to external mandates, self-regulation often accelerates best practice adoption ahead of legal requirements. Leading firms establish ethics committees tasked with reviewing new AI initiatives against codes of conduct—sometimes including external advisors from academia or civil society—to proactively navigate emerging dilemmas rather than reacting after issues arise.

Developers benefit from open-source toolkits designed for governance tasks such as bias detection (e.g., IBM's AI Fairness 360), interpretability (LIME or SHAP), and secure model deployment (TensorFlow Privacy). Integrating these tools into continuous integration pipelines enables earlier detection of compliance gaps during development instead of post-deployment firefighting.

Collaboration remains equally vital. Cross-industry consortiums like the Partnership on AI facilitate sharing of effective governance strategies among sectors facing similar challenges—healthcare providers exchange insights on privacy-preserving techniques with financial institutions; manufacturing firms learn explainability methods from autonomous vehicle developers.

While the landscape of standards and governance continues to evolve rapidly, it forms the backbone of sustainable AI automation ecosystems. Organizations investing time and resources now to understand these frameworks not only reduce operational risks but also gain competitive advantage through trustworthiness—a currency increasingly valued by customers, regulators, and investors alike.

Without disciplined governance guiding design choices and operational practices around AI automation tools, businesses expose themselves not only to technical failures but also reputational harm that can stifle long-term growth. Moving forward requires embracing complexity while grounding efforts in practical compliance steps—a balance crucial for thriving amid accelerating waves of digital transformation reshaping industries today.

AI ethics and policy development

Ethics and policy development in AI automation require more than a checklist approach; they demand the integration of moral reasoning into the core of technological innovation. As AI systems are rapidly deployed across business operations, gaps have emerged where efficiency gains sometimes come at the cost of fairness, accountability, and societal trust. Addressing these challenges calls for nuanced policies that strike a balance between fostering innovation and ensuring responsibility—policies that neither stifle creativity nor allow unchecked algorithmic power.

A fundamental challenge is defining ethical boundaries for autonomous decision-making. Take, for example, an AI system screening loan applications: it must avoid perpetuating historical biases embedded in its training data. Yet, determining which biases are ethically unacceptable is complex. Fairness metrics vary widely—should the system aim for equal false positive rates across demographic groups, or prioritize equal opportunity in approval rates? Organizations need to engage diverse stakeholders— including ethicists, affected communities, and regulators— to navigate these questions thoughtfully and avoid one-size-fits-all solutions that risk ignoring context-specific harms.

Transparency and explainability present another critical dimension for policy development. Stakeholders increasingly seek clarity on how AI models arrive at their conclusions to build trust and enable recourse when outcomes seem unjust. This requires businesses to invest in explainability tools without compromising proprietary algorithms or security. Techniques like SHAP (SHapley Additive exPlanations) provide local interpretability by quantifying feature contributions for individual predictions, while global methods such as LIME offer insights into overall model behavior. Integrating these approaches into operational workflows helps auditors and end-users alike understand decisions—a necessity especially in regulated sectors like finance or healthcare.

Data governance also forms a vital pillar of ethical AI policy. Consent mechanisms should be granular and user-centric, empowering individuals to control not only whether their data is used but also how it is processed within automated systems. Many companies underestimate this complexity, treating consent as a one-time checkbox rather than a dynamic agreement requiring ongoing transparency. Emerging blockchain-based solutions create immutable audit trails of data usage permissions, aligning practices with regulations like GDPR and CCPA while bolstering user confidence.

On the regulatory front, governments worldwide are strengthening frameworks aimed at ethical AI deployment. The European Union's Artificial Intelligence Act introduces risk-based classifications for AI applications, imposing stricter oversight on high-risk systems such as biometric identification and critical infrastructure management. Compliance obligations span rigorous pre-market testing to mandatory post-deployment monitoring. In contrast, countries like Singapore emphasize voluntary codes of conduct paired with incentives for responsible innovation—reflecting cultural and economic priorities that shape varied approaches to enforcement.

Corporate governance structures must evolve accordingly. Ethics committees or AI oversight boards have become fixtures in leading firms' organizational charts, tasked not just with project approval but with assessing societal impacts, overseeing bias audits, and recommending mitigation strategies throughout development cycles. However, implementation can be uneven; some organizations treat these bodies as symbolic rather than integral partners, risking reputational harm when ethical breaches occur despite nominal safeguards.

Equipping the workforce with ethical AI knowledge remains essential yet challenging. Most engineers and data scientists focus primarily on technical problem-solving without formal grounding in moral philosophy or social implications. Interdisciplinary education programs that blend computer science with ethics, law, and social sciences are gaining traction to bridge this gap. Companies investing in such initiatives report fewer compliance incidents alongside increased employee engagement as teams recognize their role in shaping trustworthy technology.

Emerging dilemmas continue to push policy boundaries—for instance, generative AI's ability to produce synthetic content at scale raises questions about intellectual property rights over machine-generated works and the authenticity of AI-created media influencing public opinion. Policies must keep pace with rapid innovation cycles while remaining flexible enough to adapt as unforeseen consequences arise.

Collaboration within industry fosters shared understanding of best practices in ethical AI development. Initiatives like the Partnership on AI bring together diverse stakeholders —from major tech firms to academia—to draft consensus principles addressing transparency, fairness, privacy, and societal impact. These collaborative frameworks offer adaptable templates that businesses can tailor locally while benefiting from collective expertise that reduces redundant efforts.

Ethical AI also intersects deeply with social justice concerns. Without deliberate design choices, automation risks amplifying inequalities rather than alleviating them. For example, hiring algorithms trained on historical workforce data may inadvertently disadvantage underrepresented groups unless corrected through debiasing techniques or inclusive datasets. Policy frameworks increasingly acknowledge this responsibility by encouraging affirmative measures instead of mere neutrality.

Accountability mechanisms complement ethical principles and policy mandates by establishing clear lines of responsibility when automated decisions cause harm. Legal liability—whether resting with developers, vendors, or end-user organizations—remains contested but must be clarified through contracts and regulation alike. Documentation standards such as model cards support this process by transparently recording design intentions and limitations.

embedding ethics into AI policy development is an ongoing journey requiring vigilance and adaptability. Real-world monitoring creates feedback loops that detect emerging risks early; continuous stakeholder engagement ensures policies evolve alongside societal norms rather than lag behind technological progress.

Confronting these complexities is no small feat—but companies committed to robust ethical frameworks gain competitive advantage through trustworthiness valued by customers and regulators alike. As Satya Nadella observed: "AI will empower people like never before—but only if it is built responsibly." Without a solid ethical foundation underpinning automation strategies, businesses risk undermining not just individual projects but their broader license to operate in a digitally transformed economy.

At its core, ethics and policy development form the scaffolding for sustainable AI-powered automation— balancing human values with technological capabilities to shape a future where innovation uplifts rather than divides.

AI and the evolving business model

AI-powered automation is reshaping the fundamental way businesses operate, prompting a reevaluation of traditional models. The integration of intelligent systems not only streamlines workflows but also transforms how value is created, delivered, and captured. To fully grasp this transformation, it's essential to examine how AI influences core elements such as product development cycles, customer engagement, revenue streams, and organizational structures.

Take the subscription economy, for example—a model built on consistent customer engagement and recurring revenue. AI amplifies this model by enabling hyper-personalization at scale. Machine learning algorithms analyze user behavior in real time, allowing platforms to adjust offerings or pricing dynamically. Netflix's recommendation engine illustrates this well: by tailoring content to individual tastes, it reduces churn and converts a commodity service into a highly personalized experience. This evolution shifts businesses from one-off transactions to relationship-driven models where customer lifetime value becomes paramount.

Another significant change lies in how companies monetize data and insights alongside or instead of physical goods and standalone services. Industrial equipment manufacturers, for instance, are transitioning from selling machines to offering "product-as-a-service" models powered by AI-driven predictive maintenance. Rolls-Royce's "Power-by-the-Hour" program uses IoT sensors combined with AI analytics to monitor jet engines remotely and forecast failures before they occur. This approach minimizes client downtime while generating steady revenue streams, exemplifying a move from ownership toward outcome-based contracts.

The financial sector mirrors this shift through AI-enhanced fintech platforms that optimize lending decisions using machine learning credit risk models. Beyond traditional credit scores, these models incorporate alternative data—such as transaction histories and social media activity—to reach underserved markets and reduce defaults. LendingClub's automated underwriting process cuts approval times from weeks to hours, fundamentally changing how credit is allocated and priced.

Operations also undergo profound transformation as traditional supply chains evolve into intelligent networks powered by AI for real-time demand forecasting and dynamic routing. Amazon demonstrates this by combining robotics with AI-driven logistics optimization: robots pick products while algorithms determine the best delivery routes on the fly. This integration shortens lead times and lowers inventory costs, but it also compels organizations to rethink supplier relationships and internal capabilities.

Alongside technological advances, organizational design adapts to new realities. Hierarchical decision-making gives way to more agile frameworks supported by data democratization and AI-assisted insights accessible across teams. Employees shift from performing routine tasks toward managing exceptions and interpreting complex algorithmic outputs. Companies like Google promote "data fluency" among all staff, blending human intuition with algorithmic precision to gain strategic advantage.

The rise of platform ecosystems further highlights AI's impact on business models. Rather than controlling every link in the value chain, firms increasingly act as orchestrators of interconnected services powered by APIs and machine intelligence. Salesforce's AppExchange marketplace exemplifies this trend by integrating third-party AI-enhanced apps into its CRM platform, expanding its value proposition without building every feature internally.

Importantly, AI opens new avenues for competitive advantage beyond cost reduction or efficiency gains alone. Strategic differentiation now depends on leveraging proprietary data combined with advanced algorithms to create barriers that competitors find difficult to replicate quickly. Tesla's fleet data, collected from millions of driven miles, continuously feeds its autonomous driving algorithms—forming a feedback loop that reinforces market leadership in ways others struggle to match.

However, evolving business models around AI brings challenges that require careful management:

- Data governance must balance protecting sensitive information with fostering innovation.

- Organizations need to weigh automation benefits against potential workforce displacement.

- Ethical considerations arise around transparency and fairness in algorithmic decisions.

- Legacy contracts often require renegotiation to accommodate new service paradigms like outcome-based pricing.

To implement AI effectively, companies should map their current value chains to identify where automation can unlock new revenue streams or cost structures—not just incremental improvements. Cross-functional workshops can help explore scenarios such as servitization (selling outcomes), platformization (orchestrating ecosystems), or hybrid models combining digital products with personalized services.

Take this example, a mid-sized manufacturer might rethink its business model through a stepwise approach:

1. Assess current revenue streams: Determine which products rely on one-time sales versus recurring service contracts.

2. Evaluate customer pain points: Use surveys or interviews enhanced by natural language processing tools to analyze feedback at scale.

3. Pilot predictive maintenance: Equip machinery with IoT sensors feeding data into machine learning models that predict failures.

4. Develop subscription offerings: Convert maintenance visits into monthly service plans guaranteeing uptime with automated alerts.

5. Integrate a customer portal: Build an online dashboard providing real-time performance insights accessible anywhere.

6. Redesign sales incentives: Shift compensation toward rewarding long-term account growth instead of volume-based transactions.

7. Monitor financial impacts: Track KPIs such as renewal rates, reduced downtime costs, and customer satisfaction linked to automated interventions.

This pragmatic roadmap aligns technology adoption closely with business goals rather than treating automation as isolated projects.

incorporating AI-powered automation demands a strategic overhaul that goes beyond optimizing efficiency. It requires reimagining value propositions—engaging customers dynamically through intelligent platforms; monetizing continuously via personalized services; optimizing operations with interconnected smart systems; and empowering people within agile organizations enhanced by algorithmic insights.

As Satya Nadella observes about digital transformation at Microsoft: "Every company is becoming an AI company." Understanding how these shifts redefine foundational business logic equips leaders not just to survive disruption but to proactively shape future markets through smart automation embedded in evolving business models.

This fundamental reconfiguration underscores that embracing AI-powered automation means adopting a new paradigm where technology co-creates economic value continuously—not merely executes routine tasks—and ultimately rewires competitive dynamics across industries without exception.

Global collaboration and AI innovation

Global collaboration driven by AI innovation is rapidly transforming the competitive and cooperative dynamics of business worldwide. The traditional approach—where companies closely guarded proprietary technology—is giving way to more open, interconnected ecosystems that leverage shared AI advancements to fuel collective growth. Leading organizations increasingly understand that accelerating innovation relies not only on internal R&D but also on partnerships spanning industries, regions, and sectors.

This shift is evident in the rise of cross-border AI research consortia and innovation hubs designed to pool expertise and resources. For example, the Partnership on AI—a coalition including tech giants like Microsoft, Google, and IBM alongside nonprofits—advances responsible AI through shared knowledge and joint initiatives. Such alliances address complex challenges like fairness, safety, and robustness—issues no single entity can solve alone. They also help establish common standards and best practices essential for interoperability across diverse platforms.

On a practical level, businesses tap into these collaborative networks to accelerate their automation capabilities far more effectively than working in isolation. Startups gain access to cutting-edge algorithms developed by university labs; multinational corporations integrate localized AI solutions sourced from specialized regional players; government agencies co-invest with private firms in AI-powered infrastructure projects. These arrangements lower barriers to entry while expanding the scope of innovation beyond what individual organizations could achieve independently.

Open-source AI frameworks like TensorFlow and PyTorch exemplify this collaborative spirit. Initially developed by Google and Facebook respectively, they now underpin thousands of companies' automation initiatives worldwide. By democratizing access to advanced machine learning methods, these tools enable firms from emerging markets to build competitive products without prohibitive upfront costs. This creates a virtuous cycle: contributors continuously enhance the codebase while users innovate at the application level.

Global data-sharing agreements are also evolving within regulatory frameworks that balance privacy with innovation needs. Since data is the lifeblood of AI systems, collaborations enabling secure exchange of anonymized or aggregated datasets multiply opportunities for more accurate models in fields such as healthcare diagnostics or supply chain forecasting. Take this example, multinational pharmaceutical companies collaborate on AI-driven drug discovery by pooling datasets under strict compliance protocols.

Operating within these collaborative frameworks requires navigating geopolitical complexities and intellectual property concerns with care. Organizations need robust governance structures to clarify ownership rights over jointly developed algorithms or data-derived insights while maintaining transparency about usage boundaries. Risk mitigation plans must also address heightened cybersecurity threats arising from increased data exchanges among partners.

The rise of cloud platforms further amplifies this trend by providing scalable infrastructures where collaborators can seamlessly co-develop automation solutions regardless of physical location. Major providers like AWS, Azure, and Google Cloud offer integrated toolkits combining machine learning services with workflow orchestration engines—making it easier than ever to prototype and deploy cross-organizational applications efficiently.

A compelling example is found in the automotive industry, where manufacturers work alongside tech companies across continents on autonomous vehicle software stacks. Tesla's proprietary approach contrasts with Volkswagen's open collaboration model through initiatives like Baidu's Apollo project in China—bringing together universities, suppliers, and other stakeholders in a shared AI ecosystem aimed at rapid progress toward driverless technologies.

Within organizations, there is also a move toward "networked innovation" structures that break down silos between departments and external partners alike. This supports knowledge sharing both inside and outside organizational boundaries—boosting creativity in automation design tailored for global markets yet sensitive to local nuances.

To navigate this landscape effectively, businesses can take practical steps such as:

1. Mapping existing partnerships to identify collaborators' strengths relevant to AI-enabled workflows.

2. Engaging in sector-specific consortia focused on shared challenges like ethical AI or predictive maintenance.

3. Investing in interoperable platforms by adopting cloud-native architectures supporting API-driven integrations.

4. Establishing clear IP agreements that define co-ownership models upfront.

5. Developing secure data exchange protocols aligned with international encryption standards and regulations.

6. Encouraging cross-functional teams to maintain ongoing dialogue between internal experts and external innovators.

This approach helps companies not only keep pace with rapidly evolving technologies but also influence industry-wide standards shaping future business models powered by intelligent automation.

In an era defined by rapid disruption, harnessing collective intelligence through global collaboration becomes a critical differentiator—and a source of resilience amid the uncertainties inherent in scaling new technologies.

Moving forward demands embracing openness balanced with discipline: blending innovative cooperation with rigorous safeguards around ethics, security, and equitable value sharing so that AI-driven progress benefits all participants fairly—not just a privileged few.

As Bill Gates once observed: "We always overestimate the change that will occur in the next two years and underestimate the change that will occur in the next ten." By collaborating globally, organizations can accelerate reaching transformative milestones far sooner than isolated efforts alone—turning ambitious visions into practical realities that will shape business evolution through smart automation at an unprecedented scale.

CHAPTER 18: CREATING AN AI-DRIVEN CULTURE

Fostering innovation mindsets

Innovation goes beyond simply adopting new technology; it demands cultivating a mindset that welcomes change, encourages experimentation, and embraces creative problem-solving. When businesses treat AI-powered automation as just another tool, they risk overlooking its broader potential. True innovation requires embedding curiosity and a readiness to challenge established processes into the very fabric of the organization.

Take Adobe's transformation with their Creative Cloud suite as an example. Early in the transition from a product-based to a service-oriented model, Adobe encouraged teams to continuously rethink workflows. This cultural shift paved the way for integrating AI features like Adobe Sensei, which automates repetitive design tasks and provides intelligent recommendations. Such advancements were possible because employees were empowered to explore new approaches rather than cling to familiar routines.

Leaders can nurture this innovation mindset by promoting small-scale pilots that invite experimentation without fear of failure. Setting up "innovation labs" or dedicated teams to explore how AI can optimize niche workflows allows organizations to test ideas before scaling successful ones company-wide. Google's "20% time" exemplifies this approach, giving employees freedom to pursue passion projects that may not yield immediate profits but often spark breakthroughs later applied across core operations.

Structured brainstorming sessions focused on automation within existing processes also drive innovation. Techniques like mind mapping or design thinking workshops bring together diverse perspectives—from frontline staff familiar with daily challenges to data scientists uncovering hidden analytical opportunities. Take this example, Siemens formed cross-functional teams that identified bottlenecks in manufacturing ripe for robotic process automation (RPA), resulting in significant reductions in cycle times.

Risk aversion remains a common barrier; organizations frequently prioritize stability over innovation, especially under tight deadlines or budget pressures. Overcoming this requires redefining failure as a valuable source of learning essential for iterative progress. Sharing internal stories where experiments fell short but yielded insights helps normalize risk-taking and build resilience.

Leadership plays a crucial role by modeling curiosity and openness. When executives actively engage with AI initiatives—attending demos or cross-department meetings —they demonstrate genuine commitment beyond mere rhetoric. Transparency about challenges encountered during implementation fosters trust and encourages collaborative problem-solving rather than blame.

Aligning measurement systems with innovation goals sustains momentum. Beyond tracking efficiency gains or cost savings, incorporating softer metrics—such as the number of new ideas generated each quarter or employee participation rates in pilot programs—shifts focus toward ongoing creativity and process improvement rather than immediate results.

At an individual level, cultivating an innovation mindset involves continuous learning, whether through formal training on emerging AI tools or informal peer knowledge sharing. Platforms like Coursera and Udacity offer accessible courses on machine learning fundamentals and automation techniques, empowering employees across departments to contribute meaningfully.

Imagine a mid-sized logistics company aiming to automate inventory management. Instead of imposing a top-down solution, they assemble a cross-disciplinary "innovation squad" including warehouse workers, IT staff, and data analysts. This team rapidly prototypes AI-powered demand forecasting algorithms while testing process changes on the floor, iterating based on real-time feedback until they develop an approach tailored uniquely to their operations.

fostering an innovation mindset transforms AI adoption from a checklist task into an evolving journey driven by curiosity and continual refinement. It turns organizations into living laboratories for intelligent automation rather than static implementers.

Embracing this mindset means accepting ambiguity while maintaining focus—a paradox that distinguishes leaders from followers in the fast-paced world of AI-driven business transformation.

Emphasizing continuous learning

Continuous learning is essential to the success of any AI-driven automation initiative. Without ongoing education, even the most advanced tools risk being underused or becoming outdated as technology evolves rapidly. Instead of treating training as a one-time event, organizations need to weave learning into everyday workflows, turning knowledge acquisition into a regular habit rather than an afterthought.

Take, for example, a multinational manufacturing company that deployed AI-based predictive maintenance systems. Initial excitement soon faded when shop floor technicians found it difficult to interpret alerts or adjust machinery based on automated recommendations. The issue wasn't the technology itself but a lack of continuous training to bridge the gap between complex algorithms and their practical application. To address this, the company introduced microlearning modules—short, targeted lessons delivered via mobile devices—allowing workers to build relevant skills in manageable segments between shifts. This approach led to higher machine uptime and boosted confidence among frontline staff, demonstrating how ongoing education directly enhances operational performance.

Building a culture that values continuous learning also means offering resources tailored to different expertise levels. Take this example, finance teams might benefit from focused sessions on AI-enhanced fraud detection models, while marketing professionals gain from hands-on workshops showcasing automated customer segmentation tools. Learning management systems (LMS) that track progress and recommend personalized courses ensure employees engage with content relevant to their roles instead of generic tutorials.

However, technical knowledge alone isn't enough. Soft skills like critical thinking and adaptability are equally important in an AI-augmented workplace. Effective training programs incorporate scenario-based exercises where participants analyze real-world challenges—such as identifying biases in AI outputs or troubleshooting model errors—and collaborate on solutions. IBM's "AI Skills Academy" exemplifies this approach by combining simulations with core technical instruction, fostering not only competence but also ethical awareness and problem-solving agility.

Leadership plays a pivotal role in amplifying learning initiatives. When executives actively participate—whether by attending workshops or sponsoring innovation challenges—they reinforce that growth is valued throughout the organization. Microsoft CEO Satya Nadella's emphasis on a "growth mindset" illustrates how continuous learning can drive innovation and resilience amid rapid technological change.

Practical steps to encourage continuous learning can start small: hosting regular "lunch-and-learns," creating internal forums for sharing AI success stories and lessons learned, and establishing peer mentoring programs where experienced users support newcomers in mastering automation tools. For example, Salesforce formed community groups focused on leveraging Einstein Analytics features; these informal networks accelerated adoption and uncovered creative use cases beyond initial expectations.

Tracking progress requires more than just attendance records; collecting qualitative feedback helps identify which topics resonate and where gaps remain. Pulse surveys asking employees how empowered they feel using AI systems provide valuable insights for dynamically adjusting training content rather than relying solely on static plans developed months in advance.

A structured approach to embedding continuous learning might include:

1. Assessing current skill levels related to AI tool usage across departments.

2. Identifying specific knowledge gaps affecting performance or adoption.

3. Curating targeted educational content from

internal experts or external providers.

4. Scheduling recurring training sessions aligned with real-time project phases instead of fixed intervals.

5. Encouraging hands-on practice through sandbox environments where employees can safely experiment with automation workflows.

6. Soliciting ongoing feedback to refine materials and delivery methods.

7. Recognizing and rewarding learners to reinforce positive behaviors and sustain motivation over time.

It's important to remember that continuous learning extends beyond formal training sessions. Fostering curiosity through internal newsletters featuring emerging trends, curated reading lists highlighting breakthrough research, or guest speaker series from industry pioneers adds valuable layers of insight that keep teams informed and adaptable.

In a world where algorithms update overnight and platforms release new features weekly, relying on yesterday's expertise risks falling behind tomorrow's competition. Organizations committed to lifelong learning are better positioned not only to implement AI-powered automation effectively but also to innovate beyond initial deployments—turning incremental improvements into lasting competitive advantage.

championing continuous learning cultivates agile workforces ready to embrace change proactively rather than reactively—a crucial distinction for businesses striving not just to survive but to thrive amid the rapidly evolving landscape of intelligent automation solutions.

Building interdisciplinary teams

Successful AI-powered automation rarely flourishes within

isolated teams. Instead, it thrives through interdisciplinary collaboration that unites diverse expertise—from data scientists and software engineers to business strategists and frontline operators. Bringing these perspectives together creates a fertile ground for innovation, producing solutions that are both technically robust and aligned with real-world business needs.

Take, for example, a retail company implementing AI-driven inventory management. While data analysts can develop forecasting models based on historical sales, their predictions may fall short without input from supply chain managers who grasp seasonality nuances or procurement officers familiar with supplier lead times. When these roles engage in ongoing dialogue, the team can organically adjust —tweaking algorithms to reflect sudden market shifts or integrating vendor constraints—resulting in more reliable and practical automation workflows.

Building such interdisciplinary teams starts with identifying the right skill sets relevant to your project goals. A typical group might include:

- AI and machine learning specialists who design and train models

- Software developers responsible for integrating AI solutions into existing systems

- Domain experts providing essential context about business processes

- Change management professionals guiding organizational adoption

- Data engineers ensuring clean, accessible data pipelines

Overlooking any of these perspectives often creates gaps that delay deployment or weaken solution effectiveness. Non-technical roles, in particular, are frequently underestimated —change managers foster user buy-in, while domain experts validate whether automated decisions make operational sense.

Another key challenge is fostering effective communication across disciplines. Different vocabularies and priorities can lead to misunderstandings; what seems like a minor technical adjustment may have significant business implications. Regular cross-functional workshops promote shared understanding. Methods such as user story mapping or design thinking sessions help teams visualize workflows collaboratively and articulate requirements clearly.

Collaboration tools also play a vital role in bridging gaps. Platforms like JIRA or Asana facilitate transparent task tracking across departments, while shared documentation tools such as Confluence or Notion serve as living knowledge bases accessible to all stakeholders. Version control systems like Git enable developers to manage code updates smoothly without disrupting others' work—small but crucial factors in maintaining harmony among mixed expertise.

Consider how an interdisciplinary approach improved outcomes for a financial institution automating fraud detection. Although data scientists developed sophisticated anomaly detection algorithms, the initial rollout faltered because compliance officers identified certain false positives as regulatory risks. By involving compliance experts in daily stand-ups, the team established immediate feedback loops; they clarified which alerts required escalation versus those safe to dismiss automatically. This collaboration reduced unnecessary investigations by 30%, saving valuable time and resources.

In practice, creating effective interdisciplinary teams requires leadership support and clear role definitions, combined with flexibility for team members to learn beyond their usual domains. Rotating members into short-term assignments outside their core expertise builds empathy—for example, having software engineers shadow customer support agents reveals pain points that technology might better address.

Recruitment strategies should emphasize soft skills such as adaptability and communication alongside technical proficiency. According to Deloitte's 2022 report on AI implementation success factors, companies excelling in cross-functional teamwork achieved 25% faster project completion rates and higher user satisfaction after deployment compared to those relying on homogeneous groups.

Organizations may also benefit from external partnerships where consultants or academic collaborators fill specialized gaps temporarily while internal staff gain skills through exposure and mentoring. Some firms establish innovation hubs where multidisciplinary squads experiment with pilot projects free from daily pressures—a practice that accelerates ideation cycles and uncovers unforeseen challenges early.

At a granular level, defining workflows within interdisciplinary teams is equally important. Assign clear ownership for each automation component while establishing integration checkpoints to prevent silos from reemerging in new forms. For example:

- Data engineers prepare datasets weekly
- Machine learning experts retrain models monthly using fresh inputs
- Business analysts monitor key performance indicators daily
- Change managers coordinate training sessions biweekly

This rhythm sustains momentum without overwhelming participants juggling multiple responsibilities.

embracing interdisciplinarity means cultivating an ecosystem where diverse perspectives challenge assumptions constructively and collectively refine solutions through iterative feedback loops. Though friction from differing viewpoints may feel uncomfortable at first, it often sparks breakthroughs unattainable within isolated specialties.

A CEO from a leading logistics firm once reflected during an internal meeting: "Our biggest AI wins didn't come from perfecting technology first but from bringing everyone— engineers, dispatchers, salespeople—into the room so their realities shaped what we built." This insight underscores why interdisciplinary teams are essential for navigating the complexities of AI automation initiatives.

To nurture this collaborative environment effectively:

1. Map all stakeholders affected by the automation effort before kickoff

2. Assign liaison roles to bridge communication between technical teams and end users

3. Schedule recurring alignment-focused touchpoints rather than just status updates

4. Encourage informal knowledge sharing through chat channels or lunch-and-learns highlighting cross-domain insights

5. Celebrate small wins publicly, recognizing contributions from multiple disciplines equally

6. Invest in conflict resolution training, acknowledging that diverse perspectives naturally lead to disagreements needing constructive navigation

Neglecting interdisciplinarity risks producing technically elegant yet impractical AI systems destined to underperform or face user rejection—a costly outcome in today's competitive landscape demanding agility paired with deep domain insight.

AI-powered automation requires not only coding skill but orchestration of human intelligence spread across specialties. Embracing this reality will distinguish organizations that thrive amid rapid technological change from those left scrambling behind fragmented efforts lacking holistic vision and stakeholder engagement essential for lasting success.

Promoting transparency in AI use

Transparency in AI use is fundamental to building trust both within organizations and with external stakeholders such as customers and regulators. Without clear insight into how AI systems arrive at their decisions, businesses risk losing credibility and facing compliance issues. Transparency goes beyond merely acknowledging the presence of AI; it involves providing detailed information about algorithms, data sources, and decision-making processes.

Consider AI-driven credit risk assessments in banking. When loan officers or customers lack understanding of why an application is approved or denied, frustration arises. More critically, undisclosed biases can remain hidden until they cause reputational damage or regulatory penalties. To address this, firms adopt explainable AI (XAI) frameworks that translate complex model outputs into understandable factors. Instead of presenting an opaque "credit score," these systems highlight key variables—such as income stability or repayment history—that influence decisions. This clarity supports informed choices and strengthens user confidence.

Transparency also requires thorough documentation of data

lineage: tracking where input data originates, how it is processed, and any transformations applied before entering models. Data provenance audits not only aid internal governance but also fulfill external regulatory demands under frameworks like GDPR or CCPA. Tools such as Apache Atlas or open-source platforms like DataHub help automate lineage capture, creating searchable records that streamline compliance efforts.

On an operational level, embedding transparency means designing dashboards that reveal AI system status and rationale behind decisions to relevant stakeholders. For example, a customer service chatbot might display confidence scores for suggested responses alongside user feedback metrics. Such interfaces enable product owners to detect anomalies—like rising error rates or biased outputs—and iterate on models proactively rather than reacting after failures occur.

Yet transparency presents challenges. Overloading non-technical audiences with technical details can cause confusion, while disclosing too much may risk exposing proprietary information. Striking the right balance calls for carefully curated communication—often through tiered transparency that offers detailed reports internally for developers and auditors, alongside high-level summaries tailored for executives or customers.

Successful implementation typically involves collaboration across legal, data science, and user experience teams to develop transparency protocols aligned with organizational culture and regulatory context. Microsoft's Responsible AI principles exemplify this approach by providing customers with comprehensive documentation on ethical considerations and model behavior within Azure AI services, setting industry standards for openness without compromising competitive advantage.

Transparency also plays a crucial role in identifying and mitigating bias. When stakeholders can examine decision pathways, they are better positioned to detect unfair patterns—for instance, if an AI recruiting tool inadvertently disadvantages certain demographic groups due to biased training data. Regular fairness audits depend on transparent access to model features and outcomes; without this clarity, organizations risk perpetuating systemic inequalities hidden beneath algorithmic complexity.

Practically, teams can integrate transparency throughout development using tools such as:

- Model cards summarizing a model's scope, performance across subgroups, intended use cases, and limitations

- Interactive visualization methods like LIME (Local Interpretable Model-Agnostic Explanations) or SHAP (SHapley Additive exPlanations) that reveal feature impacts on individual predictions

- Comprehensive logging of model inputs and decisions to facilitate retrospective analysis when issues arise

Take an e-commerce platform employing AI-driven dynamic pricing. Without transparent explanations for price changes, customers may perceive unfairness, leading to churn. Publishing clear pricing policies alongside real-time dashboards showing demand-supply correlations helps maintain trust while supporting competitive agility.

Beyond compliance and customer relations, transparency fosters an internal culture of accountability. Knowing their models will be openly scrutinized motivates developers to rigorously test data quality and anticipate edge cases rather than rushing deployments based on unchecked assumptions.

To embed transparency effectively, organizations should incorporate checkpoints within governance frameworks by:

1. Establishing documentation standards from project inception

2. Assigning roles responsible for maintaining accessible audit trails

3. Scheduling periodic reviews of model explanations aligned with business impact assessments

4. Training non-technical staff to interpret AI outputs and promote organization-wide literacy

Neglecting these practices risks creating "black box" systems that breed distrust among employees who feel alienated by opaque automation decisions—undermining adoption rates and the productivity gains AI investments aim to deliver.

Transparency is not merely a technical necessity but a strategic imperative that connects ethical responsibility with sustainable success in automated enterprises. By opening the proverbial curtains on AI operations, companies invite collaboration across teams and stakeholders—enabling smarter decisions grounded in clarity rather than uncertainty.

In doing so, organizations build resilient ecosystems where technology enhances human judgment instead of replacing it blindly—a vital shift for long-term value creation amid accelerating digital transformation pressures.

Encouraging experimentation

Encouraging experimentation within an AI-driven culture involves cultivating an environment where trial, error, and iteration are embraced as essential drivers of innovation. Organizations that avoid experimentation risk stagnation, missing opportunities to refine automation workflows or discover unexpected efficiencies. One effective strategy is to create dedicated spaces—both physical and virtual—where teams can safely explore new tools, algorithms, or process adjustments without fear of immediate consequences. Take this example, Google's well-known "20% time" policy allows engineers to dedicate part of their workweek to personal projects, some of which have become core company products. This concept can be adapted for AI initiatives by enabling data scientists and automation specialists to prototype novel solutions in sandboxed environments.

Implementing a structured yet flexible experimentation framework requires clear guidelines on scope and objectives alongside mechanisms for rapid feedback. A practical example is A/B testing in operational processes: introducing an AI-driven chatbot to a subset of customers while others continue using traditional support channels. Tracking key performance indicators such as response times, customer satisfaction, or resolution rates offers measurable insights into the new system's effectiveness. This iterative approach drives continuous improvement; when one method falls short, teams can quickly pivot without being hindered by rigid project plans.

Leadership plays a vital role in fostering this mindset by modeling risk-taking behaviors and rewarding constructive failure. Recognizing experiments that reveal limitations or expose hidden issues reinforces learning and encourages openness about setbacks. Atlassian's regular "ShipIt Days," where employees showcase experimental projects and share lessons learned regardless of success, exemplify this approach. Applying similar practices in AI adoption supports iterative model tuning and exploration of unconventional data sources without fear of punitive consequences. Documenting these experiments also builds organizational knowledge repositories that future teams can reference, minimizing duplicated efforts and accelerating maturity.

At the same time, experimentation must strike a balance

between freedom and accountability; unrestricted tinkering can lead to resource drain or disorganization if left unchecked. Lightweight governance protocols help maintain focus on business objectives while granting autonomy. One effective method is hypothesis-driven development: each experiment begins with a clear statement such as "Introducing predictive maintenance AI will reduce downtime by 15% within three months." Predefined success criteria and timelines foster discipline amid creative exploration.

On the technical front, modern MLOps platforms facilitate experimentation at scale by automating model training pipelines, managing version control, and monitoring real-time performance metrics. Tools like MLflow and Kubeflow allow teams to run multiple model variants simultaneously, objectively compare results, and roll back changes when needed. This infrastructure reduces friction in rapidly testing ideas—enabling the fail-fast approach critical for staying competitive.

Cross-functional collaboration further enriches experimentation outcomes. When data scientists work closely with domain experts—such as marketing professionals or supply chain managers—they gain valuable contextual insights often missing from purely technical perspectives. This synergy sharpens hypotheses and ensures prototypes align closely with practical needs rather than theoretical ideals.

Early adopters offer compelling examples of how experimentation uncovers unexpected value beyond initial goals. One manufacturing company initially used computer vision models for defect detection in quality inspections but discovered secondary benefits: predictive analytics derived from inspection data helped optimize equipment maintenance schedules. This bonus insight fueled further investment.

embedding experimentation requires nurturing psychological safety at every organizational level so employees feel empowered to propose unconventional ideas without fear of judgment. Training programs focused on agile methodologies and design thinking support this culture by combining curiosity with structured problem-solving techniques.

Through repeated cycles of experimenting, learning, and adapting, companies evolve beyond static implementations toward dynamic ecosystems where AI-powered automation grows organically alongside changing business landscapes. Such cultures build resilience against disruption by refusing to settle for the status quo—instead turning setbacks into fuel for innovation.

In practice, building this culture starts with simple steps:

- Allocating dedicated time for AI pilots outside core production

- Defining clear hypotheses with measurable outcomes before launching tests

- Candidly documenting all results in shared knowledge bases

- Publicly recognizing both successful innovations and instructive failures

- Investing in tools that support rapid prototyping and continuous integration

Encouraging experimentation does more than improve technology deployment; it reinvigorates workforce engagement by transforming AI projects from mandated tasks into collaborative ventures where creativity drives tangible business impact.

Storytelling and communication

Storytelling and communication are essential to the success of AI-powered automation initiatives, transforming technical complexity into narratives that resonate across all levels of an organization. When teams understand not only the "what" but also the "why" behind automation efforts, engagement deepens, resistance fades, and alignment strengthens. Take, for example, a mid-sized logistics firm that struggled to convey the benefits of its new AI-driven routing system. Rather than overwhelming staff with dry specifications or abstract metrics, leadership shared stories focused on real experiences: a dispatcher's frustration with manual route recalculations and a driver's stress from frequent overtime. This human-centered approach shifted skepticism to curiosity, paving the way for adoption.

The strength of storytelling lies in its ability to translate data and algorithms into relatable experiences. While technical teams may get lost in code and performance benchmarks, business leaders and frontline employees connect more naturally with narratives that highlight tangible outcomes —such as reduced delays, cost savings, or improved customer satisfaction. Crafting these stories requires close collaboration among data scientists, project managers, and communications specialists who can simplify complex concepts without oversimplifying them. Take this example, instead of stating "Our predictive maintenance model improves uptime by 12%," sharing how unexpected machine failures sharply declined—saving thousands in repair costs and downtime—creates clearer understanding and greater impact.

Visual storytelling enhances verbal communication by offering intuitive representations that cross language barriers. Dashboards featuring dynamic charts, annotated flow diagrams of automated workflows, or interactive simulations allow stakeholders to observe AI's influence unfolding in real time. Consider a financial services company rolling out an AI fraud detection tool: their launch included a dashboard highlighting suspicious transaction patterns paired with case summaries explaining how the system flagged anomalies missed by human auditors. Such visuals invite questions, foster transparency, and build trust —especially important for technologies often met with skepticism.

Effective communication goes beyond simply delivering information; it fosters dialogue that surfaces concerns and ideas. Regular workshops or town hall sessions where users share feedback on automation tools encourage continuous improvement and reinforce a culture of openness. For example, a retailer implementing an AI chatbot for customer service discovered early user frustrations around misunderstood queries; addressing these issues required iterative tuning informed by frontline employee input gathered during feedback forums. These conversations often reveal gaps between technical expectations and operational realities—insights that remain hidden when development occurs in isolation.

Tailoring messages to diverse audiences within an organization is equally important. Executives focus on strategic ROI metrics; IT teams prioritize system integration challenges; end users care about daily workflow impacts. Segmenting communications ensures relevance without overwhelming recipients with unnecessary detail. For example, monthly executive summaries might highlight cost savings and risk reductions through concise infographics, while training sessions for staff emphasize hands-on demonstrations covering ease of use and troubleshooting tips.

Incorporating storytelling into training materials further grounds learning in context rather than abstraction. Instead of generic tutorials on AI tool features, embedding scenarios drawn from real business challenges helps users connect theory with practice. Imagine an HR department adopting an automated candidate screening platform through role-playing exercises where participants evaluate fictitious profiles enhanced by AI scoring—this experiential method reinforces understanding far more effectively than static manuals.

The narrative thread extends beyond internal audiences to external stakeholders such as clients or investors who increasingly scrutinize companies' digital transformation journeys. Transparent communication about AI initiatives can boost brand reputation by demonstrating innovation alongside responsibility. One software provider publicly shared case studies detailing how their automation solutions improved client efficiency while respecting data privacy protocols—building credibility crucial for winning new business.

Storytelling also plays a subtle yet vital role in managing change fatigue—a common challenge when multiple automation projects launch simultaneously. Framing each deployment as part of a larger mission to empower employees rather than replace them helps maintain morale amid uncertainty or disruption. Leaders who share personal anecdotes about overcoming their own initial doubts add authenticity to messages encouraging AI adoption.

At the same time, authenticity is paramount; overhyping capabilities or glossing over limitations risks backlash when reality fails to meet expectations. Balanced narratives that acknowledge challenges alongside benefits foster realistic optimism rather than blind enthusiasm—laying the groundwork for long-term trust.

To embed storytelling effectively within AI programs organizations should:

- Develop persona-driven case studies illustrating diverse user experiences

- Use multimedia formats (videos, podcasts) capturing voices across departments

- Create feedback loops where stories evolve based on stakeholder input

- Train leaders in narrative techniques tailored to technical content

- Align messaging calendars with key project milestones for timely communication

effective storytelling bridges the divide between cutting-edge technology and human experience—it transforms abstract automation into compelling journeys where every participant understands their role and stakes involved. In doing so, it sparks collaboration essential for sustained success amid the complexities of AI integration.

Communication here is not just a soft skill; it is an operational imperative that shapes how organizations internalize innovation and convert potential into measurable outcomes through shared understanding.

Recognizing and rewarding AI initiatives

Recognition and reward systems play a crucial role in embedding AI initiatives within an organization, transforming isolated projects into lasting cultural change. When employees receive genuine appreciation for their contributions to automation goals, motivation grows and innovation thrives. Yet, effective recognition goes beyond bonuses or plaques—it taps into deeper drivers of engagement such as purpose, autonomy, and mastery.

Take, for example, a mid-sized manufacturing company that formed a cross-functional AI task force to optimize production scheduling. Initial efforts faced skepticism and uneven participation. To address this, leadership launched a program that publicly acknowledged team members who developed impactful automation scripts or contributed valuable ideas during brainstorming sessions. Importantly, recognition was based on peer nominations as well as top-down awards. This approach led to a significant increase in participation, encouraging knowledge sharing and sparking new initiatives beyond the original objectives.

Reward strategies should align closely with organizational values and the specific nature of AI work. In environments where iterative experimentation is vital, gamification elements like leaderboards, badges, or milestone celebrations can be highly effective. Conversely, professional development incentives—such as funded certifications or conference attendance—resonate strongly with teams focused on building AI skills.

One practical method is establishing an "AI Innovation Champion" program. This designates individuals across departments who demonstrate leadership in adopting or promoting automation solutions. These champions gain not only formal recognition but also early access to new tools and a voice in strategic decisions, fostering internal evangelists who accelerate adoption organically.

Using metrics to highlight contributions adds transparency and fairness to recognition efforts. Dashboards tracking key performance indicators—such as process improvement rates, error reductions, or time saved—provide objective data managers can draw upon when nominating candidates for rewards. This visibility helps avoid perceptions of favoritism and reinforces merit-based advancement.

Recognition should also extend beyond individual achievements to celebrate team successes. Automation often requires collaboration among data scientists, IT staff, business analysts, and end users; acknowledging cross-disciplinary accomplishments builds camaraderie and helps break down silos that can hinder innovation.

A frequent misstep is focusing solely on short-term wins

while overlooking incremental progress that may be less visible but equally important—for instance, refining data pipelines or improving model accuracy through repeated testing. Encouraging leaders to recognize these behind-the-scenes contributions sustains morale during complex projects where outcomes may not immediately reflect the effort invested.

Integrating recognition programs with existing performance management frameworks ensures they feel cohesive rather than disconnected or arbitrary. Incorporating AI milestones into regular reviews maintains focus and accountability while linking accomplishments to career advancement.

The psychological aspect of recognition also matters: public acknowledgment satisfies social needs for status and belonging but should be balanced with private feedback tailored to individual preferences. Some employees thrive on public praise; others respond better to one-on-one discussions highlighting personal growth alongside strengths.

Incentives need not rely solely on monetary rewards. Non-financial tokens—such as additional vacation days, flexible work options tied to project milestones, or symbolic artifacts like "automation pioneer" plaques—can powerfully convey appreciation for AI contributions.

Leaders have a vital role in modeling recognition behaviors themselves. Sharing success stories at town halls, sending personalized thank-you notes after project milestones, or spotlighting achievements in company newsletters all deepen a culture of appreciation around AI adoption.

Take this example, a global retail chain implemented an automated inventory forecasting system involving store managers in pilot phases. Management held quarterly award ceremonies where those who optimized stock levels most effectively received commendations linked to store performance bonuses—a clear demonstration of tying automation success directly to business impact.

Organizations can formalize recognition through a multi-tiered framework:

- Tier 1: Immediate peer-to-peer shout-outs via collaboration platforms celebrating daily wins

- Tier 2: Monthly manager-nominated awards highlighting measurable contributions

- Tier 3: Quarterly executive honors recognizing strategic breakthroughs

Maintaining these layers fosters continuous momentum rather than sporadic bursts of acknowledgment.

recognizing and rewarding AI initiatives does more than mark achievement—it drives behavioral change by reinforcing what matters most: creative problem-solving, cross-disciplinary collaboration, persistence through complexity, and alignment with broader business goals. Without this reinforcement loop, even technically successful projects risk fading into forgotten experiments instead of sparking lasting transformation.

To build effective programs:

- Define clear criteria directly linked to AI project goals

- Use data-driven evidence of impact whenever possible

- Balance public recognition with personalized feedback

- Celebrate both individual and team achievements

- Tie rewards to professional growth opportunities

Harnessing human motivation remains one of the most powerful levers for accelerating AI-powered automation across organizations—and rewarding those who drive progress secures their loyalty while inspiring others to follow suit.

Celebrating diversity in AI

Diversity in AI initiatives is more than a matter of meeting quotas; it is a strategic necessity that drives innovation and strengthens resilience in automation projects. When teams bring together varied perspectives—across cultural backgrounds, disciplines, and cognitive styles—they open pathways to creative problem-solving that homogeneous groups often overlook. This diversity leads to AI solutions that better mirror the complexity of real-world users and scenarios, reducing blind spots that can cause bias or ineffective outcomes.

Take, for example, a fintech startup that initially developed a credit-scoring AI using a narrow dataset largely representing one demographic. Upon deployment, significant accuracy gaps emerged for minority applicants, risking regulatory issues and reputational damage. In response, the company broadened its team to include social scientists, domain experts from diverse communities, and engineers with varied lived experiences. This shift not only produced fairer algorithms but also revealed new market opportunities —demonstrating that ethical considerations and business growth can go hand in hand.

Fostering such diversity involves more than intentional recruitment; it requires cultivating inclusive environments where all voices shape project direction. Implementing "AI design thinking" workshops with mixed teams can help uncover assumptions embedded in data selection or model objectives. In these sessions, participants challenge each other's viewpoints constructively, building accountability for equitable outcomes early in development rather than addressing problems after launch.

From a governance standpoint, diversity closely aligns with transparency and fairness demands increasingly emphasized by regulators worldwide. Incorporating diverse perspectives into AI auditing processes strengthens compliance while building trust among stakeholders. One effective approach is rotating "ethics review boards" composed of employees from various departments and backgrounds who regularly evaluate AI projects for potential biases or unintended consequences.

On the technical side, diversity influences feature engineering and dataset curation as well. Teams attuned to cultural nuances are better positioned to spot proxies for sensitive attributes that might inadvertently skew model behavior. Take this example, natural language processing systems risk misinterpretation if dialectal variations are overlooked—a pitfall avoided only when diverse expertise informs data annotation and validation stages.

Supporting diversity also means addressing systemic barriers like unequal access to AI education or career advancement opportunities within organizations. Mentorship programs targeting underrepresented groups help nurture future leaders who will sustain inclusive innovation. Partnerships with universities or advocacy organizations further expand talent pipelines while demonstrating genuine corporate commitment beyond mere rhetoric.

Leaders can take practical steps such as conducting regular "inclusion audits" on AI teams and projects—tracking representation alongside qualitative feedback on workplace culture—and integrating these insights into performance reviews and resource allocation decisions. Transparency around hiring goals and project decisions fosters accountability and empowers employees to raise concerns safely.

Celebrating diversity extends beyond internal dynamics to how companies engage customers through automated systems. Customizable interfaces accommodating different languages, accessibility needs, or cultural preferences show respect for user heterogeneity while boosting adoption rates. For example, a multinational e-commerce platform saw significant increases in customer satisfaction after introducing localized chatbots trained on region-specific dialects combined with culturally aware product recommendations.

To put these principles into action:

- Set measurable diversity targets linked explicitly to AI project milestones

- Create cross-functional working groups combining technical experts with social scientists or ethicists

- Conduct iterative bias impact assessments throughout model training

- Promote ongoing education on unconscious bias tailored to AI contexts

- Design user testing protocols that reflect the demographic variety of end customers

True progress in automation depends on embracing the complexity of human society—acknowledging differences rather than smoothing them away creates systems capable of adapting and thriving amid change rather than collapsing under hidden assumptions or exclusions.

As Verna Myers famously said: "Diversity is being invited to the party; inclusion is being asked to dance." In AI automation efforts, both are essential—not only ethically but pragmatically—for building solutions that endure and serve all stakeholders effectively.

CHAPTER 19:
CASE STUDIES OF
LEADING THE WAY
IN COMPANIES

Tech industry leaders

The tech industry has consistently led the way in AI-powered automation, not only as early adopters but as relentless innovators shaping the tools and frameworks that others depend on. Companies like Google, Microsoft, and Amazon have evolved from traditional software and retail giants into AI-first enterprises, embedding machine learning models across everything from search algorithms to cloud services. Their journeys reveal key patterns for businesses seeking to harness automation effectively: continuous iteration, a culture that views failure as feedback, and an unwavering commitment to scalability.

Google's use of AI in data center energy management offers a compelling example. Rather than relying on manual monitoring or static algorithms, Google developed

DeepMind's reinforcement learning models to continuously optimize cooling systems in real time. This innovation reportedly cut energy consumption for cooling by 40%. Such results highlight how combining domain expertise with AI automation can enhance decision-making, extending far beyond human intuition through predictive capabilities. Yet scaling these solutions requires robust infrastructure and agile teams capable of swiftly translating algorithmic insights into operational adjustments.

Microsoft provides another instructive case with its Azure platform. By offering Cognitive Services—plug-and-play APIs for vision recognition, language understanding, and anomaly detection—Microsoft lowered the barriers for businesses seeking AI automation. This democratization fuels innovation across industries but also raises challenges around data privacy and model customization. To address these concerns, Microsoft invested heavily in documentation, community support forums, and layered security measures—lessons vital for enterprises balancing automation benefits against regulatory demands.

Amazon's fulfillment centers showcase robotic process integration at scale. Autonomous robots transport shelves to human packers, significantly reducing walking time and streamlining workflows. Behind this smooth operation lies complex orchestration software powered by AI-driven scheduling algorithms that dynamically balance task allocation amid fluctuating demand. This collaboration between humans and machines illustrates how leading tech companies blend machine efficiency with human oversight rather than pursuing outright replacement.

These principles are evident in practical coding examples as well. Within Azure's ecosystem, developers often automate routine data preprocessing before feeding data into machine learning pipelines. Take this example:

```python
import pandas as pd
from azureml.core import Workspace, Dataset

\#\# Load workspace configuration
ws = Workspace.from_config()

\#\# Access dataset registered in Azure
dataset = Dataset.get_by_name(ws, name='customer_data')

\#\# Convert to pandas DataFrame for preprocessing
df = dataset.to_pandas_dataframe()

\#\# Example: Fill missing values automatically
df.fillna(method='ffill', inplace=True)

\#\# Save preprocessed data locally or upload back to Azure
Blob Storage for training pipeline
df.to_csv('cleaned_customer_data.csv', index=False)
```

This snippet demonstrates not just automation but embedding AI-aware practices into everyday workflows—a hallmark of tech leaders who integrate AI initiatives deeply within core business operations rather than isolating them.

Open-source communities supported by these tech giants further accelerate the adoption and refinement of AI tools. Platforms like Google's TensorFlow and Facebook's

PyTorch have transformed access to deep learning models worldwide. While open collaboration encourages rapid experimentation, it demands vigilance to maintain code quality and alignment with strategic objectives—a balance maintained through rigorous governance frameworks.

Strategically, these companies emphasize modularity —designing automation components reusable across applications—which reduces duplication and fosters agility. This approach shifts automation from isolated projects toward scalable platforms that support continuous innovation cycles.

Still, challenges remain. For example, a facial recognition system prematurely released without addressing bias issues sparked public backlash and internal reassessment. This incident underscores that technical expertise must be paired with ethical rigor—a theme championed by thought leaders like Fei-Fei Li who advocate for "human-centered AI." Embedding ethics directly into development processes ensures solutions are effective while remaining socially responsible.

Leadership styles also influence these successes profoundly. Satya Nadella's tenure at Microsoft exemplifies transformational leadership—encouraging cross-disciplinary teams to break down silos and promote widespread AI literacy instead of confining it to specialists. This cultural shift accelerated adoption rates and fostered meaningful collaboration among engineers, product managers, and end users alike.

Talent strategies further reinforce innovation by emphasizing diversity in expertise—from data scientists skilled in advanced analytics to UX designers focused on intuitive interfaces—each contributing essential perspectives for building robust automated systems. Technical depth combined with broad domain knowledge forms the foundation for sustainable progress.

In summary, tech industry leaders thrive not merely through advanced algorithms but by integrating AI-powered automation holistically into their business strategies; cultivating inclusive cultures that embrace experimentation; upholding ethical standards; leveraging open ecosystems; and assembling interdisciplinary teams guided by visionary leadership.

This comprehensive approach creates a blueprint adaptable to organizations of varying scales and contexts—where the constant is a deliberate fusion of technological mastery with strategic agility that drives lasting competitive advantage.

Healthcare innovators

Healthcare is a sector where AI-powered automation is reshaping patient outcomes and operational efficiency in profound ways. Unlike many industries, healthcare automation must carefully navigate regulatory compliance, sensitive data, and the high stakes involved in clinical decision-making. Yet, innovators who have embraced AI demonstrate that thoughtful integration can drive significant improvements across areas ranging from diagnostics to administrative workflows.

Take IBM Watson Health as an example. Despite early hype, Watson's experience highlighted the necessity of combining AI with deep domain expertise and ongoing refinement. Initially promoted as a revolutionary diagnostic tool capable of analyzing vast medical literature to recommend treatments, Watson exposed the gap between algorithmic promise and real-world clinical practice. Over time, IBM shifted focus toward more targeted applications —such as oncology decision support and imaging analysis— helping radiologists detect anomalies more accurately while reducing false positives. This evolution underscores how healthcare AI must be carefully tailored rather than broadly applied.

Radiology departments provide a clear illustration of this approach. Many hospitals now use convolutional neural networks (CNNs) trained on thousands of annotated X-rays or MRIs to identify tumors or fractures. This automation accelerates initial screenings by generating prioritized lists that highlight cases needing urgent attention. Although final diagnoses still depend on human expertise, this triage process can cut turnaround times by 30-40%. Typically, the workflow involves collecting labeled imaging data, training CNN models like ResNet or DenseNet on GPUs, integrating them into Picture Archiving and Communication Systems (PACS), and presenting flagged images with confidence scores. Beyond speeding diagnosis, this system helps reduce clinician burnout by efficiently filtering routine cases.

Another area benefiting from AI is documentation—a chronic challenge in healthcare administration. Clinicians often spend excessive hours completing electronic health records (EHRs), detracting from patient care. Solutions like Nuance's Dragon Medical One combine speech recognition with natural language processing (NLP) algorithms to transcribe and structure notes in real time. The process typically unfolds as follows: physicians dictate notes during or after consultations; advanced acoustic models convert speech to text; NLP parses medical terminology and maps phrases to standardized codes such as ICD-10 or CPT; finally, structured fields within EHR platforms are auto-populated. By reducing manual input, these tools accelerate billing cycles, improve coding accuracy, and ease cognitive burdens on providers.

Pharmaceutical companies also harness AI automation extensively within drug discovery pipelines. Insilico Medicine offers a compelling example: their platform employs generative adversarial networks (GANs) to design novel molecules with specific therapeutic properties. Unlike traditional trial-and-error approaches that can take years of lab testing, AI-driven simulations rapidly explore chemical space by virtually screening millions of compounds before synthesis. Key steps include defining disease-related target proteins, generating candidate molecules optimized for binding affinity and bioavailability, iteratively refining designs through reinforcement learning, and prioritizing candidates for laboratory validation based on predicted efficacy. This automation dramatically compresses timelines —sometimes cutting drug discovery phases from over five years to under two.

Supply chain management is another critical domain where AI-driven automation adds value by optimizing inventory and forecasting demand—particularly vital for hospitals managing essential supplies such as PPE or medications. For example, Kaiser Permanente uses predictive analytics models that combine historical usage data with external factors like seasonal illnesses or pandemics to dynamically adjust orders. Their system aggregates multi-source data including supplier information and patient admission rates, applies time-series forecasting techniques such as ARIMA or LSTM networks, and automates purchase orders aligned with predicted demand spikes. This proactive strategy ensures resource availability while minimizing excess inventory costs—a crucial balance during crises like COVID-19 surges.

Despite these successes, healthcare innovators face ongoing challenges around data privacy governed by HIPAA regulations and ethical concerns related to algorithmic bias that could worsen health disparities. Transparent model validation protocols coupled with clinician oversight remain essential safeguards against unintended consequences.

The overarching lesson from healthcare's AI pioneers is that success depends not merely on deploying advanced technology but embedding it thoughtfully within workflows that honor clinical nuance and human judgment.

Automation acts as a supplement rather than a substitute —enhancing speed, precision, and scalability without compromising safety or empathy.

these innovations demonstrate how deeply integrated automation can transform sectors where lives hinge on swift yet accurate decisions. Healthcare's experience sets a valuable precedent for other industries seeking to leverage AI responsibly while unlocking significant gains in efficiency and outcomes.

Retail and e-commerce transformations

Retail and e-commerce are among the industries most visibly transformed by AI-powered automation, revolutionizing everything from inventory management to customer engagement. In markets where consumer preferences shift rapidly, success hinges on speed, personalization, and operational agility. Unlike healthcare's cautious approach, retail embraces automation at a relentless pace, fueled by intense competition and razor-thin margins.

Amazon's fulfillment centers exemplify this transformation. Robotic automation works alongside AI-driven logistics to manage a vast network of inventory movement. Autonomous mobile robots retrieve shelves stocked with millions of products and deliver them to human pickers, drastically reducing walking time. Meanwhile, AI algorithms optimize picking routes in real time based on order priority and worker availability. The warehouse management system coordinates this complex workflow: it processes incoming orders, assigns tasks using AI-optimized scheduling, guides robots via SLAM (simultaneous localization and mapping) techniques to locate storage pods, and continuously streams data for performance monitoring. This seamless fusion of robotics and AI cuts processing times and boosts throughput without significantly increasing labor costs.

Beyond warehouse operations, AI enhances demand forecasting to help retailers avoid costly stockouts or excess inventory. Zara leverages machine learning models that analyze point-of-sale data alongside external factors such as weather and social media trends to predict regional demand fluctuations. These models often employ gradient boosting algorithms trained on multi-year sales datasets segmented by geography, product category, and seasonality. Feeding these predictions into automated replenishment systems enables Zara to restock efficiently according to local preferences—an essential advantage in fast fashion where trends change quickly.

Personalization remains a cornerstone of AI-driven automation in e-commerce. While Netflix-style recommendation engines are common, some retailers push further. Stitch Fix combines customer style profiles gathered through questionnaires with real-time feedback from purchase histories and returns. Using ensemble machine learning models that mix decision trees and neural networks, the platform generates curated clothing selections tailored to each subscriber. Although automated stylist recommendations drive scale, human experts oversee quality control, blending algorithmic efficiency with human intuition to maximize customer satisfaction.

Chatbots have evolved from simple scripted responses into intelligent virtual shopping assistants capable of nuanced interactions powered by natural language processing (NLP). Sephora's chatbot not only answers product questions but also guides users through makeup tutorials or schedules in-store appointments via conversational interfaces embedded in messaging apps or voice assistants like Alexa. Behind the scenes, intent recognition models trained on extensive conversational datasets specific to beauty retail combine with sentiment analysis to dynamically adjust tone. These tools maintain 24/7 customer engagement while freeing representatives to focus on more complex inquiries.

Automation also streamlines the checkout experience to reduce friction and cart abandonment. Amazon Go's cashierless stores utilize computer vision and sensor fusion technologies that detect products taken from shelves without barcode scans or traditional checkout lines. Convolutional neural networks analyze video feeds in real time to track customer movements while weight sensors verify product removal. Payment is automatically charged via linked accounts as customers leave—creating a seamless experience powered by tightly integrated AI systems that maintain accuracy even in crowded environments.

Inventory management extends into post-sale returns— a notorious challenge for online retailers due to logistics complexity and fraud risks. Automated returns platforms apply machine learning classifiers trained on historical return reasons along with image recognition algorithms that assess product condition from customer-uploaded photos. These systems flag suspicious claims for manual review while expediting straightforward returns through automatic refunds or exchanges, balancing efficiency with fraud prevention.

Small- and medium-sized enterprises (SMEs) increasingly benefit from AI automation tools once exclusive to industry giants through cloud-based SaaS platforms offering modular solutions for marketing automation, inventory tracking, or customer analytics. Shopify's AI-powered sales forecasting plugins enable store owners to anticipate seasonal spikes using intuitive dashboards without deep technical knowledge. While these democratized tools lower barriers, success depends on careful customization; off-the-shelf solutions often falter if businesses fail to align features with unique workflows.

However, rapid adoption of automation carries challenges

around data privacy—particularly given the extensive profiling involved in personalization—and supply chain vulnerabilities exposed by overreliance on algorithmic predictions during disruptions like pandemics or geopolitical events. Companies must balance agility with resilience; maintaining diverse supplier networks alongside human oversight remains crucial.

A practical example of implementing demand forecasting automation starts with consolidating historical sales data into clean datasets segmented by SKU (stock keeping unit), region, and time period—ideally monthly granularity over at least two years. Next comes feature engineering: incorporating promotional calendars, holidays, competitor pricing scraped from web sources, and even Google Trends indices for related keywords adds predictive power. Models such as XGBoost or Facebook's Prophet can be trained iteratively; evaluation metrics like Mean Absolute Percentage Error (MAPE) guide selection before deploying predictions into replenishment planning software via APIs or custom connectors.

retail and e-commerce demonstrate how AI-powered automation unlocks new levels of operational excellence while enhancing customer experiences in hyper-competitive markets. Success depends not on chasing every new technology but on thoughtfully embedding automation within business processes—combining cutting-edge tools with domain expertise and strategic flexibility.

This integration creates value beyond efficiency gains: it fosters loyalty through personalized experiences while optimizing costs across complex global supply chains—a balance every retailer strives for yet few fully master without deliberate design and ongoing refinement.

Financial services advancements

Financial services have long been a fertile ground

for technological innovation, but the integration of AI-powered automation has accelerated transformation at an unprecedented pace. From risk assessment to fraud detection, AI is fundamentally reshaping how banks, insurers, and investment firms operate—delivering sharper insights, faster transactions, and vastly improved customer experiences. Tasks that once required hours of manual analysis now unfold in seconds as machine learning algorithms sift through terabytes of data.

Credit scoring offers a clear example of this shift. Traditional models depend heavily on static data points like credit history and income levels. In contrast, modern AI-driven systems enhance accuracy by incorporating alternative data sources such as social media activity, purchasing behavior, and smartphone usage patterns. These models leverage advanced classification techniques—random forests or gradient boosting machines—to assign risk scores with greater precision. Take this example, Upstart, a fintech lender, uses AI to approve loans 75% faster than traditional methods while reducing default rates by nearly 30%. This combination of speed and accuracy enables financial institutions to scale lending decisions without compromising quality.

AI's operational benefits extend well beyond underwriting. Fraud detection illustrates an area where milliseconds matter. Classic rule-based systems often generate high false-positive rates, overwhelming compliance teams with alerts that consume time and resources. In response, anomaly detection powered by unsupervised machine learning techniques—such as autoencoders or clustering algorithms—learns normal transaction patterns to flag deviations with far greater specificity. JP Morgan Chase reportedly employs AI to monitor billions of transactions daily, enabling real-time identification of suspicious activities that might have previously slipped through manual reviews.

Implementing these AI solutions often requires carefully integrating new pipelines with legacy core banking systems —a complex task given regulatory constraints and system intricacies. One large multinational bank addressed this challenge by designing a hybrid architecture where AI microservices interface with existing transaction databases via APIs. This approach preserves transactional integrity while enabling scalable analytics. Developers deploy AI components modularly using containerization tools like Docker combined with orchestration platforms such as Kubernetes, allowing updates without downtime or system disruption.

Budget forecasting is another domain ripe for automation that delivers immediate returns on investment. Financial planners traditionally grapple with sprawling spreadsheets prone to human error and version control issues. Today's predictive analytics models ingest historical expenditure data alongside macroeconomic indicators to generate probabilistic forecasts under various scenarios—employing Bayesian networks or recurrent neural networks (RNNs) trained on temporal financial data streams. Visualization platforms then translate these predictions into intuitive dashboards, enabling CFOs to interactively test variables like interest rate hikes and their effects on liquidity ratios.

The following Python example illustrates a simple workflow for budget forecasting using an LSTM model—a specialized RNN suited for sequential financial data:

```python
import numpy as np

import pandas as pd

from keras.models import Sequential

from keras.layers import LSTM, Dense
```

```python
from sklearn.preprocessing import MinMaxScaler

\#\# Load monthly expenditure data
data = pd.read_csv('monthly_expense.csv')
values = data['expense'].values.reshape(-1, 1)

\#\# Normalize data between 0 and 1
scaler = MinMaxScaler(feature_range=(0,1))
scaled_values = scaler.fit_transform(values)

\#\# Prepare training sequences: past 12 months to predict next month
X_train = []
y_train = []
for i in range(12, len(scaled_values)):
X_train.append(scaled_values[i-12:i])
y_train.append(scaled_values[i])

X_train = np.array(X_train)
y_train = np.array(y_train)

\#\# Define LSTM model architecture
model = Sequential()
model.add(LSTM(50, activation='relu', input_shape=(12, 1)))
```

```
model.add(Dense(1))
model.compile(optimizer='adam', loss='mse')

\#\# Train model
model.fit(X_train, y_train, epochs=50)

\#\# Predict next month's budget
last_12_months = scaled_values[-12:].reshape(1,12,1)
predicted_scaled = model.predict(last_12_months)
predicted_expense = scaler.inverse_transform(predicted_scaled)
print(f"Predicted expense for next month: predicted_expense[0][0]:.2f")
```
` ` `

This snippet demonstrates the full process—from data normalization to prediction—offering a replicable template for finance teams exploring AI-driven forecasting.

Automation also plays a crucial role in compliance reporting, alleviating significant burdens while enhancing accuracy. Regulatory frameworks such as Basel III and GDPR require timely disclosure of capital adequacy and customer privacy metrics—areas well suited to automation through natural language generation (NLG) combined with structured databases. By extracting real-time compliance figures from operational systems and automatically generating human-readable summary reports via SQL querying engines integrated with NLG templates (often programmed in Python or JavaScript), institutions can meet regulatory demands more efficiently.

Risk management has embraced automation beyond number crunching into dynamic scenario simulation using reinforcement learning algorithms. These agents continuously learn from market fluctuations and adjust hedging strategies in real time rather than relying solely on static rulebooks crafted years ago. While computationally intensive, this approach reduces unexpected losses by adapting proactively to changing conditions.

Even payroll processing benefits from automation improvements. Intelligent bots cross-verify timesheets against attendance records using optical character recognition (OCR) integrated with robotic process automation (RPA) tools like UiPath or Automation Anywhere before triggering payments—all while maintaining audit trails required by internal controls.

Investment advisors increasingly integrate AI tools as well. Robo-advisors combine client preferences with market trend analysis powered by sentiment analysis drawn from news feeds and social media monitoring platforms such as Meltwater or Brandwatch. By automating portfolio rebalancing based on predefined risk thresholds calculated through Monte Carlo simulations embedded in Python scripts or MATLAB environments, advisors deliver personalized wealth management at scale.

Despite these advances, challenges remain. Transparency issues arise when complex machine learning models become opaque "black boxes," complicating auditors' ability to justify decisions. Cybersecurity risks grow as systems integrate numerous external data sources. Additionally, staff resistance may slow adoption if employees fear replacement rather than augmentation.

Still, the benefits overwhelmingly favor business efficiency and strategic agility. As investor Peter Lynch famously advised: "Invest in what you know." In this context, that means embracing intelligent automation tailored precisely to the unique needs of your financial ecosystem rather than relying on generic off-the-shelf solutions.

AI's role in financial services transcends faster number crunching; it reimagines entire workflows—from underwriting loans more swiftly than ever before to instantly detecting fraudulent transactions among billions processed daily—all while helping businesses manage regulatory demands more effectively than traditional methods ever could. Those who master these innovations position themselves not only ahead technologically but also financially—unlocking unprecedented levels of profitability driven by precision and speed unseen in any industry sector before.

Manufacturing process optimizers

Manufacturing has always depended on precision and efficiency, but AI-powered automation is reshaping what those concepts mean in practice. Where traditional production lines relied on fixed schedules and manual quality checks, smart systems now optimize every phase —from raw material sourcing to final assembly. This shift is driven by AI tools that enable predictive maintenance, adaptive scheduling, and real-time quality control.

Take predictive maintenance as an example. Machine downtime costs manufacturers billions each year, yet maintenance traditionally followed fixed intervals or reacted only after failures occurred. Modern AI models analyze continuous sensor data—such as vibration levels, temperature changes, and acoustic signals—using machine learning algorithms to detect subtle anomalies well before breakdowns happen. Siemens, for instance, applies these techniques to their gas turbines, allowing operators to schedule maintenance precisely when needed rather than relying on conservative estimates. The results speak for themselves: downtime can drop by up to 30%, and inventory costs shrink as unnecessary part replacements are avoided.

Achieving this level of insight requires more than just sensors—it demands robust data pipelines capable of handling large volumes of time-series information efficiently. Typically, IoT-enabled devices are installed on critical machinery, streaming data into a centralized platform, often cloud-based for scalability. Algorithms such as Random Forest classifiers or Long Short-Term Memory (LSTM) networks then analyze patterns that signal wear or malfunction.

A straightforward Python example using an Isolation Forest model shows how anomaly detection might work on vibration sensor readings:

```python
import pandas as pd

from sklearn.ensemble import IsolationForest


\#\# Load sensor data (timestamp, vibration_level)

data = pd.read_csv('machine_vibration.csv')


\#\# Use only vibration_level for anomaly detection

X = data[['vibration_level']]


\#\# Train Isolation Forest

model = IsolationForest(contamination=0.01)

model.fit(X)


\#\# Predict anomalies (-1 for anomaly, 1 for normal)
```

```
data['anomaly'] = model.predict(X)

\#\# Extract timestamps where anomalies detected
anomalies = data[data['anomaly'] == -1]
print(anomalies[['timestamp', 'vibration_level']])
```
` ` `

This snippet illustrates how manufacturers can quickly start flagging irregular equipment behavior without deep AI expertise—a crucial step toward gaining early wins in automation adoption.

Beyond maintenance, adaptive scheduling plays a vital role in boosting manufacturing throughput. Traditional scheduling struggles with sudden order changes or supply delays, but AI-driven systems dynamically adjust workflows by balancing machine availability, labor capacity, and delivery deadlines. This flexibility leads to shorter lead times and reduced inventory costs.

BMW's Munich plant provides a compelling example. There, an AI-based scheduling system integrates production data with supplier statuses and customer orders daily. By combining constraint satisfaction algorithms with reinforcement learning agents that evolve optimal scheduling policies over time, the plant significantly cut idle times and improved output consistency—even amid unpredictable demand surges.

Implementing such systems starts with digitizing existing workflows—process mining tools help by extracting event logs from ERP or MES (Manufacturing Execution Systems). These logs feed optimization models trained on historical production outcomes, creating feedback loops that drive continuous improvement.

Quality control also benefits greatly from AI-driven automation powered by computer vision. Manual inspections are prone to fatigue-induced errors and limited throughput, whereas high-resolution cameras paired with convolutional neural networks (CNNs) can instantly detect defects like cracks, surface blemishes, or misalignments right on the production line.

Fanuc demonstrates this approach by integrating vision-based defect detection directly into robotic arms assembling circuit boards. As thousands of components pass through inspection stations at high speed, CNNs analyze images in real time with accuracy surpassing human inspectors.

Here's a simplified Python example using TensorFlow to illustrate the concept:

```python
import tensorflow as tf

from tensorflow.keras.models import load_model

from tensorflow.keras.preprocessing import image

import numpy as np


\#\# Load pre-trained defect detection model

model = load_model('defect_detection_cnn.h5')


\#\# Load and preprocess image from assembly line camera

img_path = 'component_sample.jpg'

img = image.load_img(img_path, target_size=(224, 224))

x = image.img_to_array(img)

x = np.expand_dims(x, axis=0) / 255.0
```

```
\#\# Predict defect presence probability

prediction = model.predict(x)

print(f"Defect probability: prediction[0][0]:.2f")
` ` `
```

While this example is simplified compared to industrial-grade deployments— which require large labeled datasets and robust edge computing infrastructure—it shows how manufacturing teams can prototype automated quality checks internally before scaling up.

Despite these advances, integration challenges remain significant. Many factories still operate legacy equipment lacking connectivity options, necessitating retrofits or middleware solutions. Workforce adaptation is equally important; technicians must learn not only to use new tools but also to interpret AI outputs meaningfully within operational contexts.

Companies that navigate these challenges successfully reap substantial benefits: shorter production cycles reduce working capital tied up in inventory; fewer unexpected downtimes improve customer satisfaction through reliable deliveries; enhanced quality lowers warranty claims and reputational risks.

Another accelerating trend is the rise of digital twins—a virtual replica of physical assets that simulates production scenarios under varying conditions without disrupting actual operations. Engineers can experiment with layout changes or process adjustments virtually, deploying validated improvements onsite with confidence.

automating manufacturing processes goes beyond robots replacing manual labor. It embeds intelligence throughout the value chain, enabling proactive decision-making instead of reactive firefighting. Enterprises embracing these technologies position themselves not just to survive market volatility but to thrive through agility and precision enabled by AI-enhanced workflows.

At its core, modern manufacturing optimization harnesses data-driven insights at every step—from early detection of machine health issues to dynamic orchestration of complex schedules and flawless product quality—redefining operational excellence far beyond what was possible even a decade ago.

Telecommunication breakthroughs

Telecommunications have been profoundly transformed by AI-powered automation, reshaping network management, customer experience, and service delivery. The complexity of modern telecom infrastructures—with extensive fiber optics, mobile networks, and satellite links—requires solutions that surpass human capabilities. In this context, AI plays a foundational role, enabling networks to be scalable, efficient, and adaptive.

At the forefront of AI innovation is network optimization. Traditional manual configurations and reactive maintenance can no longer keep pace with surging data traffic and rapid 5G deployment. Telecom providers now deploy AI algorithms that analyze vast telemetry datasets—such as signal strength variations, packet loss rates, and user mobility patterns—to dynamically adjust network parameters. For example, AT&T uses machine learning models to predict congestion points before they arise, allowing for proactive bandwidth allocation and load balancing. This leads to reduced latency and improved quality of service even during peak usage periods.

Building such predictive models involves a layered data pipeline. Raw network logs are first preprocessed to extract key features like throughput per cell tower or fluctuations in user density. These features then feed into classification or regression models—random forests for anomaly detection or deep neural networks for recognizing complex patterns. Unlike traditional threshold-based alerts, these AI-driven systems can detect subtle early signs of network faults or performance degradations.

A simple Python example illustrates this approach by using Isolation Forests to detect anomalies in network metrics:

```python
import pandas as pd

from sklearn.ensemble import IsolationForest


\#\# Load network performance data with features like latency, throughput

data = pd.read_csv('network_metrics.csv')


\#\# Select relevant features

X = data[['latency_ms', 'throughput_mbps', 'packet_loss']]


\#\# Train Isolation Forest model to detect anomalies (outliers)

model = IsolationForest(contamination=0.02)

model.fit(X)


\#\# Predict anomalies: -1 indicates anomaly

data['anomaly'] = model.predict(X)


\#\# Filter detected anomalies
```

```
anomalies = data[data['anomaly'] == -1]

print(anomalies[['timestamp',                'latency_ms',
'throughput_mbps']])
```
` ` `

Though straightforward, this example highlights how telecom engineers can automate monitoring to flag irregularities faster and more reliably than manual inspections.

Beyond fault detection, AI also enhances capacity planning. Mobile operators must anticipate usage trends across regions to deploy infrastructure efficiently. Verizon, for instance, employs time-series forecasting models—combining ARIMA with LSTM networks—to predict shifts in subscriber demand related to events like sports games or festivals. Accurate forecasts help inform decisions about activating temporary cell sites or implementing dynamic spectrum sharing.

Improving customer experience represents another vital application of AI in telecom. Chatbots powered by natural language processing handle millions of support queries daily across SMS, voice assistants, and web portals. These virtual agents address routine issues such as bill inquiries or service resets, freeing human agents to focus on complex cases. Telefónica's Aura virtual assistant exemplifies this evolution by combining contextual understanding with sentiment analysis to provide personalized interactions while quickly escalating sensitive matters.

Robotic process automation (RPA) streamlines backend workflows as well. In the order-to-activation process, for example, RPA bots verify account eligibility, coordinate inventory checks, schedule installation appointments, and update CRM systems—all without human intervention. This automation drastically reduces turnaround times from days to hours.

AI also plays a critical role in fraud detection within telecom ecosystems vulnerable to subscription fraud and identity theft. Machine learning classifiers analyze call detail records (CDRs) to identify anomalous calling patterns indicative of SIM cloning or unauthorized account use. Continuously adapting to evolving fraud signatures, these systems outperform traditional rule-based filters that often generate false positives.

Network security benefits from AI-driven intrusion detection systems (IDS) that scan massive traffic flows for cyber threats in real time. Operators employ unsupervised learning techniques like autoencoders or clustering algorithms to isolate malicious activity hidden within legitimate data—a necessity amid increasingly sophisticated attacks targeting telecom infrastructure.

A key enabler of many AI applications is edge computing combined with 5G's low-latency capabilities. Instead of routing all data to centralized clouds—which introduces delays—AI inference engines embedded at base stations or edge nodes execute real-time decisions locally. Huawei, for example, has piloted edge AI platforms that autonomously adjust beamforming parameters based on user location patterns detected moments earlier.

Despite these advances, integrating AI with legacy systems remains a persistent challenge for many telecom operators. Numerous organizations still rely on monolithic OSS/BSS platforms that are difficult to retrofit with AI modules directly. Middleware solutions that bridge traditional databases with modern APIs enable incremental automation without disruptive overhauls.

Equally important is employee adaptation: network engineers are transitioning from routine monitoring tasks toward supervising AI outputs and interpreting predictive alerts within operational contexts—a shift resembling a pilot-in-the-loop model rather than fully autonomous control.

Telecom companies investing in these technologies not only improve operational efficiency but also unlock new revenue streams through AI-powered services—such as personalized data plans that dynamically adjust based on predicted consumption or intelligent roaming pricing tailored to travel behaviors.

telecommunications is evolving into an intelligent ecosystem where AI-driven automation harmonizes hardware assets, software platforms, and human expertise to deliver seamless connectivity experiences demanded by today's hyperconnected world.

This transformation goes beyond faster internet or clearer calls; it marks a shift toward self-optimizing networks capable of instant adaptation to environmental changes and user needs—a paradigm made possible only through deep integration of artificial intelligence across every layer of telecom operation and management.

Energy sector innovations

The energy sector's adoption of AI-powered automation is transforming how power generation, distribution, and consumption are managed. Moving beyond traditional systems that depend heavily on manual oversight and fixed schedules, modern energy infrastructures now leverage AI to optimize performance in real time, achieving a finely tuned balance between supply and demand. This shift not only enhances efficiency but also addresses pressing challenges such as sustainability and grid resilience.

Central to this transformation is smart grid technology, which applies AI algorithms to analyze extensive data streams from sensors embedded throughout the network. These sensors track a variety of factors including voltage fluctuations, equipment health, weather conditions, and consumer usage patterns. Take a wind farm as an example: turbines continuously generate operational data—blade angles, rotational speeds, ambient temperatures—that AI models process to dynamically adjust turbine settings. This maximizes output while minimizing wear and tear. Siemens' digital twin platform illustrates this approach by simulating equipment behavior under different scenarios and forecasting maintenance needs before failures occur.

Load forecasting offers a practical demonstration of AI's impact. Energy providers must carefully match generation with consumption, but conventional methods often struggle with variability introduced by renewables like solar and wind. AI techniques such as gradient boosting regression or long short-term memory (LSTM) networks excel at capturing complex temporal patterns and nonlinear relationships in consumption data.

Consider this simplified Python example using a random forest regressor for load prediction:

```python
import pandas as pd

from sklearn.ensemble import RandomForestRegressor

from sklearn.model_selection import train_test_split

from sklearn.metrics import mean_absolute_error


\#\# Load historical load and weather data

data = pd.read_csv('energy_load_weather.csv')


\#\# Features: temperature, humidity, day_of_week encoded numerically

X = data[['temperature', 'humidity', 'day_of_week']]
```

```
y = data['load_mw']

\#\# Split into training/testing sets
X_train, X_test, y_train, y_test = train_test_split(X, y,
test_size=0.2)

\#\# Train random forest model
model = RandomForestRegressor(n_estimators=100)
model.fit(X_train, y_train)

\#\# Predict load values on test set
y_pred = model.predict(X_test)

\#\# Evaluate prediction accuracy
mae = mean_absolute_error(y_test, y_pred)
print(f"Mean Absolute Error: mae:.2f MW")
` ` `
```

While this example abstracts many complexities, it highlights how incorporating weather variables can improve forecast accuracy—enabling utilities to adjust generation schedules or dispatch reserves more effectively.

AI's predictive capabilities also enhance energy storage management. Grid-scale batteries must carefully balance charge and discharge cycles to extend lifespan while meeting variable demand. Reinforcement learning algorithms are well-suited to this task, learning optimal policies through simulated trial-and-error interactions and adapting strategies in response to changing market prices or grid conditions.

Demand response programs benefit from AI automation as well. By analyzing detailed consumption patterns—down to individual households or devices—utilities can deliver personalized incentives or control signals that encourage shifting usage away from peak hours. This approach alleviates infrastructure stress without compromising consumer comfort, relying on finely tuned algorithms that process real-time feedback.

The rise of distributed energy resources (DERs) such as rooftop solar panels, small wind turbines, and electric vehicles introduces further complexity. Managing these decentralized assets demands platforms capable of aggregating diverse inputs and orchestrating their operation cohesively. AutoGrid's flexibility management system exemplifies this by employing machine learning models to predict DER availability and coordinate dispatch across thousands of units simultaneously.

As energy systems become increasingly digital and interconnected, cybersecurity takes on renewed importance. AI-driven anomaly detection tools monitor network traffic for signs of cyberattacks targeting control systems or data integrity. Methods like autoencoders and clustering quickly identify deviations from normal patterns—an essential capability given the growing threats power grids face amid geopolitical tensions.

On the regulatory side, compliance grows more complex with evolving standards designed to reduce carbon footprints and improve transparency around renewable integration. Automation tools embed compliance checks into operational workflows—flagging potential issues early to avoid costly penalties while streamlining reporting through automated document generation.

A significant challenge remains in integrating legacy

infrastructure. Many utilities operate aging equipment not originally designed for digital connectivity. Middleware solutions that translate between older protocols and modern IoT frameworks play a crucial role in enabling incremental upgrades without disruptive downtime—making it possible to harness AI benefits while preserving existing assets.

Alongside technological change, workforce transformation unfolds within energy companies adopting automation. Routine monitoring roles give way to specialists who interpret AI-generated insights and develop adaptive strategies responsive to complex market dynamics. This shift demands a new blend of domain expertise combined with data fluency.

Beyond operational savings, AI opens new financial opportunities for utilities. Dynamic pricing models powered by real-time market analysis can unlock revenue streams, while offering value-added services such as predictive maintenance contracts for distributed generators owned by consumers themselves creates fresh business prospects.

Together, the integration of artificial intelligence within energy systems marks more than just incremental efficiency gains. It represents a fundamental shift toward resilient, sustainable power ecosystems where human oversight works in harmony with autonomous optimization—paving the way for cleaner grids capable of meeting tomorrow's demands while ensuring reliability today.

Lessons learned from failures

Failures in AI-powered automation projects often reveal critical lessons that businesses can leverage to harness this technology more effectively. A frequent challenge is underestimating data quality issues. Inaccurate, incomplete, or biased datasets can derail machine learning models even before they are deployed. Take this example, a retail chain that tried to automate inventory replenishment based its predictions on sales data plagued by inconsistent timestamps and missing entries. This led to stockouts of high-demand items and overstocking of slow movers —outcomes that increased costs and hurt customer satisfaction. This example highlights the importance of rigorous data auditing and preprocessing before any modeling begins.

Integration with legacy systems presents another common obstacle. A manufacturing firm invested heavily in an AI-driven predictive maintenance platform without accounting for compatibility with its decades-old equipment monitoring infrastructure. Lacking middleware or suitable APIs to bridge the gap, system communication failures caused inaccurate alerts and unplanned downtime, effectively negating automation benefits. For organizations facing similar challenges, incremental modernization paired with carefully planned integration layers can prevent such costly disruptions.

Scope creep also undermines many AI initiatives. The impulse to include every possible feature upfront often results in extended timelines and depleted resources without delivering clear business value. One financial services company sought to automate end-to-end loan processing but encountered repeated redesigns and testing cycles due to unclear objectives and shifting requirements. Taking an agile approach—starting with small pilot projects targeting well-defined use cases—helps maintain momentum while allowing iterative improvements.

Human factors are equally significant. Employee resistance driven by concerns over job security or skepticism about AI's reliability can stall adoption efforts. An insurance firm experienced reluctance from claims adjusters to trust automated decision support tools until transparency measures were embedded into workflows alongside targeted training that emphasized augmentation rather than replacement. Fostering a culture that embraces collaboration between humans and machines is vital for successful change management.

Financial constraints often tighten midway through projects as unforeseen costs arise—from additional data collection to specialized talent acquisition or extended testing phases. A startup developing a natural language processing application underestimated cloud infrastructure scaling expenses, leading to budget overruns and forced project downscaling. Building comprehensive budgets that include contingency funds for technical challenges can help mitigate these risks.

Finally, the absence of continuous monitoring after deployment frequently dooms automation efforts to stagnation or failure over time. Models degrade as business conditions evolve—a phenomenon known as model drift—and ignoring this leads to unnoticed declines in performance until significant damage occurs. For example, a logistics provider's route optimization AI lost accuracy following seasonal traffic pattern shifts but lacked alert systems or retraining pipelines to respond promptly.

Together, these lessons emphasize that successful AI automation requires more than just technology investment; it demands meticulous preparation, realistic planning, attention to organizational dynamics, and ongoing stewardship post-launch. Ignoring these aspects risks wasting resources on implementations that fall short of promised returns or create new operational challenges.

In practical terms, start your next AI project with thorough data validation using tools like Python's pandas profiling or open-source frameworks such as Great Expectations to detect anomalies early. When legacy system integration is unavoidable, design middleware connectors based on RESTful APIs or message brokers like Apache Kafka to ensure smooth interoperability without extensive system overhauls.

Define project scope around high-impact bottlenecks where measurable improvements justify the effort—whether automating invoice processing cycles from days down to hours or reducing customer support ticket resolution times through chatbot assistance.

Maintain transparent communication with stakeholders throughout the project; share progress metrics regularly and establish feedback loops so end-users can raise concerns or suggest improvements easily.

Budget realistically by accounting for hidden costs: fluctuating cloud hosting fees, competitive salaries for data scientists and ML engineers, and schedule inflation due to unforeseen delays.

Deploy monitoring dashboards linked directly to model outputs using tools like MLflow or Grafana so that anomalies trigger immediate alerts for remediation teams—preventing silent degradations that damage efficiency and trust.

failures in AI projects should not be viewed as endpoints but as catalysts for refining strategy execution—the hard-earned wisdom that transforms organizations from experimental adopters into industry leaders capable of sustainable innovation through automation.

Mastering these lessons turns initial setbacks into stepping stones toward resilient, scalable AI ecosystems that consistently deliver value in an ever-changing business landscape.

CHAPTER 20: CONCLUSION AND ROAD AHEAD

Key takeaways from the book

Understanding the core lessons from AI-powered automation grounds the entire discussion in practical wisdom. Successful automation depends not only on deploying advanced technologies but also on aligning them carefully with specific business needs and executing thoughtfully. Central to this is data quality —without clean, well-structured data, even the most sophisticated AI models struggle to perform effectively. Take this example, investing time upfront with tools like Python's pandas profiling or Great Expectations to audit and cleanse datasets can prevent costly errors down the line.

Equally important is integrating AI solutions smoothly with existing infrastructure. Many organizations still rely on legacy systems that require custom middleware or APIs to connect old and new technologies without disrupting operations. Consider a manufacturing company that avoided a full system overhaul by developing

RESTful connectors between its monitoring equipment and predictive maintenance AI; this incremental approach enabled seamless communication and delivered immediate return on investment.

Maintaining clear project scope is another essential insight. Spreading efforts too thin across numerous automation goals often results in delays, budget overruns, and diluted outcomes. Focusing on well-defined, high-impact processes —such as automating invoice approvals or streamlining customer support ticket routing—yields measurable improvements without overwhelming teams or resources. Applying agile methodologies, with rapid pilots followed by iterative refinement, helps keep projects tightly aligned with business value.

The human element plays a critical role as well. Employee resistance usually arises from uncertainty rather than outright opposition to technology. Being transparent about how AI supports jobs instead of replacing them, combined with hands-on training and open communication, encourages collaboration between people and machines. An insurance company's experience demonstrates this clearly: by embedding explainability into decision support tools and providing targeted upskilling, they transformed skeptics into advocates.

Financial realism cannot be overlooked either. Budgets must account not just for initial software licenses or hardware but also for less visible costs such as cloud scaling fees, specialized talent recruitment, ongoing maintenance, and contingency funds for unforeseen challenges. A startup's premature shutdown of its NLP application due to underestimating infrastructure expenses illustrates the consequences of insufficient financial planning.

Sustained success requires continuous monitoring after deployment rather than viewing implementation as a one-off achievement. Model drift—where evolving market conditions degrade AI accuracy over time—demands automated alerting systems and retraining pipelines to preserve performance. Logistics companies that neglect these factors risk losing optimization benefits amid changing traffic patterns or supply constraints.

Taken together, these insights reveal that AI automation is less about hype and more about disciplined execution grounded in preparation, realistic planning, human engagement, financial prudence, and ongoing stewardship. This holistic approach transforms AI initiatives from speculative experiments into resilient drivers of lasting business advantage.

To apply these principles practically, start with a comprehensive data health check using open-source profiling libraries before selecting automation targets based on bottleneck severity and potential ROI. Design integration layers focused on flexibility and minimal disruption through modern API standards or messaging platforms like Apache Kafka. Keep projects lean by defining clear objectives prioritized around quick wins while embedding transparency into workforce training early on.

Develop detailed budget plans that include contingency reserves for unexpected resource demands—recognizing that cloud hosting costs can fluctuate and top-tier machine learning talent commands premium salaries in competitive markets. After deployment, implement monitoring dashboards powered by tools such as MLflow or Grafana to provide real-time model insights alongside proactive alert mechanisms for anomalies.

Above all, cultivate a culture that views setbacks as learning opportunities rather than failures—fostering continuous improvement through iteration—a hallmark of mature organizations successfully advancing AI at scale.

By mastering these guiding principles, your path toward sustainable automation becomes not only achievable but advantageous in an increasingly competitive landscape where agility defines survival.

Revisiting the role of leadership

The practical implications of this approach are clear. Leaders need to develop fluency in AI concepts—not to become data scientists themselves, but to grasp the technology's capabilities and limitations well enough to ask meaningful questions. This understanding improves decision-making, from selecting pilot projects aligned with strategic priorities to managing risk and reward across portfolios. When a CEO clearly communicates why automating a supply chain bottleneck matters—in terms of customer satisfaction, inventory turnover, and cost savings—it builds momentum that reaches beyond IT into marketing, operations, and finance.

Equally crucial is an awareness of the human dynamics automation triggers. Resistance often stems from fear of obsolescence or loss of control rather than simple inertia. Leaders who engage transparently with their workforce—explaining how AI tools augment rather than replace roles—can reduce anxiety and build trust. Take this example, at a global logistics firm, leadership introduced AI-powered route optimization alongside retraining programs for drivers and dispatchers instead of rolling out changes silently. The result was higher adoption rates and unexpected ideas from frontline employees who felt valued rather than sidelined.

Leadership also requires fostering cross-functional collaboration. Automation rarely fits neatly within one department; it impacts multiple areas with differing priorities. Executives who establish interdisciplinary steering committees create spaces for diverse perspectives that identify risks early and uncover innovative use cases overlooked by narrow viewpoints. A financial services company exemplifies this: marketing teamed up with data science not only to automate campaign targeting but also to refine product design based on evolving customer behavior patterns revealed through AI insights.

Another vital trait of effective leaders guiding automation journeys is strategic patience. The lure of rapid ROI can push organizations into premature scale-ups or overly ambitious pilots without sufficient groundwork. Leaders must resist "shiny object syndrome," insisting on incremental wins supported by rigorous measurement frameworks. IBM's experience with Watson illustrates this balance well; initial hype gave way to carefully measured deployments focused on specific business problems like claims processing before expanding more broadly.

Resource allocation under strong leadership goes beyond budgeting capital; it extends into talent development and culture building. The scarcity of skilled AI professionals makes internal upskilling as essential as external hiring— a challenge intensified by global competition for expertise. Leaders who invest early in training programs build pipelines aligned with organizational needs, rather than relying heavily on expensive consultants whose departure can leave knowledge gaps.

Finally, leadership accountability ensures that ethical considerations remain central amid automation's excitement. Deliberate oversight is required around data privacy, algorithmic fairness, and transparency, embedded within senior governance structures. Fei-Fei Li captures this responsibility succinctly: "The future of AI depends not only on technical advances but on thoughtful governance." Neglecting these aspects risks reputational damage and regulatory backlash that can derail promising initiatives.

Putting these leadership principles into practice involves

deliberate steps:

- Develop executive education sessions tailored to your industry's specific AI opportunities.

- Establish cross-departmental governance bodies with clear charters to prioritize projects.

- Design communication strategies that emphasize ongoing dialogue about changes affecting staff roles.

- Create staged investment plans tied explicitly to milestone achievements validated through data.

- Launch internal mentorship programs pairing data scientists with domain experts.

- Integrate ethical review checkpoints into project workflows before scaling.

Leadership is not about dictating automation outcomes from an ivory tower; it's about empowering teams while navigating complexity with clarity and accountability. Those who embrace this multifaceted role transform AI-powered automation from a technological challenge into a catalyst for sustainable competitive advantage.

At its core, effective leadership turns potential disruption into orchestrated transformation—balancing technical insight with emotional intelligence to harness automation's full value without losing sight of the people driving change forward.

The human element in AI-driven businesses

Automation's promise extends far beyond algorithms and data—it fundamentally centers on people. The human element in AI-driven businesses shapes not only how technology is deployed but also how value is created, sustained, and expanded. To fully grasp this dynamic, it is essential to consider workforce dynamics, cultural adaptation, and leadership engagement—factors that breathe life into automated systems.

Essentially of AI integration lies a paradox: while automation seeks to reduce manual intervention, it often heightens the need for human creativity, judgment, and oversight. Take JPMorgan Chase's COiN platform as an example. This AI system processes thousands of contracts in seconds—tasks that would take lawyers countless hours—yet humans remain indispensable for interpreting nuanced clauses and making final decisions. This hybrid approach enhances efficiency without relinquishing control, illustrating a broader trend where human expertise amplifies AI capabilities rather than being replaced by them.

Embracing this symbiosis involves more than redefining roles; it calls for reimagining workplace culture. Organizations that view employees as collaborators in automation, rather than obstacles, unlock unexpected benefits. A mid-sized manufacturing firm's experience with AI-powered predictive maintenance tools demonstrates this well. Initially met with skepticism by technicians concerned about job security, the company shifted tactics by involving them early as "automation champions." These technicians offered valuable insights that refined sensor placements and alert thresholds, resulting in higher system accuracy and improved morale. This example shows how fostering ownership can transform resistance into advocacy.

Clear communication plays a pivotal role in this cultural shift. Employees need to understand which tasks are automated and which still require human input to avoid confusion or disengagement. Transparency about AI's limitations helps counter unrealistic expectations or undue fears. Take this example, a retail chain deploying chatbots for customer service briefed frontline staff on chatbot capabilities and trained them to handle escalations effectively—an approach that maintained service quality while freeing employees to focus on complex issues.

Sustainable AI adoption also depends on training programs tailored to evolving skill requirements. Upskilling initiatives should go beyond technical expertise to emphasize soft skills like problem-solving and ethical reasoning critical for oversight roles. Accenture's internal academy offers a practical model: employees across departments complete modules blending data literacy with decision-making frameworks for AI governance, building confidence alongside competence.

AI further introduces challenges related to workforce diversity and inclusion that organizations must address thoughtfully. Algorithms can unintentionally perpetuate bias if trained on data reflecting historical inequalities—a risk exemplified by Amazon's discontinued recruitment tool that showed gender bias. Active human oversight combined with diverse teams reviewing AI outputs helps identify and mitigate such issues early.

Leadership plays a crucial role that goes beyond setting strategic direction; it requires empathy toward these human complexities. Leaders who engage authentically with employee concerns foster trust essential for smooth transitions—often through iterative dialogue like town halls or feedback loops rather than top-down mandates alone. One logistics company instituted weekly "AI open forums," creating space to share successes and address anxieties openly; this transparency encouraged collective problem-solving instead of fear-driven resistance.

Human-centered design principles are gaining traction in developing AI interfaces tailored to user needs rather than forcing users to adapt rigidly around technology constraints. User experience research uncovers pain points such as alert fatigue from excessive notifications or unclear dashboard metrics; addressing these improves adoption rates as well as operational outcomes.

Finally, ethical stewardship intersects deeply with the human dimension of automation efforts. Organizations must balance efficiency gains against potential impacts on employment quality and privacy rights—concerns requiring multidisciplinary input beyond technologists alone. Establishing ethics committees that include HR representatives, legal advisors, frontline workers, and data scientists ensures automated solutions align with organizational values while respecting individual dignity.

Integrating AI into business processes is not a zero-sum contest between humans and machines; it reshapes how people collaborate with technology toward shared goals. Companies that recognize this duality will be better positioned to cultivate resilient cultures where innovation thrives without sacrificing humanity's essential role at the heart of value creation.

The true challenge lies in orchestrating collaboration between intelligent systems and individuals empowered not just to coexist but to co-create—unlocking automation's full potential beyond cost savings into sustained competitive advantage grounded firmly in the human experience itself.

The importance of agility and adaptability

Change in today's business environment doesn't simply occur—it accelerates, twists unpredictably, and often catches organizations off guard. Agility and adaptability are not mere buzzwords; they are essential survival mechanisms. Companies bound by rigid structures risk falling behind, as AI-powered automation demands flexibility across strategic, operational, and cultural dimensions.

True agility goes beyond quick reactions; it requires embedding responsiveness directly into workflows. Take, for example, an e-commerce retailer that implemented AI-driven inventory management. When global supply chain disruptions arose unexpectedly, the system swiftly adjusted reorder points based on real-time shifts in demand patterns. The IT team wasn't forced to scramble rewriting code or intervene manually. Instead, automation flexed naturally with evolving conditions, preventing costly stockouts or overstocks. This kind of built-in agility empowers businesses to pivot smoothly rather than freeze under pressure.

However, adaptability depends as much on human judgment as it does on machine efficiency. Automation tools can highlight anomalies or suggest optimal courses of action, but frontline teams must interpret these insights in light of market realities and customer nuances that AI may overlook. Take this example, a logistics company deployed route optimization algorithms prioritizing shortest distances. Drivers challenged the recommendations because some routes regularly faced delays due to traffic or weather conditions not fully captured in the data. By incorporating driver feedback, the company created a hybrid approach blending algorithmic precision with practical experience— illustrating adaptability as a collaborative interplay between technology and people.

Fostering this mindset begins with leadership but must permeate every organizational layer. Agile companies encourage decentralized decision-making, empowering teams closest to operations to adjust automated processes rapidly without bureaucratic delays. One effective method is forming "automation squads" responsible for continuously monitoring key performance indicators and iterating workflows based on evolving needs instead of waiting for top-down instructions. These squads often rely on dashboards updated hourly or daily—frequently powered by AI themselves—to spot inefficiencies early and respond proactively.

When paired with regular review cycles, tools such as Python scripts for data analysis or Excel macros for reporting transform from static solutions into living assets. Finance teams automating month-end reports not only reduce manual workloads but also establish weekly checkpoints where analysts examine flagged anomalies and refine formulas accordingly. This iterative process marries technical rigor with adaptive thinking.

Organizational culture plays a pivotal role in supporting such adaptability. A tolerance for experimentation and failure is crucial because agile adaptation requires quickly trying new approaches—even if some fall short initially. Consider a mid-sized SaaS company that rolled out AI chatbots for customer support on an aggressive timeline. Early performance was uneven; bots frequently misunderstood customer intents, frustrating users. Rather than abandoning automation in favor of human agents exclusively, the team implemented rapid feedback loops to capture errors, retrain models weekly, and incrementally improve conversation flows. Within three months, customer satisfaction climbed substantially as the bots evolved responsively.

This example highlights that adaptability doesn't mean expecting flawless automation from day one; it means building systems designed for continuous improvement grounded in real-world interactions.

Another important aspect of agility lies in technology choices favoring modularity and scalability over monolithic systems that lock companies into rigid paths. Cloud-native architectures enable components like AI inference engines or data pipelines to be swapped without disrupting entire workflows—a critical capability when new algorithms emerge or business priorities shift quickly.

From a practical perspective, executives should champion investments not only in cutting-edge AI but also in infrastructure that supports rapid iteration: containerization tools like Docker, orchestration frameworks such as Kubernetes, and robust API integrations open doors for plug-and-play enhancements rather than costly system rewrites.

Financial planning must also adapt to this dynamic environment. Budgets should include buffers for experimentation phases alongside projections based on incremental ROI improvements instead of all-or-nothing bets on automation success stories.

At its core, agility combines technological foresight with organizational flexibility—not merely reacting faster but anticipating change proactively and embedding adaptability within core processes.

Equally important is cultivating an employee mindset aligned with this ethos. Training programs should emphasize problem-solving skills alongside technical proficiency, empowering staff to collaborate actively with intelligent systems rather than passively follow automated mandates.

A practical next step involves establishing periodic "change readiness" assessments—surveys coupled with workshops—to gauge how prepared departments are to embrace iterative process adjustments driven by AI insights.

agility and adaptability redefine competitive advantage from static efficiency gains toward a continuous capability for evolution. Organizations mastering this duality don't just survive disruption—they transform it into growth opportunities that keep them ahead of peers stuck in inflexible paradigms.

The most resilient businesses view automation not as a fixed endpoint but as an ongoing journey demanding openness to learning, experimentation, recalibration—and sometimes course correction—to sustain long-term success amid relentless technological and market pressures.

Inspiration for future projects

Innovation often emerges where ambition meets constraint. When embarking on AI-powered automation projects, it's more productive to focus on iterative experiments than on crafting perfect solutions from the outset. Rather than waiting for every variable to align, capturing small wins can build momentum that drives broader success. Take this example, a regional logistics firm began an AI pilot by optimizing delivery time windows on just a few routes instead of tackling their entire network. This focused approach enabled rapid data collection, swift refinement of machine learning models, and measurable improvements in punctuality within weeks—laying the groundwork for later expansion.

Begin by identifying tangible business challenges that cause daily frustration or drain resources. Look past flashy AI features and ask where bottlenecks consistently arise, which processes yield frequent errors, or which tasks demand excessive human effort. Pinpointing these pain points creates a clear starting line. One finance team, for example, found manual invoice validation to be both time-consuming and prone to transcription errors. By introducing robotic process automation (RPA) bots to extract invoice data from PDFs, they cut processing time by over 60% while dramatically improving accuracy. Their success stemmed from initially focusing narrowly before scaling once the concept was proven.

Technology alone does not guarantee success; how teams adopt and adapt it is equally crucial. Early cross-functional collaboration is essential since automation projects rarely thrive in silos. Involving IT, operations, finance, and frontline staff ensures diverse perspectives inform development, preventing costly oversights such as missing edge cases or ignoring compliance requirements.

For example, when a retail chain rolled out AI-driven inventory forecasting, shop floor managers highlighted seasonal variations not fully reflected in historical data. Incorporating this tacit knowledge into the model improved forecast accuracy significantly.

Lower barriers to experimentation by leveraging open-source tools and cloud platforms. Services like Google Cloud AutoML or Microsoft Azure Cognitive Services provide modular AI components accessible without large data science teams. Python libraries such as scikit-learn or TensorFlow allow developers with basic programming skills to prototype predictive models quickly. One small business started building a chatbot by training intent recognition with open-source natural language processing tools, then connected it to customer service workflows—iterating based on user feedback rather than aiming for perfect accuracy from day one.

Data is your most valuable asset; its quality must be treated as non-negotiable. Early failures often stem from inconsistent, incomplete, or outdated datasets that skew algorithm results. Establish rigorous processes for data cleansing and validation upfront, including automated scripts to detect anomalies or missing values regularly. An ecommerce company automating customer segmentation discovered gaps caused by inconsistent tracking across channels; addressing these issues boosted marketing campaign effectiveness dramatically.

Building dashboards that deliver real-time visibility into automation performance—tracking metrics like cycle times, error rates, and user interactions—is vital for continuous improvement. Tools such as Power BI or Tableau can integrate with backend AI outputs to provide stakeholders at all levels with visual insights beyond anecdotal feedback. This ongoing monitoring phase is where many projects either flourish through refinement or falter from neglect.

Change management plays an indispensable role in encouraging teams to embrace AI-powered workflows. Training sessions tailored to varying skill levels combined with clear communication emphasizing benefits help ease transitions. In one manufacturing plant introducing automated quality inspections using computer vision, leadership paired technical demos with hands-on workshops so operators understood how technology augmented rather than replaced their expertise.

Strategically, align automation initiatives with measurable business objectives—whether increasing throughput by 20%, halving manual errors, or speeding customer response times—to maintain focus and justify investments confidently when discussing ROI internally.

A practical roadmap might include:

1. Selecting a high-impact process suitable for automation based on frequency and complexity.

2. Assembling a cross-disciplinary team that includes end-users and IT specialists.

3. Choosing scalable tools balancing ease of use with integration capabilities.

4. Conducting small-scale pilots that capture detailed performance data.

5. Analyzing outcomes rigorously while soliciting frontline feedback.

6. Iteratively refining models and workflows before broader deployment.

Finally, cultivating curiosity throughout your organization transforms each project into a learning opportunity rather than a risk-averse endeavor limited by fear of failure or perfectionism. Early setbacks often reveal valuable lessons about model biases or unexpected workflows needing adjustment—as when an insurance company's claims-processing bot initially struggled with outlier cases until human analysts helped retrain its decision criteria.

As AI-powered automation reshapes business boundaries—from optimizing existing processes to enabling entirely new service models—the key to future success lies in combining nimble experimentation with disciplined evaluation. Financial gains follow when leaders create environments where innovation is not just tolerated but systematically nurtured through both structure and creativity.

This mindset turns automation from a technological hurdle into a strategic advantage—one defined not solely by the tools deployed but by an organization's willingness to continuously explore what comes next.

Example Walkthrough: Automating Invoice Data Capture With Python and OCR

Automating manual invoice processing using Python alongside Optical Character Recognition (OCR) illustrates a practical application:

- Step 1: Gather sample invoices in PDF format representing typical supplier layouts.

- Step 2: Extract raw text from PDFs using the open-source Tesseract OCR engine accessed via the pytesseract Python wrapper:

```python
import pytesseract

from pdf2image import convert_from_path


pages = convert_from_path('invoice_sample.pdf', 300)

for page_number, page_data in enumerate(pages):
```

```
text = pytesseract.image_to_string(page_data)
print(f'Page page_number + 1 Text:', text)
```
` ` `

- Step 3: Use regular expressions to identify key fields such as invoice number, date, and total amount:

` ` `python
```
import re

invoice_text = """...""" \# Extracted text string here

invoice_number = re.search(r'Invoice Number:*(+)', invoice_text)
date = re.search(r'Date:*(2/2/4)', invoice_text)
total = re.search(r'Total Due:*\?([,.]+)', invoice_text)

print(f"Invoice Number: invoice_number.group(1)")
print(f"Date: date.group(1)")
print(f"Total Due: total.group(1)")
```
` ` `

- Step 4: Export the structured data into Excel using pandas:

` ` `python
```
import pandas as pd

data =
'Invoice Number': [invoice_number.group(1)],
```

```
'Date': [date.group(1)],

'Total Due': [total.group(1)]


df = pd.DataFrame(data)

df.to_excel('processed_invoices.xlsx', index=False)
` ` `
```

By automating these steps within your workflow, you reduce manual entry errors while significantly accelerating financial reconciliation cycles. Such pilot projects set the stage for scaling more complex AI-powered finance automations aligned closely with business goals.

The driving force behind successful future projects is embracing manageable scope paired with relentless curiosity—a combination that ensures steady progress toward greater efficiency and value creation through AI-powered automation.

Encouraging sustainable practices

Sustainability in AI-powered automation is far more than a buzzword; it's a vital business imperative that balances long-term viability with ethical responsibility. While rapid technological adoption often eclipses concerns about resource consumption, environmental impact, and social equity, embedding sustainability into automation projects requires intentional decisions around infrastructure, data management, and operational design.

A logical starting point is assessing the energy footprint of AI systems. Cloud providers increasingly offer tools to estimate and optimize the carbon emissions generated by data processing. Take this example, Google Cloud's Carbon Footprint tool enables companies to monitor emissions from their AI workloads almost in real-time. With this visibility, organizations can make greener choices—such as scheduling non-urgent model training during periods when renewable energy is more available or opting for more energy-efficient algorithms. One financial firm, for example, cut compute demand and related emissions by nearly 40% by switching to incremental learning techniques instead of full retraining of machine learning models.

Data strategy also plays a crucial role in sustainable automation. Collecting and storing excessive data "just in case" leads to unnecessary storage costs and higher energy consumption without guaranteed returns. Implementing clear data lifecycle policies that archive or delete obsolete information—while maintaining privacy compliance—can significantly reduce overhead. An ecommerce company addressed rising storage expenses by automating the deletion of transaction logs beyond retention periods and compressing image assets with AI-powered optimization tools, which substantially lowered data center loads.

Sustainability goes beyond infrastructure to encompass responsible resource use across business ecosystems. For example, procurement workflows enhanced by AI-driven supplier risk assessments can evaluate vendors based on environmental records and labor practices. This integration aligns operational efficiency with corporate social responsibility, reducing reputational risks tied to unethical supply chains.

A practical way to embed sustainability is by incorporating specific criteria into automation rulesets. A logistics company illustrates this approach by programming its route optimization algorithms not only to minimize delivery times but also to reduce fuel consumption—prioritizing low-emission vehicles on certain routes during high-pollution alerts. This dual focus achieves both cost savings and environmental stewardship.

Ongoing monitoring is essential for maintaining sustainable practices. Dashboards that track sustainability KPIs alongside traditional performance metrics allow for continuous adjustment and accountability. Tools like Microsoft Power BI can integrate carbon intensity data with process efficiency indicators, offering decision-makers a comprehensive view of financial and ecological impacts.

Equally important is cultivating awareness among employees involved in automation initiatives. Workshops or internal communications highlighting how small behavioral changes—such as adjusting batch sizes for automated tasks or setting realistic model update frequencies—can collectively reduce resource use help embed sustainability into organizational culture.

An often-overlooked aspect is hardware lifecycle management. AI infrastructure extends beyond software; physical components like servers and GPUs carry embodied carbon costs from manufacture through disposal. Companies relying on cloud services should seek transparency regarding hardware refresh cycles and recycling programs, while those with on-premises systems can align refurbishment schedules with sustainability goals.

To help organizations implement these principles systematically, consider the following steps:

1. Audit current AI workflows for energy consumption using provider dashboards or third-party tools.

2. Identify non-critical processes where compute can be deferred or reduced without disrupting business operations.

3. Establish clear data governance policies emphasizing minimal necessary retention alongside privacy compliance.

4. Incorporate sustainability metrics into project KPIs alongside speed, accuracy, and cost-efficiency.

5. Involve cross-functional teams—including IT, compliance, operations, and sustainability officers —in automation design discussions.

6. Pilot eco-friendly algorithmic techniques such as quantization or pruning to lower computational demands without compromising performance.

7. Transparently track progress with real-time dashboards accessible across organizational levels.

Sustainable automation should be woven into the fabric of projects from inception through deployment and ongoing operation—not treated as an afterthought retrofitted onto existing models. Striking this balance ensures AI-driven gains do not come at the expense of future resources or societal trust—a commitment increasingly demanded by stakeholders ranging from investors to customers.

Leading technology companies offer instructive examples: Apple has committed to running all corporate operations carbon-neutral, including substantial investments in renewable energy powering cloud services behind its AI applications; Microsoft's "green AI" research benchmarks aim to reduce training time and resource use across the industry.

For business leaders, integrating sustainability upfront not only mitigates risks but unlocks new opportunities as consumer preferences shift toward environmentally conscious brands and regulatory pressures intensify worldwide.

In this light, sustainability elevates automation from a purely transactional endeavor to a transformational force— optimizing workflows while reshaping entire ecosystems for responsible growth.

Example Walkthrough: Integrating Sustainability Metrics into Automation Dashboards

Consider a mid-size retail chain automating inventory replenishment through predictive analytics hosted on Azure Cloud:

- Step 1: Configure Azure Cost Management + Billing to monitor cloud resource consumption tied to AI model training and inference for inventory forecasting.

- Step 2: Gather external datasets reflecting regional grid carbon intensity (grams CO_2 per kWh) from APIs like electricityMap or governmental open data sources.

- Step 3: Build a Power BI dashboard combining forecast accuracy KPIs (e.g., mean absolute percentage error), compute hours per forecasting run, and estimated CO_2 emissions calculated as:

CO_2 Emissions (kg) = Compute Hours x Average Power Consumption (kW) x Grid Carbon Intensity (g/kWh) / 1000

- Step 4: Set alert thresholds within Power BI to notify operations managers if emissions exceed targets during specific periods (e.g., peak pollution days).

- Step 5: Use insights from the dashboard to experiment with scheduling batch forecasting jobs during greener time windows or employing lighter-weight models without significantly compromising accuracy.

This approach yields financial benefits through optimized inventory management while driving measurable reductions in environmental impact—turning data into actionable insights that support responsible business practices.

Sustainability has become an essential dimension embedded throughout AI automation strategies—an ethos that amplifies value beyond efficiency gains alone, fostering resilient and conscientious enterprises prepared for the future.

Final thoughts: Embracing change

Embracing change in AI-powered automation goes beyond adapting to a passing trend; it requires a fundamental, ongoing transformation that reshapes the core of business itself. This shift demands not only technological upgrades but also a deep evolution in mindset across organizations. Leaders who understand this and act decisively position their companies to fully harness AI's potential rather than simply responding to disruption.

Take, for example, a mid-sized manufacturing firm that faced stagnant productivity despite heavy investment in automation tools. The issue wasn't the technology, but the teams' reluctance to rethink workflows and experiment with new roles alongside machines. When leadership shifted from enforcing rigid processes to encouraging curiosity and resilience, employees began collaborating with AI systems instead of competing against them. This cultural change sparked innovation, reduced downtime, and uncovered efficiencies hidden by entrenched habits.

Resistance is natural and expected. Concerns about job security or fears of obsolescence persist despite evidence that AI more often augments human capabilities than replaces them entirely. Transparent communication and upskilling initiatives help build trust. One company's monthly "AI impact forum" allowed employees to share experiences with new tools, exchange tips, and voice concerns directly to project leads—transforming anxiety into engagement.

It's important to recognize that AI-driven transformation

is rarely linear; setbacks are part of the process. A company might roll out a chatbot only to find it struggles with nuanced customer queries or discover that predictive maintenance models falter due to initial data quality issues. When framed constructively rather than punitively, these failures become valuable learning opportunities.

To embed a culture that embraces change, practical steps include:

1. Modeling adaptability at the top: Leaders openly acknowledge uncertainties while championing experimentation, setting a tone that tolerates risk.

2. Encouraging iterative learning: Establish short feedback loops after automation rollouts to capture lessons and make quick adjustments.

3. Empowering continuous education: Offer accessible training focused on emerging AI tools relevant across roles.

4. Aligning incentives: Reward behaviors that foster collaboration between humans and AI rather than penalizing early missteps.

5. Embedding transparency: Regularly share automation goals, progress metrics, and challenges at all levels of the organization.

When these practices become part of everyday operations, change shifts from being feared to anticipated—a space where agility transforms from an operational headache into a competitive advantage.

Looking at industry evolution reveals a consistent pattern: those who thrive amid technological revolutions accept uncertainty as part of growth rather than an obstacle. As management thinker Peter Drucker famously said decades ago, "The greatest danger in times of turbulence is not the turbulence—it is to act with yesterday's logic." Today's environment calls for embracing continuous transformation powered by AI-driven automation.

organizations combining technological capability with cultural readiness unlock sustainable value far beyond immediate efficiency gains. The ability to pivot swiftly in response to market shifts or unexpected disruptions fosters resilience—not just survival—in volatile times. Change isn't a one-time hurdle; it's the foundation for lasting innovation.

The true payoff comes when leaders stop asking if they should automate and instead focus on evolving their people, processes, and purpose alongside intelligent machines— embracing change as essential to business excellence in the digital age.

This structure provides a comprehensive exploration of AI-powered automation in business, covering various aspects from initial concept to future applications.

The evolution of AI automation reveals a compelling progression. Early on, businesses depended on simple mechanization like assembly lines in manufacturing. Later, rule-based automation emerged in the late 20th century, using scripted processes to manage repetitive tasks without adapting to new circumstances. The real breakthrough arrived with machine learning, which allowed systems to learn from data rather than follow fixed instructions. For example, spam filters evolved from relying on keyword matching to employing sophisticated probabilistic models that detect emerging spam patterns dynamically. Today's AI solutions combine this adaptability with vast computational power and cloud connectivity, making scalable automation accessible even for small enterprises.

In today's competitive landscape, adopting AI-driven automation has become less of an option and more of a necessity. Gains in operational efficiency are tangible and directly impact profit margins and customer satisfaction. Companies deploying AI-powered chatbots often report significantly faster response times alongside higher customer engagement rates. Meanwhile, supply chains optimized through predictive analytics reduce stockouts and cut logistics costs. Failing to embrace these advancements risks losing ground to more agile competitors who harness AI as a powerful multiplier.

Understanding the technology behind these improvements clarifies how such benefits arise. Machine learning algorithms sift through large datasets to identify patterns for predicting outcomes or classifying information—a bank detecting fraudulent transactions in milliseconds provides a prime example. Natural language processing (NLP) enables machines to understand human language, powering virtual assistants that schedule meetings or respond automatically to support inquiries. Computer vision analyzes images and video streams for purposes like quality control or security monitoring without fatigue or distraction. When combined within robotic process automation frameworks, these technologies orchestrate complex workflows from start to finish.

AI automation offers advantages beyond mere speed. It reduces human error by standardizing execution—machines don't suffer from distractions or biases inherent in manual processes. Scalability shifts dramatically: tasks that once required dozens of clerks can now be handled by configuring software robots within hours. Also, AI systems continuously improve through feedback loops that adjust parameters as new data arrives, unlike traditional automation that remains static unless manually reprogrammed.

Despite these benefits, misconceptions about AI persist among business leaders and employees:

- AI will replace all jobs: In fact, most

implementations augment human roles rather than eliminate them.

- Automation is too complex or costly: Cloud-based solutions and intuitive platforms have significantly lowered barriers.

- Data privacy becomes impossible: Proper governance frameworks ensure compliance with regulations such as GDPR.

- AI lacks transparency: Emerging explainability tools are making decision-making processes more interpretable.

Addressing these myths helps create an informed environment conducive to successful adoption.

This book explores these themes beginning with foundational concepts before delving into technology breakdowns and methods for identifying opportunities. Financial analyses support investment decisions, while strategic frameworks guide implementation considering organizational culture and workforce dynamics. Industry-specific chapters cover applications in marketing, finance, HR, supply chain management, and innovation pipelines— each enriched with actionable examples and case studies from leading enterprises.

Take this example, consider invoice processing automation using Python combined with optical character recognition (OCR). A simple script leveraging open-source libraries like Tesseract can extract text from scanned invoices automatically:

```python
import pytesseract

from PIL import Image
```

```
\#\# Load image file
invoice_image = Image.open('invoice_sample.png')

\#\# Extract text using OCR
text = pytesseract.image_to_string(invoice_image)

\#\# Basic parsing example - extracting invoice number
import re
match = re.search(r'Invoice Number:*(+)', text)
if match:
invoice_number = match.group(1)
print(f"Extracted Invoice Number: invoice_number")
else:
print("Invoice number not found.")
` ` `
```

This example demonstrates how automating data capture reduces manual entry errors while accelerating accounting workflows—a microcosm of broader efficiencies achievable at scale.

In supply chain management, predictive demand forecasting applies machine learning models such as ARIMA or LSTM networks to analyze historical sales data and anticipate inventory needs precisely:

1. Collect time-series sales data spanning multiple years.

2. Cleanse the dataset to address anomalies or missing

entries.

3. Train the forecasting model using the chosen algorithm.

4. Validate model accuracy against recent sales figures.

5. Integrate model outputs directly into procurement systems for automated reorder triggers.

Such integration drastically shortens lead times compared to traditional spreadsheet-based planning.

The promise of AI-powered automation lies in combining adaptable technology with strategic business insight—neither element alone suffices fully without the other's support.

Recognizing this interplay sets the stage for leveraging artificial intelligence as a catalyst for smarter workflows rather than merely faster ones—a crucial distinction that separates successful digital transformations from superficial upgrades delivering limited value.

www.ingramcontent.com/pod-product-compliance
Lightning Source LLC
LaVergne TN
LVHW051219050326
832903LV00028B/2157